11,13, 39-42,

D0930602

**CONTENDING APPROACHES TO
WORLD SYSTEM ANALYSIS**

SAGE FOCUS EDITIONS

Contending Approaches to World System Analysis

EDITOR

WILLIAM R. THOMPSON

SAGE PUBLICATIONS
Beverly Hills / London / New Delhi

Copyright © 1983 by Sage Publications, Inc.

For information address:

SAGE Publications, Inc.
275 South Beverly Drive
Beverly Hills, California 90212

SAGE Publications India Pvt. Ltd.
C-236 Defence Colony
New Delhi 110 024, India

SAGE Publications Ltd
28 Banner Street
London EC1Y 8QE, England

Printed in the United States of America

Library of Congress Cataloging in Publication Data

Main entry under title:

Contending approaches to world system analysis.

    (Sage focus editions ; 62)
    Bibliography: p.
    1. International organization—Research. I. Thompson, William R.
JX1954.W67   1983   341.2′072   83-8669

ISBN 0-8039-2018-0
ISBN 0-8039-2019-9 (pbk.)

FIRST PRINTING

Contents

Part III: Discussion and Debate

Introduction

World System Analysis With and Without the Hyphen

This volume has been assembled in an effort to support three basic and related propositions. One, world system analysis represents a definite advance on the various ways in which we have collectively attempted to account for "international" political and economic behavior. Two, there is more than one way to approach the analysis of the world system. Yet it is also fair to say that none of the perspectives that have been developed so far represents anything resembling a finished product. On the contrary, much remains to be done in terms of more fully elaborating how and why things work the way they do. Three, given the strengths and especially the weaknesses of the currently available frameworks for world system analysis, we might do well to consider avoiding an exclusive commitment to any prevailing orthodoxy on how the world system has developed and is developing. Students of the world system need to be sensitive, particularly in an era of crude theoretical construction, not only to their own assumptions, but also to the assumptions of different perspectives—even though some of these different perspectives may not be able to satisfy a strict definition of world system analysis. Each of these propositions requires some further clarification.

THE COMMON DENOMINATORS AND PROMISE OF WORLD SYSTEM ANALYSIS

What is world system analysis? One is tempted to answer this question by noting that multiple perspectives exist and, as a consequence, that any attempt to produce an all-encompassing response might satisfy a few analysts while certainly dissatisfying many others. But such a response would surely constitute more of an evasion than an appropriate reply to the query. There are, moreover, at least three common denominators that can serve to delineate the basic nature of world system analysis.

First, it is asserted that a world system exists, that the system is characterized by more or less interdependent political, economic, and cultural subsystems, and that the modern or contemporary world system began to take definite shape sometime around the late fifteenth century. Since that time, the system and its subsystems have continued to expand in the geographic coverage sense and to evolve in the functional sense. The system structures have also maintained a strong element of continuity despite the passage of a number of centuries. A world system analysis of, say, seventeenth century behavior is therefore likely not only to yield information about the seventeenth century but to shed light on subsequent and earlier behavior as well.

The role of history is critical to this endeavor—not merely for the limited sake of descriptive narrative, but also because the contemporary world system is so embedded in its own specific historical development that any analyst attempting to decipher its structures and processes must first develop a sense of the developmental flow over the entire 500 or so years of its existence. In other words, an attempt to explain the system's behavior solely at an ahistorical, abstract level is as likely to be unsuccessful as an attempt to explain the genesis of the twentieth century's second world war without also knowing something about that century's first world war.

Yet it must be emphasized that there is more to this endeavor than simply developing a sense of history. Analysts have always been fond of finding analogies in, or comparing the differences among, different historical epochs. Scholars may, for example, find value in contrasting the current U.S.-Soviet confrontation with the Athenian-Spartan conflict or in distilling current strategic principles from the Roman experience. While not wishing to deny the potential utility of comparative historical system analysis, it needs to be stressed that there is an important difference between pursuing and discussing historical analogies and tracing the historical development of a specific system. Developments in the sixteenth, seventeenth, eighteenth, and nineteenth centuries are not important to an analysis of the world system in the twentieth century because of the presence or absence of interesting similarities. Rather, the structures and processes of the twentieth century simply (although sometimes not so simply) reflect the latest twists and modifications of the same structures and processes found in the four earlier centuries. An understanding of the significance of warfare in the 1939-1945 period is thus enhanced not only by information on warfare in the 1914-1918 period but also by an appreciation of markedly similar world wars in the 1793-1815 and 1689-1713 periods because they are all manifestations of a remarkably consistent, systemic process.

World system analysis can be viewed in part as a reaction against current tendencies to suppress or misinterpret history in an embarrassingly large number of social science models. A prime example is the extrapolation of economic and political development models from the European experience with the expectation that these models will somehow serve equally well in the seventeenth, mid-nineteenth, or late twentieth centuries despite significant differences in the systemic opportunities for development. Ironically, however, not only can one argue that opportunities conducive to development in the seventeenth century may be inoperative or relatively nonexistent in the twentieth century, but also that we have much to learn and unlearn about the way things worked in the seventeenth century.[1] History is vital to the world system enterprise, but much of the historical knowledge that is presently available is written from such different perspectives that it must at the very least be reinterpreted and often quite substantially.

A second major assumption of world system analysis is that behavior within the system can best be explained in terms of world system structure and its critical processes. Other levels of analysis—the individual, the group, the nation, or society—are not condemned to analytical oblivion by this premise. On the contrary, the operating assumption is that analysts must at some point decipher the pervasive structural context within which all behavior is conducted, regardless of the level of interaction. The outcomes of crisis decision making, for instance, may be explained in terms of the psychological pathologies and orientations of critical decision makers, the interaction of small groups, the standard operating procedures of bureaucratic organizations, or the action and reaction processes of several states in confrontation. But the lessons derived from these analyses, particularly if major powers are involved, may easily be misconstrued if it is assumed that crises in 1914, 1938, and 1962 are all equivalent phenomena without due regard to important differences in world system structure or world system time.

World system time (Thompson, 1983) does not refer to the more conventional chronologies measured by calendars, clocks, or even the revolution of the earth around the sun but to time in terms of the regular rhythms and cycles of the world system's major processes. All world system analysts may not agree on which cycles exist or on which ones are most important, but they all rely heavily on a few major cycles such as those that are asserted to characterize the concentration of capabilities or long-term fluctuations in economic growth and prices. Examining behavior from these vantage points leads to the correlation of certain types of behavior with specific cyclical phases. Thus if it is contended that a particular oscillating process exerts a crucial influence on behavior, an investigator must be more concerned with where his or her subjects are in terms of the pertinent cycle as opposed to the year, decade, or century in which the activities happen to be taking place. Of course, not every world system process is cyclical in nature, but many of the most important ones do appear to be subject to relatively regular periodicities.

A third feature of world system analysis is its willingness (some might even say eagerness) to cross traditional disciplinary frontiers. Some analysts prefer to view the study of the world system as a multidisciplinary effort eventually capable of incorporating that older version of multidisciplinary work in the social sciences—international relations. Others regard world system analysis as a unidisciplinary movement in its own right. However viewed, world system analysis reflects a considerable amount of dissatisfaction with the artificial Balkanization of the study of social, economic, and political interaction and the evident analytical limitations imposed by disciplinary barriers and binders. It is hardly a novel observation that it has always been difficult to disentangle economics and politics. Yet many economists proceed as if it is possible to make sense of economic behavior in isolation from political structures and influences. Naturally, the converse charge for political scientists is equally appropriate.

Similarly, the analysis of "domestic-internal" events and processes has for too long been regarded as an inherently different realm from the analysis of "international-external" events and processes. This engrained propensity has always been an analytical fiction of dubious convenience or advantage. In an increasingly interdependent world, the analytical and real-world costs of maintaining this fiction become more apparent on a daily basis.

In these respects, world system analysis might be somewhat awkwardly described as a historical-sociological approach to political economy with a decided emphasis on the systemic level of analysis as the principal point of view. Whereas traditional disciplines tend to exclude certain topics as beyond their pale and to compartmentalize other topics within their own discipline, world system analysis tends to avoid excessive respect to specialized academic turfs. The sheer diversity of topics of interest to world system analysts necessitates incursions and extended trespassing in an equally large number of fields.

To be sure, there are very sound reasons for academic specialization. World system analysts, needless to say, are more than likely to make their share of the same commission and ommission errors that specialists as well as later generations of more sophisticated world system analysts can be expected to correct. Ideally, however, the analytical insights derived through a world system perspective will outweigh the sins and mistakes of what must presently appear to resemble a virulent outbreak of academic imperialism and poaching.

Why then should world system analysis be considered an improvement on current modes of analysis? The answer to this question is inherent to the three common denominators outlined above. World system analysis emphasizes structures and processes that, while not altogether ignored in the past, have never received adequate and integrated attention. To the extent that world system arguments prove to be well supported by the evidence, a respectable proportion of social science knowledge will require considerable revision. In the process, our understanding of world history will undergo equally extensive revision. At the same time, a strong appreciation for the necessity of structured historical information and analysis will have been reintroduced into areas of inquiry that in too many cases have been divorced from considering the immediate past in the attempt to explain the immediate present. Finally, the potential of world system analysis for reintegrting a large number of frustratingly separate fields of study and levels of analysis is unusually promising. Only time and a great deal more work will determine whether this promise can be fully realized.

MULTIPLE PERSPECTIVES ON WORLD SYSTEM ANALYSIS

Currently, there are several ways to approach problems of interest to world system analysis, and still other paths, no doubt, will appear in the not too distant future. Two world system schools of thought, nevertheless, can be said to predominate, albeit to varying degrees, at the present time.

Easily the most widely known approach to world system analysis is the *world-economy perspective,* which is frequently associated with the work of Wallerstein (1974, 1979, 1980). This variety of world-system analysis (with a hyphen) constitutes a large-scale and long-term framework for the study of selected systemic structures, cycles, and secular trends. Three central processes are stressed: the historical development of a core-periphery devision of labor, the episodic rise and fall of hegemonic powers, and the gradual geographic expansion, coupled with the periodic growth and stagnation, of the world economy.

At the root of these processes lie the more fundamental processes of capitalism, which is defined as the attempt to obtain a maximum price and profit for market sales by increasing production efficiency and by capital accumulation.

The core of the world-economy consists of those states in which agro-industrial production is the most efficient and where the complexity of economic activities and the level of capital accumulation is the greatest. As a consequence, the core receives the most favorable proportion of the system's economic surplus through its exploitation of the periphery, which, in turn, is compelled to specialize in the supply of less well rewarded raw materials and labor.

During what is described as the first stage (1450-1600/50) of the modern world-economy's development, the conjuncture of feudal disintegration; changes in climate, population, and technology; the economic need for geographic expansion; and the political multicentricity of Europe facilitated the movement away from the traditional Mediterranean locus toward the establishment of the system's core in northwestern Europe. Parts of Eastern Europe and Latin America emerged as the initial periphery. Systemwide stagnation during a second stage (1600/50-1730/50), however, forced a general consolidation and retrenchment in an economy still predominately agrarian. The emphasis on industrial production became more salient in a third stage (1750/1815-1917). In turn, the increased need for raw materials and markets led to the further geographical expansion of the world-economy and the peripheral incorporation of much of the rest of the world. After 1917, the third stage was superseded by a fourth and ongoing stage characterized primarily by a consolidation of the world-economy's industrial base.

In addition to the core-periphery division of labor and the persistent political multicentricity of the interstate system, a third important source of systemic structure is attributed to the ascent and decline of hegemonic core powers. Although there seems to be some disagreement about the fifteenth- and sixteenth-century role of the Habsburgs, the world-economy framework usually identifies three periods of hegemonic power: the United Provinces of Netherlands (1625-1672/75), Great Britain (1763-1815/c. 1850-1873), and the United States (1945-1965/67).

These periods of unusual levels of system dominance are based on the short-lived concentration within a single state of superiority in agro-industrial productivity, commerce, and finance/investment. The brevity of dominance is explained largely in terms of the high overhead costs of hegemony, the diffusion of capital, and the strong probability of relative improvements in the economic capabilities of rival core states. The cyclical decline of hegemonic control, in turn, is given responsibility for ushering in a period of power diffusion, increased freedom of maneuver for the core states, and increased exploitation of the periphery—all compounded by a phase of general economic contraction or stagnation. Attempts to restructure the world market in each core actor's interest lead to acute competition and conflict and, eventually, world war between the core powers.

A second and comparatively less well known approach to world system analysis is the *long cycle of world leadership perspective,* which is most readily associated with the work of Modelski (1978, 1981, 1982). The long cycle viewpoint emphasizes the post-1500 development and gradual evolution of a modern global political system. The primary issues of political concern in this nonterritorially based system have centered on managing such problems as those connected with long-range transactions and the frictions of interdependence. Order, security, territorial rights, and trade stability therefore tend to head the systemic political agenda.

The crux of the long cycle approach, however, stems from the observation that global problem management is neither constant nor random. It has been characterized instead by a regular rhythm, the long cycle of world leadership, for nearly 500 years. The rhythm of the long cycle, in turn, is predicated in large part on interrelated fluctuations in the systemic concentration of power and major bouts of global warfare. At the end of a war fought to determine the constitution of the global political system (1494-1516, 1586-1608, 1689-1713, 1793-1815, and 1914-1918/1939-1945), a single state, the world power, emerges with monopoly control over the seapower capabilities essential to the capacity for global reach and order keeping. Enjoying the advantages of the system's lead economy and legitimized to an increasing extent by postwar peace settlements, the world power becomes the system's primary supplier of security and assumes the responsibility for crafting the institutional frameworks of order as exemplified by international organizations and the rules of international economic exchanges.

Over time, the initial preponderance (always less than hegemonic in extent) erodes as the relative capability shares of the system's most significant other actors, the global powers, improve. Consequently, the unipolar power structure of the system is transformed gradually into a multipolar distribution, just as monopolistic leadership gives way to oligopolistic competition and rivalry. Yet the slide into the next bout of global warfare is not exactly a linear progression, for each long cycle goes through four successive, 25- to 30-year seasons. The supply of global order tends to exceed the demand for order in the first phase (*world power*), but as priorities and commitments change, nationalistic challenges to the global order and the world power's leadership create a deficit (the demand for order is greater than its supply) in the second phase (*delegitimation*). Even though the leader's relative capability position continues to decline in the third quarter (*deconcentration*), potential challengers are not yet ready to press their claims to the benefits of leadership, thus creating another period of relative order surplus, as in the lull before a storm. The long cycle is completed by the conclusion of an intensive struggle for succession in the fourth quarter (*global war*) from which a new world power and reconcentrated capability distribution emerges.[2]

These fluctuations in the global political system, it is further argued, also have important implications for fluctuations in the world economy. Since political and economic activities must by and large draw on the same population and resource base, it is difficult to focus attention and resources in both spheres simultaneously and to the same extent. Thus periods of intense political preoccupation (for example, during global war) alternate with periods of economic growth and expansion. Accordingly, rising prices, resource scarcities, and relatively few economic innovations are expected in the second (delegitimation) and fourth (global war) phases. The opposite situation—falling prices, relative resource abundance, and the development of new leading economic sectors—is therefore associated with the first (world power) and third (deconcentration) quarters. In this fashion, the Kondratieff economic long wave is reinterpreted as a reflection of the reciprocal transmission of instabilities in the global political structure to the world economy's structure and vice versa.

Both of these frameworks represent ambitious and impressive attacks on unraveling the dynamics of the modern world system. Both also have flaws that limit the maximum extent of their appeal. The world-economy school of thought's emphasis on capitalism and capital accumulation narrows the system's motors of change to a version of the profit motive. Noneconomic forces and processes frequently are relegated to subordinate or residual categories of analysis. To adopt the framework, one must accept this initial choice of model reductionism—something that is difficult for many analysts to do. In addition, the emphasis on the significance of global reach and seapower, so critical to the long cycle approach, while not totally ignored in world-economy analyses, is granted little prominence.[3] While neither perspective has any claim to infallibility, it is quite possible that the world-economy school's orientation toward continental developments is obscuring an important point.

The long cycle approach invokes an even more radical revision of our established images of post-1500 historical developments than does the more Eurocentric world-economy perspective. This is not necessarily a flaw but it certainly limits the approach's intuitive appeal. Much more problematic is the absence of a definitive statement on the sources of the long cycle decay. So far, analysts within this perspective have devoted more attention to demonstrating the existence of the capability concentration and deconcentration cycle than they have to exploring what drives it. This allocation of resources, limited by the hitherto small number of investigators, reflects an explicit strategy, but this explanation does little to relieve analytical discomfort or to assuage skepticism about the ultimate utility of the framework. Furthermore, students of the world's economic division of labor will find much more of direct interest in the world-economy framework than can be extracted at present from the long cycle perspective.

Criticisms such as these can be found elsewhere and usually in much more detail. The point to be made in the present context is not that the leading perspectives are vulnerable to criticism. This position, we may safely assume, is perfectly noncontroversial. But rather than devoting forests of paper and rivers of ink to their respective inadequacies and leaving it at that, a more constructive route involves regarding these perspectives as incomplete statements still very much in the process of being developed. Criticism from within and outside world system schools of thought is both welcome and necessary, but the real challenge lies in attempting to improve upon the analytical tools currently at our disposal.

Several research strategies to accomplish this task are conceivable. Students within the predominant schools of thought undoubtedly will continue to sharpen their own frameworks by giving more attention to theoretical specification, operationalization, and hypothesis testing. A second avenue well worth exploring is the possibility of narrowing the conceptual gap between the world-economy and long cycle perspectives. Still another path to improvement lies in recognizing that a variety of non-world system approaches and investigations possess varying degrees of compatibility with the thrust of world system analysis. Indeed, a number of non-world system analyses require only limited translation and reinterpretation to serve world system analytical purposes.[4] Moreover, in addition to searching for compatibilities and convergence, it should also be possible to improve upon world system analysis by considering and/or coopting the useful elements and features of these other, related approaches.

The chapters presented in this volume pursue some mixture of these various avenues. At the same time, they are clearly pursuing a variety of substantive research agendas as well. Despite the diversity of interests and perspectives, it does seem warranted to cluster the thirteen chapters into three groups. The first group shares a principal focus on the economic dimension of the world system's structures (especially the core-periphery division of labor and its implications), while the second group stresses other considerations such as war and world order from primarily noneconomic orientations. Finally, the third group of chapters reflects an explicitly critical or evaluative focus on the perceived advantages and disadvantages of different world system analytical strategies.[5] Nevertheless, I hasten to point out that noneconomic and economic considerations, respectively, are hardly absent from the first two clusters of chapters. Nor does the last group possess anything resembling a monopoly on the criticisms expressed in this volume.

ACCENTING THE ECONOMIC DIMENSION

One of the important factors in accounting for the appeal of world system analysis—both with and without the hyphen—is a growing sense of dissatisfaction with more conventional modes of analysis. André Gunder Frank expresses this mood of discontent in his discussion of what he views as widespread crises of theory, ideology, and ideas in general. One need not espouse Frank's own preferences or conclusions in order to appreciate what may well be his most telling criticism—the failure of prevailing frameworks "to view past, present, and future as sequences in a single historical process." For Frank, the continued development of a world system perspective is essential so that we may examine accurately "the here and now in the context of a then and there."

Albert Bergesen's essay accepts Frank's premise in principle but, at the same time, takes issue with one significant aspect of it by focusing on the theoretical implications and conceptual distinctions between societal-bound class relations and core-periphery exchange relations. Bergesen suggests that both the "external" (unequal exchange) emphasis of Amin, Frank, and Wallerstein and the "internal" (class) emphasis of more orthodox critics of the world-economy framework represent variations on nineteenth-century fixations on societal formations. As a consequence, they misinterpret the transformations brought about by the development and expansion of the world-economy. If class is viewed as a function of the ownership and control of the means of production, one can examine the creation of a global class structure in which most of the world's means of production have been dominated by the world system's core states. It is this more fundamental structure that, according to Bergesen, makes possible the by-product of unequal exchange between core and periphery.

Christopher Chase-Dunn takes Frank's premise one step further. Not content with the current looseness of the emerging world-economy approach to world system analysis, Chase-Dunn wishes to construct a formal and empirically testable theory of capitalist development. He begins with Marx's model of capitalist accumulation and then attempts to elaborate on this theoretical "kernel" by introducing a set of noneconomic considerations ("organizational, political, market, interstate, and world class relations") that are ignored by Marx but which he views as promising complications from a world-system perspective. Chase-Dunn readily admits that the desired synthesis is not forthcoming in this essay. Instead, he attempts to specify which variables and processes undergo substantial change in the qualitative transformation of social systems (i.e., feudalism to capitalism to socialism). Two areas of investigation are emphasized: the uneven interaction between commodification and organizational rationalization processes and, partially contrary to Bergesen's argument in the preceding chapter, the cross-cutting nature of intrasocietal class and core-periphery exploitation. Both areas produce interesting theoretical complications, but neither avenue of inquiry is regarded, as yet, as capable of capturing fully the essence of the capitalist development process.

Dependencia theorizing predates the advent of world system theorizing but the linkages between dependencia schools of thought and the world-economy perspective on the world system are quite overt and close. This is hardly surprising since the world-economy framework as developed by Wallerstein and others seeks to provide a general explanation of core-periphery dependency structures. Accordingly, and in contrast to the more abstract discussions advanced by Chase-Dunn and Bergesen, the chapter written by David Sylvan, Duncan Snidal, Bruce Russett, Steven Jackson, and Raymond Duvall presents a preliminary empirical test of some of the dependent development consequences of unequal exchange between core and periphery. Based on a complex, cross-sectional modeling effort, the authors find, as expected, that foreign capitalist and cultural penetration of peripheral countries leads to export commodity concentration and can reinforce the concentration of trading partners. Somewhat less anticipated, however, is the difficulty they encounter in generalizing about the direct effects of penetration on internal economic distortions. Some linkages are traced to structural disintegration and uneven development but, it is concluded, a number of intervening contextual factors appear to be responsible for penetration working different ways in different social and economic settings. As such, their findings serve as a useful warning of the problems and challenges of generalizing about the influence of world system structures across space and time.

ACCENTING OTHER DIMENSIONS

George Modelski's chapter reviews much of the progress made to date in developing and elaborating the long cycle of world leadership perspective that he introduced in the mid-1970s. Particular attention in this essay is paid to the prerequisites of a capacity for global reach (secure oceanic position, ocean-going seapower, vigorous economy, innovative nation-state organization, and the absence of an overriding cultural or ideological mission) and to differentiating the concepts and functions of leadership and order from anarchy, self-help, and hegemony. Following a summarization of the long cycle process, its sequential phases, and some possible explanatory models, Modelski's focus returns to a comparative discussion briefly outlining how he views the long cycle framework as differing from classical inter-national relations theories, philosophies of history, societally oriented social theories, and the world-economy perspective. The overview concludes with some commentary on two of the topics that tend to trouble critics of the long cycle: the connections between world politics and world economics and the predictive potential of the long cycle framework.

William R. Thompson's chapter concentrates on the question of how international systems are transformed. In contrast to the fairly amorphous treatment of this topic in the more conventional inter-national politics literature, Thompson argues that there is growing interest and some amount of convergence—within and outside of world system schools of thought—on the fundamental role of recur-ring fluctuations in capability concentration as one of the primary processes of structural change in the world system. After reviewing several perspectives on systemic change and their points of agree-ment, it is contended that analytical sensitivity to the existence of structural periodicities in the history of the world system leads to markedly different ways of studying war—one of the more important consequences of systemic change. In support of this argument, two non-world-system studies (Singer et al., 1972; Doran and Parsons, 1980) are reexamined from a long cycle point of view. As anticipated, the introduction of a world system perspective leads to new and different findings, interpretations, and conclusions about the rela-tionship between war and structural change.

Charles Doran's chapter constitutes a direct response to some of the questions raised in the preceding chapter about the relationship between Doran's relative cycle of power theory and the extensive-ness of major power warfare. The basic question is how may we best go about integrating our sometimes rival, sometimes overlapping explanations of national and systemic behavior. In general, Doran's position seems to be that there are no meaningful cyclical movements at the systemic level that cannot be better explained at the nation-state level. Although Doran implies that world system analysts tend to exaggerate the influence of the system's leading actors, he argues that when leading states undergo severe role pressure and political stress, as is argued in the cycle of relative power theory, the entire system will experience political stress. The most spectacular examples of this phenomena and the brief intervals during which nation-states and their international system are most closely wedded are the periodic wars fought to resist attempts at hegemony. But even in these cases, the primary reason for attempts to establish hegemony must be traced back to the would-be hegemonic power's position on the relative cycle of power.

Jack Levy's chapter continues in a relatively similar vein through his attempts to isolate the set of assumptions/propositions that underlie an older and more conventional perspective emphasizing a focus on the behavior of the international system's oligarchy, the great powers. In explicit contrast to the world-economy and long cycle frameworks on the world system, Levy points out that a *great power framework* stresses the overriding primacy of politics and security issues, the prominence of Europe as the historically predominant source of security threats, and the greater likelihood of pluralism and balance of power activity as opposed to fluctuations in power concentration. Given its Eurocentric and political biases, the great power framework also grants primary significance to a different set of wars and influential actors. Thus even though (or because) the world-economy, long cycle, and great power perspectives have been designed to treat different questions, they do generate some mutually contradictory hypotheses that can eventually, Levy believes, be empirically tested.

While the two chapters discussed above stress the contradictions and disagreements encountered in comparing various types of world system analyses with more conventional frameworks, Richard Falk and Samuel Kim find that the evolving *World Order Models Project* (WOMP) perspective on world order possesses some degree of compatibility with world system analysis. WOMP analysts are particularly interested in delineating and facilitating the processes of transformation through which the values and institutions needed for a normatively preferred world order can be created. In addition to sharing dissatisfaction with other prevailing frameworks and explicit interests in structural change, historical processes, and holistic conceptions of the world system, WOMP and world system analyses have mutually complementary interests in determining not only where we have been and where we presently are, but also where we might wish to be in the future. As Falk and Kim note, in order to understand how to make the transition from here to there, it is essential that we develop "a sophisticated awareness of the dynamics of the existing order."

DISCUSSION AND DEBATE

The variety of perspectives displayed in the first two clusters of essays very much continues to characterize the third and last group of papers. The first chapter in this section, written by David P. Rapkin, advances the position that no currently available framework possesses sufficient breadth to account for the world system's economic and political processes. While acknowledging that the alternative approaches tend to emphasize different but related topics (capitalism and uneven development versus war and order), Rapkin criticizes the world-economy framework for relegating political processes to the role of a fairly static backdrop for economic forces. At the same time, however, conventional theorizing about international politics also has little to say about the long-term political processes of the world system. In this respect, the long cycle perspective is regarded as a marked improvement on the classical paradigm. But the long cycle perspective is flawed as well by insufficient attention to economic motivations, nonmajor powers, and uneven development. What is needed, according to Rapkin, are multiple assumptions, concepts, explanatory logics, and research strategies formulated not only at the systemic level but also at the state level. In particular, an auxiliary theory of the hegemonic state is needed in order to better explain the internal factors that lead to variable strategies of leadership in the world system.

Aristide R. Zolberg, as is clearly illustrated by his chapter, adopts an entirely different stance. Zolberg is prepared to accept the validity and necessity of analyzing the interpenetration of state and system from a global level, but he argues that both the world-economy and long cycle approaches represent backward steps for social science analysis. Because he has criticized the world-economy perspective for its inadequate treatment of political structures and processes in another place (Zolberg, 1981), much of the attention of the current essay is focused upon the long cycle approach. More specifically, Zolberg criticizes long cycle analysis for paying too little attention to the exchange between political and nonpolitical spheres of activity and for insisting on a historical series of repetitions that do not match his perception of the reality of European politicostrategic events. Even so, Zolberg's most fundamental criticism, and one that he direct to both perspectives, is that an "all-encompassing theory at the world-historical level is an impossible dream." History, it is argued, cannot provide explanations but only interpretations of isolated points in time. When this principle is disregarded by treating the past five hundred years as successive cycles/stages of the same world/global system, world system analysts fall into the trap of forcing a broad range of variation among multiple factors and conditions into an overly narrow, reified, and formalized conceptualization.

Not surprisingly, George Modelski finds this line of argument less than persuasive. In his brief rejoinder, Modelski addresses some of Zolberg's specific complaints about the long cycle framework. One important assumption that is frequently overlooked is the long cycle perspective's distinction between global and regional interactions. For example, a world power might be a leader on the global level, as in the initial case of sixteenth-century Portugal, but not necessarily the most powerful actor on the European continent. This often confused point is partially related to the seapower specialization of global leaders but it also reflects the world power's need for, and interest in, some degree of extracontinental freedom of maneuver as opposed to the heavy regional commitments of European land powers. In any event, there is no reason to expect that each long cycle will be identical in all respects for the cyclical sequence is characterized by a definitely progressive institutionalization of the world power role. Furthermore, Modelski points out that a discussion of political-economic linkages is not totally absent from the long cycle perspective, which argues that (a) world powers have the system's lead economies and (b) trade takes place within a political framework initially provided by the world power. More generally, nevertheless, the differences between Zolberg's and Modelski's perspectives are summarized by Modelski's qualified rejection of Zolberg's premise that history cannot be systematized by social scientists.[6] Modelski's primarily contrary view is that the contemporary task is precisely one of making statements about the behavior of identifiable, or time- and space-defined, social systems—one of which is the modern global political system.

Finally, a still different and somewhat exasperated opinion on the subject of multiple perspectives is articulated in Immanuel Wallerstein's chapter. For Wallerstein, arguments over the relative emphasis on economic versus political factors run the risk of completely missing the point of what he chooses to refer to as *the* world-systems perspective. Reflecting in part a total rejection of the conventional divisions of labor within the social sciences, Wallerstein asserts that once one replaces the society/state with the world system as the primary unit of analysis, it no longer makes any sense to speak of different logics for the world-economy and the interstate system. Both concepts refer presumably to different structural aspects of the same, singular world-system in which it is extremely difficult to differentiate what is "economic" from what is "political." Instead of engaging in "semantic juggling," Wallerstein would prefer that we proceed with the "hard work of describing complex reality in politically useful ways."

Needless to say, the essays of this volume raise a respectable number of historical, theoretical, epistemological, and ideological issues. And as is customary, more questions are raised than answered. But the basic point remains that there is more than one way to do world system analysis, and most analysts will agree that there is considerable room for improving the ways in which we conduct world system analyses. Whatever one's assessment of the current state of affairs, we are far more likely to make analytical progress by confronting the contradictions of the sometimes conflicting, sometimes complementary, multiple perspectives currently available. It is hoped that the implicit and explicit ideas and tensions revealed in this volume's collection of essays will contribute to the ongoing debate on how best to interpret the past, present, and future of the world system's "reality." The essays may not be able to resolve the analytical disputes, but they can make us more aware of the need to work on resolving the disagreements and to take greater advantage of the points of agreement.

NOTES

1. This point is central to an understanding of the origins of the world-economy approach to world system analysis as is indicated by Wallerstein's contribution to this volume. But concern with these types of issues is by no means unique to world system analysis (see Tilly, 1975a, 1975b).

2. Modelski now prefers to regard the "global war" quarter as the initial quarter of a new long cycle—as opposed to the fourth quarter of a concluding long cycle. Precisely where one wishes to break into the sequence of phases will depend on the nature and purposes of the analysis. The sequence of phases remains the same.

3. Wallerstein (1982), however, seems to be willing to give a bit more credit to the role of seapower than has been the case in the past.

4. A number of works come immediately to mind: "hegemonic stability" analyses (Gilpin, 1981; Kindleberger, 1973, 1981; Keohane, 1980, 1982; Krasner, 1976, 1982b; McKeown, 1983) and international regime analyses (see Krasner, 1982a). Other fairly recent studies of immediate interest include McNeill (1982), Olson (1982), Padfield (1979), and Weber (1981)—the last of which manages to inject elements of Parsons and Lasswell into the study of the Kondratieff phenomenon.

5. The critical orientation of the last group of chapters is not accidental. In contrast to the other authors, Professors Wallerstein and Zolberg were invited to read and comment as they saw fit on ten of the first eleven chapters (Professor Doran's response to the Thompson chapter was prepared after they had completed their reviews). Professor Modelski had reserved the right to reply to any extensive commentary on his contribution thus accounting for his brief rejoinder to the Zolberg chapter.

6. Modelski and Zolberg agree that there is little point in searching for universal laws of history.

REFERENCES

DORAN, C. F. and W. PARSONS (1980) "War and the cycle of relative power." American Political Science Review 74 (December): 947-965.
GILPIN, R. (1981) War and Change in World Politics. Cambridge: Cambridge University Press.
KEOHANE, R. O. (1980) "The theory of hegemonic stability and changes in international economic regimes, 1967-1977," pp. 131-162 in O. R. Holsti, R. M. Siverson, and A. L. George (eds.) Change in the International System. Boulder, CO: Westview.
———(1982) "Hegemonic leadership and U.S. foreign policy in the 'long decade' of the 1950s," pp. 49-76 in W. P. Avery and D. P. Rapkin (eds.) America in a Changing World Political Economy. New York: Longman.
KINDLEBERGER, C. P. (1981) "Dominance and leadership in the international economy: exploitation, public goods, and free rides." International Studies Quarterly 25 (June): 242-254.
———(1973) The World in Depression, 1929-1939. Berkeley: University of California Press.
KRASNER, S. D. [ed.] (1982a) International Regimes. A special issue of International Organization 36 (Spring).
———(1982b) "American policy and global economic stability," pp. 29-48 in W. P. Avery and D. P. Rapkin (eds.) America in a Changing World Political Economy. New York: Longman.
———(1976) "State power and the structure of international trade." World Politics 28 (April): 317-347.
McKEOWN, T. J. (1983) "Hegemonic stability theory and 19th century tariff levels in Europe." International Organization 37 (Winter): 73-91.
McNEILL, W. H. (1982) The Pursuit of Power. Chicago: University of Chicago Press.
MODELSKI, G. (1982) "Long cycles and the strategy of United States international economic policy," pp. 97-116 in W. P. Avery and D. P. Rapkin (eds.) America in a Changing World Political Economy. New York: Longman.
———(1981) "Long cycles, Kondratieffs, alternating innovations and their implications for U.S. foreign policy," in C. W. Kegley, Jr., and P. J. McGowan (eds.) The Political Economy of Foreign Policy Behavior. Beverly Hills, CA: Sage.
———(1978) "The long cycle of global politics and the nation-state." Comparative Studies in Society and History 20 (April): 214-235.
OLSON, M. (1982) The Rise and Decline of Nations. New Haven, CT: Yale University Press.
PADFIELD, P. (1979) Tide of Empires: Decisive Naval Campaigns in the Rise of the West, 1481-1654. London: Routledge & Kegan Paul.
SINGER, J. D., S. BREMER, and J. STUCKEY (1972) "Capability distribution, uncertainty and major power war, 1820-1965," pp. 19-48 in B. Russett (ed.) Peace, War, and Numbers. Beverly Hills, CA: Sage.
THOMPSON, W. R. (1983) "The world-economy and the long cycle of world leadership: the question of world system time," in P. J. McGowan and C. W. Kegley, Jr. (eds.) Foreign Policy and the Modern World system. Beverly Hills, CA: Sage.
TILLY, C. (1975a) "Reflections on the history of European state-making," pp. 3-83 in C. Tilly (ed.) The Formation of National States in Western Europe. Princeton, NJ: Princeton University Press.
———(1975b) "Western state-making and theories of political transformation," pp. 601-638 in C. Tilly (ed.) The Formation of National States in Western Europe.

Princeton, NJ: Princeton University Press.
WALLERSTEIN, I. (1982) "The three instances of hegemony in the history of the capitalist world-economy." Fernand Braudel Center, State University of New York, Binghamton. (mimeo)
———(1980) The Modern World-System II: Mercantilism and the Consolidation of the European World-Economy, 1600-1750. New York: Academic.
———(1979) The Capitalist World-Economy. Cambridge: Cambridge University Press.
———(1974) The Modern World-System I: Capitalist Agriculture and the Origins of the European World-Economy in the Sixteenth Century. New York: Academic.
WEBER, R. P. (1981) "Society and economy in the western world system." Social Forces 59 (June): 1130-1148.
ZOLBERG, A. R. (1981) "Origins of the modern world system: a missing link." World Politics 33 (January): 253-281.

PART I

Accenting the Economic Dimension

1

World System in Crisis

ANDRE GUNDER FRANK

The new political economic crisis throughout the world is also producing a crisis—or at least crises—of ideology and theory that cries out for alternative social theory approaches to guide political practice. In the so-called first world of the industrial-capitalist West (including Japan, Australia, and New Zealand), the deepest economic crisis in over a generation is reviving long-forgotten memories of the interwar Great Depression, if not yet of the two world wars themselves. The push of economic and political crisis in the second world of the East—as well as the pull of the West in crisis—is increasingly reintegrating the "socialist" economies into the changing capitalist international division of labor. Both of these crises, as well as the failure of two "development decades" in the Third World, are imposing political oppression on the peoples in most of the countries of the South, raising their doubts about the values of national liberation and the prospects for socialism. The various "parts" of the world are economically more and more integrated into a single economic system through the intervention of increasingly powerful and repressive states. Yet paradoxically, a new wave of nationalism is threatening international relations among, and challenging authority within, national states all around the world. These real social crises in various parts of the world—or are they reflections of a crisis in a single world system?—are also producing crises in received theory and ideology throughout the world.

The manifestly increasing—and increasingly manifest—inadequacy of partial theories to analyze this reality in crisis and the related crises of ideology to guide political practice in different parts of the world (to say nothing of the world as a whole) cries out for alternative theory and ideology. The publication, and indeed the title, of *The Crisis of*

*Democracy: Report on the Governability of Democracies to the
Trilateral Commission* (Crozier et al., 1975); *The Alternative,* by
the East German Communist Rudolph Bahro (1979); *The Limits to
Growth* (Meadows et al., 1974); and *Reshaping the International
Order* by the Club of Rome, as well as the call for a new international
economic order by Third World governments in the United Nations,
is a visible manifestation of crises or crisis and resulting search for
alternatives on the theoretical and ideological levels. Though all of
these authors seek to read and help shape the future, none of them
draws much on the past or tries to view past, present, and future as a
sequence in a single historical process. Moreover, with the notable
exception of Bahro, these ideological efforts have been undertaken—
and sometimes very self-consciously so—on behalf of the already
ruling classes or dominant groups in the West and South.

In response to the same crisis, an alternative, more modest
approach—if not yet a theory and intentionally not an ideology—is
emerging at least incipiently out of the historical-social scientific
efforts of some independent scholars in the West and South (and
perhaps the East?). This approach, which recognizes the exploitative
and oppressive class basis of past and present development, seeks to
offer a historical perspective and an analytical approach to the
examination of the past, present, and future development of the whole
world within a *single modern world system.* This system is driven by
capital accumulation, whose dynamic and structural characteristics
simultaneously generate cycles of expansion and stagnation or crisis
in a process of periodically uneven development and unequal geographical and sectoral development among the various interrelated
parts of the single world system. In this unequal development, the
structural role of some parts of the world system is transformed, particularly when the recurrent crises of accumulation and development
oblige the system to undergo structural transformations among its
various parts.

Although much of the analytical work on this modern world system
is intentionally historical, all of its authors (to be cited below) self-
consciously and explicity regard their theoretical concern to be the
clarification of contemporary events—and, indeed, future tendencies—
in the development of the present world in crisis. Indeed, in the
contemporary history of social thought, the development of this
approach to the study of the modern world system should be regarded
as an outgrowth of the world in crisis.

Economic, social, political, and, therefore, ideological crises seem
to be coming to a head in and with regard to the South, East, and West
of the world. Although each of these crises may appear limited to one

or another particular part of the world—and although they are reviewed here separately and successively, part by part—all these crises may be only partial manifestations of a larger general crisis in the development of the single modern world system.

THE THIRD WORLD

"Development" and "modernization" theory have proven inappropriate in a world in which the gap between rich and poor is growing by leaps and bounds and the number of poor and the depth of their poverty are increasing. The failure of these theories and models has now been publicly recognized by their most authorized spokesmen (e.g., Leontief, 1977, for the United Nations; the World Bank President McNamara, 1977; and former U.S. Secretary of State Henry Kissinger [in his interview on SALT and Iran in the *Economist,* February 3 and 10, 1979]).

In his 1977 address to the Board of Governors of the World Bank, President McNamara (1977: 7) soberly observed:

> Development, despite all the efforts of the past 25 years, has failed to close the gap in per capita incomes between developed and developing countries. . . . The proposition is true. But the conclusion to be drawn from it is not that development efforts have failed, but rather that "closing the gap" was never a realistic objective in the first place. . . . It was simply not a feasible goal. Nor is it one today. . . . Even if developing countries manage to double their per capita growth rate, while the industrial world maintains its historical growth, it will take nearly a century to close the absolute income gap between them. Among the fastest growing developing countries, only 7 would be able to close the gap within 100 years, and only another 9 within 1,000 years.

Since the 1973-1975 recession in the developed capitalist countries, their growth rates have declined, however; and the growth rates of the non-oil-exporting, (under)developing countries in the Third World have been cut in half.

For the world's poor, the past has been dismal and future prospects are dim. The *World Development Report, 1978* of the World Bank (1978) observes beginning on its first page:

> The past quarter center has seen great progress in developing countries. . . . But much remains to be accomplished. Most countries have not yet completed the transition to modern economies and societies, and their growth is hindered by a variety of domestic and international factors. Moreover, about 800 million people still live in absolute poverty. These people are living at the very margin of existence—with inadequate shelter, education, and health care. . . . Many of these

people have experienced no improvement in their living standards; and in countries where economic growth has been slow, the living standards of the poor may even have deteriorated.

But as recent events in Iran and the end of the "miracle" in Brazil suggest, even with rapid growth here and there, one economic "miracle" and "take off" into development after another turns out to be a snare and a delusion based on ruthless exploitation, cruel oppression, and/or the marginalization of the majority of the population from "development." This experience, which is only sharpened by the present crisis, has now raised serious doubts about the very concept of development as a progressive, integral, and integrating social process in most of the (Third) world (which was first called "backward," "poor," or "colonial," and then through successive euphomisms "undeveloped," "underdeveloped," "developing," "new," "emerging," and "less developed" [LDCs]). At the same time, though structural impediments to development and dependence certainly are and remain real in the Third World, the usefulness of structuralist, dependence, and new dependence theories of underdevelopment as guides to policy seems to have been undermined by the world crisis of the 1970s (Frank, 1977; Leys, 1977). The original sin, inherited from a view of the world divided into parts (or at least the Achilles heel of these conceptions of dependence or of these dependent conceptions), has always been the implicit and sometimes explicit notion of some sort of "independent" alternative for the Third World. This theoretical alternative never existed in fact—certainly not on the "noncapitalist" path and now apparently not even through "socialist" revolutions as we have known them. The new crisis of real-world development now renders our partial development and parochial dependence theories as well as their related policy solutions invalid and inapplicable.

The recent call for national and/or collective "self-reliance" (but without autarky) within a capitalist "new international economic order" appears to be the consequence of ideological desperation and the desperate appeal to ideology. For instance, Angola's economic support is still largely derived from the payments of foreign exchange that the U.S. Gulf Oil Company makes for petroleum produced in Cabinda under the protection of troops from Cuba. In the meantime, with regard to the model of self-reliance in Africa, *Business Week* (December 25, 1978) reports "Tanzania: A Economy on the Brink of Collapse," the *International Herald Tribune* (May 7, 1979) headlines "Amid Economic Difficulties, Tanzania Seen Improving Ties to U.S. [and] is taking a new look at Western finance and expertise," and the Corporate Assessment of Investment Potential in Sub-Saharan African by Business International (January 1979) places Tanzania in sixth place "in descending order of investment interest [among] countries with the greatest investment potential, 1978-1988." No wonder that Tanzanian President Nyerere commemorated the tenth anniversary of his proclamation of the goal of self-reliance and *ujama* (freedom) in the Arusha Declaration by soberly observing tht "Tanzania is certainly neither socialist nor self-reliance. . . . Our nation is still economically dependent. . . . [The goal of socialism] is not even in sight" (International Herald Tribune April 21, 1977).

With regard to existing and prospective socialist countries elsewhere, the Stalinist theories of historical progression by inevitable stages through feudalism, capitalism, socialism, and communism; the transitional existence of two world markets, one capitalist and the other socialist; and the post-Stalin Soviet amendment proposing a "noncapitalist path" in the transition to socialism have certainly been relegated to the dustbin of history by experience. Khruschev's hope of "burying" the West has itself been buried; and the Soviet Union is trying to compensate for its comparative economic and political/ideological weakness (which marks the "popular democracies" of Eastern Europe even more) through increasing mililtary strength (which threatens not only its potential enemies in the West but also its supposed allies in the East). The Maoist theory and praxis of "new democracy," "walking on two legs," "cultural revolution," and "three worlds" (two superpowers, the other industrialized countries, and the Third World including China) has been most seriously challenged by events inside and outside China and has recently been denounced even by the erstwhile, most faithful Albanian Workers Party. The world-embracing, albeit not universal, sympathy with the Cuban guerrilla and popular movements, Korean *suche* self-reliance, and Vietnamese national liberation as models have given way to increasingly searching critiques and heartfelt doubts among many of their previously enthusiastic supporters around the world. Trotskyist and new left movements of many varieties have left a trail of disillusioned or disaffected militants to be reintegrated into the establishment because the latter seemed to tremble in one country after another in 1968 and its aftermath. Now, after the largely self-inflicted electoral defeats of the Communist parties in France, Spain, and Italy (as well as in Japan on the municipal level), observers from left to right, including *Business International* (beginning with foresight in 1977) and the American press, have observed the "Last Days of Eurocommunism?" (International Herald Tribune, April 28, 1979). They are writing off "Eurocommunism" (which was neither "euro" nor "communist") as a nonstarter (and obliging the Secretary General of the French Communist Party, Georges Marchais, to issue "denials" of Eurocommunism's demise at the May 1979 party congress that celebrated the postmortem of the left alliance with the socialist and followed Marchais's lead in another about turn in the direction of Moscow).

Deng Xiaoping's theatrics on his 1979 tour of the United States, part of the Chinese effort to get Western technology and credits (to support the drive to make China a world industrial power by the year 2000) highlight the direction of Chinese development over the last decade. Since the defeat of the Cultural Revolution and the downfall of Lin Piao in 1971 (apparently for favoring a rapproachement with the Soviet Union instead of with the United States), the way was cleared for Chou en Lai's "conciliatory" line: of ping pong diplomacy, the invitation to Nixon to visit China, the launching of the four (industry, agriculture, technology, and defense) modernization programs (no longer so much through self-reliance as with foreign aid and trade, which has quadrupled since 1970 and 85 percent of which is with capitalist countries), and the rehabilitation and reinstatement of the victims of the cultural revolution. Deng Xiaoping is now taking China on a "great leap backward" to 1957, to the year before the Great Leap Forward, in the attempt to get a better running start to leap to great-power status by the twenty-first century.

THE SECOND WORLD

In the wake of their own economic and related political problems, the "socialist" economies of the Soviet Union and Eastern Europe are implementing a détente with the West (albeit a competition with China); they are seeking to import Western technology and to pay for it with exports produced by cheap labor through thousands of bilateral production agreements with Western firms and tripartite ones involving Third World states as well. Even so, the East European and Soviet demand for Western technology is growing so rapidly that their cumulative balance-of-payments deficit and debt with the West has grown from U.S. $8 billion in 1972 to over U.S. $50 billion in 1978, despite the Eastern balance of payments surplus with the South, which the East uses in part to offset its deficit with the West. Moreover, as Brezhnev correctly observed, "Because of the broad economic links between capitalist and socialist countries, the ill effects of the current crisis in the West have also had an impact on the socialist world." Zhikov, his colleague and president of the Bulgarian State Council, adds, "It may be hoped that the crisis in the West may come to a rapid end." The Eurocommunist parties in the West, for their part, not only hope the crisis will go away; they also do the best they can to help capital overcome the crisis economically by imposing austerity measures on labor (as in Spain and Italy) and to face the crisis politically by strengthening the state and its repressive power (which the Communist Party of Italy is now the first to defend and expand).

One is left to wonder how and why the official pronouncements of self-styled Communist and revolutionary socialist centers, parties, and movements continue to claim that "the situation is excellent" (Bejing), "socialism is advancing stronger than ever" (Moscow), and "revolutionary possibilities are around the corner" (Trotskyists), at least in southern Europe. These pronouncements continue in the face of the domestic and foreign policies—now including repression at home and wars abroad—that mark contemporary socialist countries, communist parties, and revolutionary movements and in the face of a grave crisis of Marxism that is costing socialism countless millions of supporters around the world.

The theoretical, ideological, and political dilemmas of socialism today derive from and may be summarized by the complete abandonment of the famous means and end of the *Communist Manifesto:* "Workers of the world unite." Both the theory and the praxis of proletarian internationalism as a means to communism have been replaced by "socialism in (my) one country." Moreover, communism itself as the goal of social development has in practice and apparently even in theory been replaced by "socialism." Though for Marx and Engles and for Lenin socialism meant no more than an unstable, transitionary process or stage on the road to communism, socialism has been converted into an end station or steady state. Some socialists claim to have arrived already, and other, more realistic ones (ironically called "idealists" by the former), such as Mao, claim only that their country is or was in the transition to socialism, which requires repeated and successful cultural revolutions (of which the first one in China failed). In prerevolutionary Chile it was customary to talk of the transition to the transition to socialism before the military coup violently destroyed these illusions and placed only "restricted democracy" on the agenda as the distant goal to be achieved. In a (vain?) attempt to escape a similar fate, the Eurocommunists with the Italians at their head therefore proposed a "historic compromise" as their goal. Of course, if socialism no longer means the transition to communism through proletarian internationalism but is an established state in one country and a distant goal for others, it becomes endlessly debatable how you recognize such a state if you see one and how you get there if you do not. Thus socialists become like the person who looks for his or her lost key under the nearest street light because he or she can see more quickly and more easily in the light than in the dark; the key to socialism was lost somewhere in the darkness and the goal of communism is lost with it.

The more the "Marxist" theory that is supposed to guide and justify this "socialist" praxis is examined in the plain light of day, the more indistinguishable "Marxism" becomes from the orthodox, everyday, bourgeois capitalist theory and praxis of "national development." It is ironic in view of the stated goals of Marxism—but perhaps not surprising in terms of its analysis—that with the exception of the state-promoted capitalist ascension of noncolonial Japan into the charmed circle of industrial powers, only the "socialist" countries have been able to achieve (or as in the case of China, realistically aspire to) participation in the world capitalist economy on a basis that is even remotely equal to that of the developed capitalist countries. *None* of the (under)developing/capitalist Third World countries have escaped dependent capitalist underdevelopment, nor do any of them show any prospects of doing so in the foreseeable future, despite Brazilian, Korean, Iranian, or Mexican miracles or oil booms. Only some socialist economies can now knock on the door of or challenge the capitalist inner sanctum (and only because they were temporarily isolated from the workings of the capitalist international division of labor). This was ironically not because they preferred isolation but mainly because the capitalist powers forced it on them during the Cold War in reaction to the socialist transformations of domestic property and productive and political relations (which are the other reason for their "success"). Even the most nationalist-dependent and state-capitalist Third World countries like Nasser's Egypt never attempted such transformations. The further irony is if Deng's China, Phan's Vietnam, Tito's Yugoslavia, Kadar's Hungary, Gierek's Poland, and perhaps last but not least Brezhnev, Andropov, and/or his successor's USSR are any guide, these countries do not want to use socialism to challenge the West in its time of crisis; instead, they wish to join as competitive partners in the capitalist world system on as nearly equal terms as possible and in the process lend the capitalists an economic, political, and thereby also ideological hand in overcoming the world crisis of capitalism. Someone in the German Democratic Republic suggested that socialist would win the race with the West as soon as they stopped running in the same direction. This situation may simply be the inevitable result of treading the path of "socialism in one country" while confronting the cruel ironies of an ancient Greek tragedy in the guise of the modern world system.

THE FIRST WORLD

The industrial capitalist countries of the West appeared to enter a long crisis of capital accumulation over a decade ago. Realization of the same, however, spread only with the onset of the 1973-1975 recession (with its 15 million unemployed compared to 5 million in the mid-1960s) and its negative growth rates; it was reinforced by a "recovery" period, during which growth returned to only half of its previous rate, investment stagnated, and unemployment rose to 17 million—while inflation continued. The faltering stagflation recovery has made business, government, and the public generally conscioius of the fact that these economic problems and their social consequences are not simply short and passing cyclical phenomena but an undeniable fact of life. There is now widespread consciousness in the West that the days of "bigger and better" rapid growth are a thing of the past; and as *Time* magazine correctly observed, was "the last year of the past."

This economic crisis has also brought on a crisis in economics, which in the words of *Business Week* has been brought to complete "bankruptcy" as a source of economic forecasting, analysis, or policy. On the other hand, this bankruptcy of economics manifests itself most visibly in the face of simultaneous unemployment or stagnation and inflation—dubbed "stagflation" or in 1975 even "slumpflation"—in every Western capitalist country. On the other hand, the growth, inflation, and exchange rates differ and fluctuate from one country to the next, thwarting all attempts to analyze, let alone regulate, the international monetary and economic system. The periodic "economic summits" among the leaders of the principal Western industrial powers are no more than the open admission of the failure of international economic coordination and analysis; they are reminiscent of the complete failure of the World Economic Conference held in London in 1931 during the Great Depression.

The "theoretical" problem is that the Keynesian economic theory and policy offer only deflationary remedies for inflation and reflationary ones for unemployment. Keynesianism is based on the assumption of competition, while the increasingly monopolized structure of the economy generates simultaneous inflation and unemployment. Moreover, the Keynesian theory and policy are essentially limited to national economies, in which states can wield substantial regulatory influence. But the world capitalist crisis is international, and no single nation-state (since the relative decline of the United States) or any supranational institution (which are useless in the face of the speculative, private banking Eurocurrency market and nationalist state economic policies) can stabilize the world economy. It is ironic that Keynesianism was born during the Depression to combat depression because it became univerally accepted and "successful" only during—and because of—the postwar expansion. At the first sign of renewed world recession Keynesianism has proven itself to be a delusion.

The bankruptcy of Keynesianism and of "post-Keynesian synthesis" (with neoclassical economics) is also the theoretical reason for the current reactionary exhumation of the simplistic neoclassical and monetarist economic theory of the 1920s. This revival of old theory is highlighted by the award of Nobel prizes in economics to

Fredrich von Hayek, whose theoretical work was done before the Great Depression, and Milton Friedman, whose lone voice echoed in the desert until the new world economic crisis put his unpopular and antipopulist theories on the agenda of business board rooms and government cabinet rooms in one capitalist country after another. The real reason for the recent recourse to 50-year-old theories is that capital now wants them to legitimize its attack on the welfare state and "unproductive" expenditures on social services, which capital claims to need for "productive" investment in industry, including armaments.

The onset of economic crisis—with its low and sometimes negative growth rates, permanent inflation, and structural unemployment— and the reinstatement of outworn economic theories and policies have also generated a serious ideological crisis in the West. Right-wing and middle-of-the-road political parties can no longer plausibly offer the bigger and better American way of life; and left-wing parties are afraid to offer a fundamental challenge to the former, lest the political center of gravity shift even further to the right or toward fascism in response. Thus across the political spectrum in the West everybody's best offer is the lesser evil. In other words, a game of musical chairs develops in which every political party and faction rushes to sit in the just vacated chair to the right, except that a few of them violate the rules of the game by moving two or three seats to the right at one jump, sowing confusion and making those who shift right more slowly appear to be almost radically left by comparison. But offering and choosing the lesser evil by moving to the next political chair on the right can only be a stopgap measure in the face of deepening crisis until some political force(s) find some new, "positive"-sounding ideology with which to legitimize their increasingly reactionary crisis policies. So far, such new (national socialist?) ideology and organization have not been developed or, at least, have not found widespread support. But what will happen after the next and perhaps deeper recession, say by 1984? Will George Orwell's Big Brother be watching?

Beyond these crises in the theories and models or ideologies of development in the South, socialism in the East, and growth in the West, and beyond the increasingly far-reaching repercussions of each region's crisis in the other two, another double-barreled critical phenomenon is looming up in all three: nationalism, or regionalism and religion, or a combination of both, as under Islam. Perhaps more than an additional crisis phenomenon, the rapid intensification of nationalism and the rapid spread of religious sentiment must more properly be regarded as ostrichlike reactions to global, regional, national, and local crisis, which though themselves are largely inspired by fear should be equally fear inspiring in their possible consequences in and for our single world system and its different parts. Indeed, Orwell's Big Brother was watching only over compliance with national duty in one-third of the world, as it shifted alliances and conflicts with the other two parts and therefore changed the definition of national duty in each of them.

All efforts to build a supranational state or even a single superimperialist political system has so far failed. In contrast, nationalist, ethnic, religious, and regional forces are increasingly threatening even the existing states despite the spread—and through the reincorporation of the socialist countries, increasingly so—of the single world economic system based on a capitalist international division of labor, not only through international trade but also in the transnational organization of production. Nationalist ideology seems to have more appeal and mobilizes far greater numbers of people around the Third World than does socialist ideology; and where the two conflict, as they increasingly seem to now that the postwar era of national liberation is drawing to a close, socialism is increasingly being sacrificed on the altar of nationalism as in Somalia, Ethiopia, and Eritrea. The participation of the socialist states in these conflicts suggest that they are far from immune to the current nationalist virus; and international relations, now including wars, among the socialist countries prove that they have been seriously bitten by the nationalist bug. Indeed, for societies that claim to have virtually resolved class conflict and the national questions nationalism paradoxically appears most rampant today in the socialist "bloc." Moreover, nationalism is becoming an increasingly potent force within most socialist countries, which may soon be subjected to serious threats and challenges from various nationalities. It is ironic, though perhaps not surprising, that in these supposedly atheist societies, where class conflict has been suppressed albeit not overcome through the negation of political pluralism, nationalism sometimes cum religion is becoming a, if not the, major vehicle for the expression of social discontent and the challenge of state authority.

The West, however, cannot afford to throw many stones at the East. In one Western country after another national, regional, ethnic, and religious movements—*within* Britain, Belgium, France, Spain, Italy, Canada, and even the Hispanic United States—are challenging state authority or are being used to shift the exercise of state power toward a more reactionary basis. Ironically, but again perhaps not too surprisingly, the world-crisis-generated frustrations (as they are perceived on the national, regional and local levels) are channeled into nationalist and religious and even subnational regionalist movements that are likely to strengthen state authoritarianism and weaken still further both national and particularly international collaboration. For this reason as well, therefore, the crisis of the modern world capitalist system is likely to become more acute in the foreseeable future.

"Crisis" does not mean "the end"; on the contrary, it refers to the critical time during which the end will be avoided through new adaptations if possible; only failing these does the end become unavoidable. The *Concise Oxford English Dictionary* defines Crisis as: "Turning point, especially of disease. Moment of danger or suspense in politics, etc. as cabinet, financial. From Greek KRISIS, decision." The crisis is a period in which a diseased social, economic, and political body or system cannot live on as before and is obliged, on pain of death, to undergo transformations that will give it a new lease on life. Therefore, this period of crisis is a historical moment of danger and suspense during which the crucial decisions and transformations are made that will determine the future development of the system and its new social, economic, and political basis.

In the capitalist world economy of the modern world system, accumulation on a world scale can no longer proceed as it did in the postwar era of expansion until and unless unequal development and dependent accumulation are put on a new footing. Among the most important elements of the emerging international division of labor are the reincorporation of the socialist economies in the world market and the transfer to certain world market industries both to them and to selected parts of the Third World, where wages are lower and labor discipline is higher; and the "rationalization" of industrial production in the West itself through investment in labor-saving technology, such as microchips, and the use of the resultant unemployment to depress wages in the industrial capitalist countries themselves. It was not an accident that when trade among the industrial capitalist countries declined by nearly 15 percent in 1975, industrial exports to the socialist countries and the Third World increased sufficiently so that total world trade declined by only 5 percent. Profits from exports to and work in the East and the South have continued to provide a significant safety net for business and safety valve for government in the West since then, while stagnating investment has shifted from expanding and new production facilities to the rationalization of existing ones with excess capacity.

The concomitant social and political transformations that necessarily accompany this new international division of labor include militarism, war and East-West competition in the South, détente and a Washington-Beijing-Tokyo axis with the East, and technological rationalization and economic austerity policies in the "national interest" without the erstwhile legitimation of a red scare but of a new defense gap instead (reminiscent of the phony missile gap of the 1960s, but apparently forgetting the subsequent credibility gap, in the West). It is to be expected that all this economic, social, and political transformation poses serious challenges to existing policy, theory, and ideology.

It would be too much to ask and naive to expect far-reaching and complete answers to these problems from any alternative body or system of theory at this early stage of the crisis. There is a growing body of historical social scientific analysis, however, that will, it is hoped, offer the beginnings of an alternative analytic perspective. This emerging approach and analysis are reflected in the very titles of the recent books on *Accumulation on a World Scale* (Amin, 1974), *Unequal Development* (Amin, 1976), *The Modern World System* (Wallerstein, 1974), *The Capitalist World Economy* (Wallerstein, 1979), *The New International Division of Labour* (Fröbel et al., 1977), *World Accumulation, 1492-1789* (Frank, 1978), *Dependent Accumulation and Underdevelopment* (Frank, 1979), *Crisis in the World Economy* (Frank, 1980), and *Crisis in the Third World* (Frank, 1981).

Interestingly, though certainly not accidentally, the intellectual and political development of these authors has come from a practical theoretical concern with the Third World and a political commitment to socialist transformation there and elsewhere. Amin, Frank, Wallerstein, and Foëbel et al. all started with the politically committed study in or of one part of the Third World and then went on to examine the problematique of the Third World as a whole. All of these authors, and increasingly many others, such as Christian Palloix (1971) in France, Giovanni Arrighi (1978) in Italy, and Amya Bagchi (1977) and Ranjit Sau (1978) in India, who began their concern in or with the dependence of the Third World, soon found that they were unable to analyze its problematique adequately unless they expanded their purview to the analysis of the world capitalist system and perhaps the modern world system as a whole. In doing so (and simultaneously with the aggravation of the world crisis, which seemed to shift the focal points of the political process from Lin Piao's surrounding villages to the world cities, that is, from the periphery to the semi-periphery and the core of the system), these authors also shifted their theoretical concerns toward the system and its apparent motor force at the center, without however giving up their political commitment to its periphery (though the worldwide crisis of Marxism and socialism, of course, does not leave them untouched).

The present concern of these and other authors in the analysis of the world system may be summarized in a schematic way, which probably does not do justice to the complexity or the constant evolution of their analysis, as follows:

(1) *There is only one system, which is worldwide.* It was formed by the expansion from a European core through the incorporation of

one part of the American, African, and Asian periphery after another. Several times some parts of the system withdrew temporarily, but so far they seem to have been and still are subject to subsequent reincorporation.

(2) *The economic structure of the system seems to be based on a core, a periphery, and some semi-peripheries between them.* (The analytic utility of this formulation, which is partly inherited from the study of dependence, is perhaps the most doubtful aspect of this approach.) The strength of the state seems to be roughly proportional and the degree of exploitation of labor and its contractual freedom seem to vary inversely with the state's distance from the core; but all attempts at the formation of a systemwide or even imperial state or of accumulation without exploitation have thus far failed. Participation in the system core, periphery, and semi-periphery has involved a wide variety of changing forms of labor, productive, and trade relations, whose content has been modified, and whose forms have been maintained, to suit the exigencies of capitalist accumulation on a world scale. The questions arises whether "postcapitalist/socialist" relations of production are any the less suited to fill this need than "precapitalist/feudal" or any other "noncapitalist" relations have been.

(3) *Placement at the core, semi-periphery, and periphery of various parts of the world has changed over time and continues to do so, albeit under some apparently systemic restrictions.* Leadership at the core has moved from the Mediterranean to Northwest Europe and Britain and then on to the United States, whose relative though not absolute position is already under challenge again. There has been frequent and substantial movement from semi-periphery both upward into the core and downward into the periphery, and some downward movement from core to semi-periphery (Spain in the seventeenth century, Britain in the twentieth?); but there has never been a move directly from periphery to core, and none is yet visible on the horizon today, even though a new international division of labor seems to be emerging today just as it has already several times in the past.

(4) *The development of the system has been characterized by long waves of expansion and stagnation or contraction from its birth in the crisis of European feudalism until today.* In the past, each stagnation or crisis has involved a far-reaching transformation of the system as a whole and its various parts, including the composition, membership, and systemic function of core, semi-periphery, and periphery. It may be possible to identify waves of different duration, one within or on top of the other, and certainly of short cycles within the waves. Today we are at the beginning of a cyclical downturn

within a contraction or crisis that began in the mid-1960s and which may in turn be part of a period of contraction or retrenchment that began around 1913 within a longer wave. If all these downward phases were to operate simultaneously, they would have far-reaching implications for future economic, social, political, and cultural, as well as ideological and theoretical, development of the world system.

(5) *Theoretical analysis of and informed political praxis in the class and national struggles within the present critical situation can benefit from a historical perspective and the development of a body of theory that permits the examination of the here and now in the context of a then and there.* This would encompass the entire modern development of the world system. For instance, this world historical perspective can help us analyze contemporary modifications in the division of labor within a single but spatially and sectorally unequal worldwide economy in response to still another major crisis in a single but historically uneven process of capital accumulation. By contrast, received theories would still encourage or even oblige us to examine many different national problems and their *international* relations at a time when these theories themselves are in crisis—precisely because in practice and therefore also in theory these problems escape short-run national (and even a combination of many national) definitions, analyses, and, above all, policies. Moreover, class interest, policies, and conflicts still seem to present themselves for resolution and therefore for analysis only within national—and by extension international—political contexts. By contrast, in reality the class structure and particularly economic and political power of the ruling class—which controls the means and processes of accumulation through economic production, social reproduction, and political repression—should perhaps be analyzed (and combatted) on the world-wide basis of a single economic, social, and political system. By implication, of course, the people in the "socialist" countries have not yet achieved liberation from the capitalist world system, and they are not likely to be able to do so on the national basis of "socialism in one country" after another. On the other hand, the renewed rise of nationalism (including ethnic and regional movements) and religion appears to be, but probably is not, the manifestation of increased self-generated affirmation in existing autonomous social units (which more often than not have no real economic, social, political, or ethnic existence in the contemporary world). From a world system perspective, by contrast, nationalism and religion appeal more visibly as a combination of two defensive reactions: one reaction competitively pits some nationalist holders of economic and political power against others who are perceived as deriving increasingly more benefit from the unequal process of world accumulation. The other nationalist reaction protectively counters the threat that the possible mobiliza-

tion of the exploited and oppressed direct producers near and far ("at home" and "abroad") pose to the present holders of economic and political power by defusing or derailing this worldwide, interclass struggle through mobilizations on national, ethnic, regional, and/or religious intraclass lines. While an effective worldwide, interclass struggle would challenge and threaten the very basis and operation of the world capitalist system, much international but intraclass conflict now helps to maintain the exploitative and oppressive nature of the system worldwide and therefore also nationally and locally. By contributing to the development of world system analysis, we only wish to add another modest grain of sand to the continued and cumulative antisystemic struggle for human liberation from this system.

REFERENCES

AMIN, S (1976) Unequal Development. Brighton: Harvester.
———(1974) Accumulation on a World Scale. New York: Monthly Review Press.
ARRIGHI, G. (1978) The Geometry of Imperialism. London: New Left Books.
BAGCHI, A. K. (1977) "Cost of economic growth as viewed from less developed countries." Paper delivered to the Fifth World Congress of the International Economic Association, Tokyo.
BAHRO, R. (1979) The Alternative. London: New Left Books.
Business International (1979) Strategies for Africa: A Corporate Assessment of Investment Potential in Sub-Saharan Africa. New York: Author.
CROZIER, J. J., S. P. HUNTINGTON, and J. WATANUKI (1975) The Crisis of Democracy. New York: New York University Press.
FRANK, A. G. (1981) Crisis in the Third World. New York: Holmes & Meier.
———(1980) Crisis in the World Economy. New York: Holmes & Meier.
———(1979) Dependent Accumulation and Underdevelopment. New York: Monthly Review Press.
———(1978) World Accumulation, 1492-1789. New York: Monthly Review Press.
———(1977) "Dependence is dead. Long live dependence and the class struggle." World Development 5, 4: 355-370.
FROBEL, F., J. HEINRICHS, and O. KREYE (1977) Die Neue Internationale Arbeitseilung. Reinbeck bie Hamburg: Rowohlt.
LEONTIEF, W. (1977) The Future of the World Economy. New York: Oxford University Press.
LEYS, C. (1977) "Underdevelopment and dependency: critical notes." Journal of Contemporary Asia 7, 1: 92-107.
McNAMARA, R. S. (1977) Address to the Board of Governors. Washington, DC: World Bank Group, September 26.
PALLOIX, C (1975) L'Internationalisation du Capital. Paris: Maspero.
———(1971) L'Economie Mondiale Capitaliste. 2 vols. Paris: Maspero.
SAU, R. (1978) Unequal Exchange, Imperialism and Underdevelopment: An Essay on the Political Economy of World Capitalism. Bombay: Oxford University Press.
TINBERGEN, J. (1976) Reshaping the International Order (RIO): A Report to the Club of Rome. New York: Dutton.
WALLERSTEIN, I. (1979) The Capitalist World-Economy. Cambridge: Cambridge University Press.
———(1974) The Modern World System. New York: Academic.
World Bank (1978) World Development Report, 1978. Washington, DC: World Bank.

2

The Class Structure
of the World-System

ALBERT BERGESEN

In the course of developing the concept of a capitalist world-system a debate has arisen over the relative emphasis to be placed upon social relations of production versus relations of exchange as the determinate social relations of capitalism on a world scale. Some argue that the world-economy is composed of a core-periphery division of labor, a view that emphasizes unequal exchange relations between developed core states and an underdeveloped periphery. Others argue that relations of production (class relations) precede economic exchange, making class relations the determinate social relation of world capitalism.

These different conceptions of the world economy have come to the fore in a number of critiques of the world-system perspective represented by Immanuel Wallerstein, André Gunder Frank, and Samir Amin. Laclau (1971) and Brenner (1977) for instance, have criticized the market and exchange emphasis involved in conceptualizing world capitalism as a world division of labor. They urge more attention to questions of class and modes of production. In response, both Wallerstein (1977) and Frank (1978) have argued that production and exchange are part of the same overall process of capital accumulation, so that it makes little sense to speak of one having priority over the other. Frank (1978) has also suggested a formulation based on a little of both, arguing that underdevelopment is a mixture of unequal

AUTHOR'S NOTE: I would like to thank Chris Chase-Dunn, Walter Goldfrank, Charles Tilly, John Meyer, and Mike Hout for comments on an earlier draft of this chapter.

exchange relations with the metropolitan core and certain class configurations within the periphery.

The argument over whether world capitalism is shaped more by class relations or exchange relations has stagnated, with the more traditional Marxists insisting upon the importance of class relations and the world-system camp continuing to emphasize the core-periphery division of labor and unequal exchange. One reason the debate is getting nowhere is that both sides have been talking past each other and ignoring important points the other has made. This is because they are referring to social processes at quite different levels of analysis, with one side emphasizing class relations *within* societies and the other unequal exchange relations *between* societies. Their emphasis upon class relations is important, but the traditional Marxists fail to see how this position leads them to focus only upon questions of power and control *within* social formations, thereby avoiding the possibility of power and coercive relations *between* core and periphery. Similarly, the world-system camp (Wallerstein, Frank, Amin) correctly perceives the necessity of focusing upon the world economy as whole, but they only see relations of trade and exchange between core and peripheral areas.

In actual fact, both positions are correct. One has identified the correct set of social relations, *class,* while the other the correct level of analysis, *world.* What is needed is to combine the best of both positions and identify the world-system's distinctive *world class relations.*

One reason we do not do this is our continued attachment to the nineteenth-century conception of collective existence, which made societal realities the relevant totality of social relations. If we continue to see the world economy from the societal point of view our present intellectual logjam will continue: Some will realize the theoretical priority of social relations of production but will be limited to identifying those class relations only within societal formations, while others will focus on the world as a whole but will be limited to seeing it only in terms of exchange relations and a division of labor.

In short, we are not going to get beyond haggling over "internal" class relations versus "external" exchange relations until we let go of the theoretical primacy of social formations and move up to considering *global formations, global relations of production,* and a *global mode of production* defined by distinctly *global class relations.*

GLOBOLOGY AND GLOBAL
RELATIONS OF PRODUCTION

If sociology is the science of social systems, social formations, and societal modes of production, then *globology* can be called the science of the global or world-system, global formations, and the global mode of production. At present we are somewhere between the sociology of the past and the globology of the future, for although we are increasingly concerned with the structure and process of the world-system, we continue to conceive of these global realities in essentially societal terms. Perhaps the clearest example of our present position somewhat beyond sociology but not yet to globology is the world-system perspective associated with the thinking of Wallerstein (1974, 1979, 1980), Frank (1978), and Amin (1980). For these world-system theorists, the fundamental units in their model of world order are high-wage, capital-intensive, developed countries specializing in manufactures—the *core*—and low-wage, labor-intensive, underdeveloped countries usually, but not always, specializing in raw materials for export—the *periphery*. A semipheripheral zone, which is something of a mix of core and peripheral economic activities, is also discussed. From this point of view the substance of world economic order is thought to reside in the flow of commodities between core and peripheral zones, constituting an unequal exchange that is understood to be the principal mechanism creating and perpetuating unequal world development, as surplus value is shifted to the core in these unequal exchanges.

The important point is that at the level of the world economy as a whole, unequal exchange relations (flows of commodities between core and periphery) are seen as the world economy's distinctive global social relation, since this is the principal tie or link between core and periphery. This is only a partial picture of the world economy, however; and most important, ignores the question of the possibility of distinctly global class relations that make the core-periphery division of labor physically possible. At the most general level my point here is the same one sociologists made about the classical economists' theory of the division of labor in the nineteenth century: Human interaction and a resultant division of labor do not create social order; rather social order precedes and creates the division of labor. Whether one is speaking of Durkheim's precontractual understandings, Weber's cultural basis of economic motives, or Marx's class relations, the position is the same: collective reality precedes interaction and gives it whatever shape and content it has. For Marx class structure preceded the division of labor, and this same general point holds for the core-periphery division of labor today: It too was created and continues to be reproduced by another set of a priori social relations, or better, global relations—global class relations. The present Wallerstein/Frank/Amin emphasis on the core-periphery division of labor is in some sense a reproduction of the classicial economists' model of a division of labor, except now we are dealing with a division between manufacturing and raw-material-producing countries rather than with a division of labor among individuals. Here countries, or global economic zones, are the equivalent of individuals in a global, rather than national, division of labor. It is, of course, not exactly the same since the exchanges are thought to be unequal (Emmanuel, 1972) and as such not mutually beneficial to both parties. But even with the idea of unequal exchange the fundamental point remains that we are still operating within the confines of an essentially nineteenth-century theoretical framework, where the determinant collective reality, determinant class structures, and determinant modes of production are in the form of societal formations or aggregations of them in the idea of core and peripheral zones.

This is nowhere more apparent then when we see how Wallerstein, Amin, and Frank apply the idea of a mode of production to the world-economy. Everyone readily accepts the idea of the world-economy as a singular empirical reality. How it is to be characterized, though, is another matter. Wallerstein does speak of a capitalist world mode of production, but a mode of production defined by the presence of a world division of labor rather than world class relations. "A capitalist mode [referring here to the world-economy] is one in which production is for exchange, that is it is determined by its profitability on a market. . . . As a formal structure, a world-economy is defined as a single division of labor" (Wallerstein, 1979: 159). Others, like Samir Amin and André Gunder Frank, see the world economy as composed of a number of different modes of production linked together in the larger capitalist world-economy. Samir Amin (1980: 18) is quite explicit: "Thus we find more than two classes in the arena, because we are dealing here not with a single mode of production—the capitalist mode—but with several modes linked together in a capitalist system." For him the overall ensemble of relations that comprise the world-system is a combination of capitalist modes in the center and precapitalist modes in the periphery.

This picture of the capitalist world-economy as a number of different modes of production is also held by Laclau (1971), who conventionally defines capitalism in terms of the wage relation. He thereby concludes that colonial Latin America was not capitalist as many of the direct producers were not separated from their means of production, because in

> the plantations of the West Indies, the economy was based on a mode of production constituted of slave labour, while in the mining areas there developed disguised forms of slavery and other types of forced labour which bore not the slightest resemblance to the formation of a capitalist proleteriat [Laclau, 1971: 30].

If Latin America is noncapitalist and one sticks with the image of linear diachronic stages of capitalist development (Bergesen, 1980), Latin America must be located earlier in the development scheme. Accordingly Laclau (1971: 30) speaks of the "pre-capitalist character of the dominant relations of production in Latin America" and "the feudal regime of haciendas." For Laclau and others (e.g., Amin, 1980: 17), the capitalist mode of production in the core preserves precapitalist modes of production in the periphery, as the development of capitalism in the core results in an intensification of precapitalist, hence feudal, relations of production in the periphery.

> Thus, far from expansion of the external market acting as a disintegrating force on feudalism, its effect was rather to accentuate and consolidate it [Laclau, 1971: 30].

Now we have a strange variation of Frank's famous "development of underdevelopment": the development of *pre*development. We get into this awkward situation only when we see separate modes of production in the core and in the periphery. Even extensive core-periphery contact does not seem to suggest one mode of production, but rather a "world capitalist system . . . that . . . includes, *at the level of its definition,* various modes of production" (Laclau, 1971: 37).

One of the principal stumbling blocks to considering different areas, or economic zones, or local modes of production, as components of one global mode of production is the importance assigned to the wage relation as the defining characteristic of capitalism. If we want to consider the early centuries of the world-economy as part of a singular capitalist world mode of production, we face the problem that Laclau pointed out: The wage relation is not found in the coerced labor of plantations, mines, and haciendas. For Brenner (1977: 49), who also urges an emphasis upon class relations, capitalism occurs,

> only with free wage labour—with the producers separated from their means of subsistence and means of production . . . [and] . . . the strictest barriers to the accumulation of capital . . . [removed] . . . that large masses of means of production and means of subsistence . . . are "free" and . . . subject to being combined at the highest technological level.

If we assume that the fundamental issue here is freeing the means of production, the question becomes one of whether the wage relation is the universal means for this separation or a very specific historical relation that was present in but one sector of the overall world-economy—the industrial core we traditionally identify as capitalism. (This whole issue may be a moot point since wage labor eventually appears throughout the whole system.)

I would like to argue here that colonialism, with its uprooting of local peoples, destruction of local social formations, and reorganization of production through plantations, mines, and large-scale ranches, represents a very fundamental means for separating primary producers from their local means of production. In effect, the long history of colonialism and imperialism is the history of separating producers from their local means of production and reorganizing their labor power under the rational control of the core. Fogel and Engerman's (1974) analysis of plantation rationality suggests that peripheral labor is in fact being recombined at the "highest technological level" under slavery, such that wage labor may not be the only means facilitating a rational recombination of labor power. A similar point is made by Wallerstein, who argues there are different forms of labor control in different sectors of the world-system.

Within the linear theory of societal development, coerced labor is clearly prior to what we call capitalism, and from the diachronic point of view of European development, it makes sense to contrast feudalism or slavery with wage labor as different modes of production. But from the synchronic global point of view, the slavery of sugar and cotton plantations exists simultaneously with European wage labor. The development of these two societal modes of production is in fact part of the same process of world development; as such, each should be considered to be a component of a singular global mode of production. The very distinction between wage labor and slavery as different modes of production is a direct consequence of their temporal sequence in the history of European development. From the European point of view slavery and feudalism do temporally precede the wage relation, and as such can be considered an earlier stage in the development of a society's productive forces. But these stages of capitalist development are not universal. They are a reflection of the European experience. For what, after all, is the transition from slavery to feudalism to capitalism but the concrete historical transition from Greco-Roman antiquity to the Middle Ages to nineteenth-century Britain and Europe? What happens if the slavery of cotton or sugar plantations, the feudalism of the haciendas, and British wage labor all appear at the same time? And further, are all part of the same world economy? Slavery in the American south harvesting cotton that is spun into cloth by British wage laborers is a matter of two "modes of production" existing simultaneously, not of one preceding the other. The significance of the wage relation as a distinguishing characteristic for a new mode of production is due to its position as the successor to slavery and feudalism within European development, that is, its role as a means of cordoning off different forms of exploitation within European social formations.

While the distinction between coerced and wage labor is helpful in marking the advent of European capitalism, it may prove to be something of a hinderance for an understanding of the world-economy if for no other reason than the fact that it keeps slaves producing cotton and wage earners weaving it into cloth as two separate modes of production, when it is increasingly obvious they are part of *one* world-economy and, I would argue, of one global mode of production. We can go either way. The world-economy can be seen as containing different modes of production or it can be considered a singular mode. If we let go of nineteenth-century societal realities then we can also let go of the idea that slavery *precedes* capitalism and go on to figure out how wage and slave labor coexist as components of one global mode of production. If not, we will continue to see the world as many different modes of production.

We face a similar problem in later centuries when it comes to deciding how to deal with the presence of "socialist modes of production" in the existing socialisms of the Soviet Union, Poland, Cuba, and elsewhere. Although there continue to be arguments about the exact nature of existing socialist relations of production (Sweezy, 1980; Szymanski, 1980; among the many), these social formations are nonetheless active participants in the world-economy (Frank, 1977). Further, there is some suspicion that rather than representing antisystemic forces, socialist states are functioning components of the overall world-economy (Chase-Dunn, 1980) and conceivably the highest level of rationality and centralization of capital in the world-economy (Bergesen, 1981). Within the world-economy, then, there has been slavery, capitalism, and now socialist states. How these different *societal* modes of production are in fact components of one singular global mode of production is a question we have hardly begun to ask.

What is required to move us beyond this present conception of the world-economy as a division of labor among states and economic zones is to let go of the primacy of societal reality and move up to world collective reality: that is, conceive of the world economy as a singular social (or better, world or global) formation, with its own class structure that in turn creates the secondary reality of the core-periphery division of labor. As nineteenth-century social theory generated an intellectual revolution by inverting the direction of causality in utilitarianism—assuming the presence of social structure that determined the activity of individuals—so globology means to invert the present conception of the world-economy by identifying those global class relations that *precede, make possible,* and *reproduce* patterns of trade and unequal exchange between developed and underdeveloped countries. We must do to the idea of a world division of labor what the social theorists of the last century did to the national division of labor of the classical economists: invert it; turn it into a dependent variable and as such, into a derivation from the operation of determinate global social structure and determinate global relations of production.

Let us be clear on what I am saying. The world-economy is certainly a division of labor. No one observing the flow of commodities between core and periphery could deny this. But the world economy is also its own mode of production. *The world-economy has a collective reality above and beyond the patterns of trade and exchange between its developed and underdeveloped zones, so that the continuing emphasis of Wallerstein, Frank, and Amin on unequal exchange mistakenly roots the exploitative nature of the world-economy in unequal commodity flows when in fact it resides in the more fundamental global class relation of core ownership and control of peripheral production.*

GLOBAL CLASS RELATIONS

Class is a question of ownership and control of the means of production, and we can just as easily speak of the global means of production as of the societal means of production, which means we can just as easily speak of global class structure as of societal class structure. When we focus on global relations of production we are freed from seeing the question of production in only national, societal, or regional terms. *Most of the world's means of production have been under the control of the core, making the core-periphery relation a class relation rather than an unequal exchange relation.*

Since the inception of the world-system in the sixteenth century, world production has become increasingly socialized as local economies on different continents became part of one larger world economy. Along with this continued socialization of world production it is also true that ownership and control of world production have remained, by and large, in the hands of a world minority, the developed core states. If we take the point of view of *all* the world's people, this ownership of the global means of production by the core represents private ownership of the global means of production, where private means something less than the whole, less than the totality of human kind. Within social formations private ownership has meaning in terms of the historical bourgeoisie who owned and controlled industrial production in the core and later in the periphery. But from a global point of view, private refers to the core as a whole. In effect, class need not be only a social relation between factory owners and their wage laborers; it can also be a relation between whole sectors of the world-economy, that is, between core and periphery. Presently we speak of class relations in the core and periphery—core bourgeoisie, core proletariat, peripheral bourgeoisie, and peripheral proletariat. This is fine, as far as it goes, but it does not preclude the designation of core-periphery relations themselves as class relations.

Now it may very well be that "class" is the wrong term to describe the coercive aspect of core-periphery relations. Class may be too well associated with the capital-labor relation as it has historically manifested itself with the appearance of the historical bourgeoisie and proletariat to be easily transferred to characterizing the relationship between whole zones of the world-economy. But something like class will have to be formulated to account for the core-periphery power relationship that at present is not encompassed in the idea of unequal exchange.

If we consider the world as a whole, the most significant social relation since the sixteenth century would have to be the colonial—and then neocolonial—domination and control by the European core of most of the rest of the world. It was colonialism that dismantled local autonomous, and quasi-autonomous, modes of production and reassembled them as parts of the growing world-economy. And it was through colonialism that most parts of the world lost control of their local economies—and their labor power—and came to be organized in mines, plantations, haciendas, and large-scale ranches producing various raw materials for export to the core.

Class struggle involves the loss of control by direct producers over their own means of production, and on a world scale European colonialism is a manifestation of *world class struggle* whereby most of the world's direct producers lost control of their production process and were subordinated to the needs of the core. If you examine Latin America before and after the conquest, how can the transformation of Aztec and Inca civilizations into gold and silver mines, haciendas, and plantations be seen as anything else than a loss by direct producers of control of their means of production? What else then is colonialism but ownership of the global means of production, particularly if by 1914 some 84 percent of the world's territory had been, or was, under colonial control? Colonialism and neocolonialism are the single most pronounced and dominant global class relation.

The reality of global class relations, and particularly of global class struggle, is nowhere clearer than in the "making" of the capitalist world-economy. This bringing together of Europe, the Americas, and Africa in the first wave of colonialism represents one of the most traumatic events in world history, as the mashing and pounding of local modes of production to make them cogs in the larger world economy dwarfs the destruction and exploitation involved in the making of nineteenth-century capitalism in Britain and Europe.

The global mode of production had to be physically constructed. What in later centuries appears as a self-propelling international division of labor (the core-periphery division of labor) can only be understood from the point of view of the global class struggle involved in bringing this capitalist world-economy into being. Just as important is the continuing global class relation of owning and controlling peripheral production (multinationals, foreign investment, and so on), which reproduces the inequality of world development and the unequal exchange of the world division of labor. It is global class structure that continually undergirds the commodity flows we observe and determines the inequality of their exchange. Unequal exchange does not arise on its own; it is not the product of centuries of unequal trade and exchange between developed and underdeveloped countries. Unequal exchange between the European metropolis and the Aztec and Inca periphery did not create mines, haciendas, plantations, and the infrastructure of underdevelopment. These transformations were the products of forceful colonial domination. Further, unequal exchange is not only the by-product of early global class struggles, but its continued existence is determined by the core-periphery class structure that encompasses, or frames, these exchanges. Unequal exchange occurs within the confines of global class structures, not in a world vacuum devoid of any global social organization. The simple picture of the world-economy as a core-periphery division of labor is a kind of *Robinson Crusoe* fiction on a world level, as if we were dealing with a world-economy of Crusoe like core and peripheral islanders, trading and exchanging island commodities independent of the global structures of domination that makes that very exchange possible.

Finally, it needs to be pointed out that social causality has dramatically shifted from the diachronic succession of stages of *societal* development to the synchronic structural relations of the global mode of production. As each unincorporated area is brought into the global mode of production, its independent history of evolution ends, as all stages of diachronic societal development are superseded by the synchrony of the core-periphery class relation. The shift from societal to global dynamics is theoretically fundamental because the global mode of production cannot be seen as a stage of development that arises out of any earlier societal stage. Internal development is interrupted, and the development that follows—if one wants to focus upon national societies or particular regions—is part and parcel of the development of the global mode of production itself. Sociology and social development end for the region when it is brought within the global mode of production, regardless of its particular level of development. *Past diachronic societal development now becomes upward mobility in the synchrony of the global stratification system.*

In effect, the emergence of the modern world-system nullified the internal evolutionary dynamics of autonomous societies as they were one by one incorporated into the emerging world-economy. Autonomous internal societal development, whether by Marxian class struggle or Parsonian structural differentiation, ends when that social formation becomes part of the world-system, for at that point the principal determinant of its development shifts from internal social relations (including class relations) to global social relations (particularly the core-periphery class relation).

It is important to realize that with the appearance of the modern world-economy in the sixteenth century, at one and the same time the global mode of production became the historical successor to the feudal mode of production in Europe, to more primitive hunter-gatherer modes of production in North America, and to the agrarian civilization and tribute modes of production in Mexico and Peru. In this sense the global model of production is not the historical successor to any particular stage of societal development but rather an emergent phenomenon at an entirely new level of analysis. While we have been most cognizant of the effect of the world-economy on the underdevelopment of the Third World, it needs to be remembered that this larger world structure also determines the direction of development for European core states as well, for after the sixteenth century the development of all societies that are more than nominally a part of the world-economy is determined by the dynamics of this emerging global mode of production and not by the logic of their own internal development.

CONCLUSION

If we continue viewing questions of production only as societal realities, we doom ourselves to limiting class analysis to only national or regional realities and perpetuate the present interpretation of world capitalism as a division of labor or as an ensemble of so many different modes of production. If, however, we see the class relation between core and periphery that defines the global mode of production, we can finally leave our nineteenth-century fixation on social formations and societal realities and begin to understand truly the workings of the world-economy and the global mode of production.

REFERENCES

AMIN, S. (1980) "The class structure of the contemporary imperialist system." Monthly Review 31 (January): 9-26.

BERGESEN, A. (1981) "Progressive and exploitative: the dual nature of socialist states." Social Problems 28 (June).

———(1980) "From utilitarianism to globology: the shift from the individual to the world as a whole as the primordial unit of analysis," in Albert Bergesen (ed.) Studies of the Modern World-System. New York: Academic.

BRENNER, R. (1977) "The origins of capitalist development: a critique of neo-Smithian Marxism." New Left Review 104 (July-August): 25-92.

CHASE-DUNN, C. (1980) "Socialist states in the capitalist world-economy." Social Problems 27 (June): 505-525.

EMMANUEL, A. (1972) Unequal Exchange: A Study of the Imperialism of Trade. New York: Monthly Review Press.

FOGEL, R. and S. ENGERMAN (1974) Time on the Cross. Boston: Little, Brown.

FRANK, A. G. (1979) Dependent Accumulation and Underdevelopment. New York: Monthly Review Press.

———(1978) World Accumulation, 1492-1789. New York: Monthly Review Press.

———(1977) "Long live transideological enterprise." Review 1 (Summer): 91-140.

LACLAU, E. (1971) "Feudalism and capitalism in Latin America." New Left Review 67 (May/June): 19-38.

SWEEZY, P. (1980) Post-Revolutionary Society. New York: Monthly Review Press.

SZYMANSKI, A. (1980) Is the Red Flag Still Flying? The Political Economy of the Soviet Union Today. London: Zed Press.

WALLERSTEIN, I. (1980) The Modern World-System II. New York: Academic.

———(1979) The Capitalist World-Economy. New York: Cambridge University Press.

———(1977) "How do we know class struggle when we see it." Insurgent Sociologist (Spring): 104-106.

———(1974) The Modern World-System. New York: Academic.

3

The Kernel of the Capitalist World-Economy: Three Approaches

CHRISTOPHER CHASE-DUNN

This chapter addresses the problem of moving our analysis of the world-system from an orienting perspective that is used to interpret history toward a new, or renewed, theory of the underlying laws of development. As it has emerged from its originators and main proponents (Immanuel Wallerstein and his colleagues at the Fernand Braudel Center), the world-system perspective is a set of orienting concepts and implied processes that are applied to periods or locales in combination with attention to the particularity of the historical situation. This methodological approach seems to assume that the world-system itself only loosely conforms to a systemic dynamic, and thus overly formalistic theory-building is thought to be inappropriate. This approach has proven fruitful for generating new and greatly improved interpretations of world history. It may be possible, however, to utilize the historical insights that have been generated by these interpretations and the conceptual developments that have accompanied them to rethink the question of the underlying laws of capitalist development.

I do not propose a voyage into the purely rationalistic universe of Althusserian structuralism, although some of the distinctions from that school may be useful. What I do propose is a rethinking of the basic model of capitalist development making use of the empirical evidence of historical scholarship and comparative research to test different formulations. This essay is not itself a formulation of such a theory. Rather, it explores three approaches to the problem of theorizing about the deep structure of the capitalist world-economy.

MOTIVATIONAL AND
METHODOLOGICAL ASSUMPTIONS

First, why do we want to formulate a theory of world-system development? I would adduce that there are both scientific and humane reasons. The scientific reasons have to do with explanation and prediction. A formalized theory is more useful than a loosely defined set of orienting concepts because it can more easily be confronted with evidence and thus is more readily improved. Such a theory could also be useful in the transformation of the very system that is its subject.

The specification of the underlying contradictory tendencies of capitalist development can help us distinguish the "crises" that result in the reorganization of capitalism on a larger and more integrated scale from the movements that contribute to its transformation to a different and, it is hoped, more humane kind of social system. This last end of theory is not an unintended consequence. Rather it is a desired consequence that should, in part, direct the theory-building project.

I shall approach this task by distinguishing among several levels of models and theories that should be employed in the attempt to reformulate the developmental laws of capitalism. Then I will discuss three approaches to theorizing the structure: the formulation of logical boundaries, the problem of world classes, and the relationship between commodification and rationalization. The epistemological assumptions I use are simple but not uncontroversial (Bach, 1980). I shall assume that the ultimate goal is an essentialist specification of the basic nature of capitalism as a historically unique social system. The method for attaining this goal is to combine the rationalistic critique of prior theories with the use of comparative empirical research.

In terms of the controversy among Louis Althusser (1970), E. P. Thompson (1978) and Perry Anderson (1980), I am adopting the methodological position of Anderson, with perhaps an added dose of American empiricism. The comparative research method I wish to employ is not "raw empiricism," however. It is informed by theoretical critique and an awareness of the dialectical nature of social processes (Wright, 1978: 9-26; Chase-Dunn, 1982a).

The full development of a world-system theory would involve an axiomatic theory of capitalist development that would make falsifiable predictions. Alternative formulations could be tested against the evidence of world history. My own predilection is to begin with the Marxian model of development as explicated in the volumes of *Capital.* The ultimate goal is to reformulate Marx to take into account the processes of capitalist development that were unknown or neglected by him. This requires (1) a clear specification of Marx's model, (2) a critique of its inadequacies in the light of our knowledge of world-system processes, (3) a reformulation of the concepts and basic axioms, and (4) testing the new formulation against contemporary and historical social reality. This program cannot be carried out here. Rather, I wish to explore three directions that might eventually lead toward the above program.

WORLD-SYSTEM PERSPECTIVE AND TYPES OF MODELS

The world-system perspective assumes that the unit of analysis that develops, and thus that can be characterized as having deep structural tendencies of motion, is the capitalist world-economy. The study of this whole social system can be accomplished in many ways. We may focus on a particular locale or period to enquire as to how world-system processes interact with unique local patterns. We may also describe the development of the whole system in terms of both processes that are thought to be structurally based and exogenous influences that are the result of unique historical conjunctures. In addition, we may posit the existence of certain regularities of growth, differentiation, integration, and conflict—cycles and trends of development—that may be observed at the empirical level. Several outlines of the structural constants, cycles, and trends exhibited by the world-economy as a whole have been published (Hopkins and Wallerstein, 1982; Chase-Dunn and Rubinson, 1977, 1979).

These hypothesized variable characteristics may be studied by a modified method of comparison over time based partly on the logic of time-series analysis (Chase-Dunn, 1979). Several such empirical studies, have been carried out (Bergesen and Schoenberg, 1980; McGowan, 1981; Thompson and Zuk, 1982; Chase-Dunn, forthcoming). These studies have great potential for determining the descriptive correlations in time between different cycles and trends, and also as a source of inferences about causal relationships between surface-level variables and the deep structural tendencies of development itself (Chase-Dunn, 1980).

What is needed is one or more theories of world-system development that are specified at a general level. Modelski and Thompson (1980) have begun the task of elaborating a supply-and-demand theory of the long political cycles that occur in the world-economy. I will here begin the task of constructing a theory starting from Marx's model of capital accumulation. The works of Arghiri Emmanuel (1972), André Gunder Frank (1979), Samir Amin (1976, 1980), Ernest Mandel (1980), and, of course, Immanuel Wallerstein (1979) are germane to this task.

MARX'S MODEL OF CAPITALIST ACCUMULATION

Marx begins his explication of the laws of capitalist development with a dialectical analysis of a fundamental institution of capitalism—the commodity. From this institutional form, which contains the secrets of the deep structure, he derives the law of value, the roles of capital and labor, and the accumulation of capital through the production and appropriation of surplus value. This theoretical formulation has several advantages. It is elegant. It focuses on what are indubitably essential features of the capitalist mode of production—market exchange, commodified labor, and the concentration of means of production in "private" hands.

The problem with Marx's formulation is not so much what it includes but what it leaves out. Marx seeks to overcome the vacuities of classical political economy by conceptualizing capitalism as a historical system that came into existence through the use of force (see Part 8 of Volume 1 of *Capital*) and which will pass out of existence through the development of its own internal contradictions. But in seeking analytical elegance in his specification of the underlying laws of capitalist development, Marx abstracts from a number of processes that probably ought to be included within the model of development. For example, in Volume 1 of *Capital* Marx assumes: (1) the existence of an English-type caretaker state that does not directly interfere in the process of development, (2) no international trade—a closed system, (3) a completely competitive relationship among capitals, and (4) the complete commodification of labor power such that there exists only a class of workers with no institutional power to obtain more than the subsistence wage, and a class of capitalists who own and control all means of production.

Certainly simplifying assumptions are required in any theory that attempts to specify the essential laws of development of a mode of production. We cannot include sunspots or climate change in our theory. Some processes must be designated as exogenous, while others, it is hoped, capture the kernel of the system. The problem I am raising is that Marx may have distorted the kernel somewhat by his choice of simplifying assumptions.

My reading of the world-system perspective leads me to question the wisdom of several of Marx's theoretical decisions. It is not a matter of the simplifying assumptions being incorrect in one or another empirical situation. This is true of every theoretical abstraction. It is rather that the essential processes of capitalist development may be distorted by the particular assumptions made by Marx. Marx attributed a great deal to historical specificity, as have many Marxists since (e.g., E. P. Thompson, 1978). His theory was an abstraction from the complications of history. The approach I will outline here will do the same thing, except that it will draw the boundaries between the essential endogenous process of capitalism and the historical excrescences in a different way.

The hard task is to reformulate a new theory of the essential kernel of capitalism. Bertell Ollman (1976) has convincingly argued that Marx held to a philosophy of "internal relations" in which the characteristics of certain essential parts contain relations that express the basic nature of the whole system under analysis. Some Marxists (Dobb, 1947; Brenner, 1977) have argued that the key social relation for capitalist society is the relationship between capital and labor as it occurs within the firm, or as Marxists say, at the point of production. This is undoubtedly an important relationship, and a spate of excellent new studies have focused on the labor process as it has developed in contemporary capitalism (Braverman, 1974; Edwards, 1979; Burowoy, 1979). The world-system perspective encourages us, however, to notice how control institutions (relations of production) are structured beyond the point of production, in states, and, indeed, are institutionalized in the territorial division of labor that constitutes the core-periphery hierarchy.

ADDITIONS TO MARX'S MODEL

The conception of the world-system as a multilayered system of competing groups has been very helpful in accounting for the historical development of capitalism. Here I would suggest that the processes of state formation, nation-building, class formation, and the reproduction of the core-periphery hierarchy can be theorized as fundamental to the capitalist mode of production itself. Obviously these processes are beyond the scope of a narrowly economic view of capitalism, but it is precisely the transcendence of such an economistic theory that is necessary if we are to understand the development of capitalism as a whole system.

The disadvantage of this inclusion of processes formerly thought to be historical into the basic model of capitalist development is that it complicates the model greatly. Instead of a kernel social relation located at the point of production we have a much more complicated set of organizational, political, market, interstate, and world class relations. This kind of theory has been developed to a certain extent by Althusserian structuralists, particularly Nicos Poulantzas (1975). And much current work on the capitalist state can be useful in formulating such a theory (see especially von Braunmuehl, 1978). But what is needed is a new synthesis of these processes that has the virtues of Marx's original theory: simplicity and the identification of a relational core. So far this synthesis has not been achieved. Here I will explore three possible approaches after elaborating a bit on what I mean by asserting a connection between the accumulation process and the other processes mentioned above.

One of the key insights into capitalist development stimulated by Immanuel Wallerstein's (1979) theoretical writings is that commodity production regularly takes place in an arena that is partially structured by noneconomic relationships. There has never been an empirically existing perfect market within the capitalist system. Instead, capitalism is structured as a set of power relations, sometimes taking the form of price-setting markets, but just as often constituted as institutionalized power or authority relations among classes and states. Thus capitalism is a competitive system in which no single organization exercises long-term monopoly control over production and consumption, but within certain organizational realms monopoly power is temporarily exercised. This organizational power is most often institutionalized within state structures or guaranteed by property laws that are backed up by states. Thus mercantilism is not a stage of capitalist development, but, with some variations in form and extent, is a constant feature of capitalism. In the long run, however, these extra-economic sources of control are themselves subjected to competition in the arena of the capitalist system.

Thus the organizational structures of states and firms, and the structured relations among classes, are, in the long run, subjected to the competing-down process that occurs in the interstate system and the world market (Chase-Dunn, 1981). This accounts for certain regularities that can be observed in the world-economy. Not only are peripheries underdeveloped, but the uneven development of core countries results in the rise and fall of hegemonic core powers. This is because the correct combination for success in the capitalist system depends, not only on efficient production for the market, but also on the right mix of state investment in infrastructure, regulation of classes, and exercise of military power and diplomacy in the interstate system.

Marx's simplifying assumption that workers in a pure capitalist system receive only the wages necessary for the reproduction of the labor force abstracts from the process of class struggle that occurs *within* the capitalist system. Marx had a rather simplified model of class struggle in which trade union movements would more or less automatically develop into socialist challenges to the logic of capitalism itself. By now it is obvious that trade unions by themselves do not challenge the basic logic of capitalism, although they do raise the wage bill paid by capital. This suggests that the process by which laborers resist their perfect commodification should be seen as a normal part of capitalist development itself. Their differential success in this is known to be mediated primarily by the extent to which they are able to gain access to state power that guarantees their rights to bargain with capital.

These political rights have been forthcoming in most core countries, and it is probably true that state repression of the work force has always been lighter in the core than in the periphery. The differences in access to state power correspond to the levels of protection from exploitation that workers across the world-economy have been able to get. These systematic variations must be taken into account in any theory of accumulation, uneven development, and crisis. Wright's (1978: 147-154) explication of the different theories of crisis refers to one cause of the decline of the rate profit as the "profit-squeeze" model, in which workers are effective in maintaining a wage level that discourages new capital investment. This is an example of the inclusion of class struggle consequences into the model of accumulation itself.

Another consequence of the systematic inclusion of extra-economic determinants of class position is that it enables us to better understand exploitation in the periphery. A great debate has emerged among Marxists about the outer boundaries of the capitalist mode of production. Some claim that the fully developed capitalist mode of production can exist only where the wage system is dominant. Thus the slavery and serfdom that emerged in peripheral areas during the expansion of the capitalist world-system are classified as "precapitalist." When we include noneconomic dimensions of class into our definition of capitalist production we can abandon the assumption of a perfect price-setting labor market. Intraclass stratification into "segmented labor markets" is often structured by extra-economic institutions such as nationalism, racism, ethnic solidarities, or trade unions. In the periphery extra-economic coercion is a much greater part of production relations. Even so, the cost of slave or serf labor and their relative efficiencies or inefficiencies enter into the calculation of profitability. The elimination of these extreme forms of labor coercion in the periphery has by no means equalized the levels of coercion exercised over core and peripheral workers. The wage differential beyond differences in productivity analyzed by Arghiri Emmanuel (1972) is produced by the differential exercise of coercion in the world-system. Peripheral states generally exercise greater controls over worker organizations, and the core-periphery division of labor itself (differences in productivity as well as in wages) structures the great inequalities that exist between core and periphery. These differences, which may be partly conceptualized as stratification *within* the world proletariat, are produced both by the direct exercise of core power through state action and multinational corporate politics *and* as the indirect consequences of the reproduced core-periphery division of labor.

The world-system perspective contends that the core-periphery hierarchy and the exploitation of the periphery by the core are necessary to the reproduction of capitalism as a system. Thus rather than a temporary stage on the road to fully developed core capitalism, the "primary accumulation" (Frank, 1979) by which the core exploits the periphery is one of the prime mechanisms that allow the continuation of expanded reproduction in the core. The relative harmony of capitalists and workers in the core (which can be observed in the interclass alliances typified by social democratic regimes or the predominantly nonantagonistic class struggle that has taken place in the United States) is possible because of the key role performed by exploitation of the periphery. It is undeniable that the greater proportion of surplus value produced in the world-economy is, and has long been, produced in the core, but the exploitation of the periphery both creates extra amounts of surplus value that can be redistributed in many indirect forms to core workers and reinforces the ideologies of nationalism and "national development" that cement class alliances in the core.[1] It is implied by the above argument that decreases in the exploitation of the periphery by the core will have potentially revolutionary consequences for core countries and for the capitalist world-system as a whole.

Criticisms of this portrayal of the world class structure follow from a strict reading of Marx. If capitalism equals wage labor, then great numbers of self-employed or politically coerced workers in the periphery can be defined as outside the capitalist mode of production. Great exigeses (Taylor, 1979) are written to define and illuminate the articulation between the capitalist mode of production (i.e., core capitalism) and these other activities that are obviously connected to it but do not constitute it.

This is precisely the problem that the proposed new synthesis should solve. And this is not done by asserting that there is no essence, but rather by searching for a way of conceptualizing the real essence correctly.

I would like to apologize for being unable to deliver the synthesis that the above discussion proposes. Instead, I will beg the reader's indulgence to suggest three directions that might be followed in the formulation of such a synthesis. The first direction is a dead end, but it took me some effort to realize that, and so I will describe the path. For those who prefer paths with more potential I suggest turning to the second and third, though even there the discussion is inconclusive.

Alternatives eliminated are better than directions unexplored, so let me turn to the discussion of a purely formalistic approach to the problem of modeling the deep structure of the world-sytem.

TYPES OF FORMALIZATION

The discussion of essences often proceeds at a metaphysical level on which great ideas clash and the victors seem to emerge more on the basis of clever argument or style of prose than in terms of a confrontation with evidence. This feature of the discourse on the deep structure of social systems causes some scholars to shy away from "epochal concepts" (Stinchcombe, 1978) and to limit their studies to processes that operate on a smaller scale or over a shorter period of time. Nevertheless, there has been a renaissance of the study of large-scale, long-run social change. Immanuel Wallerstein's spatial metaphor for conceptualizing social relations is a useful tool, as the discussion of the spatial boundaries of the capitalist world-economy reveals (Sokolovsky, forthcoming), but social systems also have "logical boundaries," transitions between qualitatively different social relations and processes, that must be combined with the spatial metaphor. This is most apparent in the contemporary global capitalist system and its potential transformation into world socialism (Chase-Dunn, 1982b).

A clear specification of the underlying structural tendencies of capitalist development is necessary to distinguish institutional forms and social movements that reproduce capitalism (or allow it to intensify or to expand to a larger scale) from those forms and movements that act to transform the capitalist system into a qualitatively different system. Here the Althusserians have given us an important distinction— that between the mode of production (the basic essence of capitalism as a system) and the social formation (the concretely existent set of social institutions that contain historical survivals of earlier modes of production and nascent elements of modes of production of the future). This distinction posits the existence of a historical essence—the basic tendential laws of capitalist development.

This discussion focuses on the "boundaries" between different systems that are often discussed in terms of periods of transition (Hilton, 1976). It is argued that these boundaries must be specified clearly in order to operationalize and test propositions about processes that operate within a single system, and also in order to understand how fundamental social change—the qualitative transformation of social systems—occurs.

Let us give a rather abstract and brief sketch of the history of capitalism as a system in order to locate our discussion of the problem of logical boundaries. We assume, following Immanuel Wallerstein, that capitalism emerged as a complete social system in Europe and Latin America in the long sixteenth century. This system, which was imperialistic and composed of a hierarchical division of labor between core and peripheral areas from the beginning, emerged from European feudalism, a somewhat unique social system that was itself a devolved combination of the Roman world-empire and the Germanic tribal societies (Anderson, 1974).[2] The period of the fifteenth and sixteenth centuries was one of transition in which the logic of capitalism fought it out and eventually dominated the logic of European feudalism and the non-European socioeconomic systems that were integrated into peripheral positions within the nascent capitalist world-economy at that time. This imagery abstracts grossly from the historical struggles that occurred, but theorizing requires abstraction. Our abstraction seeks to combine Wallerstein's spatial metaphor with the structuralist notion of modes of production.

The peripheralization of Eastern Europe was possible because the timing of the process of infeudation there was delayed due to the weaker influence of the Roman Empire. The so-called "second serfdom" of Eastern Europe was really its first serfdom (Anderson, 1974). The development of feudalism out of the slavic village communities corresponded, in Poland, with the emergence of the capitalist world-economy such that serfdom became a form of labor control utilized for the production of commodities for export to the core.

From its base in Europe and Latin America capitalism expanded in a series of waves eventually to include the whole globe by the end of the nineteenth century. But the process of expansion was also accompanied by a process of the deepening of capitalist relations in the areas in which it had already become dominant, that is, in Europe and Latin America. The commodification of production and the increased rationalization of production for sale not only was expanded to new areas by trade and by force but was also intensified to include more and more areas of life within the capitalist world-economy. In the core this meant the more thorough subjugation of the labor process to the logic of efficient and profitable commodity production (Marx, 1976: 1025-1038) and in the periphery it meant the partial decline of the directly coercive aspects of labor control and the rise of more opaque, market-mediated wage-labor relations. Capitalist slavery and serfdom were eventually replaced by less directly repressive forms of labor control. The process of proletarianization deepened in both the core and the periphery as subsistence production and home production (worker's gardens, nonmonetized family labor, and the like) became commodified, making workers more and more exclusively dependent on their abilities to sell their labor power. In the periphery, at times "precapitalist" forms of labor control were either created anew or revitalized to produce peripheral commodities for export to the core. In addition, many "part-time proletarians" received low wages made possible by their partial dependence on village communities that served as labor reserves for the sector of the economy producing peripheral commodities (Murray, 1980).

Thus the expansion of capitalism during some phases reproduced "precapitalist" forms of production, while during other phases it broke these forms down and replaced them with production relations more similar to those of the core. Proletarianization and the commodification of life have therefore increased in both the core and the periphery, with a certain lag and the retention of more coercive types of labor control in the periphery. These are more coercive relative to the core but less coercive relative to the earlier periphery.

At the level of the core-periphery hierarchy capitalist production relations have similarly become less directly coercive and more formally organized as market relations between equals, even though unequal power of core and peripheral states in the interstate system, and the "market advantages" of core capitalism employing capital-intensive technology and skilled highly paid labor, remains great. Nevertheless, neocolonialism is not colonialism. the sovereignty of contemporary peripheral nation-states may often be in question, but it is undoubtedly greater than when colonial empires carved up the world-economy. Similarly, "peripheral industrialization" and "dependent development" (Evans, 1979) may not constitute the end of the core-periphery economic domination, but they certainly involve more corelike capitalist relations of production than did the purely extractive peripheral industries of earlier centuries.

In this brief description of the spread and deepening of capitalist relations of production we can see the importance of specifying both the spatial and logical boundaries of capitalism. The intensification of commodified relations within both the core and the periphery of the capitalist system is an important process that may have consequences for the ability of capitalism to reproduce itself. An exclusively spatial metaphor for conceptualizing production relations can blur the distinction between commodity production and home production for use. I am not agreeing with the orthodox (Leclau, 1977) that home production or village economies are "outside" the capitalist mode of production. Rather, I am arguing that articulation of wage-labor production with nonwage forms is an important feature of capitalism that may reach certain limits as commodity production deepens and widens.

Socialism is a mode of production that subjects investment decisions and distribution to a logic of societal use value, and, as such, socialist movements reintroduce noncommodified relations into the interstices of capitalist relations. But the complete institutionalization of a socialist mode of production awaits the day when this qualitatively different logic becomes dominant in the world-system. Thus the question of logical boundaries is important for allowing us to see how a particular organizational form may reproduce capitalist relations and/or contribute to the transformation of capitalism. A particular institution may, of course, do both at the same time. Thus labor unions have forced the expansion of mechanization and growth of commodity production at the same time as they have placed constraints on capitalist control of a certain share of surplus value. Similarly "socialist" states may reproduce the logic of commodity production on a national scale (state capitalism) while at the same time creating a more socialist logic of distribution, at least within their political boundaries (Chase-Dunn, 1982b). Thus logical boundaries must be specified that enable us to understand the qualitative distinction between capitalism and socialism in a dialectical way.

We can borrow a metaphor from biological systems in order to begin this task. Lenski (1978) and Alker (1979) have argued that social systems are reproduced by "genetic" codes. These theorists share a cybernetic conception of essence in which social information becomes coded in cultural institutions and symbolic systems. Materialists may accept the imagery of the genetic theory of deep structure and reproduction without accepting its culturalist content. For Marx the genetic structure of social systems was inherent in the institutions by which material life was reproduced. He posited a tension between the technical and social forces of production (technology, labor process) and the relations of production (those political institutions that allow exploitation to take place). Cultural institutions were thought to be reflections of the more basic struggle over material production, at least in all class societies. Thus the essential nature of a particular mode of production could be understood from an analysis of the typical institutions of production and exploitation. A deep structure theory that follows the materialist approach will start with an analysis of class relations. These are conceptualized differently by different Marxists, and these differences have profound effects on the understanding of modes of production and of the transition between modes of production (Hilton, 1976).

Immanuel Wallerstein's (1979) theoretical essays have displayed a reluctance to discuss the problem of the mode of production. Instead, Wallerstein has elaborated a now large collection of complex and loosely defined concepts for interpreting the history of capitalism. He and Terence Hopkins (1982) have suggested a number of charac-

teristic trends and cyclical features of the capitalist world-economy
as a whole (see also Chase-Dunn and Rubinson, 1979). However, the
causal relations between the trends and cycles have not been pos-
tulated, nor have these empirically conceived patterns been linked to
a theory of the logic of capitalism as a system.

What is a model of deep structure? We have various formal alternatives that may be useful. A theory may be specified axiomatically
as a series of propositions and derived hypotheses. Nowak (1971)
has thus formalized parts of Marx's accumulation model of capitalist
development. Such an axiomatic theory can employ the kind of
dialectical causal logic developed by Wright (1978: 15-26). Or a
theory may posit the existence of a set of basic processes in terms of
causal relations among a number of variables. The equations that
describe this kind of model may be written and alternative specifications are easily posited. Let us take this second form and imagine that
we have decided upon a set of key variables for representing the
underlying model of capitalist development. We then have a number
of equations that posit causal relations among basic variables under
specified scope conditions. If our logic is dialectical (Alker, 1979),
we may model complicated, non-Aristotelian relations among variables. The problem of dialectically qualitative transformation of one
such system into another is difficult to model, but here we may get
some help from the mathematics of "catastrophe theory."

Let us think about what it would mean to specify the *logical boundaries* of such a formalization of the capitalist system. We can ask
what would have to change to constitute a different system. In principle, I suspect that the historicists are partly right: The underlying
model is *always* changing to a certain extent. I shall assume that this
constant "background" change is small. The problem of stages of
capitalist development might be approached in terms of larger
changes in the parameters specifying relations between variables.
And qualitative transformation should refer to a more fundamental
change in the model such that wholly different processes with different variables are created or become dominant in the overall direction
of development.

Of course, many problems are raised by such a formal approach to
system transformation. We want to distinguish between changes in
the model that may reproduce the same system using new organizational forms (and on a greater scale) from changes that transform it
into a different system. At the level of formalization any degree of
change can be arbitrarily designated as a transformation, and so we
must establish criteria for transformation that link the characteristics
of a formal model with the outcomes and concrete processes of the
system we are modeling. The distinction between epiphenomenal

versus transformative change cannot be divorced from the substantive content of a theory of capitalist development, but the discussion of such a formalized approach may be suggestive of ways to conceptualize substantive theoretical criteria. The formalization approach outlined above is inadequate in itself, except for the implication that a theory of transformation must contain both the logic of capitalism *and the logic of socialism*. The process of socialist development and dynamics is, of course, difficult to model because it is a potential system rather than (I would argue) an existing one. But if we follow Marx's lead we should be able to discern the way in which capitalism contains the seeds of socialism, and this will imply the nature of a socialist system.

Thus the main implication of this discussion of logical boundaries is that a purely formalistic approach in the absence of a substantive theory of the deep structure of capitalism is not sufficient. Unfortunately, the explication of a reformulated theory of capitalism development in the light of the insights of the world-system perspective is only in its infancy. Let us now proceed to examine two alternative starting points toward a theory of the logic of capitalism.

The above discussion implies that we require a substantive core of assertions on which to base our theory of world-system development. It might be possible to work backward from the hypothesized empirical-level cycles and trends, though more research on these phenomena ought to be done first, and a large number of possible deep structure theories could account for any set of empirical relationships. I will proceed in the other direction, from prior theorizing, although it should be emphasized that this deductive kind of theoretical development should not remain a self-contained universe. Different formulations must eventually contend with one another to account for empirical evidence. We are a long way from such clarity, however, and the first task is to think through some general theoretical approaches. Below I outline two. This is not done to be difficult, but because I have yet to decide which direction might prove to be more fruitful.

A question that poses nicely the problem I wish to confront is "what is capital?" For Marx capital was understood as a social relationship, an institutionalization of control through property ownership of the means of production. Capital contained within itself the relationship with labor, a market in which propertyless workers sell their labor time to capital-owners. How do we wish to modify this definition in the light of the insights provided by viewing capitalism as a world-system? This question can be confronted on two levels and I will try both to see which one works best. The first uses insights about the state and interstate system to reformulate the nature of capital. This involves the analysis of the commodity and the Weberian process of rationalization. The second approaches the problem of domination more directly by analyzing the relationship between classes and the core-periphery hierarchy.

COMMODIFICATION AND RATIONALIZATION

Marx began with the commodity. The commodity is a standardized product produced for exchange in a price-setting market, in which the conditions of production are subject to reorganization as a result of changes in input costs. A work of art is not a commodity because it is not standardized or reproducible. Your mother is not a commodity because she is not replaceable on the market. There are no perfect commodities, but many social objects approximate commodities. It is uncontestably the case that the deepening of capitalist relations involves the commodification of ever more areas of human life. Production for use in the home is replaced by the purchase of commodities. Economists commonly project the character of commodities onto everything. Children become consumer durables. Some sociologists carry on in the same manner, although they differentiate between purely economic and "social" exchange (Blau, 1964).

All of human life is not organized in the commodity form. Some things represent collective "goods" or transcendant values that have no calculable market price. Many relationships, even in "advanced" countries, involve real transcendant solidarity that is not reducible to a business deal. Friendship, love, and patriotism are often described in the language of exchange, but part of the nature of these relationships involves a merging of the individual identities (the constitution of a corporate entity) such that the terms of exchange among parts are undefined—and undefinable.

Marx observed that the market, especially the market for labor, while it formally represented an exchange among equals, is actually an institutional mystification of the main type of exploitation that typifies capitalist society: the extraction of surplus value. His great contribution was to show how the formal equality of the market could produce socially structured inequality. I have mentioned above that Marx's model of capitalist accumulation assumes a perfectly operating system of markets for labor and other commodified objects. This assumption has led to the narrow view, held by both Marxists and non-Marxists, that capitalism is a market system in which "private" ownership of the means of production exploits labor power to accumulate capital. The public/private distinction is fundamental to the definition of "independent producers" and to the distinction, therefore, between production for use and production of exchange. It is assumed that in a market economy independent producers seeking to maximize their own return exchange commodities with one another. The production of use-values, on the other hand, assumes some unity of interests, either because an individual or family is producing for itself rather than for the market, or because the unit producing use-values does so according to a set of norms that are formulated on principles other than strict economic efficiency. Thus use-values may be produced by a traditional division of labor in an Indian village in which "prices" are set by long tradition, or by a socialist society in which investment decisions and exchange terms are determined by a calculus of social need.

Max Weber's analysis of capitalist society was not formulated explicitly as a theory of deep structure. Nevertheless, many interpreters of Weber's work have argued that the kernel that he saw as the basis of modern capitalism is the tendency toward rationalization of activities. Organizational means are constantly subjected to restructuring according to their calculated efficiency in the attainment of organizational ends. The image conjured up by such a general focus is often the large corporation or the large public bureaucracy, but Weber's rationalization process is also revealed in the development of law in national societies.

The world-system perspective on capitalism suggests that we should seek our kernel in the specific laws of competition and integration that characterize capitalism as a model of production. Since the market principle is historically only part of the determination of success and failure in this system, we should incorporate the dynamics of nonmarket processes that are important to success into our conceptualization of the kernel social relations. It has been pointed out by some critics of Immanuel Wallerstein that states and the interstate system (which are the political bases of world capitalism) operate according to somewhat different principles than do firms and classes struggling to survive and succeed in the arena of the world-economy (Skocpol, 1977; Zolberg, 1981). I have argued elsewhere that the logic of competition and conflict in the interstate system and the logic of competition in the world market can be understood as interdependent determinants of the dynamics of world development (Chase-Dunn, 1981). I would here like to ground this idea in an analysis of the commodity-form and Weber's notion of rationalization. These two concepts, thought to be different ways of understanding the nature of modern capitalism, may perhaps be combined to clarify the secret of capital as it really operates in the modern world-system.

One advantage of Weber's notion of rationalization over Marx's commodification is that it does not presume the nature of the goal. A modern formal organization may pursue either profit or the salvation of souls. This allows for organizational efficiency and calculation in the service of integrative "social" ends, as well as for private accumulation. It must be observed that capitalist society produces and reproduces many collective solidarities at the same time as it produces individuals and "private" purposes. The most obvious and powerful instance of this is the nation, and its formal embodiment, the state. The state, in law and in some consciousness, aggregates the interests of constituent parties and pursues the "general" or "universal" interest.

The world-system perspective, focusing on the interstate system rather than on the state, makes us acutely aware of the partial and competitive nature of the so-called universal purposes embodied in states. In formally representing only its own citizens, each nation-state is merely a political organization contending with others in a larger arena. But the myth of the nation as a transcendent solidarity is an important determinant of success or failure in this struggle. States must be able to legitimate their actions and to mobilize participation in order to survive or prevail in the world-economy. Those that do this less efficiently and/or less effectively are likely to lose out in competitive struggle. The notion of *partial rationality*—the efficient and effective construction of organizational forms to serve transcendent but still "private" ends—interacts with the logic of comparative advantage in the world market to produce the dynamic of growth and to determine the winners and losers. Rationality is partial and private because the logic of comparative costs and maximalization for "social" ends remains calculated on the basis of a subgroup operating competitively in a larger arena.

It might be argued that rationality is really the underlying principle of socialism rather than of capitalism. From this perspective the addition of "social" desiderata to planning schemes and the inclusion of broader welfare goals in the operation of states represents the appearance of the logic of socialism within the interstices of capitalism. I prefer a different formulation, however. Capitalism's main principle is the production of commodities for the market, but as Polanyi (1944) recognized, the expansion of markets and the commodification of land, labor, and wealth produce a need for social integration and regulation. Thus the expansion of markets brings into being new institutions to regulate the market in the interests of "society." What Polanyi did not see is that as long as capitalism survives as a system, *the scale of the market principle outstrips the scale of the rationality principle*. Partial rationality is precisely the socialization of certain aspects of subunits within a larger competitive arena.

This outstripping of rationality by the market has been a recurring feature of capitalism since its development in Europe in medieval times. Medieval urban communes, artisan guilds, religious communities, firms taken over by workers, labor unions, political parties, and socialist states have created "social" forms of distribution to protect their members against market forces. These organizations were eventually outmaneuvered by the expansion of markets, and those that survived were forced to adopt organizational forms more suited to competition within the expanded setting. The present competitive interstate system and world market expose contemporary "socialist" ✓ states to this contradiction: whether to "develop" within the logic of the capitalist world-system or to invest resources in the transformation of the social context along more collectively rational and democratic lines.

I am willing to characterize Weber's rationalization principle as socialist as long as it is remembered that, at least up to now in history, this has been only a partial rationality, and it has continually been outstripped by the expansion of the market principle. The implication of this is that socialism can become dominant in the world-system only when there is an organization capable of aggregating the "universal," not partial, interests of the human species—a world government. In this light the reproduction of national solidarities by the operation of the capitalist system has created an extremely tenacious barrier.

WORLD CLASSES AND THE
CORE-PERIPHERY RELATIONSHIP

Another possibility for conceptualizing the kernel of capitalism is to focus on the way in which exploitation and domination are structured—the interaction of interclass and intraclass conflict in the world-system. Albert Bergesen (this volume) has argued that the core-periphery relationship can be conceptualized as a kind of class relationship. He shows convincingly that the relationship between the core and the periphery is not simply an exchange between equal partners. Structured power has created and sustained the hierarchical division of labor between the core and the periphery.

Nevertheless, rather than collapsing the categories of class and core-periphery, it may be more helpful to use them both and to study their interaction. First, what is the difference between the two? The capitalist/proletarian relationship is based on ownership and/or control of productive property versus a class of workers who do not own means of production and must sell their labor power. This institutional situation is understood to have come into existence through the use of extra-economic coercion and to be sustained by the normal processes of capitalist growth. The core-periphery relationship is analytically understood as a territorial division of labor in which core areas specialize in capital-intensive production using skilled highly paid labor, and peripheral areas specialize in labor-intensive production using low-wage and relatively unskilled labor.[3] Similarly, the core-periphery relationship is thought to have been brought into existence by extra-economic plunder and colonialism but is sustained by the normal operation of the capitalist system.

The world class structure is composed of capitalists (owners and controllers of means of production) and propertyless workers. This class system also includes small commodity producers who control their own means of production but who do not employ the labor of others, and a growing middle class of skilled and/or professionally certified workers.

The territorial core-periphery hierarchy cross-cuts this world class structure and interacts with it in important ways. Thus the categories of core capitalist-peripheral capitalist and core worker-peripheral workers are useful for an analysis of the dynamics of world capitalism. It is important to realize that people may be proletarians without receiving a formal wage. The serfs and slaves that produced surplus value for peripheral capitalists in earlier centuries were treated as commodities in the sense that their labor process was directed by a logic of capital accumulation, even though they did not have the juridical freedom to sell their labor-time to capital. Coercion beyond the operation of free labor markets remains an important condition for wage differentials in the contemporary world. After all, if there were no extra-economic barriers to labor migration, carpenters in the United States would not earn ten times more than carpenters in Mexico. It is not the operation of a perfect labor market that determines proletarian status but the subjection of labor to the logic of profitmaking, and this is accomplished by a wide variety of institutional inventions.

The combination of capital/labor relations and core-periphery relations produces many of the consequences that are fundamental to the capitalist development process. The dynamics of the interstate system and the process of uneven development are largely the result of interclass and intraclass conflict and competition. Class alliances or "relative harmonies" between capital and labor within core countries cause and are caused by the strong states and relatively well-integrated nations of the core. The more coercive and exploitative interclass relations of the periphery are partly the result of alliances between peripheral and core capitalists, as are the weaker states and less integrated nations of the periphery. State socialism, the most important of the anticapitalist movements that have emerged within the capitalist world-system, was possible because of the "combined and uneven development" that occurred in semi-peripheral areas, where cross-cutting contradictions (conflicts among capitalists and between capitalists and workers) were exacerbated by an intermediate position in the core-periphery hierarchy.

The interstate system, composed of powerful core states that contend with one another for hegemony, is an important structural basis of the continued competition within the world capitalist class. No state represents the "general" interests of the capitalist class as a whole. Rather fractions of the world capitalist class control particular states, often in alliance with middle-class workers. This multicentric structure of the world capitalist class allows the process of uneven development to continue. The rise and fall of hegemonic core states and changes in the structure of international alliances allow for flexibility in the world polity and accommodate changes in the distribution of comparative advantage in commodity production. A single world capitalist state would be likely politically to sustain the interests of those capitalist class fractions that controlled it and thus to impede the shift in productive advantage from less to more (market) efficient producers. Similarly, such a state would probably become the single object of orientation of anticapitalist movements. Thus unlike the present interstate system, in which welfare claims by workers or other interest groups often lead to loss of centrality in the world market and capital flight, in a world capitalist state the aggregation of workers' interests would likely be more effective in actually transforming the logic of the political economy toward a more democratic and collectively rational system.

The world-system perspective contends that the core-periphery hierarchy, rather than being a passing phase in the transition of "backward" areas toward core-type capitalism, is a permanent, necessary, and reproduced feature of the capitalist mode of production. This contention is supported by historical studies and comparative research (see Bornschier and Hoby, 1981), which have substantiated André Gunder Frank's notion of the "development of underdevelopment" and the ideas of dependency theory. The periphery of the world-economy has certainly "developed" and changed greatly since the incorporation of Latin America, Asia, and Africa into the capitalist world-economy, but the hierarchical relationship between the core and the periphery remains.

What is the function of this territorial hierarchy for capitalism as a system? It has probably never been the case, even in the heyday of pure plunder, that more surplus product was extracted from the periphery than was produced in the core. Most of the surplus value accumulated in the core is produced by core workers using relatively more productive technology. Nevertheless, the surplus product extracted from the periphery has played a crucial role in allowing the relatively peaceful process of expanded reproduction in the core to proceed. This has occurred in three ways: (1) by reducing the level of conflict and competition among core capitalists within core states, (2) by allowing adjustments to power relations among core states to be settled without destroying the interstate system, and (3) by promoting a relative harmony between capital and labor in the core.

This last point is politically sensitive because it is contrary to much Marxist class analysis and it raises the question of long-run versus short-run class interests. There has been much discussion about whether or not core workers exploit peripheral workers or benefit from their exploitation (Emmanuel, 1972: 271-342). It is clear that core workers do benefit from the exploitation of the periphery in a number of different ways. They are able to buy peripheral products cheaply. The territorial division of labor between the core and the periphery enables core workers to have cleaner and more skilled jobs. The profits from imperialism enable core capitalists to respond more flexibly to worker demands for higher wages. The greater affluence of the core allows core states to devote more resources to welfare and to maintain a relatively greater degree of pluralism and democracy.

Thus the Marxists who have maintained that lack of socialist militancy among core workers is entirely due to "false consciousness" based on nationalism and antisocialist propaganda are wrong, although this status-based mechanism of ideological hegemony is also important in maintaining class harmony in the core. Thus the objective structuring of interests based on the cross-cutting nature of class and core-periphery exploitation has stabilized the capitalist world-economy. The other side of this is the implication that limitations on the ability of core capitalists to keep on exploiting the periphery may have revolutionary consequences for class relations within core countries.

CONCLUSION

What can we conclude from the above attempts to seek the kernel of capitalist development? My discussion of commodification and rationalization did not lead to a new formulation but I think it may prove fruitful to continue this line of thought. We need to think more clearly about the logic of organizations, including states, operating in the context of a commodity economy. One good idea came out of this discussion—historically the scope and scale of the market outrun the scale of organizational integration, and thus attempts to socialize market forces must themselves adapt to the competitive struggle.

The discussion of interclass and intraclass relations similarly did not find a new formulation of the kernel. Rather the Marxian emphasis on the capital/labor relationship at the point of production was cast into a larger structure of world classes, the core-periphery hierarchy, and the interstate system. This rather complex description of capitalist production relations lacks the political focus and theoretical elegance of Marx's formulation and this is to be lamented. It may, however, be a better representation of the real structure of the system in which we live and, therefore, more useful, even if less immediately compelling.

The task undertaken in this essay was to search for the real kernel of capitalist development in the light of insights generated by the world-system perspective. The supposition that a kernel exists is based on the philosophy of internal relations that Ollman (1976) argues is held by Marx. This philosophy contends that "the whole is bound up, in some sense, in each of its parts." The world-system perspective, on the other hand, has started from the other end, from the whole, and has sought to derive the parts. At this level of abstraction we can only gain suggestions about what to look for. Everyone wants to connect the larger and the smaller in social life in some meaningful and useful way. Even though the above discussion does not locate the key social relationship or set of relations within capitalism that can explain its dynamics, further thought and investigation may soon produce a new synthesis for social science.

NOTES

1. Albert Szymanski (1981: ch. 14) shows evidence against several propositions that support the "necessity of imperialism" argument. He does not, however, contradict the claim that the core-periphery hierarchy allows capitalist accumulation to proceed as a result of its effects on class peace in the core. His study of the "aristocracy of labor" thesis (1981: ch. 14) does not successfully disprove the fact that core workers benefit from the core-periphery hierarchy, and in fact he admits that the concentration of cleaner, better-paid jobs in the core is an important part of the depolarization of class confict within core countries.

2. The European feudal system was not, during its classic period, a world-system in the strict Wallersteinian sense. The manorial economy was composed of economically self-sufficient units, and thus there was no territorial division of labor exchanging fundamental products. This weakly integrated system was fertile ground for the emergence and eventual hegemony of capitalist production.

3. This is similar to Kautsky's discussion of commodity circuits between urban and rural areas within a regional division of labor (see Lipton, 1977: 115-121).

REFERENCES

ALKER, H. (1979) "Logic, dialectics, politics: some recent controversies." Paper presented at the Moscow Congress of the International Political Science Association, Moscow, April.
ALTHUSSER, L. (1970) Reading Capital. London: New Left Books.
AMIN, S. (1980) Class and Nation, Historically and in the Current Crisis. New York: Monthly Review Press.

————(1976) Unequal Development. New York: Monthly Review Press.
ANDERSON, P. (1980) Arguments Within English Marxism. London: New Left Books.
————(1974) Passages from Antiquity to Feudalism. London: New Left Books.
BACH, R. (1980) "On the holism of a world-systems perspective," pp. 289-310 in T. K. Hopkins and I. Wallerstein (eds.) Processes of the World-System. Beverly Hills, CA: Sage.
BERGESEN, A. J. and R. SCHOENBERG (1980) "Long waves of colonial expansion and contraction, 1415-1969," pp. 231-278 in A. J. Bergesen (ed.) Studies of the Modern World-System. New York: Academic.
BLAU, P. M. (1964) Exchange and Power in Social Life. New York: John Wiley.
BORNSCHIER, V. and J. P. HOBY (1981) "Economic policy and multinational corporations in development: the measureable impacts in cross-national perspective." Social Problems 28 (April): 363-377.
BRAVERMAN, H. (1974) Labor and Monopoly Capital. New York: Monthly Review Press.
BRENNER, R. (1977) "The origins of capitalist development: a critique of neo-Smithian Marxism." New Left Review 104 (July/August): 25-92.
BUROWOY, M. (1979) Manufacturing Consent. Chicago: University of Chicago Press.
CHASE-DUNN, C. (forthcoming) "The system of world cities: 800-1975," in M. Timberlake (ed.) Urbanization in the World Economy. New York: Academic.
————(1982a) "The uses of formal comparative research on dependency theory and the world-system perspective," in H. Makler, A. Martinelli, and N. Smelser (eds.) The New International Economy. London: Sage.
————[ed.] (1982b) Socialist States in the World-System. Beverly Hills, CA: Sage.
————(1981) "Interstate system and capitalist world-economy: one logic or two?" International Studies Quarterly 25 1: 19-42.
————(1980) "Models and interpretation in world-system research: comments on Bach," pp. 311-314 in T. K. Hopkins and I. Wallerstein (eds.) Processes of the World-System. Beverly Hills, CA: Sage.
————(1979) "Comparative research on world-system characteristics." International Studies Quarterly 23, 4: 401-623.
————and R. RUBINSON (1979) "Cycles, trends and new departures in world-system development," pp. 276-296 in J. W. Meyer and M. T. Hannan (eds.) National Development and the World System: Educational, Economic and Political Change, 1950-1970. Chicago: University of Chicago Press.
————(1977) "Toward a structural perspective on the world-system." Politics and Society 7, 4: 453-476.
DOBB, M. (1947) Studies in the Development of Capitalism. New York: International Publishers.
EDWARDS, R. (1979) Contested Terrain: The Transformation of the Workplace in the Twentieth Century. New York: Basic Books.
EMMANUEL, A. (1972) Unequal Exchange: A Study of the Imperialism of Trade. New York: Monthly Review Press.
EVANS, P. (1979) Dependent Development: Multinational, State and Local Capital in Brazil. Princeton, NJ: Princeton University Press.
FRANK, A. G. (1979) Dependent Accumulation and Underdevelopment. New York: Monthly Review Press.
HILTON, R. [ed.] (1976) The Transition from Feudalism to Capitalism. New York: New Left Books.
HOPKINS, T. and I. WALLERSTEIN (1982) World-System Analysis. Beverly Hills, CA: Sage.
LECLAU, ED. (1977) Politics and Ideology in Marxist Theory. London: New Left Books.

LENSKI, G. (1978) Human Societies. New York: McGraw-Hill.
LIPTON, M. (1977) Why Poor People Stay Poor: Urban Bias in World Development. Cambridge, MA: Harvard University Press.
MANDEL, E. (1980) Long Waves of Capitalist Development: The Marxist Interpretation. London: Cambridge University Press.
MARX, K. (1976) [1867] Capital, Vol. 1. Harmondsworth, Middlesex: Penguin.
McGOWAN, P. (1981) "Pitfalls and promise in the quantitative study of the world-system: a reanalysis of Bergesen's 'long waves' of colonialism." (unpublished)
MODELSKI, G. and W. R. THOMPSON (1980) "Elaborating the long cycle theory of global politics: a cobweb model." Paper presented at the Annual Meeting of the American Political Science Association, Washington, DC, August.
MURRAY, M. (1980) The Development of Capitalism in Colonial Indochina. Berkeley: University of California Press.
NOWAK, L. (1971) "Problems of explanation in Marx's *Capital.*" Quality and Quantity 2.
OLLMAN, B. (1976) Alienation: Marx's Conception of Man in Capitalist Society. New York: Cambridge University Press.
POLANYI, K. (1944) The Great Transformation. Boston: Beacon.
POULANTZAS, N. (1975) Classes in Contemporary Capitalism. London: New Left Books.
SKOCPOL, T (1977) "Wallerstein's world capitalist system: a theoretical and historical critique." American Journal of Sociology 82, 5: 1075-1090.
SOKOLOVSKY, J. (forthcoming) "Logic, space and time: the boundaries of the capitalist world-economy," in M. Timberlake (ed.) Urbanization in the World Economy. New York: Academic.
STINCHCOMBE, A. L. (1978) Theoretical Methods in Social History. New York: Academic.
SZYMANSKI, A. (1981) The Logic of Imperialism. New York: Praeger.
TAYLOR, J. G. (1979) From Modernization to Modes of Production. London: Macmillan.
THOMPSON, E. P. (1978) The Poverty of Theory and Other Essays. New York: Monthly Review Press.
THOMPSON, W. R. and G. ZUK (1982) "War, inflation and the Kondratieff long wave." Journal of Conflict Resolution 26 (December): 621-644.
von BRAUNMUEL, C. (1978) "On the analysis of the bourgeois nation state within the world market context," pp. 160-177 in J. Holloway and S. Piccioto (eds.) State and Capital: A Marxist Debate. Austin: University of Texas Press.
WALLERSTEIN, I. (1979) The Capitalist World-Economy. New York: Cambridge University Press.
WEBER, M. (1978) Economy and Society. Berkeley: University of California Press.
WRIGHT, E. O. (1978) Class, Crisis, and the State. London: New Left Books.
ZOLBERG, A. R. (1981) "Origins of the modern world system: a missing link." World Politics 23 (January): 253-281.

4

The Peripheral Economies

Penetration and Economic Distortion, 1970-1975

DAVID SYLVAN
DUNCAN SNIDAL
BRUCE M. RUSSETT
STEVEN JACKSON
RAYMOND DUVALL

In this essay we report the first set of empirical results from our effort to test a formal model of "dependencia" theory on a worldwide set of peripheral countries in the 1970-1975 period. The results apply to the effects of external penetration from the countries of the industrial center of the world economy, in creating an export enclave and in various economic "distortions" in the domestic peripheral economies. We show that the effects are, in broad outline, consistent with those described in many writings of the dependencia school. Though the results also vary in important respects from common expectations, the distortions found are substantial enough that they may affect other characteristics of peripheral countries typically anticipated by dependencia theory: inequality, marginalization, an expanded role for the state, and ultimately an ascending cycle of social conflict and political repression. Our results here deal only with the initial economic effects, however.

AUTHORS' NOTE: We are grateful to the National Science Foundation and the German Marshall Fund of the United States for support of our research. Of course, only the authors are responsible for the material in this chapter. Authors are listed here in reverse alphabetical order, but no priority is implied either here or in previous papers in which the listing was in alphabetical order. Please, in any citation of this article, list all the authors.

METHODOLOGICAL BACKGROUND

North American and European social scientists some time ago "discovered" the continent of "dependencia theory." Like Columbus, however, they have often misunderstood the character and contours of their discovery. Some have adopted it; others have ridiculed it; still others have purported to "test" it. In some instances they have added to our set of insights if not to our body of replicable knowledge; in others the misunderstandings have been dominant. Distortion and scientific impoverishment have been most common when particular propositions are extracted from dependencia theory and generalized or "tested" as totalizing statements devoid of a context specified in time, space, or social development (see such criticisms as Cardoso, 1977). Social science must, of course, make generalizations. But a perspective or "theory" as complex and dense as dependencia theory cannot easily be translated into the usual forms of North American social science. A substantial set of propositions must be carefully distilled and examined jointly.

At the heart of our project is a formal model of dependencia theory that we have presented elsewhere (Duvall et al., 1981), expressed as a system of twelve simultaneous equations and two identities. Appendix A presents the theoretical specification of the six equations to be estimated here. The model synthesizes arguments from various studies in the dependencia tradition and represents the processes that lead from external penetration to the creation of an export enclave, to structural distortions in the peripheral economy, and finally to sociopolitical distortions, the latter including social inequalities, state capitalism, and a spiraling process of political conflict and institutionalized state coercion. The model deals only with processes stemming from external penetration and, unlike theories of imperialism, makes no statements about the causes of penetration. Thus we limit ourselves to examining repercussions in the periphery of foreign penetration and do not explore the ultimate impact of these repercussions *on the center*. Also, we deal with a limited time period: namely, with part of the period that Dos Santos (1970) has characterized as the flowering of the "new dependence," and not with the centuries that preceded it.

We must also note a variety of methodological limitations. One stems from the fact that our model is cast at a fairly abstract level, and we rarely specify the relevant social actors whose behavior leads to the processes we describe. In this we may seem open to criticisms akin to those of Laclau (1971), Leys (1977), and Wuyts (1976) that the analysis is insufficiently class based and hence is a superficial theory based on distributional forms rather than on production relations. This problem is probably an unavoidable consequence of our wish to generalize about "situations of dependence" ranging from Argentina to Zambia. The mere existence of, not to mention the distinctions between, relevant actors varies so widely across cases that any attempt to specify certain types of interactions (e.g., relations between state bourgeoisie and middle peasants) is probably doomed to irrelevance. Hence we are driven to analyze the relations between actors rather than the actors themselves; for example, we employ a concept of uneven development without specifying which is the leading sector.

Nevertheless, there are at least two ways in which "causal" explanation may be inferred from the structural relationships that we have examined in our parameter estimation. First, one might argue that structural constraints dominate rational calculations and, hence, that these structural relations very nearly reveal the actual causal mechanisms that we seek as our understanding of the processes of dependent development. If, by various specific mechanisms, growth always leads, for example, to an increasingly unequal income distribution, we might argue that the ramifications of growth are so far-reaching that, regardless of the ways in which actors in dependent societies make decisions or would like to act, the processes of growth create sufficiently deep networks of pressure as to ensure that the ultimate result will be increasing income inequality. This line of reasoning is, in the final analysis, of a structural-functional character. It may be reduced to the form of a proposition such as, every dependent society must be structured in such a way as to produce this result. The origin of the "must" is problematic, unless one accepts the Darwinian proposition that societies in which it is not true do not survive. Of course, the need for the "must" only exists where one seeks "cause"; it is possible to describe dependent societies by observing that all such societies appear to satisfy the particular structural relation. However, this stands as an explanation only if, by the nature of being dependent, society must be structured in this way. As Elster (1978) has argued most forcefully, outside of perfectly competitive markets there seems very little evidence in favor of a structural-functional orientation in the analysis of social situations. The mechanisms for rooting out "deviant" cases appear not to work automatically so much as to stem, where they do occur, from the calculations of interested parties.

The second way in which cause may be inferred from the structural appearances with which we have dealt (in the terms of Amin, 1974) is by identifying the range of possible calculi by which actors might be motivated and still produce the observed appearances. That is, in this method we assume that underlying every specific appearance are calculating actors seeking to promote or protect their interests. Certain kinds of calculations may be shown as inconsistent with the observed relations; these calculations, and whatever they imply about the interests and resources of certain social actors, may be disproven on the basis of the structural results. Of course, the proof will not be conclusive, normally, as the inferential steps are sufficient to require various assumptions that in practice may be difficult to assess exactly. However, by this method we can certainly introduce strong and substantial doubts about certain kinds of purported calculations.

The more difficult problem is the constructive one of locating that set of calculations that gave rise to the observed relations. Of course, multiple underlying calculations may be consistent with the observed appearances. Moreover, multiple underlying calculations may account for the various observations. While we cannot from the structural relations deduce that deep structure (or set of deep structures: here we return again to Amin's distinction between appearances and the deep structure of explanation) that accounts for the observations, we can attempt to describe the range of possible such structures. We can attempt as well to isolate the most plausible explanation(s) from this range. It is this tactic of explanation that we pursue in the following efforts to understand dependent development. Thus we shall elaborate examples of social interactions that are consistent with the empirical results and leave it to the reader to judge the success of what is basically a meta-analysis.

The complexity of the theory presents formidable problems for empirical estimation. For example, while there are two distinguishable blocs (trade sector and domestic economy) in the partial system of equations presented here, feedback loops prevent the model from being bloc recursive. Thus all parts of the model, except the exogenous penetration variables, are reciprocally related. The model is probably underidentified, although this may be somewhat mitigated by the nonlinearities in the structural specification.[1] We have chosen not to estimate the entire model; rather, in this report we use an equation-by-equation approach that allows us to reduce the complexity of the problem and increases our ability to detect peculiarities between the specified relations and the observed data. Our estimates cannot be fully satisfactory insofar as we ignore the interrelations between equations. Technically, the estimated coefficients will be biased and inconsistent whenever such feedbacks actually exist. However, if we believe that first-order effects are typically greater than the second-order effects of feedback, we may reasonably expect that the former will still be observable despite the biases introduced by improperly excluding the latter. The existence of a broader theoretical framework (i.e., the full simultaneous model) within which to consider the estimates of each single equation provides rich assistance in seeking out problems of misspecification.[2]

A further caveat concerns the problem of measurement. Dependency theory is concerned with economic outcomes not normally captured by directly available statistics (e.g., national accounts data) and with political phenomena that are difficult to measure. We often have used complicated measurement techniques and the logic of multiple indicators to overcome these problems (our measures are briefly described in Appendix B). Such measurement procedures are sure to contain substantial measurement error, and these will cause inconsistent estimates as parameters of variables with measurement error will tend to be underestimated (Johnston, 1972: 281-282; Theil, 1971: 607-610). One advantage of piecewise estimation is that measurement errors affect only the equation in which the variable appears and are not transmitted throughout the system.

A final caveat concerns the use of cross-sectional estimates to infer the dynamic processes of concern in dependency theory. Strictly speaking, such inference is not appropriate (see Kuhl, 1959: Nerlove, 1971) and the results reported below pertain to differences in the "histories" of peripheral countries across the sample rather than in the experiences of *particular* nations through time. However, the model—viewed cross-sectionally—is concerned with the relative performance of nations according to differences in "stimuli" (e.g., penetration) received in the time period considered. In this respect the coefficients do provide information about the dynamics of dependent development in any one nation, but they should not be mistaken for the coefficients we would derive from a longitudinal estimation.[3]

To incorporate the impact of stimuli over extended periods of time, many of the equations in our model employ a Koyck "distributed lag" formulation. In this formulation the stimuli, or independent variables $(X_{t's})$, affect the outcome or dependent variables (Y_t) over an extended period of time:

$$Y_t = \alpha + \beta_t X_t + \beta_{t-1} X_{t-1} + ... + \beta_{t-\infty} X_{t-\infty} \qquad [1]$$

where $\beta_t, \beta_{t-1}, ... \beta_{t-\infty}$ reflect the decreasing impact of older values of X and hence of past history. Often we assume that there is a smooth and steady decline in the impact of more distant history on the present that can be approximated by a geometric distributed lag, i.e., where $\beta_{t-i-1} = L\beta_{t-1}$, and $0 < L < 1$. In other cases we may believe that it takes time for the impact of stimuli to have impact, and thus that L exceeds 1. Therefore, the impact of history may either increase or decrease through the time period considered in our analysis, but in either case may be modeled as:

$$Y_t = \alpha + \beta_t\, X_t + L\beta_t\, X_{t-1} + L^2\beta_t\, X_{t-2} + \ldots + L^\infty\, \beta_t\, X_{t-\infty} \qquad [2]$$

By taking the expression in equation 2 for the previous time period (Y_{t-1}), multiplying both sides by L, and then subtracting the result from equation 2, we obtain a form that can be estimated:[4]

$$Y_t = (1 - L)\,\alpha + LY_{t-1} + \beta_t\, X_t \qquad [3]$$

The coefficient (L) of the lagged dependent variable in the equations estimated below is therefore an estimate of the rate at which the impact of the independent variables declines over time. This suggests that the impact of "history" will lead to strong autoregression between Y_t and Y_{t-1}. For this reason many of the estimates reported fit very well (i.e., high R^2 and very significant coefficients for the lagged dependent variable), but we should not be overwhelmed by this. Rather, our concern should lie with the estimates of all the coefficients—especially those of the independent variables—and whether they are both in the hypothesized direction and are "significant."[5] Only in light of this can we evaluate the fit of the model and interpret the autoregressive parameter.[6]

Each of the results reported below is the product of careful estimation techniques. We began with the form of each equation as originally hypothesized (Appendix A). We then tried several variants (e.g., logging a variable, adding an interaction term, or breaking down a composite variable into separate elements) that still were consistent with verbal propositions in the dependencia literature. We routinely applied several controls (population, GNP, GNP per capita, geographical region) to capture the effect—so important in dependencia writing—of different contexts on causal relations. We paid particular attention to univariate and bivariate outliers to ensure that a few data points were not playing a crucial role in determining the estimates. Transformations were used to correct skewness in variables that might distort the results, and extreme values on variables were trimmed in several cases. The "hat matrix" (Hoaglin and Welsch, 1978) was employed to check further the stability of the results, and the residuals were checked against possible excluded variables such as size, wealth, region, and resources. The results reported in the text are those we felt were "best." We believe that we were fair in neither too zealously favoring the theory nor too enthusiastically rejecting its hypotheses. Those who wish to replicate or question our decisions may do so when our data become publicly available in machine-readable form.

One reason for our concern with outliers and residuals lies in the dispute over to what set of countries dependency theory applies. We have followed Amin (1974: 378-79) in considering all Third World states and the peripheral European states (Portugal, Spain, Malta, Yugoslavia, Greece, Israel) but excluding the socialist states (Eastern Europe, China, Cuba) except Yugoslavia. However, in looking at outliers and residuals we have tried to isolate individual countries or sets of countries to which the theory did or did not apply. Thus we started each equation with the largest sample for which we could obtain all relevant data and then dropped states that seemed distinctly different than the others on the multivariate relation for that question. Generally we tried to be conservative and resist dropping cases.

PENETRATION AND THE EXPORT ENCLAVE

Penetration of a peripheral society exists to the extent that foreign elements constitute a significant proportion of the set of elements in that society. Penetration is a mechanism of dependence, that is, a means by which conditions within are made contingent upon conditions outside the periphery. *Capitalist penetration* is one mechanism of dependence, referring to the extent of control of the effective capital stock of a given peripheral country by foreign economic actors. The *concentration* of capitalist penetration is an indication of vulnerability, being the extent to which foreign control operates through a specific set of multinational channels, reflecting reliance on different kinds of capital and nationality. *Cultural penetration* is the permeation of a country's beliefs, values, and aspirations. Hence, cultural penetration indicates foreign orientation. The *concentration* of cultural penetration is an indication of intensity, being the extent to which a single source country dominates the origination of various aspects of cultural penetration.

The export enclave in dependent societies reflects the external orientation of the dependent economy. This external orientation of economic activity seeps into every corner of social life: economic, cultural, and political. In the stereotypical case, often discussed as generally applicable by Amin (1974) and Frank (1972) among others, the dependent economy relies on the external market both for a substantial portion of its consumption (both immediate and indirect) through imports, and for a substantial portion of its realization of profits from production, through exports. We call this reliance on the external market *trade centrality*. More than just the centrality of trade is embodied in the export enclave: The enclave maintains and is maintained by a pattern of exchange on international markets that is highly concentrated. Exports are directed at one or two markets with which the enclave maintains special relations. This yields a *concentration of trading partners*. Further, the products that are exported remain within a narrow range, whether that range be in primary products (agricultural or mineral) or in manufactured products. One of the ways in which the dependent enclave gains access to the external market is through its specialization in the export of certain products, which results in a *concentration of commodities exported.*

While the stereotypical case serves to distinguish certain basic features of dependent societies from the comparable characteristics of autonomous advanced industrial societies, the stereotype also serves to obscure substantial differences in the degree to which an export enclave thrives in any particular dependent society. Countries differ in the extent to which trade is central to their economies. Countries differ also in the extent to which their trade is concentrated, both by partner and by commodity. In the first bloc of our estimating we have identified the structural relations with which we may infer the causal mechanisms by which enclaves grow and thrive in some dependent societies or wither away in others. According to dependencia theory, foreign capitalists contribute to the development of an export enclave because of their interests in obtaining raw materials and in the differential profit rates available from production for export from the peripheral country. These interests lead to alliances with the local bourgeoisie to protect the foreign interests, and thus are conditioned, in the local context, by the existing class structure of the peripheral country. Depending on the nature of colonial history, local allies may be found, for example, among elements of the bourgeoisie in the plantation and mining sectors, or among those oriented toward production for the local market. Another potential ally is the "state bourgeoisie," that is, the state bureaucracy, often in actual control of the productive process, in relative autonomy from the rest of the bourgeoisie. Sunkel and Fuenzalida (1977) and Cardoso and Faletto (1979) state especially strongly the need to look at how the internal situation, as a reflection of historical context, conditions foreign penetration.

Table 4.1 and Figure 4.1 present the results of our estimation of the first three equations, constituting the bloc of equations dealing with the development of export enclaves. We present these results with a more detailed analysis of how they may be interpreted in the light of dependency theory.

We also add, in Table 4.2, an "impact analysis," which indicates the effect of each "independent" variable. It shows the percentage change in each dependent variable associated with movement from the lowest value of a particular independent variable found in our sample to the highest value. (Remember however, that this is essentially a cross-sectional analysis and not meant to imply that we actually observe the movement of any one country's value from low to high.)

TABLE 4.1 Estimated Equations for Bloc 1

(1) $PARTCON_t$ = $-.030$ + $.155$ $\sum\limits_{i=0}^{\infty} .815^i (CAPPEN_{t-i} \times CAPCON_{t-i})$ + $.327$ $\sum\limits_{i=0}^{\infty} .815^i (CULTCON_{t-i-1})$

             (.048) (.047) i=0 (.102)   (.184) i=0 (.102)

                 $-$ $.030$ $\sum\limits_{i=0}^{\infty} .815^i (CULTSYS_{t-i-1} \times CULTCON_{t-i-1})$

                   (.016) i=0 (.102)

                $n = 34; R^2 = .74$

(2) $(COMCON_t - COMCON_{t-1})$ = $.268$ + $.00262$ $([UNEVEN_t - UNEVEN_{t-1}] \times DISINTEG_{t-1})$ + $.0628$ $(CAPPEN_{t-1})$

                     (.160) (.00075)   (.336)

                $n = 27; R^2 = .34$

(3) $logTRADCENT_t$ = $-.789$ $-$ $.136$ $\sum\limits_{i=0}^{\infty} .813^i (CAPPEN_{t-i})$ + $.252$ $\sum\limits_{i=0}^{\infty} .813^i (CAPPEN_{t-i} \times GDPCAP_{t-1}\gamma < 650)$

             (.243) (.101) i=0 (.078)   (.114) i=0 (.078)

                + $.053$ $\sum\limits_{i=0}^{\infty} .813^i (CULTSYS_{t-i-1})$ $-$ $.110$ $\sum\limits_{i=0}^{\infty} .813^i (logCOMCON_{t-i-1})$

                  (.025) i=0 (.078)   (.062) i=0 (.078)

                $n = 48; R^2 = .80$

NOTE: γ in equation 3 is a dummy variable.

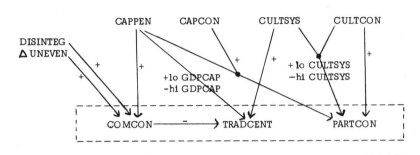

Figure 4.1   Determinants of the Export Enclave

Although the export enclave shows a strong tendency to persist over time, certain long-run trends are discernible in each of its three aspects. Both partner and commodity concentration declined gradually throughout the 1965-1975 period. The mean Hirschman concentration index *decreased* from .22 in 1965 to .17 in 1975 for trade partners and from .34 to .30 for commodities. On the other hand, the median level of trade centrality remained stable at .33 in this same period. Thus the enclaves became *less reliant on particular nations or commodities* but did not change *in overall size.*

The dominant result of the trade bloc estimation is the size and significance of the autoregressive parameter. Interpreted in light of the Koyck transform by which it is derived, it suggests the importance of penetration acting over extended periods in determining the partner concentration and trade centrality aspects of the export enclave. The autoregressive parameters for the trade centrality and partner concentration equations both were around .80. These values indicate a time horizon for the effects of penetration that is very "flat" or long run in character. (For commodity concentration the interesting questions revolve around the changes rather than the level, so the Koyck transform is not used.)

The overall declines in concentration nevertheless mask the experience of particular countries, some of whom still experience great and even increasing concentration. Among countries, partner concentration varies with both capitalist penetration and with cultural penetration. In those countries in which capitalist penetration has been very high, and very highly concentrated on one national supplier of capital, the concentration on one trading partner has also been very high. Where either the level of penetration or its degree of concentration was lower, the degree of partner concentration was also lower. In those countries in which cultural penetration has been very low, the

TABLE 4.2   Impact Analysis for Bloc 1

Dependent Variable	Independent Variables	Percentage Change (Impact) Produced by Movement from Low to High of Independent Variable's Range
Partner Concentration	CAPPEN × CAPCON	16
	CULTCON	17
	CULTCON × CULTSYS	42
Commodity Concentration	UNEVEN × DISINTEG	129
	CAPPEN	22
Trade Centrality	CULTSYS	68
	CAPPEN if rich	47
	CAPPEN if poor	40
	COMCON	40

more highly concentrated that penetration has been, the more highly concentrated is the partner concentration of trade. On the other hand, where cultural penetration has been relatively high, the more concentrated is the cultural penetration, the less concentrated is trade.

The determinants (correlates) of trade centrality are somewhat simpler in kind. In the first instance, in those countries that have experienced high levels of cultural penetration, the centrality of trade is higher than in those countries in which the penetration has not been as high. The effect of capitalist penetration on trade centrality depended qualitatively upon the level of per capita income. For countries with per capita incomes above $650 (in 1970 U.S. dollars), "middle-income countries," the higher the level of capitalist penetration the lower the level of trade centrality. For countries with per capita incomes below $650, "low-income countries," the effect of penetration might be either positive or negative. In any case, higher levels of penetration were associated with a smaller reduction in the centrality of trade in low-income than in middle-income countries.

The determinants of changes in commodity concentration reflect a marked difference in the origins of this aspect of the export enclave compared with the two previously discussed. While capitalist penetration appears to condition the rate of change in concentration here, the remaining determinants originate within the dependent economy itself. This is not to say that external influence is missing; in those countries most highly penetrated by foreign capital, the concentration of commodity exports has increased most rapidly. Moreover, the remaining internal determinants are themselves determined, in part, by external forces (to be discussed in bloc 2). Nonetheless, it is worth noting that the conditioning of changes in commodity concentration by disintegration and changes in uneven development suggest a shift in emphasis here from the primarily external to the mix of external and internal in determining the nature of the export enclave. In those countries in which the disarticulation of the economy was most severe, and in which the unevenness of development across sectors was increasing most rapidly, the increasing concentration of commodity exports also increased most rapidly.

Several noteworthy trends in the world political economy affected export enclaves. First was a general shift in the nature of capitalist penetration, away from raw materials investment and toward investment for manufacturing production, whether intended for domestic markets in the host countries (e.g., Brazil) or for the home country through some sort of "export platform" (e.g., Malaysia). Needless to say, this shift did not *end* further developments in the field of raw materials investments, but the growing nationalism of the time (as evinced in expropriations and in import substitution policies) and the wage inflation of the 1960s and early 1970s in the capitalist center countries provided a strong impetus for such a shift, except for poor and politically malleable Fourth World countries (e.g., most states on the West Coast of Africa; Dos Santos, 1970; Cardoso and Faletto, 1979; Mandel, 1975).

Concomitant with this first trend was a second one: a shift in the source of capitalist penetration, away from old metropoles and toward their competitors. Thus the United States moved in on former British and French colonies following their formal independence in the late 1950s, while France, Germany, and Japan did the same in Latin America starting in the late 1960s. Undoubtedly, this trespassing process was partly impelled by the profitability squeeze in the Trilateral countries and by other forms of "interimperialist" competition—as well, of course, as by the rebuilding of Japan and Europe (Frank, 1981; Amin, 1980).

The third, and in some ways most significant, trend was a shift in the power structure within many underdeveloped countries, away from the old raw materials exporters and their oligarchic allies and toward a "modernizing" segment of the bourgeoisie, which in some countries involved itself in domestic manufactures; in others, in the new, export platform fields. This segment of the bourgeoisie often had allies in the foreign corporations penetrating the peripheral economy and in certain technocratic elements in the state. Several factors lay behind this alteration in the power structure. One (in Africa and Asia) was the anticolonial struggle, whereby collaborating segments of the ruling classes lost much of their influence. A second reason (especially in parts of Latin America and other countries such as Iran) was a strengthened domestic labor movement, which posed challenges that could not be met by the old alliances. A third reason was a push on the part of the United States for a retooling and rationalization of the political economy of countries it deemed "vulnerable" to "Communist subversion" (whether from Cuba or China was immaterial). (In Latin America, this revamping was known as the Alliance for Progress; in Vietnam, it was known as political reform; Evans, 1979; O'Donnell, 1978a; Collier, 1979.) A fourth reason, a more conjunctural one, was the recession in world commodities that began shortly after the 1973 oil price increases; this cut into the power of the traditional export segment of the bourgeoisie, forcing them to change their economic base or else lose economic and political power. (Similarities with the Depression years are obvious.)

All three of these trends had important effects on the export enclaves in the periphery. Consider first *trade centrality*. As the form of capitalist penetration shifted, domestic manufacturing in the wealthier periphery countries grew faster than exports did; hence their trade centrality declined. This interest in developing internal markets within middle-income dependent countries may derive in part from the decline of American military hegemony in the 1960s, a decline that removed some of the guarantees of stability. Transnationals now seek those guarantees in greater diversification of their productive facilities. The distinction in the periphery between those whom MNCs choose to develop and those whom they do not comports well with Wallerstein's (1974) distinction between periphery and semiperiphery. It does not, however, fit well with the expectations of those like Amin who see in dependent development a vicious circle of external orientation and production that can never be broken. Here we find the circle being broken, presumably because it is in the interests of core capital. Much the same occurred in highly populous countries; even if their per capita incomes were not high, the size of the population guaranteed a substantial market for foreign corporations. (High-population countries, we know, are those in which domestic cultural elements as opposed to foreign ones predominate; this accounts in part for the positive relationship between systemic cultural penetration and trade centrality.) In the Fourth World, however, investment still went into traditional exports (or, in some cases like the Philippines, into labor-intensive manufacturing exports); thus some of those countries experienced an increase in trade centrality.

But it was not only foreign corporations that affected the trade centrality of underdeveloped countries. Those nations in which a few traditional exports predominated in the trade profile had those exports particularly hard hit by the commodity recession of the 1970s (thus accounting in part for the negative relationship between changes in commodity concentration and trade centrality). As pointed out before, this drop in the prices of traditional exports hit the older exporting classes hard, rendering them more vulnerable to the encroachments of a new alliance of "nizers" (von Freyhold, 1979), who were more interested in domestic manufacturing (often in cooperation with multinationals) than in raw materials exports. As a result, trade accounted for a smaller part of total economic activity.

Cultural penetration also serves to link the fortunes of the dependent economy and society with the development of the advanced industrial world. By introducing the symbols, ideals, and aspirations emanating from the core countries into the peripheral environment, cultural penetration shapes the processes of development, whether they be the economic processes of the market, the political processes of contesting authority, or the social processes of individual communication. The agents of this cultural penetration are the affluent, educated elements of the local elite in a dependent society who are "privileged" enough to travel abroad to study, learning the manner of thought as much as the substance of courses of study in advanced industrial universities. Added to this are those who learn through contact with visitors—tourists, whether visiting for business or pleasure—the nature of the syntax in which they operate. While tourists do not determine directly the nature of the dependent economy, nationals of the society who are in contact with them do. Students may not shape societies often (although occasionally they do, as in Korea), but when young elites age they become determining elites, complete with the ideological baggage of their youth. Hence to the extent that a peripheral society has been culturally penetrated, to that extent there exists a class of individuals in that society who have internalized those foreign symbols and goals that originate in the core of the world economy. This portion of a country's bourgeoisie corresponds approximately to that which Frank (1972) called the "lumpenbourgeoisie." To the extent that a country has been culturally penetrated, then, the interests of the lumpenbourgeoisie will be reflected in the development outcomes of the society.

The lumpenbourgeoisie have a collective interest in maintaining the external orientation of production in dependent economies. With their values and goals rooted in an outside world, it is not surprising that the lumpenbourgeoisie seek to maintain the intimate economic connections of their society to the means of satisfying their aspirations, the world market. This is central to Frank's original conception of the lumpenbourgeoisie. Where we extend Frank is in recognizing that the lumpenbourgeoisie exist in every area of the dependent economy, wherever elites have borrowed symbols and values from overseas. They do not reside solely within the export enclave; in industry, in the bureaucracy, and in the military foreign values thrive as well. Across all of these different locations, the interests of the lumpenbourgeoisie are one in maintaining the centrality of trade in the economy.

Turning to the second component of the export enclave, *commodity concentration,* we again find a combination of external and internal influences. Simple profit-seeking will lead both domestic and foreign capitalists in an economy with highly *uneven development* (different returns to factors of production in different sectors) to concentrate their investments in leading sectors—which are quite often the major export sectors, whether traditional or new. Similar reasoning helps to explain the link between *economic disintegration* (the absence of linkages within the peripheral economy) and changes in commodity concentration. The dynamic sectors are likely to include those originally oriented toward specialized production for the world market. This latter phenomenon, however, can be explored more deeply. Structural disintegration, after all, is a manifestation of underlying splits within a country's bourgeoisie. To be sure, the proximate cause of disintegration may be a poor transportation or communication network, but the question then recurs as to why that network was not upgraded. And to answer *that* question by saying "colonialism" is to sidestep the whole issue of *divide et impera* policies in the preindependence era. Thus we see again a feature of underdevelopment being the joint result of "external" (foreign profit seeking) and "internal" (splits in the bourgeoisie) factors.

This combination affects commodity concentration in another, related way. Capitalist penetration, as we have argued, goes into dynamic sectors. If those sectors are indeed in traditional exports, then commodity concentration will increase as a logical consequence. Furthermore, we may infer that foreign capital has an interest in increasing the specialization of countries in different productive lines to increase the efficiency of production and hence enable the realization of larger profits. This differentiation of roles in the world economy is the phenomenon to which world systems analysts rightly point when they discuss the emergence of an international division of labor. On the other hand, to the degree that the dynamic sectors are in the domestic market, capital will be pulled out of the weaker export products, leaving the dominant ones even more important in the country's trade profile. Needless to say, the oil price hikes that began in 1973 led to petroleum-exporting countries (many of them high income) increasing commodity concentration. Those "high"-income countries that were not oil producers responded to their sharply increased oil bills by pumping up their major exports as much as possible. Finally, the commodity recession of the 1970s badly hurt the leading exports of those poorest countries (the Fourth World), thus lowering commodity concentration in countries with low per capita incomes.

Two kinds of effects are suggested in the results on *partner concentration in trade.* First, trade follows the flag of capital. In 1970, it will be remembered, the capitalist world economy was in a state of transition from "old" to "new" forms of external penetration. By 1975, that transition was continuing but had gone on long enough so that the partner concentration of capitalist penetration in those countries highly penetrated to begin with conduced to partner concentration in trade as well. Trade also follows the flag of culture. Those who have accepted the values of France wish to, and push to, maintain trade relations with France to satisfy those value-driven desires. Hence, the larger the proportion of lumpenbourgeoisie that originates in France, the larger will be the demand for products from France. However, the second observation from our results suggests that alternative methods for satisfying these foreign-generated desires now exist: Luxury goods can be produced domestically in the dependent country. Indeed, our results suggest that as the size of the lumpenbourgeoisie as a whole increases, the diversion from foreign sources of supply to domestic ones must increase. Thus, the remaining trade appears less concentrated because those goods that were being acquired specifically to meet the needs of particular factions of the lumpenbourgeoisie can now be produced domestically. This suggests a novel (if not entirely positive) structural arrangement for peripheral societies, in which the resources of the lumpenbourgeoisie are now sufficiently large to enable much frivolous spending on luxury goods to be kept within the dependent economy.

Moreover, as mentioned earlier, there was a shift in the ruling coalitions of many periphery countries during this period, and in those nations in which systemic cultural penetration was high, a nationalist political reaction set in against extensive concentration of foreign culture on a specific source. This modern *Kulturkampf* was one component of the modernizing alliance's reaction against older ruling elements; it was carried out not only by directly stimulating domestic values, but also by a conscious redirection of economic ties away from older metropoles and toward newer, more aggressive ones. These two actions were not usually carried out by the same groups. The first was the particular forte of intellectuals not tied directly to the regime; the latter was more the bailiwick of the middle classes in the ruling alliance. The first group carried out its goals by means of standard cultural instruments like films and books, while the second group used the government to sponsor conferences and fund student exchanges. A good description of this process as it worked in Tunisia (a country with very high levels of systemic culture penetration) may

be found in Hennebelle (1976) and *Middle East Yearbook* (1980).
Those countries in which this process was well advanced ended up
with a strong indigenous culture, a more evenly balanced set of
foreign cultural elements, and often a high concentration of trade with
the "new" metropole.

STRUCTURAL DISTORTIONS
IN PERIPHERAL ECONOMIES

Dependencia theorists are concerned with three kinds of structural
distortions in peripheral economies: *dis-integration* of the economy,
uneven development across sectors, and *heterogeneity* of the return
to productive factors across sectors. The first two, introduced in the
previous discussion, refer respectively to lack of linkages or connec-
tedness between sectors and to different levels of economic activity
and capital accumulation across sectors. The last refers to different
rates of return to land, labor, and capital in different sectors. While
these three structural distortions are related, they are conceptually
and empirically distinct, and different propositions are advanced to
account for them. Implicit in dependencia theory is a norm of a
"good" economy in which all sectors are developed, interact with one
another, and reward factors of production equally. Dependencia
theory is hardly unique in recognizing that structural distortions are
typical of peripheral economies. It is, however, distinctive in the linkages from capitalist penetration to distortion that it asserts.

As with the presentation of results for the previous bloc, we give
both the estimated equations (in Table 4.3) and a graphic summary of
the effects (Figure 4.2) and, in Table 4.4, an impact analysis. As can
be seen, all of the independent variables have some impact on structural economic distortions in the periphery. Note that the level of
economic activity is particularly important, whereas capitalist penetration is important only in combination with other variables. This
suggests that the "external" has effects on the "internal" only in
combination with the latter. (Trade centrality of course is not
solely "external" but instead describes the country's productive
structure.)

Both the opposite effects across equations of variables such as
GDP per capita and the quadratic terms (in the uneven development
equation) mean that the independent variables do not have to cluster
together in one or two neat packages. Instead, there are 144
possible combinations of bloc 2 independent variables (2 CAPPEN,
2 UNEVEN, 2 COMCON, 2 DISINT, 3 TRADCENT, 3 GDPCAP)
which, together with the dependent variable outcomes, we shall call
syndromes. Clearly, this is far too high a number for meaningful

TABLE 4.3 Estimated Equations for Bloc 2

(4) $UNEVEN_t = 5.58 + 1.96 \sum_{i=0}^{8} .867^i (TRADCENT_{t-i}) - 1.84 \sum_{i=0}^{8} .867^i (TRADCENT^2_{t-i})$
    $ (1.04) \quad (.466) \quad\quad (.058) \quad\quad\quad\quad\quad (.527) \quad (.058)$

$ - 1.80 \sum_{i=0}^{8} .867^i (GDPCAP_{t-i}) + .144 \sum_{i=0}^{8} .867^i (GDPCAP^2_{t-i})$
$ \quad (.329) \quad (.058) \quad\quad\quad\quad\quad (.027) \quad (.058) \quad\quad\quad (.137)$

$ - .208 \sum_{i=0}^{8} .867^i (CAPPEN_{t-i} \times UNEVEN_{t-i-1})$
$ \quad (.137) \quad (.058)$

$\quad n = 47; R^2 = .98$

(5) $DISINTEG_t = 36700 - 17500 \sum_{i=0}^{8} 1.13^i (TRADCENT_{t-i}) + 1690 \sum_{i=0}^{8} 1.13^i (COMCON_{t-i-1})$
    $ (12127) \quad (5216) \quad (.047) \quad\quad\quad\quad\quad (296) \quad (.047)$

$\quad n = 22; R^2 = .97$

(6) $HETERO = .141 - .077 \sum_{i=0}^{8} 1.24^i (\log CAPPEN_{t-i}) - 2.05 \times 10^{-11} \sum_{i=0}^{8} 1.24^i (CAPPEN_{t-i} \times DISINTEG_{t-i} \times GDPCAP_{t-i})$
    $ (.076) \quad (.051) \quad (.237) \quad\quad\quad\quad (.875 \times 10^{-12}) \quad (.237)$

$\quad n = 12; R^2 = .83$

NOTE: Sample size for HETERO equation is very small because of lack of data on both CAPPEN and DISINTEG for many countries. Equations have been estimated with only one of these variables and, though biased, suggest both do contribute.

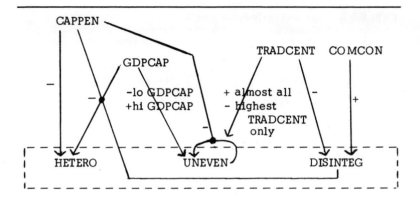

Figure 4.2 Determinants of Structural Economic Distortion

analysis; it even exceeds the total size of our universe! Instead, we shall discuss four of the most important syndromes; some OPEC capital surplus countries, some of the larger newly industralized countries (NICs), Fourth World raw materials exporters, and some NIC "export platforms." Two cautions are in order before doing this. First, as indicated above, the data do not tell us anything about the processes resulting in the statistical results we report: thus the necessity for interpretation—and also its tenuous nature. Second, our estimates, strictly speaking, refer only to levels of variables, except in those few cases where we explicitly introduce change terms. Much of the following discussion, though, is couched in terms of movements up or down from starting levels. This is a perfectly permissible procedure, and even, from the viewpoint of the dynamic quality of the dependencia perspective, a desirable one, but it is different from simply discussing correlations between levels. Table 4.5 presents the average or "modal" inputs and outputs for four development paths. We shall discuss each one in turn.

Consider first the *OPEC capital surplus countries*. These countries were characterized by a significant "petrobourgeoisie," made up of both private companies and government technocrats. In addition, of course, foreign oil companies were present in a variety of ways. There were other classes in the country as well; particularly important for our purposes are other bourgeoisie involved in nascent manufacturing industries. These latter classes began (in many cases) as offshoots of the petrobourgeoisie (e.g., family connections) but have in a number of situations become independent of their origins, since there is at least a latent conflict of interest between the two groups.

TABLE 4.4   Impact Analysis for Bloc 2

Dependent Variable	Independent Variables	Percentage Change (Impact) Produced by Movement from Low to High of Independent Variable's Range
Uneven	TRADCENT	18
Development	GDP CAP	48
	CAPPEN × UNEVEN	12
Disintegration	TRADCENT	23
	COMCON	24
Heterogeneity	CAPPEN (single term)	3
	CAPPEN × DISINTEG × GDP CAP	282

NOTE: When DISINTEG × GDPCAP is at low end and move from minimum CAPPEN to maximum CAPPEN, the impact of CAPPEN is 3%; when DISINTEG × GDPCAP is at its high end, movement from minimum to maximum CAPPEN produces an impact of 213%.

As the 1970s unfurled, economic nationalism (both for purposes of ideology and for garnering additional loot) beame more prevalent in a number of countries; OPEC nations were no exception. Gradually, more and more foreign oil companies were taken over by host governments, leaving them companies with large sums of money but nowhere (as regards oil wells) to put them. As a result, foreign oil companies moved "downstream" into petrochemicals. At the same time as the price of OPEC oil increased, recycling of petrodollars became a more attractive option for other center companies, and they began to penetrate the OPEC countries in various other fields, particularly construction and manufacturing. (The combination of nationalization and new foreign investment led to a medium degree of capitalist penetration.) As these other areas of the economy began to be built up (which led to a further moderation of trade centrality), the lead of the extractive sectors on output per worker began to be reduced (lowering of uneven development). On the other hand, the lead was enhanced in purely accounting terms by the vast increase in oil prices following 1973 (trade centrality and income effects on uneven development).

As for distintegration, the history of concentration on oil products (high commodity concentration in the previous time period) led to the ascendance of the petrobourgeoisie. Increasingly, this class fraction had drawn strength from its links (capital and technology, in particular) with foreign capitalists, thereby weakening its relations with other segments of the country's bourgeoisie and petty bourgeoisie (e.g., merchants). Indeed, as the case of Iran shows, the petrobourgeoisie often enlisted the state to help weaken and intimidate those other parts of the bourgeoisie. As political links dissolved

TABLE 4.5   Modal Levels—"Development" Paths (1970-1975)

Individual Inputs	*Individual Outputs*	*Collective Outputs*
OPEC		
Medium TRADCENT	High UNEVEN	
High GDPCAP	High UNEVEN	High UNEVEN
Medium CAPPENX	Medium UNEVEN	
High UNEVEN$_{t-1}$		
Medium TRADCENT	Medium DISINTEG	Medium-High
High COMCON	High DISINTEG	DISINTEG
Medium CAPPEN		
High DISINTEG		Low-Medium HETERO
High GDPCAP		
NICs		
Low TRADCENT	Low UNEVEN	
High GDPCAP	High UNEVEN	Medium UNEVEN
Low CAPPENX	Low UNEVEN	
Medium UNEVEN$_{t-1}$		
Low TRADCENT	High DISINTEG	Medium DISINTEG
Low COMCON	Low DISINTEG	
Low CAPPEN		
Low DISINTEG		Medium HETERO
High GDPCAP		
Fourth World		
High TRADCENT	Low UNEVEN	
Low GDPCAP	High UNEVEN	Medium UNEVEN
High CAPPENX	Low UNEVEN	
High UNEVEN$_{t-1}$		
High TRADCENT	Low DISINTEG	Medium DISINTEG
High COMCON	High DISINTEG	
High CAPPEN		
High DISINTEG		Low-Medium HETERO
Low GDPCAP		
Export Platforms		
High TRADCENT	Low UNEVEN	
Medium GDPCAP	Low UNEVEN	Low UNEVEN
High CAPPENX	Low UNEVEN	
High UNEVEN$_{t-1}$		
Medium TRADCENT	Medium DISINTEG	Medium DISINTEG
Medium COMCON	Medium DISINTEG	
High CAPPEN		
Medium DISINTEG		Medium-Low HETERO
Medium GDPCAP		

between fractions of the bourgeoisie, so too did economic ones (hence disintegration).

But even as the old links were withering, new ones were being formed. As the petrobourgeoisie and the foreign oil companies began to take some of their profits (medium trade centrality) and establish "forward" and "backward" linkages into manufacturing, construction, and petrochemicals, this set up a whole new group of sectors in the economy that were closely allied—politically and economically— with the oil export class. As a result, the aforementioned increase in structural disintegration was lessened somewhat.

Capitalist penetration into the new, allied spheres was spurred to a considerable degree by the wealth of the country (high GDP per capita). Its effect on countries with labor shortages (which covered most capital-surplus OPEC countries) was to bid up wages in those sectors so that they began to approach the wage levels in the petroleum sector itself. This effect, in turn, was enhanced by the lack of trust (for good reason) between old and new bourgeoisies, which helped to make labor more mobile and to bid up its cost (since with a split bourgeoisie, joint action against workers was obviously impaired). On top of this disintegration effect (reduced heterogeneity), should be added the fact that, considering their tremendous startup capital costs in many of the new economic sectors, multinationals did not quibble at paying top dollar for their labor. With the exception of labor shortages, these processes can be seen quite clearly in the case of Iran (see Keddie, 1981; Jazani, 1980).

Let us now consider a second developmental path, that taken by some of the larger *newly industrializing countries (NICs)*. To begin, it is vital to realize that capitalist penetration (as with any type of capitalism) is profit seeking, but that profitable fields (as defined by return on investment) are not necessarily those in which output per worker (our measure of uneven development) is high. It may be, for instance, that extensive investment in plant and machinery will lead to high per worker output, but that return on investment will not be all that great. Foreign capitalists found that, starting in the 1970s, the rate of growth in profit rates of their investments in the NICs began to decline somewhat. This occurred for several reasons, foremost among them (a) diffusion of technology to indigenous competitors (who could then produce with much lower sunk capital costs—and note that this was in part due to state-mandated indigenization requirements); (b) low wages, due in part to government repression, which limited the size of the domestic market below expectations; and (c) NIC governments were, under domestic pressure, moving to reduce somewhat the extent of foreign penetration (O'Donnell, 1979;

Cardoso and Faletto, 1979). This policy also helps to account for the low level of capitalist penetration in the NICs even though, in absolute dollar terms, it was quite high. This falling off in the rate of growth of profitability of foreign investments was coupled with various economic problems faced by foreign firms outside of NICs—secular and conjunctural declines in profit rates in the First World. Consequently, foreign capitalists began looking for more profitable sectors in NICs in which to invest. Those sectors, it turns out, were ones in which less capital was needed to start up operations and in which relatively more labor was used. Labor-intensive investments of this sort (e.g., textiles) provided higher rates of return but were not as efficient (output per worker) as were capital-intensive industries. The fact that domestic firms were going into other fields (see below) was also an incentive to get into these areas. As a result, uneven development declined somewhat from previous levels.

We suspect that the domestic bourgeoisie in the NICs did not react the same way that foreign capitalists did to the slowing of the growth rate in profitability. Remember that the state played a vital role in the "tri-pe" (Evans, 1979) and that the state bureaucracy had longer-range, more encompassing interests than those of the foreign firms. Specifically, the *técnicos* wished to guarantee a stable foreign reserve position for the country in years to come (no easy thing to do in the face of the 1973-1975 oil price increases), and, in the face of the recession engendered by the commodity bust, to guarantee some type of employment (and hence, they assumed, political) stability for the regime. Thus while return on investment was an important consideration for domestic capitalists, their alliance with the state obliged them to take a less short term point of view of the economic interests.

The result of these various calculations was that the indigenous large bourgeoisie, together with the state, responded to the oil price rise and the profitability squeeze by pushing manufacturing or more stable raw materials exports, raising trade centrality from its former low levels. These investments necessitated large amounts of liquid capital but did lead to high per-worker output and, as a result, continued growth in GDP per capita. These investments accentuated the existing unevenness of the country's economic development.

The actions detailed above had other consequences. When the state went into the business of manufactures exports (which after several years began to raise the low level of commodity concentration as the new exports were pushed), it increasingly competed with small exporters and domestic manufacturers, placing them in a serious economic squeeze and widening a major fissure in the ranks of the country's bourgeoisie. this was exacerbated by the técnicos' tendency to prefer foreign technological inputs over domestic ones. The fissure, of course, was both a sign and a cause of increased economic disintegration.

There was, nevertheless, a backlash. Even as the state pushed manufactured exports to pay for foreign oil (and thus increased trade centrality), those small manufacturers whose sectors were invaded began to join ranks, mitigating somewhat the increase in disintegration. Indeed, it may not be too much to suggest that the state helped set off a considerable degree of concentration and centralization of capital in the small (non tri-pe) sector of the bourgeoisie, which (integration) may eventually transform that sector into a powerful partner of the state.

Capitalists are always interested in low-wage sectors for obvious reasons of profitability. As we have discussed, foreign and domestic capitalists in the period under discussion were interested in moving into relatively new industries where to the extent production had previously occurred, wages were lower than in other, more heavily penetrated fields. Sources of capital for investment will be attracted by, and (to the extent we are speaking of domestic capital) a consequence of, high per capita income. Flows of capital to low-wage areas will bid up wages in those sectors, thereby reducing heterogeneity. This effect was to a degree mitigated during the time period under discussion by the competition between the tri-pe firms and the smaller segment of the domestic bourgeoisie implied by disintegration. The former group was able to compete by capital-intensive processes, and so it could afford to pay more for skilled labor. The latter group, though, had labor-intensive operations and, therefore, tried to cut costs by keeping wages low (for a good discussion of these various processes, see O'Donnell, 1978a, 1978b).

Let us now consider a third type of developmental path, that of the *Fourth World* countries (and some slightly richer ones) still primarily involved with traditional raw materials exports (but not, of course, oil). As pointed out above, the mid-1970s saw the conjunction of two situations—a commodities recession (conjunctural) and the beginnings of a shift in the domestic political coalitions among the bourgeoisie in the Fourth World countries. These changes placed foreign capitalists in a quandary. If they went with the "internalists," they risked exchanging their still potentially lucrative investments in mines and plantations for small domestic markets that were not likely to be profitable for decades to come (if then). If, however, the foreigners went with the traditional exporting class segments, they would run the risk of endangering their political standing with a group of possible winners. And to pull out altogether was to lose a considerable amount of money. What appears to have happened in a large number of cases (see Biersteker, 1980) was that foreign capitalists threw some sops to the nizers, in the form of domestic boards of directors and so forth, while at the same time modernizing their existing investments to keep afloat in the lower-commodity-price era that was unfolding. (Note that even though this may not have involved much real investment—in terms of dollars—it did result in drastic increases in relative investment: capitalist penetration.) To put it another way, there was the appearance of diversification and indigenization, combined with the reality of capitalist penetration being largely channeled into traditional exports. Investment in those traditional exports had the additional political advantage of pumping up the growth rate, thereby increasing—at least a little—GDP per capita, albeit from a low base. Since traditional exports were ones in which output per workers was low (especially in recent years given the price drop), the modernization programs that began had the effect of raising efficiency and thereby reducing uneven development. Still, this reduction in uneven development had to be seen against the backdrop of that very drop in commodity prices (which perforce lowered trade centrality); from an *accounting* perspective, traditional exports had been characterized by an even lower per worker output than previously (i.e., uneven development had increased, because what little manufacturing existed in those countries had not undergone a deterioration in efficiency).

As discussed above, the plunge in raw materials prices in the mid-1970s led to a further lowering of commodity concentration in the Fourth World. As traditional exports shrank from their high level (at least for a time); the bourgeoisie in that sector lost some of their power relative to nizers. This loss of power was exacerbated by the modernization of traditional exports begun by foreign firms, which revealed the traditional export bourgeoisie to be increasingly irrelevant as economic actors—a politically damaging characterization especially in light of increasing economic nationalism. As a result of these twin processes, domestic opponents of the export bourgeoisie (principally the nizers and their allies) saw both political and economic advantage in joining closer together against the old ruling class fragments. Hence this intraclass coalition (and, indeed, given that it could present itself as a populist movement, it attracted portions of other, nonbourgeois classes as well) became more integrated politically. One tactic employed in this process was government subventions to various members of the coalition (called industrialization assistance and similar terms), which helped to enhance economic integration (commodity concentration down; disintegration down).

Both as a reaction to these inroads (which led the export bourgeoisie to seek partners abroad) and as a result of the decisions of foreign capitalists detailed above, the commodity recession yielded a new injection of foreign capital into traditional exports. Of necessity, this reduced flows of capital and other resources between enclave and hinterland, thereby increasing disintegration from what it would otherwise have been.

Finally, a word on wages. The growing integration between the (nonexport) nizers was manifested, as we have said, in increasing state funds channeled toward light industry and other related fields. As we have also said, these small fields were ones in which foreign capitalists were not much interested—in part because national GDP per capita was so low. The result of this rechanneling of government money was that the size of the "labor aristocracy" was increased, as manufacturing workers began to get better paid and become more numerous. (The other part of the labor aristocracy, of course, was the labor force associated with the transportion of export goods—railway workers, stevedores, and so forth.) Hence the working force became more polarized into haves (relatively speaking) and have nots, and, therefore, by definition heterogeneity increased (for evidence and examples, see Amin, 1980; Saul, 1979: chs. 9, 12).

There was, finally, a fourth development path, pursued by those nations that although not in the NIC category, were no longer restricted only to traditional exports. We refer here to the so-called *export platforms,* which increasingly came to specialize in the labor-intensive assembly of products produced in part from, and destined to be sold in, the center countries. The arguments here recapitulate those presented above, so we can be brief.

In the export platforms, as in the poorer Fourth World countries still emphasizing traditional raw material exports, foreign capital continued to flow primarily into the export sector, reinforcing unevenness of development. Industrialization was occurring, but overwhelmingly as a "horizontal" phenomenon oriented toward exports rather than as a "vertical" phenomenon resulting from the import-substituting (as well as export-oriented) industrialization of the NICs with larger internal markets. But the unevenness implied by the further expansion of the export sector at the expense of the domestic market (greater trade centrality) mitigated unevenness in another sense: The new investment was in industry, in contrast to the previous export dominance of raw materials (e.g., tin and rubber in Malaysia). Moreover, as the industrialization depended mainly on cheap labor and imported components for reexport, it was not oriented toward processing the indigenous raw materials formerly dominant in exports. It therefore did little to integrate the domestic economy. Finally, whereas the industrialization created new and somewhat higher-paying jobs, the competitiveness of the products on the world market depended on keeping wage rates still basically low. Foreign capital had been attracted by the availability of cheap labor, an availability strengthened by the commodity recession that discouraged production—and thus employment—in the extractive and agricultural sectors. This was hardly the circumstance under which a labor aristocracy could arise, so low wages remained the norm throughout the economy (fairly low heterogeneity).

CONCLUSION

In examining the forces shaping export enclaves in the early 1970s we found results that substantially confirmed the expectations aroused by dependencia theory. The greater the capitalist penetration, the greater the degree of concentration on a few export commodities. Where penetration was high and stemmed principally from a single metropolitan economy, it worked to reinforce the concentration of trade with that metropolitan economy at the expense of diversification of trade partners. Concentration of cultural penetration had similar positive effects on the concentration of trade, though unlike the situation with systemic capitalist penetration, when systemic cultural penetration was high it frequently stimulated a nationalist backlash against the principal foreign source of culture. The result then was likely to be a widening of the sources of cultural influence. Cultural systemic penetration, where great, also produced the expected increase in the size of the export enclave (greater trade centrality). Capitalist penetration did likewise in the poorer countries, but in the middle-income countries it increasingly took advantage of the domestic market potential rather than merely created an export platform.

The results for internal economic distortions in Third World countries are much more complex, less easily summarized, and much more context specific. The relationships among foreign penetration (of various sorts), domestic class structure, and internal development patterns vary widely, depending especially on such factors as level of income and wages, absolute size of domestic market, the supply of valuable raw materials available for export, and the nature as well as the extent of previous penetration. Each of these influences had different implications for possible alliances among social classes, the continued supply of cheap labor, the kind of goods and services that could be marketed, and the role of the state in serving, mediating, or in part surmounting interests of dominant classes. In this we refute relatively simplistic formulations of dependencia theory and reinforce the arguments of those noted theorists, steeped in the experience of their own countries or regions, who have consistently emphasized the importance of contextual variables and have resisted broad-brushed "generalizing." At the same time, our results do not appear so idiosyncratic as to confound cautious attempts to generalize once the appropriate contextual variables are identified.

Chiefly because of the different ways it works in different social and economic contexts, we did not find capitalist penetration having many of the direct effects on the internal economy that we anticipated in our original formalization of dependencia theory. Penetration was not positively and directly associated with great heterogeneity or unevenness of development. Capitalist penetration did, however, produce some of the anticipated results indirectly. Notably, high capitalist penetration seemed to produce high commodity concentration (in the first bloc of equations) which in turn (in the second bloc) promoted structural disintegration. In addition, cultural penetration and capitalist penetration (at least in the low-income countries) promoted high trade centrality, which again (except in the most trade-dependent countries) worked to create more uneven development.

These results—typified by the importance of contextual conditions and the indirectness of many effects—certainly do not constitute a refutation of dependencia theory. Rather, their complexity conforms to what a conscientious, sophisticated reading of dependencia writings might lead one to anticipate. They provide the basis for a richer, more nuanced, but still generalizable understanding of situations of development in the contemporary periphery of the world economy. They also raise expectations of an even more complex understanding of the interactions of economic and social forces on the politics of peripheral countries. But that must be the subject of subsequent reports.

APPENDIX A: ORIGINAL FORM OF EQUATIONS FOR A FORMAL MODEL OF DEPENDENCIA THEORY

(1)   Concentration of trade partners.

$$X_{5t} = B_0 + A_0 \sum_{i=0}^{\infty} L^i X_{2_{t-i}} + A_1 \sum_{i=0}^{\infty} L^i X_{4_{t-i}}$$

(2)   Concentration of export commodities.

$$X_{6_t} = B_0 + X_{6_{t-1}} + B_1(X_{10_t} - X_{10_{t-1}})X_{11_{t-1}}$$

(3)   Trade centrality.

$$X_{7_t} = B_0 + A_0 \sum_{i=0}^{\infty} L^i X_{3_{t-i}} + A_1 \sum_{i=0}^{\infty} L^i X_{1_{t-i}}(c - X_{9_{t-i}})$$

(4) Uneven development.

$$X_{10_t} = B_0 + A_0 \sum_{i=0}^{\infty} L^i X_{8_{t-i}} + A_1 \sum_{i=0}^{\infty} L^i X_{1_{t-i}}(X_{1_{t-i}} + cX_{10_{t-i-1}})$$

(5) Economic dis-integration.

$$X_{11_t} = B_0 + A_0 \sum_{i=0}^{\infty} L^i X_{7_{t-i}} + A_1 \sum_{i=0}^{\infty} L^i X_{10_{t-i}}$$

(6) Economic heterogeneity.

$$X_{12_t} = B_0 + A_0 \sum_{i=0}^{\infty} L^i X_{1_{t-i}}(X_{9_{t-i}} X_{11_{t-i}} - c)$$

Export enclave development.

(X_8) is an identity, and so is not estimated.
L^i is a geometric lag coefficient.
c is a constant.

Other variables.

X_1 = Capitalist penetration (systemic).
X_2 = Capitalist penetration (concentration).
X_3 = Cultural penetration (systemic).
X_4 = Cultural penetration (concentration).
X_8 = Level of economic activity.

APPENDIX B

The following are thumbnail sketches of our measures; for the logic of our procedures, the data series, and the results on which we based our decisions, see Duvall et al. (1981) and the referenced papers. One methodological note: many of our equations call for multiplicative interactions of variables. This creates difficulties when there are no natural "origins" for the variables involved—as is indeed the case for many of our variables, which are composed of multiple indicators. We have tried to cope with this problem by transforming variables so that all values are positive (to avoid problems associated with the multiplication of "signs"), but we have not searched for scales for the variables that make the interaction terms "fit" best.

(1) CAPPEN (systemic capitalist penetration). An additive index composed of five series—publicly held foreign-incurred debt, foreign direct investment, capital goods imports, foreign-registered patents, and foreign-registered trademarks—each divided by an appropriate

"total," weighted by its loading in a factor analysis, and with flows in different years weighted so as to approximate stocks. A sixth series—long-term capital—was not included because of data limitations.

(2) CAPCON (concentration of capitalist penetration). As for CAPPEN, but before combining the indicators, a Hirschman-type concentration measure across the top five partners was computed for each series. By contrast, CAPPEN measures total penetration from all sources.

(3) CULTSYS (systemic cultural penetration). An additive index composed of three series—students educated abroad (lagged five years to account for their cultural "carrying" properties), foreign aid received, and foreign arms received—each divided by an appropriate "total" and weighted by its coefficient in a canonical correlation. A fourth series—foreign tourists received—was not included because of data limitations.

(4) CULTCON (concentration of cultural penetration). As for CULTSYS, but instead of computing the index for total penetration from all sources (as CULTSYS does), penetration indices were constructed for each of the top three partners, and a Hirschman-type concentration index was computed based on those partner indices.

(5) PARTCON (partner concentration of exports). A Hirschman concentration index computed on the basis of the five largest export receivers.

(6) COMCON (commodity concentration of exports). A Hirschman concentration index computed on the basis of the five largest export commodities.

(7) TRADCENT (trade centrality). The average of (a) the ratio of total exports to GDP and (b) the ratio of total imports to GDP.

(8) ENCLAVE (export enclave syndrome). PARTCON ✕ COMCON ✕ TRADCENT.

(9) GDPCAP (level of economic activity). As the label implies, this is gross domestic product divided by population.
  (a) LOINC = GDPCAP < $550 (1970 U.S. dollars)
  (b) HIINC = GDCAP ≥ $550.

(10) UNEVEN (uneven development). A measure of the absolute sectoral deviation of output per worker, using GNP/total labor force as the average and with three sectors: agriculture, industry, and services. Each sector's absolute deviation is weighted by the sector's proportion of total economic output.

(11) DISINTEG (economic dis-integration). An additive index composed of three series—railway freight ton-mileage, commercial vehicle registrations, and freight ton-mileage on scheduled domestic civil aviation services—each divided by the appropriate "totals" and weighted by its regression coefficient on an input-output table-derived measure.

(12) HETERO (economic structural heterogeneity). The absolute difference between average wages in manufacturing and average overall wages, divided by average overall wages and weighted by the proportion of labor engaged in manufacturing.

NOTES

1. The requirements for identification of systems with nonlinear structural relations are not precisely known (Fisher, 1975).

2. Our argument may be restated that we realize our model is misspecified but that our awareness of this problem provides safeguards as we work in building a properly specified model. Certainly our approach is sounder than one that simply posits single-equation relationships without emphasizing that these are embedded in and interact with a larger environment (see, for example, the otherwise good work of Chase-Dunn, 1975; Bornschier, Chase-Dunn, and Rubinson, 1978; also Kaufmann, Geller, and Chernotsky, 1975). Also, direct estimation of the more complex system does not solve the problem of misspecification unless we believe ourselves to be particularly prescient in specifying theory. (If our crystal balls are so accurate, why stoop to empirical confirmation?) Indeed, any direct estimation of the larger model (setting aside identification problems) is certain to be biased and inconsistent, and these problems are difficult to detect in such a complex system. Thus our procedure is probably the most prudent.

3. The cross-sectional and longitudinal estimates would be the same only under very strict conditions. See an earlier project paper (Jackson et al., 1979) for some discussion of the assets and liabilities of "longitudinal" versus "cross-sectional" research on dependence.

4. Whenever more than one distributed lag form appears in an equation we have made the further assumption that the geometric lag coefficient (L) is the same for both processes. Both of these assumptions ultimately require investigation in a more complete test of our model. In fact, we have reason to believe that economic and sociopolitical impacts (e.g., of capital and culture) are likely to show different lag structures.

5. The coefficients are of theoretical interest, while the R^2 is in any case problematic (see Achen, 1977; Rao and Miller, 1971). We chose to treat a 20 percent

confidence level as "significant" in this study. While higher than often used, it seems appropriate in this exploratory analysis where we have clearly specified hypotheses and where measurement problems will attenuate apparent relations and might lead us to accept the null hypothesis incorrectly.

6. The Koyck transformation results in an estimating form that includes both a lagged endogenous variable and an error term of the form $e_t + Le_{t-1}$. This will mean that least-squares estimates will be biased and inconsistent. The bias in the autoregressive term will be positive, since L is positive; the size and direction of bias in other coefficients will depend on the correlation of their respective variables with the autoregressive term. However, *because* we: (1) expect the autoregressive parameter (i.e., coefficient of Y_{t-1}) and the autocorrelation parameter (i.e., coefficient of e_{t-1}) to be the same size (i.e., both equal to L); (2) have included other exogenous variables in the equation, which tends to lessen the bias (Malinvaud, 1966: 462-465); (3) expect the autoregressive term to have a fairly large size (because history is important we expect it to be closer to 1 than to 0; see Griliches, 1961: examine his tables); and (4) are interested primarily in the sign of the coefficient rather than its precise size, our estimates should *not* be devastated by this asymptotic bias, and certainly the signs should be estimated correctly (Johnston, 1972: 307-313; Griliches, 1961). Longitudinal estimation is again ultimately desirable as a way to correct for this asymptotic bias.

REFERENCES

ACHEN, C. (1977) "Measuring representation: perils of the correlation coefficient." American Journal of Political Science 21 (November): 805-815.

AMIN, S. (1980) Class and Nation, Historically and in the Current Crisis. New York: Monthly Review Press.

———(1974) Accumulation on a World Scale: A Critique of the Theory of Underdevelopment, 2 vols. New York: Monthly Review Press.

BIERSTEKER, T. (1980) "The illusion of state power: transnational corporations and the neutralization of host country legislation." Journal of Peace Research 17 3: 207-222.

BORNSCHIER, V., C. CHASE-DUNN, and R. RUBINSON (1978) "Cross national evidence on the effects of foreign investment and aid on economic growth and inequality: a survey of findings and a reanalysis." American Journal of Sociology, 84, 3:651-683.

CARDOSO, F. H. (1977) "The consumption of dependency theory in the United States." Latin American Research Review 12, 3: 7-24.

———(1973) "Associated-dependent development: theoretical and practical implications," in A. Stepan (ed.) Authoritarian Brazil: Origins, Policies, Future. New Haven, CT: Yale University Press.

——— and E. FALETTO (1979) Dependency and Development in Latin America. Berkeley: University of California Press.

CHASE-DUNN, C. (1975) "The effects of international economic dependence on development and inequality: a cross-national study." American Sociological Review 12, 3: 7-24.

COLLIER, D. [ed.] (1979) The New Authoritarianism in Latin America. Princeton, NJ: Princeton University Press.

DOS SANTOS, T. (1970) "The structure of dependence." American Economic Review 60, 2: 231-236.

DUVALL, R., S. JACKSON, B. RUSSETT, D. SNIDAL, and D. SYLVAN (1981) "A formal model of 'dependencia' theory: Structure and measurement," in R. Merritt and B. Russett (eds.) From National Development to Global Community. London: Allen & Unwin.

ELSTER, J. (1978) "Exploring exploitation." Journal of Peace Research 15, 1: 3-18.

EVANS, P. (1979) Dependent Development: The Alliance of Multinational, State and Local Capital in Brazil. Princeton, NJ: Princeton University Press.

FISHER, F. (1975) The Identification Problem in Econometrics. Huntington, NY: Krieger.

FRANK, A. G. (1981) Reflections on the World Economic Crisis. New York: Monthly Review Press.

———(1972) Lumpenbourgeoisie and Lumpendevelopment: Dependence, Class and Politics in Latin America. New York: Monthly Review Press.

GRILICHES, Z. (1961) "A note on the serial correlation bias in estimates of distributed lags." Econometrica 29, 1: 65-73.

HENNEBELLE, G. (1976) "Arab cinema." MERIP Reports 52: 4-12.

HOAGLIN, D. and R. WELSCH (1978) "The hat matrix in regression and ANOVA." American Statistician 32, 1: 17-22.

JAZANI, B. (1980) Capitalism and Revolution in Iran. London: Zed Press.

JOHNSON, J. (1972) Econometric Methods. New York: McGraw-Hill.

KAUFMAN, R., D. GELLER, and H. CHERNOTSKY (1975). "A preliminary test of the theory of dependency." Comparative Politics 7, 3: 303-330.

KEDDIE, N. R. (1981) Roots of Revolution: An Interpretive History of Modern Iran. New Haven, CT: Yale University Press.

KUHL, E. (1959) "The validity of cross-sectionally estimated behavior equations in time series applications." Econometrica 27, 2: 197-214.

KUZNETS, S. (1963) "Quantitative aspects of the economic growth of nations: VIII, distribution of income by size." Economic Development and Cultural Change 11, 2,II: 1-80.

LACLAU, E. (1971) "Feudalism and capitalism in Latin America." New Left Review 67 (May-June): 19-38.

LEYS, C. (1977) "Underdevelopment and dependency: critical notes." Journal of Contemporary Asia 7, 1: 92-107.

MALINVAUD, E. (1966) Statistical Methods of Econometrics. Amsterdam: North-Holland.

MANDEL, E. (1975) Late Capitalism. London: NLB.

Middle East Yearbook (1980) New York: Watts.

NERLOVE, M. (1971) "Further evidence on the estimation of dynamic economic relations from a time series of cross sections." Econometrica 39, 2: 359-382.

O'DONNELL, G. (1979) "Tensions in the bureaucratic-authoritarian state and the question of democracy," in D. Collier (ed.) The New Authoritarianism in Latin America. Princeton, NJ: Princeton University Press.

———(1978a) "State and alliances in Argentina, 1956-1976." Journal of Development Studies 15, 1: 3-33.

———(1978b) "Reflections on the patterns of change in the bureaucratic-authoritarian state." Latin American Research Review 13, 1: 3-38.

RAO, P. and R. MILLER (1971) Applied Econometrics. Belmont, CA: Wadsworth.

SAUL, J. S. (1979) The State and Revolution in Eastern Africa. New York: Monthly Review Press.

SUNKEL, O. and E. FUENZALIDA (1977) "The transnationalization of capitalism and national development." Institute of Development Studies, University of Sussex. (mimeo)

THEIL, H. (1971) Principles of Econometrics. New York: John Wiley.

von FREYHOLD, M. (1979) Ujamaa Villages in Tanzania: Analysis of a Social Experiment. New York: Monthly Review Press.

WALLERSTEIN, I. (1974) The Modern World-System. New York: Academic.

WUYTS, M. (1976) "On the nature of underdevelopment: an analysis of two views on underdevelopment. Economic Research Bureau, University of Dar es Salaam. (mimeo)

PART II

Accenting Other Dimensions

5

Long Cycles of World Leadership

GEORGE MODELSKI

If the central focus for the social sciences is coordination, or organization, then it follows that the master question must be that of world coordination, or world organization. How is the world organized today? How was it coordinated in the past? How might it cohere in the future?

As an answer to the political aspects of these questions I propose a body of thought now being woven around "long cycles of world leadership." I view this as a parsimonious device for describing and analyzing the principal structures and the chief processes of modern world politics. In the present article I briefly present these concepts in the context of the modern world system and discuss the conditions for the appearance of long cycles and the evidence now at hand to document them. I sketch out the relationship of the long cycle approach to classical theories of international relations and the major schools of social thought and conclude by tracing some spinoffs from long cycle studies in several directions. These suggest that although the long cycle approach is primarily a theory of world politics, it has implications for, and the capacity for reaching out into, important questions facing other social sciences.

THE MODERN WORLD SYSTEM

Long cycles of world leadership are not universally valid laws of political behavior. Rather, they are a pattern of regularities charac-

AUTHOR'S NOTE: This chapter was written while the author was Scholar-in-Residence at the Study and Conference Center, Bellagio, Italy, April 1981. A revised version of this chapter was presented at the Annual Meeting of the American Political Science Association, New York, September 1981.

teristic of the modern world system, that is, a world system bounded
both in space and in time. Spacewise the modern world is an oceanic
system distinct from the old-world-centered, basically continental
system of premodern times. Timewise it is a system that arose in
around 1500 and may now have about reached its maturity. Structurally, moreover, the modern world system may be classified as one
of medium complexity.

If we take the basic unit of the world system to be a world region
(that is, a major cultural area such as China), the structure of relations
among such regions may be classified according to the degree of complexity they assume. If the world regions live in total isolation from
each other, the relations among them are those of zero complexity.
Depending on a variety of social and technical conditions, relations
among regions might assume positive degrees of complexity, ranging
from low to high. The degree of structural complexity in interregional
relations determines the functioning of the world system and
constitutes the criterion that distinguishes between historical world
systems.[1]

For more than a millenium prior to 1500, the (premodern) world
system was characterized by interregional interactions largely along
one single path; it was a system of low complexity. Its paradigm was
the Silk Road, a route linking China with Europe via Central Asia,
India, and the Near East, along which a volume of traffic slowly
passed in both directions but one that was frequently interrupted and
subject to the control and the exaction of the intermediaries such as
Persia or Egypt. The characteristic vector of that path network was
the caravan.

The modern system, by contrast, has been, since 1500, a structure
whose characteristic medium is the ocean, its vector, the oceanic
ship, and its specialized military resource, sea power. It is a circular
network structure of medium complexity. Although technology may
now be laying the foundations for a world system of high complexity,
such a system is not yet in place.

WORLD LEADERSHIP

If we accept the notion of a modern world system rising in about
1500 A.D. to a higher degree of complexity, the question arises: How
would that system be politically organized? In Mediterranean interregional relations city-states played a leading part in such processes.
With a population of the order of 100,000 steadily supplemented by
migrants by also frequently ravaged by severe epidemics, Venice did
manage a substantial portion of such relations in the fifteenth cen-

tury. But in the larger-scale, higher-order, more complex oceanic system an entirely new order of capabilities would be required. What were they?

Capacity for Global Reach

In the first place, a secure position on the ocean was important. It would have to be on the ocean because that was where the new action was going to be, and the lack of such a location was Venice's great handicap. Even Genoa, which had more extensive experience in Western navigation than Venice did (Genoans had helped the Portuguese explore the Atlantic islands; a Genoan founded the Portuguese navy) was too far from the ocean. But it would also have to be a secure home base, protected from direct attack and therefore capable of serving as the platform for far-reaching enterprises. The ideal such position would be that of an island; semi-insular or peninsular would be a second-best compromise solution.

In the second place, ocean-going sea power would be needed—not the coast-hugging boats and navigation procedures characteristic of the Mediterranean age, but entirely new ones. And, consequently, also in due course, naval resources capable of global reach would also be needed. That called for not only shipbuilding and navigational capacity of a new order but also a higher degree of organization (command and staff, headquarters and bases) for acting coherently on a global scale, together with navies capable of keeping out competitors and of defeating them if and when the need arose.

In the third place, the expensive navies would have to be paid for. To do that the shipping enterprises would have to be profitable and a vigorous economy would be needed to furnish and to finance the naval enterprise, to take advantage of the opportunities it afforded for worldwide trade and other exchanges, and to serve as the nursery of those innovations that would be set in motion by the lurch into the great unknown expanses of the world ocean; hence the need for a lead economy of national (as distinct from merely urban) dimensions.

In the fourth place, a political structure of some stability and weight was needed to lend coherence to a global enterprise. To accomplish such a task a political base would be required that went beyond the capacities of an individual and his or her family and kin, or even of a city-state. The need for global operations set the stage for the creation of a solidary political unit of a size and complexity not previously experienced: a lead polity, one that could be in a favorable position to innovate the necessary political techniques. This was the nation-state.

Such were the specifications for a lead unit of a modern global political system. But it we also take seriously the notion that the modern world system calls for low-saliency culture at the global level (Modelski, 1981a), the lead unit would also be one that, while requiring national solidarity and cultural cohesion for its operational efficiency, would not regard the spread of cultural homogeneity and its own values worldwide as one of its principal missions. Hence little demand for messianic fervor or for the crusading or missionary impulse.

Here then is a world leadership role cut out for those with the needed qualifications. Who possessed them and who came to fill the role of lead unit, which we have called the world power? The answer is, in order of temporal succession, first Portugal,[2] then the United Provinces of the Netherlands, followed for two centuries by Britain, and, most recently, the United States (see Table 5.1, column 5).

Each one of these lead states did, in its appointed time, meet the specifications I have listed. Each was insular or semi-insular and located on the North Atlantic, possessed in its heyday of the monopoly of sea power, backed up by a lead economy, as well as by a lead polity organized as a nation-state with a strong politico-economic vocation but no overriding cultural or ideological mission.

In this detailed specification for a lead unit in the modern world system lies a major difference between long cycle theory and the interpretation of modern capitalism proposed by Fernand Braudel (1979), who sees the key to that development not in terms of nation-states as lead unit but rather, more simply, as a succession of "dominant capitalist cities," principally Venice, Antwerp, Genoa, Amsterdam, and London.[3]

This emphasis on the qualifications required of a lead unit, specifications that may be deduced from the characteristics of the emerging world system, becomes even more important if the known world powers are contrasted with those other powerful states that, over the centuries, rose to contest world leadership and to challenge the world powers on their own ground. We would not expect them to succeed at the global level even if (or maybe because) they might have had substantial military power or great regional impact, unless they also could meet the required specification. In fact, as we look at the principal challengers in Table 5.1, column 6 (Spain, sixteenth-seventeenth century; France, seventeenth-nineteenth century; Germany, nineteenth-twentieth century)—that is, those that have fought prolonged global wars and on issues of world organization— we find that they do not meet our criteria: their access to the ocean was less direct and less secure; their sea power, while at times power-

TABLE 5.1 Long Cycles of World Leadership

(1) Cycle[a]	(2) Duration	(3) Global War	(4) Global Powers[b]	(5) World Power[c]	(6) Principal Challenger[d]
I	1494-1580	Italian Wars (1494-1516)	England, France, Portugal, Spain	Portugal	
II	1581-1688	Spanish Wars (1581-1609)	England, France, U.P. Netherlands, Spain	U.P. Netherlands	Spain
III	1689-1791	Wars of Louis XIV (1688-1713)	Britain, France, U.P. Netherlands, Spain, Russia	Britain	France
IV	1792-1913	Revolutionary and Napoleonic Wars (1792-1815)	Britain, France, Japan, Russia, United States, Germany	Britain	France
V	1914-	World Wars I and II	United States, USSR	United States	Germany

SOURCES: Modelski (1978: 225); Thompson (1980, 1981); Modelski and Thompson (1981).
a. These are "systemic" cycles; they depict the state of the global political system and open with the Global War phase. They need to be distinguished from World Power cycles, which open two phases earlier and focus on a rising world power.
b. Nation-states with significant capacity for global reach (sea power) following the Global War phase of that cycle.
c. Global power with preponderant (50 percent or over) capacity for global reach.
d. Global power acting as primary contestant in Global War.

119

ful, lacked follow through; their national economies, while large because continental size, lacked vitality and innovative capacity; and their national polities, while liable to be seized by powerful and charismatic figures, suffered from poor organization and faulty decision making, trying in vain to make up for these deficiencies by ill-founded schemes of universal mission, be it religious or ideological. If the Soviet Union were to be added to that latter list, it might be found similarly deficient.

This is not the place to follow up these assertions with detailed empirical backing. Some of these (e.g., relating to geographical position) require no elaborate proof; while for others, such as sea power (Thompson, 1980; Modelski and Thompson, 1981), party political organization (Modelski, 1983), and lead economies (Modelski, 1981, 1982), a substantial assortment of supporting data are now becoming available.

Global Political Functions

Global political problems are those that arise out of the ordering of global-level interactions, the enforcement of such order, and the attempts to disrupt or change that order. The functions that therefore devolved on world leadership include the following: the facilitation of global-level interactions, the earliest and most important form of that being the organization of intercontinental and oceanic trade, and more recently, of other forms of global economic relations; preventing disruptions in that order, specifically by organizing the distribution of sea power, which became the basic means of order keeping at the global level; as well as preventing the threats to such order from strong regional powers of continental significance. This in turn might entail the guaranteeing of the territorial security of certain key states or areas, that is, some measure of collective security; and finally, innovative means of handling these problems including better techniques of diplomacy (methods of representation, conferences and consultations, intergovernmental organizations), improved codes of conduct and rules of international behavior, as well as solutions to specific international problems such as slavery, piracy, epidemics, or famines.

Inasmuch as the ordering of global problems interests all those who partake in global interactions, activities designed to perform such functions have the potential for being in the common interest, though quite obviously they also have a potential for generating conflict. World leadership therefore in part consists in exploiting the possibilities for common interest and minimizing the areas of conflict. To the extent that it succeeds, world leadership operates in the areas of community formation and is, in the first place, a form of cooperative or innovatively cooperative activity.

If leadership in the world system is the solution to global problems in the common interest, we can regard it as a form of social differentiation, one form that the division of labor assumes in the large. While one nation-state, the world power, thus initially specializes in the production of the bulk of order produced, other nation-states, parties, interest groups and associations, households, and individuals become the consumers of such order. The producers and the consumers of global order are the essential components of the structure of world politics and the substance of that process. If we agree to regard world politics principally as a cooperative project engaged in by the producers and the consumers of global order, certain other notions quickly rule themselves out of court.

First, the notion of international anarchy, meaning literally the absence of government, or established order, in international relations becomes untenable. No one who understands how the world system has worked over the past half-millenium, or longer, can accept the idea that that system has been anarchic or lacking in an ordering principle or authority. Quite to the contrary, and as I have shown earlier and on other occasions, the world has seen, at the global level, a succession of orders of leadership—the Iberian world order, the Dutch supremacy, the long rule of Britannia, and a post-1945 order in which the role of the United States has been primary and constitutive. Anarchy means, if anything, the absence of specialized provision for the production of order; my experience and analyses point entirely the other way. While it is true that eras of transition between these orders have been difficult and beset by strife that informed contemporary observers sometimes regarded as chaotic or anarchic[4] on any overall view, what is amazing is the degree of structure created by leadership (limited, it is true, but political and governmental) and the continuity in that process going back for so many centuries.

Nor is the notion of self-help any more enlightening. Long a staple of international lawyers, self-help is indeed a marginally significant element in international relations, a manifestation of the vaunted individualism of that system of behavior. Yet in actual fact the characteristic pattern of world leadership has been the capacity for the organization of consensus and the elaboration of coalitions. For it is through collaborative behavior that enduring changes have been made or great achievements have been preserved. Critical examples of these are the role of Britain in the formation of balance-of-power coalitions in the global wars in which it was involved, and the role of the United States and Britain in the formation of the United Nations in World War II. Those states, on the other hand, that deliberately assume a posture of self-help, embodied in pure isolation (such as eighteenth-century Japan, or China in the throes of the Cultural Revolution) and proclaiming doctrines of self-reliance, have been neither strikingly successful nor notably persistent, nor widely imitated in that role by other members of the system. Self-help is no less a myth at the global level than it was the supposed cornerstone of Victorian morality; the reality is of an increasing division of labor between the producers and the consumers of global order.

The same goes for the notion of hegemony defined as domination— that is, rule for the benefit of the rulers alone and impervious to the general interest. As long as hegemony is regarded as a deviant form of world or regional leadership, in the same sense in which Aristotle (in the *Politics*) defined tyranny as a deviant form of kingship, it is a useful term; it may be understood as the condition arising when the power and the pretensions of the producers of order become excessive. It ceases to be useful when used to describe both the cases of world leadership and their aberrations. Hence the two need to be kept distinct and the concept of world leadership retained to indicate a form of world organization that, inasmuch as it accords with the common interest, is a legitimate form of world politics. In any event we do not regard world leadership as including the functions or conferring the right to govern other nations or to acquire territorial domains in the imperial manner. Where such cases occur, as, for example, large-scale British annexations in India in the nineteenth century, they may be regarded as deviations from the concept of world leadership and as signs of deterioration and decay and not as the distinguishing features of the essential and constitutive elements of modern world politics.

But we should not dismiss this matter too lightly. The fact remains that over time, in the latter part of their cycles in particular and also in their postcyclical eras, both Portugal and the United Provinces, seized larger colonial areas than they held at the peak of their power, when their territorial demands ran primarily to islands and promontories. As already mentioned, Britain, too, had much more colonial ballast at the end of its second cycle than at the beginning, and all three powers held on to their colonial possessions until after World War II. We need also add that their principal challengers, Spain and France, and even Germany, became significant colonial powers, Spain shedding its empire in the nineteenth century, Germany in 1919, and France even more recently. The point nevertheless remains valid that the colonial "Indian Summer" has been a product principally of the declining phases of the careers of the world powers and that it carries a warning, in two respects: inasmuch as the role of world powers incorporates in it the experience of earlier occupants it carries with it the liabilities incurred by such occupants, and the colonial heritage may be regarded as such a liability; and inasmuch as such experience may still be operative it may also carry in it a warning about the future.

But all of this is not to argue that the world leadership role is the only important role in the modern world system. If humankind may be divided between those that go roaming on the seas and others that stay at home, there is no general principle that says that those who leave home are more important than those who remain to tend the home hearths. It is in this sense that the contribution of the great land powers who have been the principal challengers may not be entirely gainsaid in contrast to that of the world powers. The fabric of global organization is woven from a variety of strands.

LONG CYCLES

If world leadership or, better still, the recurrent dualism between the lead powers and their principal challengers are the principal structure, then the long cycles are the central political process of the modern world system.

That there should be fluctuations in the performance of the functions of world leadership is not really surprising. Both the capacity to perform functions (on the part of producers) and the demand for the performance of these functions (by consumers) must be expected to vary, especially over the medium to long term. Even a secure insular position, for example, might be threatened by an expanding land power as Britain's was in 1804 and 1940. More exposed semi-insular powers such as Portugal and the United Provinces have been even more vulnerable to continental pressures. Sea power tends to be expensive and is liable to fall into neglect; and then comes the time of challenge from new rivals. Innovations tend to come in bunches and are followed by periods of quietude. In turn, the lack of a cultural substratum weakens and destabilizes the demand for leadership services. The stunning impact of the initial achievement—the construction of global order through victory in a massive war— carries a great weight but gradually tends to wear off; the turnover of generations and the alternation of parties in power also take their toll.

More surprising is the fact that the fluctuations that prevail and that can be documented in fact show a clear pattern, one that can be described as a long cycle. The pattern can be described as cycle because it is repetitive; it can be described as long because its observed average period over the past five cycles exceeds 100 years. In short, to the question "why cycles?" (Zolberg, 1981: 380) we cannot but reply: because they are there.

The Basic Cycle

The basic facts of the long cycle can be predicted from the relationship between world leadership and the process by which it is established and terminated. If we are right in regarding world leadership as a massive project of political investment—a construction project of global scope and significance—its establishment cannot be expected to be a simple process or an easy one. It is a process both of tearing down and of building up, a time of prodigious expenditures of time and energy. In fact, we find that global wars of past experience do fit such a prescription. We find that such great wars have each been followed by the rise of a new world power and the establishment of a new world order.

Thus the basic sequence has been as follows (compare Table 5.1, column 3). The *Italian wars* at the turn of the sixteenth century, a series of wars between France and the new Spanish monarchy but also extending to the Indian Ocean, destroyed the autonomy and the vitality of Renaissance Italy, the active zone that animated interregional relations in the Mediterranean zone in the previous half-millenium. By the same token, they also deprived Venice of the possibility of thwarting Portugal's design for an alternative trade route to Asia. That route was established after 1500 and opened the way for a reconstruction of the global system into an Iberian order in which Spain assumed at first a localized and gradually a more important position so that by 1580 it became the principal contender for the control of the global system, as well as the principal contender for the control of Europe. But both issues had to be resolved first by prolonged *Spanish wars* in the course of which leadership on global issues was assumed by the Dutch, whose revolt against Spanish domination gradually became not only the central conflict of the wars of religion in Europe but also the opportunity for undermining and overthrowing the Iberian order worldwide. By 1609 the monopolistic features of that order could no longer be maintained, and leadership at the global level was assumed by the Dutch. After the middle of the seventeenth century, the Dutch Republic came under pressure both of English and French competition, and in the *wars of Louis XIV,* the French bid failed and naval supremacy passed to Britain. The rule of Britannia ran into its own problems in the second half of the eighteenth century, the principal symptom of which was the American Revolution, aided by a surge of French naval strength. The Revolution of 1789 raised the power of France to new heights but the *Napoleonic wars* failed to overthrow and rather consolidated the global order based on British leadership. The rise of the United States after 1865 and of Germany after 1870 put that order into question, but *World Wars I and II* of the twentieth century were needed before the question was resolved in favor of the United States, and the confirmation of a new order. In the years after 1945, but especially after 1970, the principal competition has been from the Soviet Union.

So much for a condensed narrative of the global war—world power cycle. A strict proof of the existence of a long-term cyclical pattern in the world system hinges upon showing that

  (a) the global wars singled out as recurrently constitutive of a new order are in fact the only such wars and that other wars have no comparable bearing on world order and are otherwise insignificant; and
  (b) the world powers emerging out of such global wars in fact were associated with distinct world orders and that no other powers were so associated.

Such evidence as is now at hand suggests that

  (a) the wars singled out for special attention as global wars are the most important wars of the modern world system (see the list of wars in Modelski and Thompson, 1981, Table 3 and Figure 6). They are the wars with the greatest impact, causing the heaviest casualties and accounting for about four-fifths of the world's naval battles in that period. They are also politically the most significant, in each single case inaugurating a new order. Over time, there is a distinct trend toward clarification: whereas at the beginning of the era the picture is less clear though still discernible, as time goes on global wars become quite distinct and clearly distinguishable by range, scope, and impact.
  (b) I have already discussed in the previous section the unique qualifications of the world powers and the world orders they were capable of creating and did in fact generate. No alternative orders have in that time come into existence on a global scale, only certain regional orders, such as the French ascendancy in Europe (1660-1688) or the Bismarckian system after 1871, in the latter parts of their respective cycles.

The basic (systemic) cycle may be initially modeled as in Figure 5.1, as a circular movement in a space bounded by the coordinates of order (Q) and choice, or valuation (V). The motion of the global

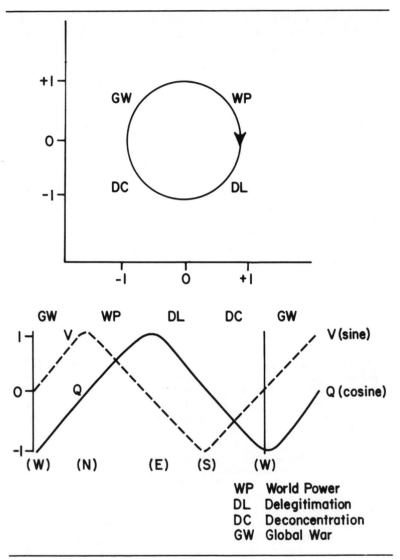

Figure 5.1 The Long Cycle

political system through its phases may then be presented as a sequence of changes along two dimensions, that of order (quantity of order in the system) and choice (valuations or preference attaching to order as compared to alternative choices). A sine curve (in lower portion of Figure 5.1) then describes the changes that occur on the V dimension, whereas the cosine describes changes in the system on the Q dimension. The V curve reaches a maximum at N (North) and a minimum at S (South); and Q curve reaches a high at E and a low at W.

We might thus identify the *global* war phase of the long cycle as one at the end of which the value of V reaches a maximum; that is to say, global war produces the maximum degree of preference for order. We may be able more precisely to describe the *world power* phase of the cycle as one at the end of which the value of Q (that is, the output of order in the global system) is maximized. The other two phases of the cycle may also be distinguished in this fashion. The phase of *delegitimation* is characterized by a decline in the preference for an order, a portent of troubles to come, runs ahead of falling world order output. The phase of *deconcentration* is characterized by conditions of severe rivalry between the powers, the output of order reaches rock-bottom but where the preferences for order have already begun to revive.[5]

The process within each cycle may therefore be described as one of *entropic decay*. The spectacular project represented by a new global order corresponds to the maximum of the periodic curve of order. Over the period of the cycle the preferences for, and then output of, order gradually decline until they reach a minimum. The system's output of order declines presumably because it receives no fresh input of energy, no new maintenance. We could also call this the *monopoly erosion model*,[6] because at its height world leadership is linked to a condition of power concentration exceeding 50 percent of disposable naval power (the world power at that point having the "command of the sea" or "first-strike capability"), hence the capacity to defeat any combination of opponents. Since we view capacity for global reach as the core of global political "production capacity," the term and the analysis of monopoly may appropriately be used in this context. But over time this capacity to mold the global system and to prevent others from molding it (and, in a more general sense, the grand innovation represented by the institution of a world power), and hence also its capacity to generate monopoly returns, erodes, and toward the end of the cycle the system moves into a condition of low concentration. Empirical evidence for cycles of global power concentration for the 1517-1970 period (in Modelski and Thompson, 1981: Figure 5) illustrates both the peaks and the valleys of the several cycles since the sixteenth century as they correspond to the rise and ebb of the several world powers.

The Cobweb Cycle

While the monopoly erosion model broadly models the process of one single cycle, it offers by itself little guidance as to why the system goes through not only one cycle but several. To explain that we might use what the economists call the "cobweb model," an analytical device that deals with exchange processes characterized by production information gaps of long duration. That is to say, production conditions of the "good" to be exchanged are such that a long period of time needs to elapse between the decision to commence production and the onset of the production process (e.g., between the planting of fruit trees and the first harvest from such trees). Furthermore, the information conditions may be such that the process is not finely tuned and tends either toward excess output or a production deficit (e.g., orderly marketing of fruit surpluses is lacking; Modelski and Thompson, 1981: 7-10). Such a system will tend toward periodicity given constant production information conditions. Empirical evidence, given a number of assumptions, seems to favor such an interpretation, and interesting leads now point toward the converging cobweb cycle as a possible model of the course taken by the global polity (Modelski and Thompson, 1981: 24-25).

The crucial assumption of the cobweb cycle is the lack of adjustment between the demand for, and the supply of, global order. This is the consequence of the underlying conditions of the low salience of culture in the modern global system (Modelski, 1981a) and hence the lack of global solidarity and underlying cultural consensus that would help stabilize the system at a deeper level. As important, it is a signal that as a political institution world leadership in the modern world has labored under severe limitations. Its legitimation is of a restricted kind, basically charismatic in character[7] and rising out of leadership in a global war, incapable of being routinized because unfortified by roles of legal-rational or of a traditional kind (even though there may be some "traditional" elements in the role of world power). There is no written or unwritten constitution that specifies the rules of world leadership or that limits, let alone controls, the exercise of power or the process of responsibility. There is even little scholarly tradition of interpretation of that role, and the prevailing doctrine of international relations, stressing either the dictates of power or the equality of all states, does little to help and much to confuse. In such conditions the production-information gap has remained huge, and major swings in public policy and public preferences in respect of world politics continue to cause instability and concern.

THE CLASSICS OF IR

The "long cycle" approach has respectable antecedents in the evolution of theoretical thought about international relations. Three bodies of literature might be mentioned in particular: *the balance of power, sea power,* and *transnationalism.* In each case we have a body of thought coming to grips not with timeless and abstract questions of the "behavior of states" in a "states-system' but rather with clearly time- and space-bounded problems of modern world politics.[8]

The Balance of Power

The *locus classicus* of scholarly reflection on international relations has long been the doctrine of balance of power. Let us distinguish two variants of it: the classical doctrine evolving from the practice of statecraft into a principle of the European political system, and twentieth-century neoclassical glossaries and elaborations, and attempts to fashion it into a universal law of international politics.

The classical doctrine is quite plain. It arose out of the wars of Louis XIV and found formal expression in the Treaty of Utrecht (1713) and in the commentaries upon it by such writers as Bolingbroke (who helped to negotiate the treaty that made it part of the public law of Europe). The standard texts may be found in Forsyth et al. (1970), who may be viewed as the principal authorities of this subject. Writers such as Vattel, who expounded the new law of nations, discussed it with fine discernment among the just causes of war, a tradition that may be seen to include even such later works as Quincy Wright's *A Study of War* (1942).

In this classical mode Europe was seen as a (regional) political system bound by common interests but subject to serious conflicts between two sets of powerful forces, those of France and those of the Habsburgs, the latter, in the eighteenth century, being the weaker side, fearful of the designs of the more active power. In the face of aggrandizement and threats to the independence of the state-members of the system and to impede the creation of an imperial system that might threaten its own independence, Britain, not having any continental possessions of its own, held the position of balancer; by intervening on the weaker side it could help keep the strong in check. Such interventions would then be justified also after France became the weaker party and needed support against Germany. That is how Winston Churchill, among others, explained the world wars of the twentieth century. Furthermore, that is how the involvement of the United States in these wars, as well as its active part in the post-1945 European economic and political recovery programs, could be accounted for, because they did amount to aiding a weaker party against a looming threat from the East.

The classical balance of power was a design for linking the stability of a critical region with the interests of world organization as represented by Britain. It can therefore be seen as a statement of a central problem of the conditions that can be generalized as those of leadership in the modern world system. Greater difficulty, on the other hand, arises with neoclassical attempts to restate it in the form of universal propositions. They are ambiguous and they tend toward overgeneralization.

Sea Power

The balance of power answered questions primarily about the workings of the European political system; it told about the world structure only by implication, without enlarging a great deal about how and why Britain was in a position to act as balancer and by doing that, was free to rearrange the global system to its own designs. For world politics is, inherently, about long-range interactions of worldwide scope and about ways of regulating and governing them by means of sea power as a globally differentiated form of military power. As in the modern world and until quite recently the only effective and cost-efficient method of global interactions involved the sea or, more precisely, the world oceans, it becomes obvious that reflections about the role of sea power must be among the basic resources of the study of world organization.

The first modern author comprehensively to expound this set of problems was Alfred Mahan. *The Infuence of Sea-power upon History 1660-1783* (1890) needs to be remembered less for its analysis of sea battles or for its tactical prescriptions than for its grasp of the world scene and for the analysis of British sea power it offered, beginning at the moment when Britain was about to take over from the Dutch and leading up, in his later work, to the time when it was about to be superseded by the United States.[9]

Contemporary theories of nuclear deterrence (on the use of strategic nuclear forces and on their control) may be seen as the most recent form of the classical doctrines of sea power.[10]

Transnationalism

Lest the balance of power and sea power overload our analysis with the ballast of the past, we need concepts that can handle processes of contemporary change. We know that the modern world system has facilitated global interactions for some half-millenium; hence globalization is hardly a novel feature of it. What we need to be able to analyze is the growth in the complexity of those interactions, growth that is quite recent and quite unprecedented, so much so that it may be necessary to ascribe to it a change in the very character of the system. The concept, and the body of writings, best suited to that task may be transnationalism, the sum of forces tending toward interdependence, that is, toward a higher degree of complexity in the world system, beyond the reality of intergovernmental relations (and studies of international organization). Students of multinational corporations first encountered it and then extended their analysis to other transnational organizations (such as parties) as well as to transgovernmental phenomena and to processes of functional differentiation at the global level (e.g., through international regimes; Keohane and Nye, 1976). Transnationalism asks essential questions about transformation processes of the global political system, and it is a convenient label under which to house such phenomena as transnational elite networks or the underpinnings of science. It sets up a useful tension between the nation-state, a creation of the modern world, and the forces supplementing it or possibly transcending it in a postmodern system.

THE MAJORS OF SOCIAL THOUGHT

If our basic question is: how is the world organized at the global level and how might it be organized to cope with conditions of varying complexity, it is also clear that the problem is not one, strictly or technically speaking, of international relations as narrowly conceived but rather one that merges at several points with major strands of modern thought. It helps to be clear where the boundaries of our field end and where the other social sciences take over because the analysis we are conducting is in fact taking place at the frontiers of this and other fields.

Is It Historicism?

If we ask broad questions about leadership and long cycles with the view of better understanding the present and the future, are we in danger of committing the "sin" of historicism? If we assert the need to specify carefully the time and space to which our statements may be made to refer, are we committed to the view that given historical conditions uniquely determine events occurring in such specified age and place?

Let us first of all adopt Karl Popper's usage of historicism and following him, define it as the tendency to pronounce "laws of history" and derive from them predictions that cannot be solidly sustained by the procedures of the social sciences. Popper (in Gardiner, 1959: 278) would call this the "historicist doctrine of the social sciences." In reply we would claim that we have no desire to indulge in false prophesy and do not claim it to be the major task of the social sciences to make historical predictions. On the other hand, we see no harm or objection if the social sciences prepare members of society toward a better understanding of the conditions that might be in store for them in the future. As Popper himself points out, prediction is possible in cases of recurrent or repetitive systems, and recurrent and cyclic systems are especially well known in biology, as in the case of the life cycle of organisms. Although in Popper's opinion "the most striking aspects of historical development are non-repetitive," he does admit that in so far as human society is "repetitive, we may perhaps make certain prophesies" (Gardiner, 1959: 279-280). Given the biological basis of human life, it cannot be held inherently inconceivable that repetitive patterns are found in human society. Within strictly defined and bounded systems (though not in "history in general"), it should not be impossible to identify significant patterns of repetition.

By maintaining that we intend to analyze carefully defined and time- and space-bounded world systems, we do not mean to suggest that such systems are in any way uniquely determined and must be understood, in historicist fashion, in terms of their unique "meaning." Rather, they need to be analyzed as particular intersections of types of social behavior explicable in terms of general social science.

Nor does our approach attempt to compete with philosophies of history of which Arnold Toynbee's may be taken as one exemplar. For Toynbee the cardinal point of departure has been the insight that the "smallest intelligible field of historical study" is whole societies he called civilizations. His problem was that while a number of these may be clearly identified in earlier history by the time we pass the year 1500 their separate identities tend to blur. As far as Western civilization is concerned and in Toynbee's view (based on the experience of earlier civilizations), it is "already far advanced in our time of trouble," which seem to have begun around 1500 and which had already produced at least two major breakdowns and a second relapse (Toynbee, in Gardiner, 1959: 203-204). The wars of religion were the first major breakdown and the "bout of internecine nationalist warfare" since the French Revolution the second. A "universal state" is looming ahead if some form of world order is not established. For Toynbee, therefore, the modern era is no more than a "time of troubles," the tail end of a waning civilization, a postscript in the story of a greater age. To this writer, though, it seems to be much more than that, surely the most exciting and promising era in the world's entire history.

The Nature of Modern Society

A major strand of social, rather than historical, thought has struggled to clarify the novel features of society that have been evolving at least for the past two centuries. Adam Smith, Auguste Comte, Karl Marx, Max Weber, and Emile Durkheim, each seized upon clusters of such features and minted concepts that have all served as exceedingly useful handles for opening our understanding of our advancing and advanced societies.

Smith and Comte gave us the notion of industrial in contrast to agrarian society; Marx launched the concept of capitalist bourgois society and saw it emerging out of feudalism; Weber delineated the outlines of modern society and set it against traditional structures; and Emile Durkheim evolved the notion of mechanistic society and how it differed from the organic. In each case tools were devised for gaining greater understanding of the advanced national societies (most often than not, the lead polity and economy of their time or its challenger) the authors knew and had studied well. What could hardly be argued was that as they wrote, and for decades if not centuries to follow, the conditions they labeled "industrial," "capitalist," "modern," or "mechanistic" were hardly representative of even a small number of the world's societies and that the world system as a whole could not be regarded as homogeneously composed of such units. Rather, only a lead society of its time would hold such characteristics and might be engaged in diffusing them elsewhere in the world, while the rest were engaged in "modernization."

The question of world organization, on the other hand, focuses attention less on certain advanced societies (though it does that too) than on the structure of the world system as a whole and at the global level. It does not, and it cannot, assume social or cultural homogeneity but rather needs to contend with problems created by high rates of innovation and growth in some parts of the system and lower rates of such innovation elsewhere. For the world system modernization is a problem rather than a solution. That is why we define modernity in the first place as an attribute of the world system and not of the national societies that may be part of it. In that sense the nineteenth-century greats, and their contemporary successors such as Talcott Parsons (1966, 1970), serve as essential background references but may not yield direct guidance on questions of world organization.

World-Economy

A separate note is required to address the distinctiveness of Immanuel Wallerstein's world-economy approach (1974, 1980a, 1980b). Inasmuch as Wallerstein does deliberately focus on structural problems of organization of what he uniquely identifies as the modern world-system, he does raise questions of direct interest. He also uses the concepts of class and core and periphery to help address the differential distribution of activity and innovation in the world in a way that echoes the themes of dependency theory, which also raises significant problems bearing on world organization. But he sees the world-economy as uniquely determining the operation of the modern world-system (making that system "capitalist"), and insofar as international relations is concerned, he is less sensitive to political structures and political innovations (e.g., parties) and does not bring out the distinctive and autonomous role of political processes at the global level (which he regards as epiphenomenal).[11]

POLITICS, ECONOMICS, CULTURE, AND SOLIDARITY

The theory of long cycles is a theory of political structure and process at the global level. It homes in on the political in part because that is where new and innovative work needs to be done—the idea of regularity in the process of international politics being so astonishing to even the more seasoned students of the subject that it needs careful and sustained work. It also concentrates on the political because that is where the strength of the political scientists lies and where the grand thinkers of modern society, have less to say and less experience and data to draw upon. The macrosociologists, in particular, leave a lot of room to fill in for specialists in world politics. In that sense we conceive of global political structures and processes as analytically distinct and in principle autonomous components of world systems, even though their degree of differentiation from national political structures leaves in many cases much to be desired.

But to say that our comparative advantage in the analysis of world systems lies in the political realm is not to say that we ignore, much less deny, the need for careful analysis of the interplay between politics and the other principal analytical structures—economics, solidarity, and culture broadly considered.[12] Entirely to the contrary we view the modern world as one exhibiting high saliency both in its political and in its economic components while slighting solidarity and culture at the global level (Modelski, 1981a) and regard this fundamental structural relationship as one key to our analysis, for instance, of the stability of the system. The role of the nation-state in its cultural aspects cannot otherwise be properly appreciated. It is in that sense that we regard the modern world as primarily a politico-economic structure, jointly determined both by the political and the economic process and only negatively shaped by the weakness of the components of solidarity and value.

This analysis already points to two principal lines of interchange between world politics and world economics in the modern world (Modelski, 1981b, 1982):

(1) The association is strong between the world power and the lead economy of the period. Each world power, in its cycle, was an economy leading in a crucial array of economic innovations, especially those bearing on global interactions such as exploration, shipping, aviation or space, and on the goods and services that might be exchanged in such contexts. The lead economy was not necessarily the largest economy of its time but was the largest in respect to the most advanced sectors, and the yield of these sectors lent crucial support to the world power.

(2) The role of world powers in organizing the framework of global economic relations is important. Each world power has had a decisive role in setting and enforcing the rules of international trade, investment and finance.

It is an implication of this analysis that fluctuations in world leadership, that is, in the output of global order, will be associated with changes in global economic relations.

I might add that equally significant is the negative association between lead economy and the principal challengers. Those latter—Spain, France, Germany (see Table 5.1)—did not lead in innovations pertinent to global interactions or exchanges. The closest case may be that of Germany before 1914, with a strong impact on naval armaments and on foreign trade and strong development, though not a decisive lead, in such leading sectors as chemicals, electricals, and motor vehicles. As a rule the principal challengers had large and wealthy, continental-type economies, relatively large populations, and a specialization toward the ground, rather than naval, end of the military technology spectrum.

This analysis finally suggests (Modelski, 1981) how the political and the economic processes might, in fact, be intermeshed, via a model of "alternating innovations," regulated in part by long-term price movements (the Kondratieffs).

One other avenue of interchange leads to the vexed question of the relationship between national and global politics and policies in the major states. Recent work tends to show that in the modern world the global political process has had a crucial relationship with the rise of national party systems (Modelski, 1983). Such evolution may be traced in ascending form through the five cycles of the world powers but, once again, would show a negative association between the principal challengers and that form of political innovation that is the party system. It would seem that the design and the consolidation of party systems gave a significant evolutionary advantage to the world powers.

Predictive Potential

Not the least interesting aspect of the theory of long cycles is its predictive potential. There is no need to overdo that facet of it, and a large dose of skepticism and caution is, of course, in order. But if there is substance to the concept of long cycle, an exploration of the predictive element is unavoidable. Even if a long cycle is long indeed, an understanding of its working helps us to establish the "system time" (Thompson, 1983): where we stand and which way "the wind is blowing." There are indeed good grounds for thinking that the distinguishing marks of the 1970s—a period awash with portents of trouble ahead—are just what we would expect from long cycle theory. The assertive nationalisms that are rising in various parts of the world are nothing other than the reverse side of the coin of delegitimation of world leadership. If present trends continue, and in the absence of significant political innovation, we would expect in the decades ahead increased fragmentation leading up to the period of deconcentration marked by severe competition among the major powers and declining attention to the common interest.

Such predictions rest, however, upon the assumption of constancy for the modern world system and that assumption cannot be taken for granted and may indeed need to be questioned. That system is now reaching maturity, and various developments signal a possible change to a new, high level of complexity. Studies of transnationalism, indeed, explore such matters quite explicitly. It is beyond the scope of this analysis to review the avenues for change to a postmodern system of high complexity. Suffice it to say the following:

(1) Such changes are unlikely to be random and will have as their point of departure the solid structures of the modern world, hence an understanding of these is a sine que non of more exhaustive investigation of such possibilities.

(2) The precise nature of such changes is hard to foretell. The most likely shape of the future will be the result of fundamental innovation in world affairs. Those enterprising enough to venture such

innovation will be in the lead tomorrow. If we could foretell that future, it could not possibly be an innovation.

IN CONCLUSION

It may be argued that the concept of long cycles of world leadership already offers promise as a focus of inquiry into international relations and world politics. This concept raises fundamental questions about how the world is politically organized, how it has been organized and how it might be organized in the future. It also gives an outline of a theory suggesting interesting answers about the nature of the modern world and the existence of certain hitherto unsuspected regularities that have informed it. It also searches out for direct linkages to the social sciences and challenges them to rethink problems of world organization.

In scope and function the theory of long cycles could be compared with the theory of tectonic plates in geology. This latter has shown that geology must be understood as having a temporal dimension subject to what is in effect a species of historical analysis. It has shown that earth-shaking events of the present cannot be properly understood without a theoretical perspective on the past. And it has offered a unifying, coherent, and science-based view of a previously amorphous field. It is hoped that long cycles of world leadership may come to fill a similar role in the contemporary view of world political organization.

NOTES

1. For Wallerstein (1980b: 744) it is "integrated production processes" organized as a "specific division of labor" that constitute the criterion that distinguishes between "historical systems." The "capitalist world-economy" constitutes one such historical system.

2. Observers tend to be surprised in particular by the appearance of Portugal in that list (see, for example, Brucan, 1980: 761). Yet not only was Portugal, in its time, the leading oceanic power with the largest naval forces, but it was also pioneering in the science and technology of discovery and exploration of the planet; without exercising "worldwide domination" it controlled the network of planetary routes until the Dutch, with the English, superseded it at the end of the sixteenth century.

3. This also makes clear that the nation-state is a product of the modern world system and of its politics in particular. The emergence of nation-states first in Europe and ultimately worldwide is the result of the process of modernity. It is confusing to regard the "states-system" as some sort of external and objective reality within which other developments occur. That is a point significant both for the conventional theory of international relations, which sees nation-states or international behavior as the basic units of analysis and therefore cannot ask questions about the emergence of the varying characteristics of nation-states, and also for the theory of modernization, because it treats nation-states as the model form of a universally valid political struc-

ture rather than as a contingent form of politcal organization evolved in the first place for the purpose of conducting efficient global operations and the need to protect or to combat them.

4. G. Lowes Dickinson published a book entitled *The International Anarchy* on the eve of World War I in 1910.

5. The long cycle is described as a set of propositions in Modelski (1980a: 4).

6. The monopoly erosion model posits some such general proposition as "over time, monopoly tends to transform into a condition of freer competition."

7. This characteristic is being ascribed to an organization, that is, the world power, rather than being, in the usual sense, the attribute of an individual leader.

8. I am stressing "oceanic" theories, that is, theories of world politics that respond to the characteristic problems of the modern world system, as do dependency theories. I find less relevant theories of empire (the model form of large-scale political organization in the premodern world) or the (essentially anti-imperial) theories of the states-system cast in the neoclassical mode.

9. I might also mention Thucydides' *History of the Peloponnesian War,* not only as an excellent study of the role of sea power but also as a suggestive analysis of how Athens' leadership in the Greek system deteriorated into an empire.

10. An early formulator of naval doctrine in this vein was Philip Howard Colomb (1831-1899). The continuities in the evolution of strategic throught may be seen, for instance, in the writings of Bernard Brodie.

11. For comparisons and contrasts of the world-economy and long cycle approaches see Rapkin (this volume) and Thompson (1983).

12. Aristide Zolberg (1980: 689, 715), therefore, incorrectly views this as a "flaw" in our analysis.

REFERENCES

BRAUDEL, F. (1979) Le Temps du Monde. Paris: Armand Colin.
BRUCAN, S. (1980) "The state and the world system." International Social Science Journal 32, 4:752-769.
FORSYTH, G. M., H.M.A. KEENS-SOPER, and P. SAVIGEAR[eds.] (1970) The Theory of International Relations. London: George Allen & Unwin.
GARDINER, P. [ed.] (1959) Theories of History. Glencoe, IL: Free Press.
KEOHANE, R. and J. NYE (1976) Power and Interdependence. Boston: Little, Brown.
MAHAN, A. (1980) The Influence of Sea Power upon History, 1660-1783. New York: Hill & Wang.
MODELSKI, G. (1983) "Long cycles of world leadership and the rise of party systems," in R. M. Goldman (ed.) Transnational Parties. Washington, DC: University Press of America.
———(1982) "Long cycles and U.S. international economic policy," in W. Avery and D. P. Rapkin (eds.) America in a Changing World Political Economy. New York: Longman.
———(1981a) "World politics and sustainable growth," in J. C. Coomer (ed.) Quest for a Sustainable Society. New York: Pergamon.
———(1981b) "Long cycles, Kondratieffs, alternating innovations: implications for U.S. foreign policy," in C. W. Kegley, Jr., and P. J. McGowan (eds.) The Political Economy of Foreign Policy Behavior. Beverly Hills, CA: Sage.
———(1980) "The theory of long cycles and U.S. strategic policy," in R. Harkavy and E. Kolodziej (eds.) American Security Policy and Policy-Making. Lexington, MA: D. C. Heath.

————(1978) "The long cycle of global politics and the nation-state." Comparative Studies in Society and History 20 (April): 214-235.

————(1972) Principles of World Politics. New York: Free Press.

MODELSKI, G. and W. R. THOMPSON (1981) "Testing cobweb models of the long cycle of world leadership." Paper delivered to the Annual Meeting of the Peace Science Society (International), Philadelphia, November.

MODELSKI, G., R. JOHNSON, and F.W. WU (1979) "The long cycle and wars, 1770-1975: a preliminary test of theory." Paper delivered at the joint Annual Meeting of the International Studies Association-West and the Western Political Science Association, Portland, Oregon, March.

PARSONS, T. (1970) The System of Modern Societies. Englewood Cliffs, NJ: Prentice-Hall.

————(1966) Societies: Evolutionary and Comparative Perspectives. Englewood Cliffs, NJ: Prentice-Hall.

THOMPSON, W. R. (1983) "The world-economy and the long cycle of world leadership: the question of world system time," in P. J. McGowan and C. W. Kegley, Jr. (eds.) Foreign Policy and the Modern World-System. Beverly Hills, CA: Sage.

————(1981) "Operationalizing long cycle theory: the basic problems and some proposed solutions for the sixteenth and late twentieth centuries." Paper delivered at the Annual Meeting of the American Political Science Association, New York.

————(1980) "Seapower in global politics, 1500-1945: problems of data collection and analysis." Paper delivered at the Annual Meeting of the International Studies Association-West, Los Angeles, March.

WALLERSTEIN, I. (1980a) The Modern World-System, Vol. 2. New York: Academic.

————(1980b) "The states in the institutional vortex of the capitalist world-economy." International Social Science Journal 32, 4:742-751.

————(1974) The Modern World-System, Vol. 1. New York: Academic.

WRIGHT, Q. (1942) A Study of War. Chicago: Chicago University Press.

ZOLBERG, A. R. (1981) The origins of the modern world system: a missing link." World Politics 33 (January): 253-281.

————(1980) "Strategic interactions and the formation of modern states: France and England." International Social Science Journal 32, 4:687-716.

6

Cycles, Capabilities, and War

An Ecumenical View

WILLIAM R. THOMPSON

A recent survey of the literature on international system transformation concludes that

> the literature on international systems has two intriguing characteristics. First, the number of studies that analyze international systems is relatively small. . . . Second, those studies that have appeared, with only a few exceptions, are largely static. Most studies of international systems concentrate on identifying and describing types of sytems.
>
> The limited attention to, and largely static treatment of, international systems could indicate a basic lack of clarity within the subject matter. Ambiguities in concepts and the absence of explicit research questions could well deter analysts from devoting time to an area of inquiry. Thus the sparse treatment of system transformation may be the consequence of a fuzziness in the use of concepts and the posing of research questions [Zinnes, 1980: 3].

Zinnes's criticisms are certainly germane to the literature she chooses to review. There is an appalling absence of agreement about what key terms mean (see Rapkin et al., 1979), and the research questions that are posed frequently are indeed fuzzy. In short, the conventional study of international systemic change lacks sufficient degrees of clarity, coherence, and the potential for cumulation. But there is a more recent cluster of analyses, for the most part unreviewed by Zinnes, that offers one way out of some of the analytical snares and collective stagnation of much previous systemic work. Despite the perhaps inevitable disagreements about analytical emphases and the primary motors of change, some consensus about the nature and significance of structural change in the world system may be emerging—with far-reaching implications for the ways in which many of us currently study international relations, politics, and economics.

Markedly similar arguments are to be found in the still fledgling if proliferating world system literature. Yet the similarities are not restricted to studies explicitly identified as belonging to world system perspectives—a factor that should serve to strengthen the analytical appeal of world system arguments and interpretations. After very briefly delineating the common ground on structural change, I will try to demonstrate some of its implications by providing two extended illustrations of how the recognition of historical patterns of systemic transformation may influence how we go about gaining an understanding of systemic war behavior.

FOUR MODELS AND A SHARED PREMISE

Consider the following sketches of systemic transformation:

(1) For scholars working within the world-economy perspective (see Wallerstein, 1974, 1980; Chase-Dunn and Rubinson, 1977; Hopkins, 1979; Research Working Group on Cyclical Rhythms and Secular Trends, 1979; Bousquet, 1980; Chase-Dunn, 1981; Hopkins and Wallerstein, 1981; Bergesen, 1983), the primary influence on the interstate system's structure is the cyclical alternation between a period of hegemony, the relative decline of the hegemonic power, and the consequent rivalry among the core powers for ascension to hegemonic power.

(2) The long cycle of world leadership perspective (Modelski, 1978, 1981a, 1981b; Rasler and Thompson, 1983; Thompson, 1983a, 1983b, 1983c) emphasizes the system-shaping significance of the distribution of capabilities responsible for making global reach possible over the past 500 years. The long cycle, the global political system's principal process, refers to the cyclical tendencies toward the structural concentration and diffusion of sea power. Initial unipolarity and world leadership gradually give way to multipolarity and rivalry. A new global order is created when a new world power emerges from a global succession struggle.

(3) Organski's (1968; Organski and Kugler, 1980) transition model divides the international system's major powers into two tiers— the dominant power and the less powerful great powers—and two camps—the satisfied and the dissatisfied. As the initial capability edge of the satisfied dominant power and its allies erodes in favor of dissatisfied challengers, war between great powers and the chance to create a new international order increases in probability.

(4) From the point of view of Gilpin's (1981) hegemonic war and change model, the distribution of relative power changes more

quickly than the international system's structure of rules and privileges does. The ensuing discrepancy between the power distribution and the status quo leads to systemic disequilibrium that can be ended only by hegemonic warfare between a declining leader and rising challengers. The outcome of hegemonic war serves to realign the international system's governance with the new distribution of power.

These four models do not share complete agreement. They disagree, for instance, about how far back in time one can trace the continuity of structural change processes at the systemic level. Long-cycle analysts begin in the late fifteenth/early sixteenth century. Some world-economy analysts identify a Habsburg hegemonic power in the latter portion of the fifteenth century, while the others are content to wait until the rise of the Dutch in the early seventeenth century. Organski sees some level of industrialization as a structural prerequisite and thus delimits his perspective to the post-1750 era. Alternatively, Gilpin's interpretation of structural change is said to be applicable to the current system only after the conclusion of the Napoleonic Wars. Analysts also disagree about the fundamental source of change. Students of the world-economy, Organski, and Gilpin share a focus on some version of uneven economic development as the root cause. Long-cycle analysts, in contrast, do not deny the existence of an uneven growth pattern but prefer instead to leave the question of what drives the system relatively open at this stage of inquiry.

Other disputes exist as well. Did France challenge British leadership or did the British challenge French hegemony in the late eighteenth century? Did the British first advance to the system's leadership position in the early eighteenth or in the early nineteenth century? Was the Thirty Years War really the first world war as Wallerstein (1980: 23) contends? How many times must the sequence of ascendancy and decline repeat itself to be described as a cycle?

Questions such as these notwithstanding—and I do not mean to make them sound trivial for they are not—there is still basic agreement that it is the concentration of political, economic, and military power and not something like the number of states in the system that essentially defines the structure of the system. The rules of the system, moreover, tend to be established during period of high capability concentration and the leadership/dominance of a single state. However conceptualized or measured, the high levels of concentration are of only temporary duration. The erosion of the system leader's competitive edge and the rise of challengers alter the prevailing distribution of capabilities. The changes in capability distribution, in turn, lead to warfare on an intensive and extensive scale in order to resolve the leadership succession question and the subsequent allocation of systemic rules, benefits, and responsibilities. The basic structural rhythm of the system, and one of the more significant and regular types of system transformation, is a periodic alternation between periods of more and less capability concentration punctuated by major wars following a process of capability deconcentration.

Common denominator or not, it is much too soon to tell to what extent this premise of structural periodicities, with its veritable host of behavioral implications, will constitute the core element of a Kuhnian paradigm shift in the way we examine international relations. It certainly represents a significant break from more conventional emphasis on the absence of regularities and even structure, but it also remains very much a minority position. Whether wide acceptance is gained no doubt ultimately will depend on the extent to which analysts, who adopt the concentration premise as an operating assumption, are successful in relating processes hitherto thought to be unrelated and in explicating processes that, so far, have resisted satisfactory explanation. Acceptance, to be sure, will also depend on convincing demonstrations of the historical fit of these structural frameworks.

For the remainder of this essay, however, I will confine my attention to the less ambitious task of demonstrating that a sensitivity to the world system's structural periodicities can lead to markedly different ways of approaching research questions on the study of war. Two examples will have to suffice. The first example, Singer, Bremer, and Stuckey's (1972) often-cited Correlates of War (COW) study of the 1820-1964 relationship between capability concentration and war, represents a set of puzzling empirical findings that can be easily resolved by selective "world system" adjustments to the 1972 research design. The second case, Doran and Parsons's (1980) analysis of the relationship between relative capability cycles and extensive war initiations, constitutes an opportunity to extend the implications of an innovative and intriguing, but less than fully persuasive, investigation into possible systemic infuences on decision maker propensities toward misperception, uncertainty, and major war involvement.

CAPABILITY CONCENTRATION AND WAR UNDERWAY

Synthesizing much of the conventional literature, Singer, Bremer, and Stuckey (1972) reduced the systemic capability concentration and war problem to the linkages between three variables: *capability concentration,* the *level of decision maker uncertainty,* and the *amount of war underway in the system.*[1] The authors argued that two of the principal contending schools of thought (predominance versus parity) agree that uncertainty levels will increase as the capabilities of the major powers become more equally distributed or less concentrated. However, disagreement characterizes the uncertainty/war linkage.

The *preponderance school* is said to assume that war is primarily due to decision maker misperceptions and miscalculations. To the extent that increasing uncertainty makes decision maker misjudgments more likely, an increase in uncertainty increases the probability of war. The expected relationship between capability concentration and war, therefore, is negative. The *parity school,* alternatively, is portrayed as assuming that environmental uncertainty, in respect to evaluating relative capabilities and identifying the composition of allied and adversarial coalitions, tends to make decision makers more cautious and therefore less likely to participate in warfare. The concentration of systemic capability distribution, accordingly, is expected to be positively related to the probability of war.

To resolve these contradictory expectations, Singer et al. (1972) proceeded to test the two rival hypotheses. Leaving the intervening variable of uncertainty levels unmeasured, the extent to which capabilities have been concentrated should be either positively (the parity position) or negatively (the preponderance position) related to the amount of warfare ongoing in the system. Unfortunately, their empirical outcome can be interpreted as supporting both the preponderance and the parity positions. Over the 1820-1964 period, the observed relationship between capability concentration and the averge annual nation-months of war underway is weakly negative (−.10). But if one analyzes the nineteenth (1820-1894) and twentieth (1895-1964) centuries separately, two differently signed relationships emerge. Strong support for the parity position (a .81 correlation coefficient) is found to characterize the nineteenth century data, while weak to moderate support (a −.23 correlation) for the preponderance position is associated with the twentieth-century observations.

Instead of resolving the theoretical dispute, Singer et al. (1972) created or discovered, an empirical puzzle.[2] Why should the concentration/war relationship change between centuries? This question is particularly interesting for world system analysis since, as noted earlier, it is argued, although not necessarily for the same reasons, that the system's most important wars are the results of systemic deconcentration processes. Since the 1972 data analysis does not support this view, are we to believe that one of the few generalizations shared by several perspectives within and outside the world system rubric is incorrect? Or must we then look for changes in systemic context that somehow differentiate the nineteenth and twentieth centuries? While this latter approach is the course advocated and pursued in a largely ad hoc fashion in the 1972 study, there may be a more simple path to clarifying the empirical puzzle. Indeed, reexamining the 1972 operationalization procedures from a world system perspective, it will be shown, eliminates the curious outcome encountered a decade ago.

In order to examine the relationship between capability concentration and war, analytical decisions about four operational questions are critical: (1) What time period should be examined? (2) Which nation-state actors are most important to the structure of the system? (3) Which capabilities are most essential to decoding the structural distribution of power? (4) Which wars are most likely to be influenced by structural changes? If a world system analyst is likely to answer these questions in a significantly different fashion from the Correlates of War project's mode, it may be equally likely that the empirical outcome will also be significantly different.

Most world system analysts probably would prefer to analyze the concentration/war relationship over the entire course of the modern world-system's existence. A long-cycle analysis (Modelski and Thompson, 1981) along related lines has in fact been undertaken for the 1517-1970 period, but concentration data that would be appropriate for either the Correlates of War project or other world system perspectives, such as the world-economy school, are not currently available and may never be available for the earlier centuries of the post-1500 era. Even so, the still respectable length of time represented by the 1820-1964 period raises a problem of its own. From both the world-economy and long cycle perspectives, 1820 to 1964 encompasses a good proportion of Britain's nineteenth-century leadership but only a few years of post-1945 American leadership. Would it make any difference if the analysis were restricted to a comparable slice of world system time such as the era bounded by the end of the Napoleonic Wars and 1945?

More important, there is no obvious rationale, from a world system perspective, to justify dividing the 1820-1964 period at 1895, especially since this procedure arbitrarily cuts off the supposed climax of the nineteenth-century deconcentration process (World War I) from the structural changes that presumably led to the twentieth century's first war between all of the system's major actors. Accordingly, the quickest way to resolve the mystery of the nineteenth-versus twentieth-century findings is to suggest that the 1895 cutting point is simply inappropriate. While this strategy might be the most convenient one, it of course does not discount the finding, however achieved, that the concentration/war relationship does not appear to be consistent over time.

Turning to the question of which elite actors to examine, there are definitely some differences of opinion on how best to proceed. Singer et al. focused on a conventional list of great powers: Austria-Hungary to 1918; Prussia/Germany to 1945; Russia/the Soviet Union, France, Great Britain, and Italy from 1860 to 1943; Japan from 1895 to 1945; the United States after 1898; and China after 1950. A world-economy analysis, emphasizing the core economic producers, conceivably would overlap to some extent, but the elite list would no doubt be somewhat shorter.[3] A long-cycle analyst, on the other hand, would eliminate Austria-Hungary, Prussia, Italy, and China as nonqualifiers on the sea power criteria.[4] The United States and Japan would be introduced at earlier points in time, while France and Britain would be dropped from the list after 1945. These changes in terms of actor selection could also be significant to the empirical outcome.

The clearest departure from the 1972 study, nevertheless, is associated with the third operational question pertaining to the choice of capabilities that need to be examined. Singer et al. adopted what might be termed an "omnibus" strategy by creating a capability index that combines six equally weighted indicators: two demographic variables (total population and the number of people living in cities of 20,000 or more), two industrial variables (energy consumption in coal ton equivalents and iron/steel production). The underlying rationale for these indicators is the assumption that great powers

> must begin with a solid territorial and demographic base, build upon that a superior industrial and/or military capability, and utilize those resources with a modicum of political competence [Singer et al., 1972: 22].

The problem with such a seemingly reasonable approach is that in recent history it has been possible to (a) create a superior industrial capability with a relatively small population and (b) exercise great political and military influence on a global scale with comparatively few armed forces personnel (see Thompson and Zuk, 1982). The world system leadership of Great Britain in the nineteenth century provides the most obvious and the most important example. Equally weighing the six indicators outlined above thus distorts the relative standing of the major actors (and the economic and politico-military history) of the nineteenth and twentieth centuries by penalizing actors who lead in some but not all conceivable categories and rewarding actors with large populations and armies. If all three of the capability dimensions are or have been equally important, the charge of distortion would, of course, be unfair. World system analysts, however, expend a fair amount of theoretical energy in attempts to demonstrate that all national capabilities are not of equal significance in terms of influencing events, processes, and other actors in the world system.

The world-economy school, for instance, emphasizes the productive, commercial, and financial superiority of the hegemonic power in determining the structure of the world economy. Such an emphasis would lead presumably to a more exclusive focus on the types of indicators, suitably supplemented by trade and financial indicators, associated with the industrial dimension of the 1972 examination.

A completely different theoretical emphasis on capabilities is advocated by long-cycle analysts. Within this perspective, global influence is predicated upon global reach capabilities, which, it is contended, are most directly indicated by naval capabilities—either in terms of capital ships or naval expenditure. Hence this version of world system analysis would stress the military dimension of the 1972 study much to the exclusion of the other capability types. But since the system's major actors have tended to specialize either in naval or land forces, there is no compelling reason to anticipate a strong correlation between rankings or capability shares based on naval expenditures versus total military expenditures/military personnel.

Finally, some attention needs to be focused on the dependent variable, the amount of war underway in the system. Distinguishing between "wars" and "nonwars" has received a great deal of attention in the past few decades, and while it naturally raises an important and still unresolved operational question, we need not dwell on definitions of war for the more restricted purposes of this essay. Singer, Bremer, and Stuckey chose to focus on interstate wars in which major powers participate as measured by the magnitude or aggregate nation-months of participation in such wars.

Two questions are raised by this decision. First, which wars should we expect to be linked to structural deconcentration processes? World system analysts usually but not always stress the infrequent but most significant global wars in which all of the system's major actors eventually participate. These wars are crucial since they represent salient opportunities to restructure the system and because their outcomes do tend to demarcate major shifts in the system's leadership structure and political framework. Minimally, then, we should expect structural deconcentration to be related to this category of warfare despite the existence of only two such wars in the 1820-1964 period. More maximally, we might sequentially expand the dependent variable to encompass wars involving major actors participating on both sides, wars involving major actors on only one side, and all other wars in precisely this hierarchical order.[5]

The second question raised by the 1972 war operationalization centers on the validity of aggregating the months of participation of each war participant regardless of their status. Adopting this procedure, a long war with at least one major actor and a number of less important states could be given greater weight than a short war in which two major adversaries participated. An extreme example of this type of measurement problem can be found in the 1972 study in which the Korean War receives the second highest score (103.34) in the 1820-1964 period—a score much higher than the 87.06 score attributed to World War I. But if World War I is correctly regarded as the most important war outcome of a century of deconcentration processes, there should be a strong incentive to avoid creating misleading outliers, especially during a period (1950-1953) when capabilities, as viewed by world system analysts, were highly concentrated.

A theoretically justified case can then be constructed, from more than one world system perspective, for altering key operational assumptions and decisions. The time has now come to determine whether some of these different choices make any difference in respect to the empirical outcomes.

Reflecting the author's own theoretical biases, the present reanalysis of the concentration/war relationship will be conducted from a long-cycle point of view. Capability concentration data, in the form of shares of naval expenditures (1816-1945) and capital ships (1946-   ), are available (Thompson, 1980, 1981) for the global powers identified earlier. For purposes of comparison with the 1972 study, capability distribution observations will be restricted to every fifth year (i.e., 1820, 1825, 1830, and so forth), and the quinquennial scores will be expressed in the format of the Ray and Singer (1973) concentration index. Two slight departures from the earlier examination will be employed, however. First, the long-cycle concentration observations will commence in 1816, the beginning of the fourth long cycle, instead of in 1820. Second, the 1855 value utilized in the 1972 study is influenced by Crimean War activity. The pre-war 1853 capability distribution score is more representative and will be substituted for the 1855 value.

With some misgivings and again largely for the sake of comparison, the amount of war underway will continue to be measured in terms of nation-months participation.[6] In light of the use of five-year observations, the average annual nation-months of war underway for every five-year interval following each capability concentration score will be analyzed. Thus the 1840 concentration score is matched with a mean value encompassing the 1840-1844 period. Rather than aggregate the nation-months of all participants, however, only the nation-months of global power participation will be counted.

Two war series will be examined—one pertaining to the less frequent participation of global powers on both sides and a second, more comparative one encompassing global power participation on at least one side of interstate wars. This procedure reflects the absence of any long-cycle rationale for anticipating a linear relationship between systemic deconcentration and all wars.[7] Periods of relatively high concentration, to be sure, are believed to be associated with less warfare than are periods of relatively low concentration. But this generalization need not imply that the movement from high to low concentration must be accompanied by a monotonic increase in warfare. Minimally, nevertheless, we should expect to find wars between global powers to be associated with periods of relatively low capability concentration. Finally, bivariate correlations between capability concentration and war will be calculated for the earlier study's nineteenth- (1816-1895) and twentieth- (1895-1964) century periods as well as for the fourth long cycle's temporal unit of analysis (1816-1945).

Table 6.1 lists the appropriate concentration and war indicator values for the 1972 study and the revised series constructed from a long-cycle perspective. Some important differences are readily apparent. The Correlates of War (COW) concentration series begins in 1820 with a relatively low .241 value, rises slightly in the mid-nineteenth century (1845-1860), and then continues to decline in the period preceding World War I. Relatively high concentration scores are reported immediately after World Wars I and II, followed by a return to a set of lower scores.

The long-cycle concentration index is not entirely dissimilar, especially in terms of the direction of change recorded in twentieth-century values, but it does deviate from the COW series most noticeably in the early and again in the latter portion of the nineteenth century.[8] Consistent with long-cycle theory, each global war period (1793-1815, 1914-1918, 1939-1945) is followed by a short-lived phase of relatively high capability concentration with marked tendencies toward decay. In addition, each of the twentieth century's two world wars is preceded by a period of declining concentration scores. But it is the nineteenth-century differences, readily detectable in Figure 6.1, that should prove to be of particular interest for our immediate purposes.

TABLE 6.1 Capability Concentration and War Underway Values, 1816-1964

Year	Capability Concentration		War Underway		
	Correlates of War	Long Cycle	Correlates of War	Long Cycle A	Long Cycle B
1816	—	.724	—	0.00	0.00
1820	.241	.481	2.92	1.46	0.00
1825	.233	.442	6.68	3.40	0.00
1830	.242	.385	0.00	0.00	0.00
1835	.243	.302	0.00	0.00	0.00
1840	.232	.287	0.00	0.00	0.00
1845	.257	.302	6.40	4.42	0.00
1850	.260	.281	9.36	5.40	5.40
1855	.276	.278	17.24	9.78	8.40
1860	.280	.344	16.82	7.02	0.00
1865	.255.	.289	12.98	5.32	0.00
1870	.233	.307	5.44	3.20	3.00
1875	.225	.304	3.52	1.76	0.00
1880	.226	.355	2.64	1.10	0.00
1885	.208	.359	2.12	1.26	0.00
1890	.203	.344	0.00	1.00	0.00
1895	.223	.361	0.00	1.34	0.00
1900	.202	.269	4.32	3.88	3.88
1905	.207	.268	3.40	3.80	3.80
1910	.212	.262	8.47	0.00	0.00
1913	.208	.200	87.06	39.23	39.23
1920	.371	.489	0.00	0.00	0.00
1925	.247	.383	0.00	0.00	0.00
1930	.241	.325	6.68	3.32	0.00
1935	.228	.221	8.73	1.92	0.00
1938	.217	.242	123.97	38.30	38.30
1946	.417	1.000	0.00	0.00	0.00
1950	.293.	1.000	103.34	7.40	0.00
1955	.331	1.000	0.52	0.16	0.00
1960	.303	.282	0.44	0.00	0.00

War Underway Indicators:
(1) Correlates of War: average annual nation-months of interstate war underway in which major powers participate on at least one side (the nation-months of all participants are aggregated).
(2) Long Cycle A: average annual nation-months of interstate war underway in which global powers participate on at least one side (only the nation-months of global power participants are aggregated).
(3) Long Cycle B: average annual nation-months of interstate war underway in which global powers participate on both sides (only the nation-months of global power participants are aggregated).

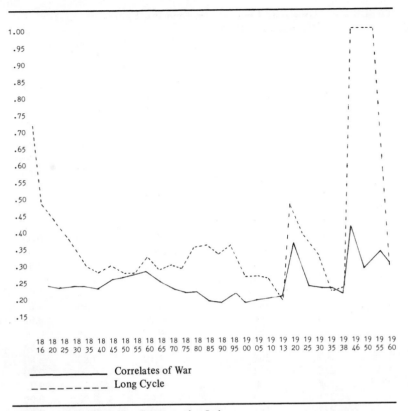

Figure 6.1 Two Capability Concentration Indexes

The nineteenth-century high points in the Singer et al. concentration index are found in the middle of the nineteenth century, while the long-cycle peak values immediately following the Napoleonic Wars, roughly a generation earlier. Equally pertinent, there is much less pre-World War I variation in the 1972 index, which ranges between .280 and .202, and the long-cycle version, with its range of .724 to .200. The war series, on the other hand, tend to be much more comparable except for the consistently similar values found in the two long-cycle series. The most obvious disagreement emerges in the 1950-1954 period—an interval that earlier had been singled out as a misleading outlier problem requiring resolution. If nothing else has been accomplished, the long-cycle war magnitude estimation procedures do restore the Korean War to its "proper" place in the political history of warfare.

With this comparative information in mind, the 1972, nineteenth-century, positive concentration/war relationship can be accounted for fairly easily if the highest nineteenth-century war values are also found in the vicinity of the COW's project's mid-century capability concentration bulge. A visual inspection of the COW war magnitude values in Table 6.1 confirms that this is precisely the case. Prior to 1895, the peak COW concentration and war values are clustered between 1845 and 1865, thereby explaining the strongly positive 1820-1895 correlation coefficient (.81) in the 1972 study. Since this same mid-century clustering pattern is not found in the long-cycle series, a different and possibly more consistent empirical outcome based on the long-cycle data seems highly possible if not probable.

Table 6.2 presents two sets of simple bivariate correlations. The first set constitutes the relationships reported in the 1972 examination. Immediately below these coefficients are the results of several design modifications introduced by adopting one of several world system perspectives. Regardless of whether one focuses on wars fought between or by global powers, the correlations between capability concentration and war underway are consistently negative. Consistent with multiple perspectives on the evolution of the world system, the magnitude of war underway does tend to increase as systemic capability concentration declines. It also does not seem to make much empirical difference how one slices the 1816-1964 time period. Coefficients of roughly comparable size and direction are found in four periods: 1816-1964, 1816-1894, 1895-1964, and 1816-1945. The anomaly of the 1972 study thus disappears once the ways in which the problem is perceived and examined are altered to match a specific interpretation of the development of the world system.[9] In this instance, the conceptualization and measurement of capabilities proved to be the main key to obtaining consistent findings across time. But the different findings could have been the product of several other design decisions just as well. Not surprisingly, the answers we find for our empirical questions must always be highly dependent upon whatever perceptual lenses are used to make sense of the world.

THE CYCLE OF RELATIVE POWER
AND EXTENSIVE WAR INITIATIONS

A different sort of example is provided by the work of Doran and Parsons (1980; Doran, 1971), who argue that the relative capabilities of the international system's major powers experience a cyclical dynamic. The causes of the cycles are multiple and include differential rates of economic and political development; absolute limitations on territorial, capital, and natural resource endowments; rigidity and overcentralization; and tendencies toward the diffusion of power (for example, the migration of population and capital). Whatever the rela-

TABLE 6.2   Systemic Capability Concentration and Average Annual Nation-Months of War Underway

Correlates of War Concentration Index	*1820-1964*	*1820-1894*	*1895-1964*	
Major power participants	−.10	.81	−.23	

Long Cycle Concentration Index	*1816-1964*	*1816-1894*	*1895-1964*	*1816-1945*
Global power participants	−.24	−.38	−.28	−.40
Global power versus global power	−.27	−.30	−.33	−.38

SOURCE: The Pearson correlation coefficients for the Correlates of War concentration index are reported in Singer et al. (1972: 33).

tive weights of the causes, they create a situation in which any given major power at any given point in time is either in a state of ascendancy, maturation, or decline vis-à-vis the capability standings of the other major powers.

The significance of locating a state's position on its relative capability trajectory, moreover, is twofold. First, a state's capacity to exercise external influence grows as it gains in power or declines as it falls behind. Second, the adoption of foreign policy roles is determined in large part by a state's position on the relative capability cycle. As the cycle evolves, roles change accordingly, requiring some amount of adjustment on the part of the state's decision makers and population. Within this context, the crux of the relative capability cycle theory is that the trauma of foreign policy role change will be the most severe at four critical points on the cycle.

As demonstrated in Figure 6.2, the critical points are found at the low, high, and the two inflection points of the cycle. Between these points, the changes in the cycle's slope are not great. Decision makers are thus in a position to project reliably their future capability positions. At each of the four critical points, however, the ability to make these simple forecasts breaks down because the trend lines shift abruptly either in terms of direction or the rate of growth. National leaders, as a consequence, are forced into contemplating the need for a change in their foreign policy role or they are forced to accept the fact that a role transformation can no longer be postponed.

In this sense, the critical points are destabilizing for decision makers, who must search for new foreign policy roles within a threatening atmosphere of uncertainty. Expansion and attempts at hegemony are most likely to occur at these points. Decision maker propensities to misperceive and overreact to the behavior of their rivals also are apt

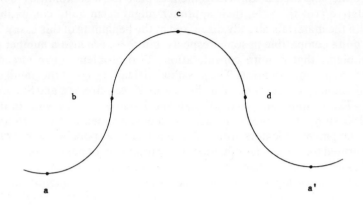

SOURCE: Based on Doran and Parsons (1980: 948).
a = low turning point, b = rising inflection point, c = high turning point; d = declining inflection point.

Figure 6.2   The Cycle of Relative Power

to be most acute in the critical points. Finally, the major power initiation of more extensive wars, expressed in terms of the status of the combatants, casualties, and/or duration, is most likely at or around the critical points as well.

While the circumstances connecting attempts at hegemony to the critical points are not made clear in the 1980 study, the authors do test the extensive war generalization. And even though it is argued that the relative power cycle applies to the post-1450 period, the test is restricted to the 1816-1975 relative capabilities and war initiation behavior of nine major powers. After locating the critical point years for each state and constructing a sixteen-year window around each point (three years before and twelve years after each point) in order to reduce the problem of indentification error, Doran and Parsons found that (1) the means for the magnitude, severity, and duration of wars initiated by major powers are higher in the critical periods than in the noncritical years; (2) the level of war extensiveness varies inversely with the temporal distance from the critical point; and (3) the inflection point periods tend to be somewhat more prone to extensive war initiations than are the turning points at the top and the bottom of the cycle.[10]

Given the Doran and Parsons emphasis on relative capabilities, the destabilizing consequences of cyclical patterns of growth and decline, and their acknowledgement of post-1450 continuities in the relative growth cycle, their approach might seem quite compatible with the materials already discussed at the beginning of this essay. It is quite compatible in some respects, but there are also a number of problems that require consideration. Two problems have already received some attention. The possible misleading use of the omnibus indicators, previously noted in the case of Singer, Bremer, and Stuckey (1972), is applicable to the Doran and Parsons case as well. In the 1980 study, the authors create a composite index of five size and development indicators: iron and steel production, population, number of armed forces, coal production, and proportion of population living in cities with more than 100,000 inhabitants. The relative capability scores and the location of the critical point years, consequently, are to some extent a function of the specific indicators employed. The problem is graphically illustrated by Doran and Parsons's finding that, by 1975, the Soviet Union and China were approximately equal in relative capability and that both were ahead of the United States.[11] Not noted by the authors but something that is evident in the plots of the nine major powers' relative capabilities (Doran and Parson, 1980: 956) is the fact that the use of the five indicators portrays the Soviet Union and China as approaching the historical peak of American relative capabilities (which their curve-fitting procedure apparently pinpoint as occurring at 1934). World system analysts would find this comparison difficult to accept; nor would they be likely, as discussed earlier, to give equal weight to such indicators as population and armed forces size.[12] Nevertheless, the question remains open as to what effect the investigation of different indicators (or, for that matter, a different set of actors) might have on the empirical results.

The perennial question of how best to measure the dependent war variable must also be raised once again. Doran and Parsons's measure of extensive war is a bit unusual. Two of their indicators, duration (number of months) and severity (number of battlefield deaths), represent fairly standard practice. The third indicator, magnitude, is less conventional in that it is restricted to the sum of the inverted quintile diplomatic ranks of the war participants. Based on the Singer and Small (1966; Small and Singer, 1973) diplomatic centrality scores, this measure gives equal weight to states in the top 20 percent, the second 20 percent, and so forth. Such an approach should help to differentiate between topdogs and underdogs, but it does very little to differentiate among the major powers, many of which are likely to be found in the upper crust of diplomatic status.

Even more curious, however, is the "and/or" character of the extensive war definition. An extensive war is said to be one lasting for a long time, killing a large number of soldiers, and/or involving a number of states with high diplomatic status. According to this definition, the 1828-1829 and 1877-1878 Russo-Turkish wars must be regarded as fairly extensive wars as must the more recent Korean and Vietnamese affairs.[13] While there is no need to dismiss these examples as insignificant exercises in bloodletting, the problem invariably reduces to one of historical proportion. A more justifiable approach might involve combining the three separate criteria in some fashion. Otherwise, it is difficult to distinguish the truly extensive wars that qualify in all three of the categories (and the ones of paramount interest to world system analysis) from those wars that rate highly according to only a single indicator.

Another problem concerns the critical points. Doran and Parsons find that the inflection points are more dangerous than the upper/lower turning points. But this is primarily an empirical observation. More preferable would be theoretically derived expectations that differentiate the behavior anticipated at each of the four critical points. It seems most unlikely, for instance, that a low turning point at the end of a major power's terminal descent (a') should produce the same sort of decision maker anxiety that might be expected at the inauguration of an ascent (a). Similarly, decision makers at points a and c should have little in common with one another other than the dilemma of being at turning points. Options open to policymakers at point c presumably will be closed to leaders at point a. Alternatively, the two inflection points (b and d) might lead to similar levels of anxiety but of a different nature. Decision makers at point d conceivably may be more likely to precipitate preemptive wars, while point b decision makers could be more likely to become involved in wars prematurely.

The last point underscores the autistic character of the critical points. While the points are located by comparing rates of growth/decline, the consequent behavioral expectations are not geared to the positional movements of competitors. Are major powers at point b more likely to attack other major powers at points c and d or vice versa? Is a major power at point a or a' unlikely to attack another major power at points b, c, or d but more likely to attack a nonmajor power? Or is it simply that the systemic probability of extensive war is greatest when the critical points of several major powers overlap? These are hardly causal questions if the research goal is one of predicting the most extensive wars—wars that tend to become extensive because, or to the extent that, major powers oppose major powers in combat.

Table 6.3 is quite suggestive in this interactive context. In the table, Doran and Parsons's critical points are listed chronologically and clustered whenever a critical point year is within ten years of the

TABLE 6.3   Doran and Parsons's Critical Points on the Relative Power Cycle, 1815-1975

Critical Point Year	Critical Point Interval	Critical Point Type	State
1821	1818-1833	d	Russia
1845	1842-1857	c	Austria-Hungary
1859	1856-1871	b	Prussia/Germany
1879	1876-1891	d	Italy
1882	1879-1894	d	Austria-Hungary
1894	1891-1906	a'	Russia
1902	1899-1914	c	Germany
1904	1901-1916	d	Great Britain
1909	1906-1921	a'	Italy
1910	1907-1922	b	United States
1910	1907-1922	a'	Austria-Hungary
1911	1908-1923	d	France
1934	1931-1946	c	United States
1939	1936-1951	b	Italy
1942	1939-1954	d	Germany
1944	1941-1956	b	Japan
1952	1949-1964	d	United States
1960	1957-1972	b	Soviet Union
1967	1964-1979	b	Japan

SOURCE: Based on information reported in Doran and Parsons (1980: 956).
NOTE: Four critical points (France, 1815 [c]; Great Britain, 1817 [c], 1975 [a'], and China, 1946 [a]) have been excluded since they may be biased by the decision to focus on the 1815-1975 period. Critical point types: a,a' = low turning point; b = rising inflection point; c = high turning point; d = declining inflection point.

preceding critical point year and the sequence is not interrupted by a world war.[14] Two obvious clusters should virtually leap out at the reader. The first major cluster, encompassing critical point years 6 through 12, captures Germany at its peak; an ascending United States; Britain and France at their descending inflection points; and Russia, Austria-Hungary, and Italy at relative nadir points. In sum, immediately prior to World War I, seven of the eight traditional great powers of the period (missing only Japan) are found to be at points that are portrayed as particularly troublesome for foreign policy management. Extrapolating to the systemic level, if each critical point increases decision maker uncertainty, the conjuncture of critical points should add up to an unusual aggregate level of uncertainty. Among similar if less numerically impressive lines, the second largest cluster, points 13 thorough 16, encompasses World War II and four important participants in that war. Is it then presumptuous to suggest that the Doran and Parson's argument might be more successful if couched at the systemic (as opposed to the national monadic) level of analysis?

An appreciation for the political history of the world system's cyclical changes in structure sensitizes analysts to such questions as who is likely to fight whom at what point or when is a major power more likely to make a bid for hegemony/leadership via the battlefield. A world system analyst is also more likely to question the wisdom of treating all relative capability trajectories as if they were somehow roughly equivalent. If it is accepted that all major powers have not been equal in strength, why should we expect Italian or Austrian elites to react to their upper turning points in the same way as British or American policymakers at their own respective point c's. Role trauma may indeed be relative. But surely there must be significant differences in decision makers' expectations in states whose apex has taken them to the every top of the system in contrast to the situation in states that have very little objective chance of ever achieving systemic leadership. This observation suggests that more theoretical elaboration is in order but it also implies the need for more systematic information about foreign policymaking in the critical point intervals.

CONCLUSION

The title of this chapter suggests quite strongly that an ecumenical viewpoint will be adopted, but a great deal of the essay has appeared to be rather critical in tone. Where, one might ask, did all the ecumenicism go? Although it is hoped that the criticisms of earlier work utilizing premises other than those advocated here are not viewed as intolerant attacks on "nonbelievers," most of the ecumenical spirit is restricted to the initial discussion of the emerging common ground on the historical regularities of systemic transformation. Despite a number of theoretical and interpretative differences that primarily are ignored in this essay, an impressive amount of overlap on a consistent form of structural change does exist. Certain wars involving all of the system's most important actors follow a period of capability deconcentration. Whatever the specific issues and goals, the wars serve the more general function of resolving the prewar ambiguities in the hierarchical leadership structure of the system. Following the wars, the system's distribution of economic, political, and military capabilities is highly concentrated, but historically persistent tendencies toward deconcentration gradually reassert themselves. The concomitant of relative capability diffusion and dispersal is a return to the conflict-laden ambiguities and uncertainties of a severely weakened leadership structure and, eventually, still another bout of warfare between the principal contenders.

Whether or not we label these historical regularities of structural change as cyclical in nature or even whether we talk about a world system as opposed to an international system matters less than whether we recognize the recurring pattern of change. For to ignore this pattern of concentration and deconcentration is tantamount to missing out on the most fundamental structural context within which the world's other processes take place. A great deal of work, needless to say, remains to be done on the precise parameters of this system-shaping rhythm. But the point remains that analysts who accept this model of systemic reality as an operating premise are likely to produce different findings—perhaps even markedly different findings—from analysts who have not incorporated it into their perspectives. There is of course nothing particularly profound or controversial about the contention that different assumptions tend to produce different results. It is another matter entirely, however, to insist that the assumption of historical structure periodicities should be and some day will be a prerequisite to the study of all the topics that we have traditionally labeled international relations, in addition to a variety of other, nontraditional topics as well. Only time will tell whether this assertion proves to be an accurate prediction or merely an empty boast of analytical imperialism.

NOTES

1. The systemic dispute over the relationship between the distribution of capabilities and war should not be confused with the different question posed by analysts (Ferris, 1973; Weede, 1976; Garnham, 1976a, 1976b) investigating the relationship between dyadic capability disparities and war. The answer for one of those research questions need have little bearing on the other question's answer.

2. The reader should be aware that I am restricting the discussion to only some of the empirical operations found in the 1972 study.

3. Russia, for instance, would not be considered a core economic power as of 1816, nor would China qualify in 1946.

4. A global power must possess a minimum of at least 5 to 10 percent (depending on the indicator) of global reach capabilities to qualify for the world's political elite status.

5. The extent to which changes in system structure influence behavior throughout the world system is very much an important and ongoing theoretical and empirical question.

6. While the nation-months indicator is less than perfect, it does provide a better indicator than does the dichotomy of the presence or absence of major power warfare. Contrary to the arguments put forward by Duvall (1976) and Bueno de Mesquita (1981), there is little justification in treating all major power wars as if they were equal in significance. The nation-months weighing scheme is one way to avoid this problem, particularly if the time period examined permits one to avoid including the long-running Vietnamese war. For a weighing scheme based on the relative capabilities of the participants, see Modelski and Thompson (1981).

7. On the contrary, Modelski and Thompson (1981) develop an argument and find empirical support for a nonlinear fluctuation with global power warfare more prevalent in the second and fourth quarters than in the first and third quarters. This pattern appears to have prevailed since the beginning of the modern world system.

8. The extremely high scores for the long cycle concentration series immediately after World War II are a function of a global elite restricted to the United States and the Soviet Union and the 1946-1959 aircraft carrier definition of a capital ship. Of the two states, only the United States possessed any of these vessels. The introduction of nuclear submarines, the latest development in capital ships, abruptly altered the concentration of naval capabilities although the extent of change is exaggerated somewhat by the use of a concentration index.

9. Other evaluations, from much different points of view, of the Singer et al. (1972) findings may be found in Bueno de Mesquita (1981) and Siverson and Sullivan (1982).

10. Doran and Parsons (1980: 960) report similar results with a more narrow ten-year window.

11. Doran and Parsons (1980: 957) also express some misgivings about the validity of these counterintuitive comparisons, but they contend that relying on different capability indicators may produce different rank orders—but it is unlikely to change the slopes of the relative power curves. They then proceed to buttress this contention by first altering their capability index (substituting defense spending and GNP per capita for armed forces size and urbanization) and second, by calculating new relative capability scores for the 1966-1975 period. The new indices, once plotted, depict more intuitively satisfactory relative positions for the United States, China, and the Soviet Union. The slopes of the old and new relative capability scores, moreover, are indeed found to be highly correlated.

12. Doran and Parsons (1980: 953) note that in their opinion no empirical or theoretical rationale could be found to justify employing other than equal weighings.

13. The two Russo-Turkish cases (1828-1829, 1877-1878) rank tenth and sixth, respectively, in terms of battle deaths in major power interstate wars. Korea and Vietnam rank third and fourth on the same indicator (see Small and Singer, 1982: 102).

14. Four critical points (two c points for France [1815] and Great Britain [1817], an a point for China [1946], and an a' point for Britain [1975]) have been excluded since they may be biased by the decision to focus on the 1815-1975 period.

REFERENCES

BERGESEN, A. L. (1983) "Modeling long waves of crisis in the world-system," in A. L. Bergesen (ed.) Crises in the World-System. Beverly Hills, CA: Sage.

BOUSQUET, N. (1980) "From hegemony to competition: cycles of the core?" pp. 46-83 in T. K. Hopkins and I. Wallerstein (eds.) Processes of the World-System. Beverly Hills, CA: Sage.

BUENO de MESQUITA, B. (1981) "Risk, power distributions and the likelihood of war." International Studies Quarterly 25 (December): 541-568.

CHASE-DUNN, C. (1981) "Interstate system and capitalist world-economy: one logic or two?" International Studies Quarterly 25 (March): 19-42.

———and R. RUBINSON (1977) "Toward a structural perspective on the world-system." Politics and Society 7, 4:453-476.

DORAN, D. F. (1971) The Politics of Assimilation. Baltimore: Johns Hopkins University Press.

———and W. PARSONS (1980) "War and the cycle of relative power." American Political Science Review 74 (December): 947-965.

DUVALL, R. (1976) "An appraisal of the methodological and statistical procedures in the Correlates of War project," in F. Hoole and D. Zinnes (eds.) Quantitative International Politics. New York: Praeger.

FERRIS, W. (1973) The Power Capabilities of Nation-States. Lexington, MA: D. H. Heath.

GARNHAM, D. (1976a) "Dyadic international war, 1816-1965." Western Political Quarterly 29 (June): 231-242.

———(1976b) "Power parity and lethal international violence, 1969-1973." Journal of Conflict Resolution 20 (September): 379-394.

GILPIN, R. (1981) War and Change in the International System. New York: Cambridge University Press.

HOPKINS, T. K. (1979) "The study of the capitalist world-economy: some introductory considerations," pp. 9-17 in W. L. Goldfrank (ed.) The World-System of Capitalism: Past and Present. Beverly Hills, CA: Sage.

———and I. WALLERSTEIN (1981) "Structural transformations of the world-economy," pp. 233-261 in R. Rubinson (ed.) Dynamics of World Development. Beverly Hills, CA: Sage.

MODELSKI, G. (1981a) "Dependency reversal in the modern world system: a long cycle perspective." Paper delivered at the NSF Conference on Dependency Reversal, Las Cruces, New Mexico.

———(1981b) "Long cycles, Kondratieffs, and alternating innovations: implications for U.S. foreign policy," pp. 63-83 in C. W. Kegley, Jr., and P. J. McGowan (eds.) The Political Economy of Foreign Policy. Beverly Hills, CA: Sage.

———(1978) "The long cycle of global politics and the nation-state." Comparative Studies in Society and History 20 (April): 214-235.

———and W. R. THOMPSON (1981) "Testing cobweb models of the long cycle of world leadership." Paper delivered at the Annual Meeting of the Peace Science Society (International), Philadelphia.

ORGANSKI, A.F.K. (1968) World Politics. New York: Alfred A. Knopf.

———and J. KUGLER (1980) The War Ledger. Chicago: University of Chicago Press.

RAPKIN, D. P., W. R. THOMPSON with J. A. CHRISTOPHERSON (1979) "Bipolarity and bipolarization in the cold war era: conceptualization, measurement, and validation." Journal of Conflict Resolution 23 (June): 261-295.

RASLER, K. A. and W. R. THOMPSON (1983) "Global wars, public debts, and the long cycle." World Politics 35 (July).

RAY, J and J. D. SINGER (1973) "Measuring the concentration of power in the international system." Sociological Methods & Research 1 (May): 403-437.

Research Working Group on Cyclical Rhythms and Secular Trends (1979) "Cyclical rhythms and secular trends of the capitalist world-economy: some premises, hypotheses, and questions." Review 2 (Spring): 483-500.

SINGER, J. D., S. BREMER, and J. STUCKEY (1972) "Capability distribution, uncertainty, and major power war, 1820-1965," pp. 19-48 in B. Russett (ed.) Peace, War, and Numbers. Beverly Hills, CA: Sage.

SINGER, J. D. and M. SMALL (1972) The Wages of War, 1816-1965. New York: John Wiley.

———(1966) "The composition and status ordering of the interntional system, 1815-1940." World Politics 18 (January): 236-282.

SIVERSON, R. M. and M. P. SULLIVAN (1982) "War, power and the international elephant." Paper delivered to the Annual Meeting of the International Studies Association, Cincinnati, Ohio.

SMALL, M. and J. D. SINGER (1982) Resort to Arms: International and Civil Wars, 1816-1980. Beverly Hills, CA: Sage.

———(1973) "The diplomatic importance of states, 1816-1970: an extension and refinement of the indicator." World Politcs 25 (July): 577-599.

THOMPSON, W. R. (1983a) "Succession crises in the global political system: a test of the transition model," in A. Bergesen (ed.) Crises in the World-System. Beverly Hills, CA: Sage.

———(1983b) "The world-economy, the long cycle, and the question of world system time," in P. J. McGowan and C. W. Kegley, Jr. (ed.) Foreign Policy and the Modern World-System. Beverly Hills, CA: Sage.

———(1983c) "Uneven economic growth, systemic challenges, and global wars." International Studies Quarterly 27 (September).

———(1981) "Operationalizing long cycle theory: the basic problems and some proposed solutions for the sixteenth and late twentieth centuries." Paper delivered at the American Political Science Association, New York.

———(1980) "Seapower in global politics, 1500-1945: problems of data collection and analysis." Paper delivered to the Annual Meeting of the International Studies Association-West, Los Angeles.

——— and G. ZUK (1982) "World power and the territorial trap hypothesis." Paper delivered at the Annual Meeting of the International Studies Association-West, San Diego.

WALLERSTEIN, I. (1980) The Modern World-System: Mercantilism and the Consolidation of the European World-Economy, 1600-1750. New York: Academic.

———(1974) The Modern World-System: Capitalist Agriculture and the Origins of the European Economy in the Sixteenth Century. New York: Academic.

WEEDE, E. (1976) "Overwhelming preponderance as a pacifying condition among contiguous Asian dyads, 1950-1969." Journal of Conflict Resolution 20 (September): 394-411.

ZINNES, D. (1980) Prerequisites for the study of system-transformation," pp. 3-21 in O. R. Holsti, R. M. Siverson, and A. L. George (eds.) Change in the International System. Boulder, CO: Westview.

7

Power Cycle Theory and the Contemporary State System

CHARLES F. DORAN

According to power cycle theory, the state passes through a series of phases of relative power and position (Doran, 1971; Doran et al., 1979; Doran and Parsons, 1980). Movement through these phases over long time periods affects the foreign policy behavior of the state, especially its propensity to become entangled in major war.

This chapter first summarizes the essentials of power cycle theory. In the following two sections I examine the principal elements of the contemporary state system relevant to the question posed by Professor Thompson in the preceding chapter, namely, the possibility of a relationship between the state power cycle and other cycles that may be operative within the system as a whole. At this point, the essay narrows the search for this relationship by questioning the empirical verifiability of certain types of cycles. It then turns to the problem of hegemonic expansion as the traumatic linkage between the state cycle and system. Finally, it concludes on the necessity of studying the interface between two quite different types of processes: balance within the central system and movement of states up and down their respective power cycles, including their entry into or exit from that system. The quintessential problem for the international relations scholar seeking to understand the maintenance of world order is how better to bring into simultaneous focus the two very different types of processes affecting the strategic calculations of the statesman: balancing within the central system via external coalition formation, and the slow movement of a state through the various historical phases of the power cycle.

Fundamental to the notion of the power cycle is that states pass through the cycle of ascendance, maturation, and decline. This cycle is traced in terms of the capability of one state relative to its principal political rivals, or, more simply, relative to the capability of the other actors in the system. Capability is the aggregate material base that underlies the power of the nation-state and consists of such elements as gross national product and military spending.

Holland, for example, after the Peace of Westphalia (1648), was a rising state in the system financing many of the major coalitions in the wars against Louis XIV, dominating the sea lanes, and exploring and settling much of the New World. But by the time of the next great attempt to heal the ruptures of European war (the Treaties of Utrecht, 1711), Dutch ascendancy had peaked, and by the mid-seventeenth century the French and the British had totally surpassed the Dutch, leaving the Netherlands in an advanced condition of international political decline (Dehio, 1965: 147). Similarly, France itself went through such a cycle of ascendancy in the seventeenth and early eighteenth centuries, peaking in terms of relative power somewhere midway between the decision of Louis XIV finally to lay down arms and the decision of Napoleon Bonaparte to take them up. War involvement neither caused the eventual decline in French power nor appreciably altered the pattern of change itself. France, however, did enter a period of long decline in power that continued into the twentieth century. In contrast, Germany passed through the entire cycle of growth, maturation, and descent in less than 100 years following Bismarck's initial phase of consolidation in the 1860s. In general, very long time periods are required to encompass these shifts of position and systemic role.

Why does change in relative national capability follow this particular pattern? Superficially the explanation is found in an understanding of the difference between change in *absolute* and *relative* capability. For most states changes in absolute capability on such measures as population size, GNP, size of the armed forces, and military spending over long time periods follows a logarithmic pattern. But in terms of the capability on these measures of one state relative to that of others, the idealized curve looks much more like Figure 7.1, in which a top (maxima) and bottom (minima) are likely to come into evidence. In other words, given logarithmic change in absolute capability for states of different sizes and rates of growth, the capability of each state relative to the others will tend to follow a curve that is convex downward.

But that which substantially underlies this pattern of change in national capability is much more complex. (1) States have different resource endowments. The larger states will eventually tend to replace the smaller states in position on the systemic hierarchy at the same

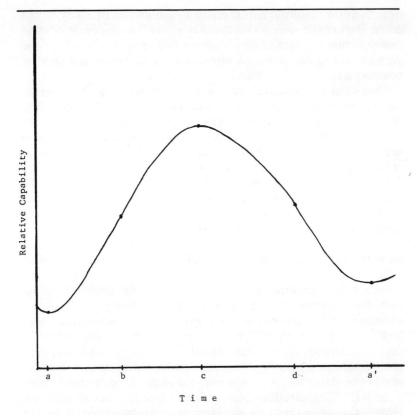

Figure 7.1 Generalized Curve of Relative Capability

SOURCE: See Doran (1971: 46-51, 191-194); Doran and Parsons (1980).

temporal point and develop at the same rate. (2) But states have not
entered the system simultaneously, nor have they developed at the
same rate. Late industrializers have surpassed early industrializers in
terms of economic size and wealth (Kuznets, 1966: Rostow, 1978).
(3) At some point, complex organizations, including nation-states,
probably experience diminishing marginal returns in terms of efficiency as they increase in size and in age. They become more rigid
institutionally and more doctrinaire ideologically. They place greater
emphasis on internal equity debates and less on productivity. Despite
efforts at reform, they allow bureaucracy to stagnate and to become
oppressive, while the vitality and the creativity within the society is
stifled. This is the reason antitrust efforts and deregulation occur in
the market place on the one hand, and why ancient empires collapsed

from their own internal bureaucratic weight and inefficiency on the other. Part of the reason that there is a "top" to the cycle of state power is that the rate of development and growth falls off for the very large and old states as opposed to their newer and smaller counterparts.

Thus change for one state on the cycle is related to changes occurring for other states on their respective power cycles. The key to the state power "cycle" theory is not the concept of repetition, although repetition of the cycle is possible, but the concept of a particular nonlinear pattern of long-term evolutionary change that is generalizable across the principal members of the state system.

These are some of the substantive explanations that underlie the pattern of rise and (relative) decline associated with the modern nation-state. In essence a function of changes in relative power of the state and thus of position on the systemic hierarchy, this pattern is significant for the internal political role the state can and is called upon to play in the system and for the stability of that system as well.

Indeed, how does the cycle of relative capability affect the probability that a state will become entangled in extensive war? According to our definition extensive war has the following characteristics: (1) high intensity, namely, a high rate of battlefield casualties; (2) long duration, namely, many nation-months of active hostilities; and (3) great magnitude, namely a high rank on an index composed of the number of states involved in a war, and their status, related multiplicatively. The question about extensive war is a causal question. How is change on the cycle of relative power responsible, at least in part, for causing extensive war? What is it about shifts up and down the cycle that would cause a nation to initiate or otherwise trigger an extensive war by its own actions and its interactions with its rivals in the system?

In order to answer this question about war causality and shifts in the relative power of the nation-state, one must consider the dynamic of the power cycle itself and the likely demands that adjustment to new systemic roles will put on the decision maker having to confront these shifts in power and systemic position. It is well known that most decision making concerning future behavior is linear. Forecasters, for example, are unable to predict turning points. It is well known from the literature on perception and misperception in foreign policy that surprises and unanticipated events can cause dangerous overreaction or miscalculation in foreign policy conduct. In the extreme, misperception can precipitate crisis and war. Given this awareness of the linear nature of conventional decision making and the significant impact that surprise has on crisis and war initiation, the dynamic of the power cycle has special interpretive value for international politics and our understanding of war causation.

By its definition the power cycle is *nonlinear.* That means that a state experiencing movement through this cycle is faced with non-linear changes in its power and its foreign policy role even though the government decision maker applies a linear conception of reality to the foreign policy situation. The clash between a linear view of the world and nonlinear reality is likely to cause intense anxiety and frustration not only to the decision maker confronting this problem of perception but for others in the society as well, including those who may be less equipped psychologically to accept abrupt alterations of societal outlook and foreign policy position. Failure on the part of the decision maker, and of others in the elite who are interested in international politics and in carving out a prominent place for the state in the system, to make the adjustments to new conditions and new realities is what is responsible for substantially increased vulnerability to war entanglement and initiation (Bueno de Mesquita, 1981). Such war causation may occur because the government overreacts to external events, becomes paranoid and excessively defensive about foreign policy initiatives, or simply becomes strident and bent upon altering its situation through the use of force before further change in its position eliminates all opportunity.

According to power cycle theory, the danger of extensive war precipitation is greatest at four critical points on the cycle, given a suitable lag for awareness to register; that is, the two inflection points occurring on either side of the cycle and the lower and upper turning points (Figure 7.1). These critical points are the source of an entirely new set of options and responsibilities for the actor, having far-reaching significance for the country itself and potentially, where the state is one of the major actors, for the system. At these critical points, or shortly thereafter, the country comes to the wrenching realization that most of the assumptions it has made about its future power base and its future role in the system are altered. Its rivals are viewed in a far different way. Its options and obligations appear transformed, and it may go from follower and ally to leader or from preponderant actor to merely one actor among equals. Adjustment does not guarantee misperception, overreaction, or outright aggression. But adjustment does significantly increase the probability that judgment may go awry. In a century or so of systemic experience, the critical points in the evolution of the power cycle are the most stressful that the country will ever experience. It follows that when major actors are involved, these critical points on a nation's power cycle become problematic for the system as a whole regarding the single most important collective preoccupation for that system—the avoidance of hegemony and extensive war. While it may take two or more actors to fight a war, a single actor by its misperception and aggressiveness can become the chief stimulus to that war. Power cycle theory helps explain why.

This brings us to the principal task of this essay—consideration of the thesis question posed by Professor Thompson in the preceding chapter. What is the relationship between the power cycle that the state undergoes and the structure of the international system? As Professor Thompson put the issue in his summary statement, is the power cycle undergone by a number of major states—a cycle that is, in turn, reflected in the long-term evolution of the international system itself? The central issue is the dynamic relationship between the state in modern history and the history of the modern state system. The theoretical literature on international relations has perhaps passed over the dynamic nexus between state and system a bit too hastily.

BALANCE, STATE, AND SYSTEM

In considering the dynamic relationship—that is, the relationship over time—between the state and system, at least four factors are important. To some extent "everything is related to everything else" in international politics, but these four factors are sufficiently distinct, or "statistically independent of each other," to be treated as autonomous sources of explanation.

(1) the numbers of actors in the central system
(2) the disparity of power between the leading actors and the rest of the system
(3) the presence or absence of balance
(4) the nature of alliance aggregation

I will discuss each of these factors separately showing the significance for state/system analysis. Subsequently I will attempt to show how each factor contributes to our understanding of the importance of the state power cycle for the international system as a whole.

Number of Actors

Superficially, and when the disparity in number is large, the easiest way of characterizing alternate international systems is by the number of actors in them. While the total size of the system is always of interest, the number of actors in the central system, or the core, is critical operationally. What distinguishes the nineteenth- and twentieth-century systems is that the former involved five actors in the core while the latter (after 1945) involved only two. This is a sufficient difference such that, in combination with other factors, the whole focus of the system changed, the degree of actor autonomy declined, and even the rules of statecraft were somewhat altered. By the mid-twentieth century two numerical trends were evident with the former trend acquiring much more importance analytically than the latter: Concentration occurred at the top of the system; diffusion in the aftermath of the colonial period occurred at the middle and lower levels of the hierarchy. By the end of the century, however, the emphasis may be quite the reverse, and the effects of diffusion may be more striking than those of concentration.

Disparity of Power

Second is the disparity of power between the leading actors and the rest of the system. Whether the actors in the central system occupy 80 percent of the total systemic GNP and military capacity or whether they occupy a position involving only 30 percent, for example, makes a great deal of difference regarding how the system operates. If the leading actors directly control a sufficient fraction of the total politically relevant capability, their impact on the system as a whole is determinative (Waltz, 1979). The rules they establish for international trade and monetary policy will be the rules everyone accepts. International law will have an oligarchic rather than a pluralistic or regional bias. The ideological, class, or territorial conflict at the top of the system will be more reflective of overall systemic preoccupations than will the same type of conflict at the bottom of the systemic ladder. As the disparity of power between the leading actors and others in the system declines, far more flexibility results; yet in a decentralized nation-state system, far greater political anarchy and local political instability may emerge as well.

Every international system may have a built-in tendency to resist either of the two trends regarding power disparity. An equilibrium among the competing units may resist natural evolutionary trends, such as those that existed briefly after 1945, toward excessively high concentration of power. Similarly, equilibrium may resist excessive decomposition of power within the central system and diffusion away from it. The resistance may take place through the ascendancy of newly powerful and visible actors from outside the inner circle. Or recombinations of units at the top may occur either through peaceful integration or forceful amalgamation. In other words, the popular image that the international system is either moving toward a unipolar consolidation of empire or toward a Dark Age collapse of all leading structure and hierarchical function is equally unlikely. Similarly unlikely, in the absence of centralized governing institutions, is the emergence of a system in which there is total equality of power among a large number of competing units. In the absence of some type of centralized governing authority, such an extreme version of power egalitarianism would probably lead to anarchy in its purest form. The natural tendency of the system is to resist such a degree of anarchy. Put simply, governments in the more vigorous units would probably attempt to impose some type of order that all could accept, at least as an alternative to structureless chaos.

Hence the disparity of power between the core and the remainder of the system is a separate matter from the number of actors within the core. But these considerations also operate together. The smaller the number of actors in the core and the greater the disparity between themselves and the rest of the system, the more significant will be their influence. Shifts or inconsistencies of power distribution within the core itself will either reinforce or undermine the leadership potential of the central system. In the extreme case, the central system can so paralyze itself with internal dispute, and this dispute is no more prone to order maintenance than is the totally decentralized, egalitarian system. But neither historical precedent nor contemporary experience suggests this degree of conflict fractionation and transmittal.

Balance

Third is the presence or absence of balance. By balance I mean an actor's intention and capacity to shift its weight against the rising power and expansionist propensity of another state or group of states. Intent is very important here. If intent is undermined by ideological commitment or by domestic political intransigence, the presence of adequate military or economic capacity is beside the point. But structure as well is critical to balance. To use Morton Kaplan's apt terminology, in a tight bipolar system balance is out of the question. Because of the degree of polarization between the United States and the Soviet Union, because of the relative equality of power between the two poles, and because of the inability of the smaller states to affect the overall power balance very much by attempting to shift their weight in the system, tight bipolarity epitomizes the absence of a balancing process at work between governments.

But balance as process may also be absent from a multipolar system. If poles are widely distributed in geopolitical terms, and if they possess an essentially regional focus (thus excluding the more globally oriented actors from much influence within their respective regions while at the same time, because of absence of capacity or intent, not allowing for a global reach on the part of the regional poles themselves), multipolarity is not likely to exhibit much balancing activity as such (Rosecrance, 1982). Such a system might be described as "rigid" multipolarity. Even though it might be constituted out of five or so regional "poles," this multipolar system would operate quite in contrast to the five-actor balance of power system of the nineteenth century, when flexibility and power shifts were the sine qua non of the central system.

A key change in the functioning of the post-1945 system came with the introduction of balance at the highest levels within the system's hierarchy for the first time. In the 1970s this event was the "revolution of alliances," which saw the Peoples Republic of China break decisively with the Soviet Union and shift its weight so as to create a rapprochement with the United States. Although China was not a global power, its enormous regional importance in Asia, and its capacity to cause the Soviet Union to redeploy troops and to increase mobilization on its long eastern border, was sufficient to convey global effects within the central system. For the first time since the advent of tight bipolarity, balancing took place with significant impact on the two superpowers. It was not so much that the United States played the "China card" as it was that both China and the United States admitted by their actions that the Soviet Union was the rising military power in the system with evident expansionist interest in Afghanistan and perhaps elsewhere. From the international political perspective both states reacted to the same potential threat irrespective of ideological differences; indeed, pragmatism in both capitals probably facilitated the balancing process. If the Reagan administration is perceived as successfully altering the military balance in favor of NATO and Japan, China is likely to move away from the United States back toward the Soviet Union once again. Thus perceived change in the relative Soviet/U.S. military relationship transformed the tight bipolar system into a system where balancing became possible, and, from the viewpoint of the threatened actors, even necessary.

Alliance Aggregation

Fourth in the series of factors critical to this discussion of state and system is the nature of alliance aggregation. Alliance aggregation is a factor somewhat independent of the foregoing factors in that, for example, alliances in the nineteenth century were comparatively small and transient while in the late twentieth century they have been much larger, more institutionalized, very asymmetric, and more durable. But a bipolar system could conceivably exist apart from the vast alliance aggregations around each of the poles. Presumably these aggregations resulted from the sense of threat that permeated the system as a whole. Variations in the degree of polarized tension between the Soviet Union and the United States have surely been a stimulus to alliance formation and disintegration. Dètente softened tensions despite different interpretations of its substance and probably had a greater impact on the politics of the alliance partners toward their respective alliance leader than on the Soviet Union or the United States toward each other.

Alliance aggregation and cohesion is one of the distinct ways in which the state becomes a functioning part of the system. Alliances are the web of which the system is composed. If power relationships provide the structure of the system and balance provides the operationally important element of process, then alliances are the visible synthesis of structure and process. When alliances are transformed, the impacts on the state and system are profound. In some ways alliances provide a more direct route to the understanding of political order within a particular system than do any of the other foregoing factors. In combination, (1) the number of actors in the central system, (2) the disparity of power between the central and peripheral system, (3) the extent of balancing activity, and (4) the nature of alliance aggregation shape the way the state interacts with the system and vice versa. Without alliances, balance, for example, would be limited to the state's internal mobilization and demobilization of resources, and the system itself would lose some of its interpretive value for international politics.

THE STATE POWER CYCLE AND THE SYSTEM

How then does the prior discussion of the system's characteristics add to our understanding of the manner in which the system reflects the existence of the power cycle at the state level? Expressed differently, in the dynamic sense, is the international system able to manifest a cycle of its own that is in some way related to the power cycle that the leading actors in the system themselves undergo? What fundamentally is the relationship over long time periods between the leading actors and the character of the international system itself?

These questions are more adequately answered in the context of an explicit examination of the four systemic factors already discussed. In a system in which the following conditions prevail, the cycle of state power for the leading actors is likely to be traced in the evolutionary pattern of the international system itself.

(1) Two or at most three states (one has never done so alone) compose the central system.
(2) The absolute and relative disparity of power between these states and the rest of the system is great; i.e., one or more of the large actors is at or near the top of its power cycle.

(3) The presence of balance does not exist to confound the initiatives exerted among the leading actors of the system. Countervailing pressures are minimal.
(4) Alliance aggregation is very substantial, reinforcing the security postures and responses to perceived threat of the leading actors.

Under these very specific circumstances, which are not likely to occur very frequently in the modern state system, the congruence of the state cycle for one or more of the leading actors and the evolution of the international system itself may be quite close. This means that the image the state has of itself is reflected in the system in terms of the conflicts fought, the agenda of negotiation undertaken, the rules of trade and finance applied, and the principal lines of communication established. As the leading actor or actors approach their zenith of power in the system, the system itself reflects the preoccupations and perspectives of the state or states.

Whether the system itself corresponds to an imperial system or a system composed of rival imperialisms very much depends upon how much (and what kind of) control the analyst would consider necessary for such designation. The activity of major states at the peak of their influence in the postcolonial phase may be more accurately described as imperialistic rather than imperialist. The degree of control exerted is always marginal in situations in which the stakes are high for all participants and in which leadership comes in the form of suasion or the threat to withdraw support rather than from the use of coercion. In spite of the Marxist interpretation, at the global level the degree of class stratification and cohesion within the international system is questionable. The divisive stress of nationalism is a stronger force. Moreover, the capacity of the leadership to sustain order in any interval is modest, in part because of rivalry at the top and because of an incommensurability between strong valued ends and the means to carry them out.

In the nuclear age this contrast between ends and means is made even more pronounced through the limits imposed on statecraft by the nuclear stalemate. The capacity of the superpowers to coerce other, including nonnuclear, states into politics that the latter regard unfavorably is extremely circumscribed even in instances in which second-strike capability does not exist on both sides. The Soviet Union is able to employ a heavy hand in the surrounding regions on its borders including most of Eastern Europe largely through access to overwhelming conventional military strength and internal manipulation of party elites. The United States exerts some influence through the international financial community based in New York and through tax and other leverage over the activities of a number of multinational corporations. But in a pluralistic society the interest of General Motors is often not the interest of the United States (and vice versa). Moreover, as the debacle over sales of pipeline equipment to the Soviet Union points up, the capacity of any goverment in the present international system to use economic sanctions unilaterally is approximately nil, especially if one weighs the opportunity costs in terms of relations with allies. All of this does not suggest that military force at the conventional and subconventional levels has lost utility as some analysts seem to believe. But the capacity to exert much leadership or to give much direction to world events from the top, even in a tight bipolar system, is subject to exaggeration.

Nonetheless, in a tight bipolar system such as that of the ancient Greek city-states, or of the system of the 1950s more than in any other type, the framework of order itself is vulnerable to the tremors set off by the two principal actors. It follows that when either or both of these states is subject to particular stress during passage along the cycle of relative capability, the entire system will experience this stress. At the critical points on the power curves of these actors, especially in terms of two or more states at such critical points, the likelihood of overreaction and misperception is substantial, and this likelihood will be directly transmitted to the system as a whole.

WHAT THE STATE/SYSTEM RELATIONSHIP IS NOT

(1) It is not cyclical movement at the level of the system independent of the nation-state. The principal source of action in the modern system is the nation-state, not supranational forces such as markets, regions, or organizations that transcend the individual units and not subnational entities or collectivities such as firms or communal movements. Cyclical variation, if it is to be correctly identified and specified, is reflected in the *behavior of nation-states relative to each other,* not in some abstract sense within the larger systemic context cut off from the primary individual units that underlie the system and are its driving mechanism. This means that, as far as international politics is concerned, so-called Kondratieff cycles located in the process of technological innovation, or in some complex way within the economic business cycle, are at the same time too broad and too narrow (Modelski, 1978). They are too broad because they are diffuse and fail to speak directly to political decision making. They are too narrow because they are restricted to economic or technical components that encompass only a small part of the state action and therefore of systemic behavior. Even if Kondratieff cycles could be identified with some precision, assuming agreement regarding their content and

measurement, such cycles avoid contact with the "politics" of international politics and therefore remain more a curiosity than an explanatory process.

(2) It is not domination by single nation-states. Just as power at the top of the system is shared today between the United States and the Soviet Union, and just as the degree of control exerted by either of these states regarding global matters is probably marginal, offset by competition, and vitiated by state action elswhere in the system, so power within the central system historically has always been shared and very partial. Britain in the eighteenth and nineteenth centuries, for example, was the primary naval and maritime state but scarcely the arbiter of the international trading and commercial system, where there were many partners and competitors. Also, Britain was not a preponderant military force since the armies on the continent were far more significant, and its stewardship of the balance of power was no more an evident success than were the efforts of Metternich prior to 1848. While writers often correctly point out that Britain found free trade arrangements to be in its own interest after the repeal of the Corn Laws (1846), these arrangements were also found to be in the interest of other trading partners, especially the most dynamic, and for this reason the free trade ideal tended to perpetuate itself although often very much compromised in form and effect. Indeed, liberal economists, at least since Marshall, have demonstrated that it is the small and isolated economies that have benefited most from the growth of a freer trading order, not the large and established economies, because the smaller economies had problems obtaining access to an adequate variety of goods, services, and factor inputs at a competitive cost when produced solely at home. Even an apparently very dependent economy such as that of British North America (Canada) found ways of profiting from freer trade after the collapse of preferential trading relationships under mercantilism. Hence the notion that, at any time since the origin of the modern state system, the system itself, either in economic or political terms, was under the primary domination of single states simply does not correspond to plausible inquiry. Power within the system has always been a matter of degree. Mid-twentieth-century interdependence has not eroded this principle but reinforced it. Indeed, increases or declines in either the rate or level of relative power are probably as important as absolute amounts are.

(3) It is not structure defined in single-variable terms. While in exploring the relationship between state and system the analyst cannot afford to overlook the critical role of military variables, national capability is a far more complex concept than this, especially when

examined over long temporal periods. Gross national product or a surrogate is, for example, at least as important in the long run as military size, because GNP provides the base from which to support military spending. But GNP does not alone index national capability, as the current difference in the power position of Japan and the Soviet Union attests (Organski and Kugler, 1980). Likewise, high per capita income is central to national capability if it is able to provide through investment or external purchase the kind of technology that supports rapid growth of capability.

To those critics who argue that such a complex of variables is the equivalent of adding apples and oranges, the answer is in the affirmative. But apples and oranges together make fruit. Military spending, population and territorial size, GNP, and high per capita income, all combine and create national capability (Singer et al., 1972). It is national capability in turn that underlies the structure of the international system. Because the analyst has a hard time measuring such a composite variable is no reason to doubt the significance of national capability as a concept. The shortcomings are in the operationalization and the data collection, not in the conceptualization.

In addition, the analyst of state/system relations must be especially careful not to select one type of variable such as naval development or spending and make it representative of overall military capability or perhaps even national capability as a whole. The problem here is that specialization within the international system occurs with some countries focusing upon one kind of military spending and other countries on others. It is well known, for example, that the continental states concentrated on their land armies in the late eighteenth century, while Britain and the other island states built navies. By selecting one type of military spending over others, conclusions about power and control can become very misleading. Indeed, one could argue that historically it has been the inability of maritime states to man and supply large armies that has driven them to exploit their comparative advantage on the sea, in the air, or in space. A country that is able to produce a higher level of several types of defense is undoubtedly likely to produce more security for itself and its allies, assuming other factors in the security equation equal.

If these considerations involve some of the items that state/system relations are not, let us now turn to events and structural situations in which the interaction has been quite close between state and system.

HEGEMONIC WAR: A TRAUMATIC LINKAGE BETWEEN POWER CYCLE AND SYSTEM

At no other time is the linkage between the power cycle and the international system so clear, or so painful, as during hegemonic war.

Hegemonic war is associated with the efforts of a single state to dominate the international system and is the most earnest challenge facing the system. On five occasions since the origins of the modern state system, single governments have sought to dominate the central system and large areas of the periphery by force. Each time the attempt has failed. But the cost of the participants of this form of extensive war has been very high.

Each of the five expansionist efforts is very clearly traced by the incidence of extensive war: (1) the Spanish-Austrian Habsburg attempt to dominate Europe, (2) Louis XIV's, (3) the Napoleonic onslaught, (4) World War I, and (5) World War II. Moreover, in the cases of the last two pairs of massive wars, a single state was involved in both, France in the former case and Germany in the latter. Although carefully collected data on war and war initiation have only been assembled for the nineteenth and twentieth centuries, a pattern of the relationship between state and system in terms of the power cycle and hegemonic war is evident as far back as the seventeenth century. Somewhere after France has passed the first inflection point of its historic rise to power, Louis XIV sought European dominance through expansion. Somewhere beyond the point of downturn (upper turning point) on the French cycle of relative capability, Napoleon launched his attack on the other principal actors in the system, including Russia. Therefore, awareness on the part of France that the rapid rise in French capability relative to rivals at the beginning of the seventeenth century was at an end and that a decline in the *rate* of relative power growth had commenced was a critical source of expansionist anxiety under Louis XIV. Napoleon, in turn, responded to an absolute downturn in French relative power in the aftermath of British industrial development and increasing naval and maritime capability. Each of these expansionist attempts followed a critical reorientation in the French foreign policy outlook.

Similarly, Germany entered upon an expansionist course following critical reorientations of foreign policy outlook and role status that were forced upon it by the dynamics of the power cycle. Germany's entry into World War I occurred on the heels of awareness that Germany's capability relative to that of the rising powers on the outskirts of the system had begun to ebb, both in terms of level and in terms of rate. Hitler expressed openly and directly to the German people in 1939 that if they failed to take this opportunity to expand across Europe, Germany would never again have such an opportunity since German power had already passed well beyond its zenith; the downturn of relative German power had begun. To a government and society less bent on a world role, such a downturn might have been taken in stride. But for a government committed to the largest possible impact on the international system, the downturn in German relative capability was ominous.

The important observation to make about this hegemonic activity is that it wedded the behavior of state and system as did no other event. Indeed, the birth of new systems (or, interpreted differently, a single evolutionary international system) emerged out of the cataclysms of hegemonic war. In none of these instances did the system succumb to the coercive strategy of these large, powerful actors. In each case a coalition of states formed in opposition to the hegemon and militarily defeated it and its allies. But the consequence for the system was that a virtual discontinuity was created in international politics by the hegemonic event. The state and the system became one in an attempt to defeat a single, large expansionist state by a collective effort that encompassed all of the members of the central system and many of the members outside. The unity of state and system came not out of domination, as the hegemon anticipated, but out of resistance to that domination by the remaining members of the system. The unity was one of action, not structure. As soon as this climactic event passed, so passed the sense of unity that had briefly characterized the relationship between state and system.

Long-term changes in the structure of the system were wrought by the power of single countries. The power of single countries was in turn shaped by the dynamic of the overall international system. One canot say that changes on the power cycle were alone responsible for the breakdown of the system, or that the system failed to contain the aggressive activities of individual states experiencing sudden stress in their historical evolution. What one can say is that the processes of order maintenance within the international system were insufficient to prevent an attack on the system by a member undergoing severe role pressure and political stress. The system, however, was strong enough in each case to resist forceful subjugation by a centralized power core.

Perhaps the relationship between the state and system in a hegemonic interval can best be expressed in existential terms. This is the interval when the system is put to its ultimate test. Afterward the system is likely to change in character. But from the state perspective this change at the systems level has already been long in process. It was fore-ordained in the dynamic of the power cycle of the major states. The event of hegemonic war was the result of the inability of head of states to understand the direction of the dynamic and to accept its implications. Such an event also signifies the inability of heads of states, faced with the prospect of hegemonic war, to coordinate their actions with an adequate mix of determination and flexibility to deter aggression *before* the shooting starts.

STATE/SYSTEM INTERFACE: BALANCE WITHIN THE CENTRAL SYSTEM, MOBILITY ALONG THE STATE/POWER CYCLE

State and system interact ultimately in two ways that shape the evolution of the international system across long time periods. For ease of reference we can think of these two most important interactions in terms of two intersecting planes, one horizontal, the other vertical. The horizontal plane is that of balance. As in the system known as the balance of power, this type of interaction is rather static in that the players are known and constant and the rules do not change. The object, where balance is possible, is to offset potential aggression by shifts of weight in the system against the expansionist state. Coalition diplomacy results. Dissociation is as important as association. Subtlety of initiative, and good intelligence about rival capabilities and intentions, remains key. The system stays in equilibrium because the players understand the importance of both pluralism and self-preservation. The system remains at peace when the credibility of balance is not destroyed by players that are either too responsive, and therefore threatening to a potential hegemon that is really a declining state in disguise, or not responsive enough, thus inviting imprudent risk taking by the similarly poorly adjusted actor. But changes on the other plane of interaction can set all of these calculations awry.

The vertical plane is composed of the movement of the major states along their respective power cycles. By its essence this plane of interaction is intensely dynamic both in terms of the numbers of states involved and in terms of the consequences for systems structure. Upward and downward mobility of major states is slow but incessant. It is also intensely upsetting to the patterns of interaction involving balance on the other plane. Movement along the power cycle introduces new actors to the central system and removes other actors. Intent upon the preservation of equilibrium among themselves in terms of rather short-term considerations, the predominant actors in the system find adjustment to new roles, status, and responsibility within the system extremely difficult. One of the consequences of this inability to cope with the dynamism of the horizontal plane is that there is sometimes an effort to bolster artificially the position of a state substantially in decline (e.g., the nineteenth-century Ottoman or pre-World War I Austria-Hungary), or to exclude from participation a state in ascendancy, because the rules of balance do not allow for such fundamental changes of structure and participation.

Hence, in viewing the relationship between state and system in ultimate terms, the analyst must recognize the difficulty heads of states experience in bringing the two planes of interaction together. Movement along the state power cycle is no less fundamental for the stability of the system than alterations of balance. But upward and downward state mobility on the power cycle has received much less scholarly attention than coalition diplomacy and power balancing. It is time that these two planes of political interaction, linking state and system, be studied together at their interface.

REFERENCES

BUENO de MESQUITA, B. (1981) The War Trap. New Haven, CT: Yale University Press.

DEHIO, L. (1965) The Precarious Balance: Four Centuries of the European Power Struggle. New York: Vintage.

DORAN, C. F. (1971) The Politics of Assimilation: Hegemony and its Aftermath. Baltimore: Johns Hopkins University Press.

———K. Q. HILL and K. MLADENKA (1979) "Threat, status disequilibrium, and national power." British Journal of International Studies 5: 37-58.

DORAN, C. F. and W. PARSONS (1980) "War and the cycle of relative power." American Political Science Review 74 (December): 947-965.

KUZNETS, S. (1966) Modern Economic Growth. New Haven, CT: Yale University Press.

MODELSKI, G. (1978) "The long cycle of global politics and the nation state." Comparative Studies in Society and History 20 (April): 214-235.

ORGANSKI, K. and J. KUGLER (1980) The War Ledger. Chicago: University of Chicago Press.

ROSECRANCE, R. (1982) "Response to Waltz." International Organization 36 (Summer): 682-685.

ROSTOW, W. W. (1978) The World Economy: History and Prospect. Austin: University of Texas Press.

SINGER, J. D., S. BREMER, and J. STUCKEY (1972) "Capability distributions, uncertainty, and major power war, 1820-1965," in B. Russett (ed.) Peace, War and Numbers. Beverly Hills, CA: Sage.

WALTZ, K. (1979) Theory of International Politics. Reading, MA: Addison-Wesley.

8

World System Analysis

A Great Power Framework

JACK S. LEVY

The study of world politics has long been dominated by the realist paradigm and its focus on the European great powers, military security, and the balance of power. This paradigm has recently come under attack on a number of grounds (Keohane and Nye, 1977; Mansbach and Vasquez, 1981). Many of these critics concede that political realism may have provided an accurate picture of international relations in earlier historical eras but argue that it is no longer relevant in the contemporary era after a revolutionary transformation of the international system. A more profound challenge to the realist paradigm is posed by the world system paradigms. These suggest that world politics in the last five centuries has never corresponded to the assumptions of the realist paradigm and has never been primarily concerned with realpolitik and the European balance of power.

After briefly summarizing some of the key assumptions of the world system paradigms and the "great power" framework of the realist paradigm, I will show that they lead to some conflicting hypotheses about the nature of international politics. One key point of contention is the definition and identification of the key actors. A major aim of this chapter is to refine the great power concept and to identify the membership of the great power system over the last five centuries, in order to facilitate future efforts to test these conflicting hypotheses against the historical evidence.

AUTHOR'S NOTE: I would like to thank Harrison Wagner, Cliff Morgan, and Jon Christopherson for their comments and criticisms on earlier drafts of this chapter.

THE COMPETING PARADIGMS

Wallerstein's Capitalist World-Economy

Wallerstein (1974, 1978), Chase-Dunn (1979, 1981), and others conceptualize a single capitalist world-economy defined in terms of the division of labor across cultural systems in a multistate system. This world-economy is dominated by economic processes and hegemonic core powers defined in terms of the division of labor rather than military power. The world-economy paradigm assumes that the most significant social, economic, and political phenomena in the modern world can best be understood in terms of the processes of capital accumulation and class formation in the context of a hierarchical core-periphery division of labor (Chase-Dunn, 1979: 602-604).

There is no autonomous international political system in Wallerstein's paradigm. Instead, all processes are conceptualized in terms of a single integrated system characterized by the reciprocal interaction of economic and political processes, although it is clearly the economic that dominate. Conflicts among core states in the system are generated by attempts to monopolize trade with particular peripheral areas and by the expansion of the periphery (Chase-Dunn, 1979: 609). World wars, the rise and fall of hegemonic core powers, and hence political reorganization derive ultimately from contradictions in the capital accumulation process and are conceptualized as the "violent reorganization of production relations on a world scale" (Chase-Dunn, 1981: 23).

The world-economy emerged five centuries ago and has been dominated since 1600 by the Netherlands, Britain, and the United States in the role of core powers. The hegemony of these powers has been challenged by second runners (the Hapsburgs in the long sixteenth century, France under Louis XIV and Napoleon, and Germany in the twentieth century). These challengers have failed primarily because of the pressures of uneven development in the world economy and the failure to supplement a politico-military strategy with a concern for control of the world market (Chase-Dunn, 1981: 36-40).

Wallerstein's world-economy paradigm constitutes a comprehensive and general theory directed toward a wide range of theoretical questions. These include social change and modernization; the transformation and evolution of the world system; the development of capitalism, industrialism, and the nation-state; the accumulation and distribution of wealth and rise of imperialism and dependency; and conflicts among the leading political entities.

Modelski's Global Politics Framework

Modelski (1978) and Thompson (1980) also posit a world system emerging in 1500 but reject the assumption that it is dominated by economic processes. Instead, there are autonomous global political processes at least equal in significance to the economic. The global polity is conceptualized as a system of exchange in which the primary goods are order and security, territorial rights, and the stability of the global economy. The system is dominated by a single "world power" on the basis of its monopoly of military power of global reach and control of world trade. The world power is also the leading economy and provides the political basis for the global economy.

The system is a dynamic one characterized by a "long cycle" of world leadership and order, with a new world power arising every century as a result of global wars. These wars are basically caused by the struggle for control of the global system. Continental challengers fail because they lack the wealth to augment the military power provided by their land armies. The world powers dominating the five cycles of the modern world system have been Portugal, the Netherlands, Britain for the eighteenth and nineteenth centuries, and the United States. Long-cycle theory attempts to provide a general explanation for the most basic global processes, including order, stability, the accumulation of wealth and power, hegemony, systemic transformation, and the causes of global wars.[1]

The Great Power Framework

The realist paradigm posits a set of assumptions consistent with a diversity of specific theoretical approaches ranging from Thucydides to Morgenthau, Schelling, and Singer. Many of these approaches cannot be compared directly to the propositions of world system theory, in that they do not deal with the same theoretical questions or attempt to explain the same empirical phenomena. It is possible, however, to construct a "great power system" with a distinct set of assumptions and propositions that can be compared with those of the capitalist world-economy or global politics frameworks.

The great powers have long been distinguished from other states and viewed as the dominant actors in international politics, by heads of states and scholars and in international law. Ranke (1833), for example, conceived of the international history of Europe as a history of great power relations, and Taylor (1954: xix) argues that "the relations of the Great Powers have determined the history of Europe." Waltz (1979: 72) concludes that "the theory, like the story, of international politics is written in terms of the Great Powers of an era."

In spite of the importance of the great powers in the traditional literature, the great power concept has never been adequately refined for systematic empirical research. There have been several thorough analytical treatments (Ranke, 1833; Modelski, 1972; Rothstein, 1968; Bull, 1977) and a number of attempts to determine the identity of the powers in historical systems (Modelski, 1974; Haas, 1968; Singer and Small, 1972; Wright, 1965). The problem is that the latter are generally unrelated to the former; attempts to identify the powers historically are conducted in the absence of any nominal or operational definition of the great power concept.[2] This raises serious questions about the validity of these systems of powers and their utility for systematic empirical research. In addition, there have been few attempts to specify the theoretical assumptions underlying the concept of a great power system or the testable propositions they generate. Let us briefly identify these assumptions and contrast their propositions with those of the world-system paradigms.

The great power framework shares the basic assumptions of the realist paradigm of international politics but focuses explicitly on the small number of leading actors in the system.[3] It is assumed that in any anarchic international system there exists a hierarchy of actors defined in terms of power. In the modern system since 1500 the dominant actors are territorial states. It is the more powerful states, the great powers, that determine the structure, major processes, and general evolution of the system.[4] It is, therefore, the actions and interactions of the great powers that are of greatest interest. Secondary states and other actors have an impact on the system largely to the extent that they affect the behavior of the great powers. This hierarchy of actors is intimately related to a hierarchy of issues dominated by military security. It is assumed that issues overlap and that the currency of military power is applicable to and effective in the resolution of other issues (Keohane and Nye, 1977). Hence the great power framework assumes that world politics is dominated by the struggle for power (Morgenthau, 1967).

The priority of military security derives from the perception of a high-threat environment, which in turn derives primarily from the anarchic structure of the international system (Rousseau, 1755; Waltz, 1954, 1979; Wolfers, 1962; Jervis, 1976: 62-76).[5] In this context, it is the great powers, because of their military capability and ability to project it, who can inflict the greatest deprivation of values and who are perceived as the most serious security threats. Consequently, the powers direct their primary attention toward each other and constitute an interdependent *system* of power and security relations, which will be called the great power system. Because they recognize the interdependence of security relations, the great powers play a major role in system management and order maintenance (Modelski, 1972, 1974; Bull, 1977). They participate with disproportionate frequency in the major international wars (Wright, 1965) and largely determine the outcome of the peace settlements that follow (Modelski, 1972: 152; Doran, 1971). In this way the great powers play the major role in the transformation of the international system and the structuring of international order.[6]

CONFLICTING HYPOTHESES

The paradigms under consideration generate hypotheses that differ in terms of the relationship between international political and economic systems, the specific identity of the key actors in past historical systems, the nature and scope of their interests, the definition and historical existence of hegemony, and the identify of general wars and their causes. These differences shall be briefly summarized but cannot be fully analyzed or empirically tested at this time.

Whereas the capitalist world-system theory of Wallerstein and Chase-Dunn rejects the existence of autonomous political processes and effectively asserts the primacy of economic processes, the great power perspective insists upon the primacy of politics and security. ✓ This manifests itself in two ways. First, it is hypothesized that the structure of the international economic system is largely determined by the structure of the international political system. It is argued, for example, that mercantilism, the international market economics of the nineteenth and twentieth centuries, the separate Soviet-bloc economic system today, and the very emergence of a world economy were all dependent upon particular configurations of international military and political power (Gilpin, 1977, 1981; Spero, 1977: 4-8). A second manifestation of the primacy of politics over economics is the priority given to security interests by the great powers themselves. While power and wealth are mutually reinforcing (Gilpin, 1981), they do come into conflict, particularly in the short run. It is hypothesized that whenever this conflict occurs it is power that takes precedence over wealth. Similarly, national political or economic interests always take precedence over private economic interests (Viner, 1948; Staley, 1935; Krasner, 1978; Blasier, 1976; Russett and Hanson, 1975). The world system theories reject these hypotheses and their underlying assumptions. Modelski and Thompson give greater emphasis to the mutual reinforcement between power and wealth, while Wallerstein and Chase-Dunn emphasize the dominant role of capitalist accumulation in its reciprocal interaction with the interstate system.

One of the primary differences between the paradigms lies in their conception of the geographical scope of the system. Because of the primacy of security interests, the fact that the primary security threats come from other great powers, and the fact that prior to the twentieth century basically all the great powers were European, the great power system was Eurocentric in a very fundamental way.[7] European security interests have always taken precedence over global political or economic interests.[8] The globally oriented world system theories explicitly reject these propositions.

The paradigms also differ in their conceptualizations of hegemony. The world system perspectives suggest that there always exists a single hegemonic power that dominates the system. Modelski and Thompson (1980) identify a succession of world powers based on their monopoly of naval strength: Portugal in the sixteenth century, the Netherlands in the seventeenth century, Britain for the next two centuries, and the United States in the twentieth century. Wallerstein and Chase-Dunn define a "hegemonic core power" in terms of the division of labor and capital accumulation and generate an identical set of hegemons beginning in the seventeenth century. The great power framework, on the other hand, defines hegemony as the dominance of Europe by a single great power in the absence of effective opposition. Hegemony is historically rare, however, because the balance-of-power system generally works fairly well in its primary functions—to prevent hegemony and maintain the independence of the powers and the integrity of the system (Gulick, 1955: 30-35; Blainey, 1973: 111-112; Morgenthau, 1967). The great power system is generally characterized by pluralism rather than by a concentration of power. Hegemony over the modern great power system has been achieved only for a short period by Napoleonic France, Louis XIV, and perhaps Philip II.

The paradigms also differ in terms of their identification of and causal explanation for the system's major wars. Modelski (1978) defines global wars as "conflicts that determine the constitution of the global political system" and traces their causes to the struggle for hegemony over the system. He identifies the following global wars: the Italian Wars (1494-1517), the War of Dutch Independence (1579-1609), the French wars of 1688-1713 and 1792-1815, and the German Wars of 1914-1918 and 1939-1945 (Modelski, 1978: 225). Chase-Dunn (1979: 609) argues that "competition and conflict among core states is causally related to attempts by individual core states to monopolize trade with particular peripheral areas and by the expansion of the periphery to new populations and areas."

The great power framework, on the other hand, identifies a different set of "general wars," defined in terms of their characteristics rather than their functional consequences for the system. These are the wars that involve nearly all the powers in intense conflict (Wright, 1965: 647-650; Blainey, 1973: 196).[9] These include the Thirty Years War (1618-1648), the Dutch War of Louis XIV (1672-1678), the War of the League of Augsburg (1688-1697), the War of the Spanish Succession (1701-1713), the War of Jenkin's Ear and the Austrian Succession (1739-1748), the Seven Years War (1755-1763), the French Revolutionary and Napoleonic Wars (1792-1815), World War I (1914-1918), and World War II (1939-1945). Unlike the world system theories, the great power framework does not advance a single theory of the causes of general war, but it does advance some restricted hypotheses. The political or military expansion of any state, to the extent that it threatens to overturn the status quo and establish its own hegemony, will always generate a broad military coalition to block that expansion and restore an equilibrium. This, of course, is the central principle of balance-of-power theory. Attempts at hegemony, therefore, are sufficient conditions for general war.[10] A related hypothesis is that economic causes of war are generally of secondary importance. A more complete theory of the causes of war requires further conceptualization and ultimately empirical confirmation.

While the three different frameworks are designed to answer different kinds of questions, they do generate some hypotheses that are mutually contradictory and that are therefore amenable to empirical test. Any tests are quite dependent, however, on the precise identification of the great power system and its membership, questions to which I now turn.

DEFINITION OF THE GREAT POWER CONCEPT

As noted earlier, the widespread recognition of the importance of the great powers is not matched by analytical precision in the use of the concept. Either no attempt at definition is undertaken or no effort is made to translate vague nominal definitions into meaningful operational criteria. This is true of modern social scientists as well as traditional theorists. Singer and Small, for example, simply resort to "intercoder agreement" as the sole criterion for the identification of their major power system (1972: 23). Rothstein (1968: 14) suggests that the primary reason for this absence of definitional precision may be traced to the fairly widespread belief that the distinction between great powers and other states is self-evident, particularly for the eighteenth and nineteenth centuries, where the indicators of military power are said to be rather unambiguous. While it is true that for any historical period the identity of *some* of the great powers is self-evident, there are frequently one or two states whose status is rather uncertain (e.g., eighteenth-century Spain or nineteenth-century Italy). Consequently, the precise identity of all of the great powers has never been as self-evident as many scholars have led themselves to believe, even for the eighteenth and nineteenth centuries, as demonstrated by the numerous contradictions in the literature. In addition, there have been a number of historical developments in the last century that have further blurred this distinction between great powers and others. In fact, it is this very *difficulty* of defining the concept of great power and devising operational indicators valid over a range of diverse historical conditions that has inhibited many from such a systematic analysis.

Nearly all definitions of great powers focus primarily on military might. Taylor (1954: xxiv), for example, asserts that "the test of a Great Power is then the test of strength for war." Modelski (1972: 149) claims that a great power "must be capable of fighting a major war." Singer and Cusack (1981) insist that the most obvious attribute of a major power is the "ability to wage war frequently, and to win most of those wars." The classic definition from which many others are clearly derived was provided by Ranke (1833: 86): A great power "must be able to maintain itself against all others, even when they are united." It is not clear what Ranke meant by "maintain," but in any case this criterion of self-sufficiency would appear to be far too demanding. There have been few states in history who have possessed capabilities sufficient to defend against a combination of all other powers. Revisionist powers seeking hegemony have invariably been defeated by opposing coalitions. Ranke's definition would exclude too many states from great power rank, though perhaps it might serve as a useful definition of a more restricted class of superpowers.

Modifications of Ranke's general conception of self-sufficiency of the powers are provided by Haas, Bull, Rothstein, and Hoffman. For Haas (1970: 122), a major power "can be totally defeated in battle by no other single power, but instead by a combination of members (usually including another major power)." By not insisting that a great power be able to withstand a coalition of powers, Haas comes much closer to the conventional but unstated notion of what it means to be a great power. However, there are some problems. Haas fails to provide empirical indicators for his concepts, and it is far from clear how he arrives at his list of major powers in a succession of international subsystems since 1649. In addition, while the notion of avoiding total defeat may be useful conceptually as a minimum standard for great power rank, it does raise the operational questions of what constitutes total defeat and whether it is a necessary or sufficient condition for major power status.[11]

There are other definitions based on the general notion of self-sufficiency that are less restrictive than the notion of total defeat. Rothstein (1968: 24-29) argues that a great power is a state that can rely on its own capabilities to provide for its security. Small powers, on the other hand, must rely on external alliances, aid, or international institutions and, therefore, do not have direct or primary control over their own destinies. This definition is similar to one criterion suggested by Hoffmann (1965: 138): Great powers can provide for their security without significantly undermining their independence, whereas smaller states must often make a choice between security and independence. This definition allows for a more reasonable conception of security than avoidance of total defeat and can incorporate the concept of deterrence as well as defense. One weakness here, however, is that it tends to underestimate the security threats posed by other great powers and the interdependence of nearly all states with regard to security matters. Before the nuclear age, at least, we have only a few instances in which one state could be self-sufficient against a coalition of other states.

The persistent danger posed by great powers to each other is recognized by Bull's (1971: 27) conceptualization: "Great Powers have been secure against the attacks of small Powers; and have had to fear only other Great Powers, and hostile combinations of Powers." While this dimension of Bull's definition constitutes an improvement over those considered above, it does share a common limitation with them. By relying on the Rankian concept of self-sufficiency, these formulations conceive of great power interests in negative terms as passive security. They minimize the importance of the great powers' capabilities and willingness to project their military power beyond their borders in order to enhance their power and other interests and structure their environment. Self-sufficiency in security matters is a necessary but not sufficient condition for great power rank. The powers have always been concerned not only with minimizing their losses but also with maximizing their gains and are willing to take risks in order to do so.[12] A state that cannot be conquered but which lacks the capability to threaten others or influence security affairs in the system as a whole (e.g., seventeenth-century Russia and perhaps the United States in the nineteenth century) would not normally be considered a great power. This is recognized in several conceptualizations. Howard (1971: 254) states that "a great power, almost by definition, is one which has the capacity to control events beyond its own borders; and that is usually based on the ability to use military force." Taylor (1954: xxiv) asserts, with some hesitation, that "a Great Power is one that can contemplate war against any other Power confidently." Similarly, Wight (1946: 18) states that "a Great Power is one that can afford to take on any other Power whatever in single combat." Haas (1974: 330-331), in an alternative formulation to that expressed earlier, defines major powers as "elite or dominant members of a system whose behavior is capable of upsetting an existing power distribution or placing a power equilibrium in jeopardy."

Thus a great power must possess both relative self-sufficiency in terms of security, including invulnerability against secondary states, and also the ability to project military power beyond its border to influence events and shape its environment. However, it is not enough to define the great power concept. It must be operationalized if the powers are to be identified and their behavior analyzed. The few attempts to provide operational criteria for the identification of the powers generally rely on indicators of military capabilities alone. This is clearly the basis for the "self-evident" classification of eighteenth- and nineteenth-century states. As Rothstein notes (1968: 14), "counting the number of available infantrymen sufficed" to differentiate the great powers. A more general formulation is suggested by Modelski (1974: 2): a great power holds at least 5 percent of the available military power in the global system. While Modelski suggests this criterion for the great powers, he uses it in his later conceptualization of global powers in a global system (Modelski and Thompson, 1980). Attempts to measure naval capabilities of the leading global powers has been undertaken by Thompson (1980). This operationalization cannot be applied directly to the great powers as conceived here because global naval power is not congruent with power in the great power system, in which land armies carry much greater weight. There would be no difficulty, or course, in redefining the criterion for the Eurocentric great power system, though we would certainly want to ask whether the 5 percent criteria is optimum. Rather serious problems would remain, though.

There is, first of all, the problem of the relative weights of the different elements of military capabilities—land-based power versus naval power, personnel versus armaments, and so on. There is also the relative importance to be given to existing military capabilities compared to military potential (Knorr, 1970). In addition, there is the difficulty of devising a single set of operational indicators of state power capabilities that would be valid over the variety of political, economic, and technological conditions of the last few centuries. The actual measurement of these indicators would present serious methodological problems. Different indicators could be used for different historical periods, but it is not clear that any measures would be of sufficient validity to permit an interval-level measurement of power capabilities that this approach would require. On a more basic level, there is the question of the validity of excluding from a measure of military power certain nonmilitary factors of considerable importance. These would include administrative skill, which determines the efficiency with which given societal resources are utilized for military purposes; the political foundations of military power, which determine the extent to which resources are made available to the military sector;[13] diplomatic skill, which helps shape the situation in which military power may have to be exerted; and other factors ranging from military reputation or prestige to national morale, all highly impervious to quantitative measurement (Knorr, 1970). The most impressive attempt thus far to measure aggregate power capabilities—that of Singer and his colleagues for the nineteenth and twentieth centuries—recognizes these problems and provides ordinal-level rankings of the most powerful states rather than actual numerical levels and differences (Stukey and Singer, 1973). Quantitative measurements from earlier historical periods would present even greater problems of validity and accuracy.

We might dismiss these analytical and methodological problems if the use of objective indicators met the minimum test of face validity. There is good reason to believe that they do not. First of all, since the ability to prevail in war is the ultimate test of military power, we would expect states ranked higher in military capabilities to emerge victorious in any military confrontation. The Arab-Israeli wars are only the most obvious counterexamples. Second, and more important for our purposes, Singer's rank-orderings of power capabilities generated by objective indicators of military capabilities do deviate from conventional wisdoms regarding the great powers. The Correlates of War project uses six equally weighted indices of power capabilities: total population, urban population, iron and steel production, fuel consumption, military personnel, and military expenditures (Stuckey and Singer, 1973: 8). These indicators do appear to reflect adequately the important dimensions of existing military capabilities and both military and industrial potential, yet the resulting rank ordering of states would seem to contradict many conventional wisdoms concerning the identity of the great powers. In 1845, for example, both Turkey and the United States rank higher than Prussia on this scale, but most scholars (including Singer and Small) identify only Prussia as a great power during this period. In 1913 China outranks France, Austria-Hungary, Italy, and Japan, but it is the latter four that are generally considered to be great powers, and not China (Singer and Small, 1972:23).

Military power may be the primary defining characteristics of great powers but it alone is not sufficient and must be supplemented with other criteria. However, we should not expect to find a set of perfectly objective criteria that can be mechanically applied to any particular historical era in order to generate a system of great powers. The aim is to minimize rather than eliminate subjectivity by providing theoretical criteria that are operationally useful yet sufficiently flexible to guide our interpretation of a rich body of historical evidence in order to identify the great powers. The validity of these criteria can be tested in part by ensuring that the results do not deviate significantly from certain well-established conventional wisdoms (e.g., the set of powers must not exclude England, France, Austria, Prussia, and Russia for the eighteenth and nineteenth centuries).

A great power is conceptualized as a state that plays a major role in international politics with respect to security-related issues. They can be differentiated from other states in terms of their military power, their interests, their behavior in general and interactions with other powers in particular, their perception by other powers, and by some international legal criteria. First of all, a great power possesses a high level of military capabilities relative to other states. This includes, at a minimum, relative self-sufficiency in terms of military security. Great powers are basically invulnerable to military threats by nonpowers and need only fear other powers. In addition, great powers have the capability to project military power beyond their borders to conduct offensive as well as defensive military operations. They can actively come to the defense of allies, wage an aggressive war against other states (including most of the powers), and generally use force or the threat of force to help shape their external environment. A state that can defend itself only on the basis of a broad territorial expanse or natural barriers to invasion but which is unable to threaten the security of other states is not a great power.

Second, great powers are distinguished from other states in terms of their interests and objectives. They define their interests in continental or global terms rather than in local or regional terms. Their conception of security goes beyond territorial defense, or even extended defense. It includes maintenance of a continental or global balance of power and perhaps even the maintenance of a global environment conducive to their own values. Great powers generally define their national interests to include systemic interests and are therefore concerned with order maintenance in the international system (Modelski, 1972, 1974; Bull, 1977). Symbolic interests of national honor and prestige are also given high priority by the great powers, for these are perceived as being essential components of national power and necessary for great power status.

Third, the great powers are distinguished from other states in terms of their behavior. They defend their interests more aggressively and with a wider range of instrumentalities, including the frequent threat or use of military force. Their behavior is also characterized by a high level of interaction with other powers. It is the great powers who account for a disproportionate number of alliances and wars in the international system (often fought against each other), particularly those designed to maintain the "balance of power" and prevent the dominance of any single state. They are also involved in major territorial partitions and compensations (e.g., partition treaties involving Spain in the late seventeenth century and Poland in the late eighteenth century), guarantees (e.g., the Barrier Treaty guaranteeing the Utrecht settlement), and informal international organizations (e.g., the Concert of Europe).

Great powers are further differentiated from other states in terms of images and perceptions as well as capabilities, interests, and behavior. The powers are perceived as such by other powers and treated as relative equals in terms of general attention and respect, protocol, negotiations, alliance agreements, and the like. The fact that great powers are perceived as equals and treated as equals by other powers is one of the most important criteria of great power rank, for it is a clear indicator of their influence on international security issues.[14]

Finally, great powers are differentiated from others in terms of certain formal criteria. These include identification as a great power by an international conference, congress, organization, or treaty; or granting of certain distinct privileges by an international organizaiton or treaty, including permanent membership or veto power. It should be emphasized that these formal criteria are neither necessary nor sufficient for great power rank and are the least important of any of the characteristics of the powers. The great powers are important because of their military power and potential and the interests and behavior that flow from that power. Great power systems existed, after all, long before the institutionalization of the great power role at the Congress of Vienna and before the formal codification of international law at the Peace of Westphalia.

It should be emphasized that this definition of great power is based on the assumed dominance of security-related issues. While the security issue area is not entirely distinct from others and "linkages" across issue areas do exist, it is possible to make some distinctions. A major role in international trade or finance does not automatically entail great power status, for commercial or financial linkages to diplomatic, strategic, and military issues may be weak at times (e.g., the Netherlands was a commercial power but not a great power with respect to security issues in the eighteenth century). Nor is status as a colonial power sufficient to qualify as a great power. While colonies may contribute greatly to national wealth and power, in some cases there may be little relation between a state's colonial holdings and its role in the great power security system. (For example, Portugal was a leading colonial power in the sixteenth century but not a great power because it took no part in European security relations.)

THE MODERN GREAT POWER SYSTEM

As I have argued elsewhere, the origins of the modern great power system can be defined as 1495 with the formation of the League of Venice in response to the French invasion of Italy (Levy, forthcoming). Hence the temporal domain of the great power system corresponds with that of the world system conceptualizations. The leading actors are different, however. The operational criteria devised earlier can be used to guide an analytical historical study to determine the membership of the modern great power system since 1495. This involves some very difficult conceptual and methodological questions. A discussion of these problems, together with a detailed historical analysis of the point of entry into and departure from the system for each great power and justification for the exclusion of other key states, can be found elsewhere (Levy, forthcoming). The results of this analytical historical inquiry are presented in Table 8.1. It is hoped that the presentation of this system of modern great powers, together with the operational criteria by which it is generated, will contribute to a productive debate regarding the identity of the leading actors in international politics for the last five centuries.

TABLE 8.1   Composition of the Modern Great Power System

France	1495-1980
England/Great Britain	1495-1980
Austrian Hapsburgs/Austria/ Austria Hungary	1495-1519; 1556-1918
Spain	1495-1519; 1556-1808
Ottoman Empire	1495-1699
United Hapsburgs	1519-1556
The Netherlands	1609-1713
Sweden	1617-1721
Russia/Soviet Union	1721-1980
Prussia/Germany/West Germany	1740-1980
Italy	1861-1943
United States	1898-1980
Japan	1905-1945
China	1949-1980

SUMMARY

The great power framework focuses attention on the leading actors with respect to security issues in any anarchic political system. Our concern here has been with the modern great power system. This system originated in Europe at the end of the fifteenth century and only in the last century evolved into a truly global security system. The paradigm does not deny the existence of other systems operating simultaneously, nor does it claim that all international behavior can be understood in the context of the great power system. It does assert, however, that security issues are paramount, that they have generally been given priority by the great powers whenever they conflict with economic or other issues, and that peace and war among these powers can best be understood in the context of the great power security system rather than a world political economy.

The revolutionary transformation of the international system in the contemporary era does raise some serious questions regarding the utility of the great power framework (Keohane and Nye, 1977; Mansbach and Vasquez; 1981), and I am not prepared to argue at this time that the great power framework still provides the best conceptualization of international politics. However, each of the world system theories asserts that the contemporary system represents in its most fundamental respects a continuation of a world system that has persisted for five centuries, and that it is characterized by the same basic structures and processes. Because of this assumed continuity of a single system by world system theorists, the invalidation of their assumptions or propositions for an earlier era would call into question the description, explanation, and predictions they provide for the contemporary era. This comparison of the assumptions and propositions of each of the paradigms will therefore help clarify the scholarly debate about the past in order to better understand the present. The different frameworks not only attempt to answer a different set of questions but also provide rather distinct answers to some overlapping questions. These questions are empirical as well as theoretical in nature and can ultimately be resolved only by subjecting contending hypotheses to well-designed empirical tests.

NOTES

1. A similar theory of order, war, and system transformation has recently been constructed by Gilpin (1981). Gilpin also speaks of a global struggle for power and wealth between hegemonic core powers and challengers. This dynamic process is driven by differential rates of growth based on the law of uneven development and is resolved by hegemonic wars. The main difference is that Gilpin tentatively rejects the notion of any regular and periodic cycles driving the system (1981: 205).

2. The notable exceptions include Modelski (1972, 1974) and Haas (1968, 1970). However, in neither case is it clear how the empirical system is derived from the nominal or operational definition.

3. While most realist theories recognize the leading role of the great powers many realists would argue that the general principles guiding the behavior of all states are the same; it is only the parameters of the powerful configurations that are different. The great power framework attempts to identify a distinct set of testable hypotheses applicable to the actions and interactions of the great powers.

4. Waltz (1979: 72) makes the more general claim that in *any* self-help system, including economic systems of oligopolistic competition as well as anarchic political systems, the structure and processes of the system are determined by the interactions of the strongest units.

5. Some realists trace this high-threat environment to an aggressive human nature (Waltz, 1954: ch. 2). This is not very useful, however. If the human nature concept is conceived broadly the hypothesis is nonfalsifiable and the concept devoid of explanatory power. If conceived narrowly the human nature concept has a marginal casual impact and is unnecessary to a theory of conflict.

6. Conceptualizations of the realist paradigm generally include the assumption that states are not only the dominant actors but also unitary actors pursuing the national interest in the absence of internal controversy or constraints (Morgenthau, 1967; Keohane and Nye, 1977; Mansbach and Vasquez, 1981). That is, state decision makers define a consistent set of foreign policy goals and agree on the means by which these goals are to be achieved. This standard assumption is unnecessarily strong. The great power framework does recognize some overlap between foreign and domestic policy and the fact that internal constraints may have some impact on the selection, pursuit, and accomplishment of foreign policy objectives (Krasner, 1978). It allows,

therefore, some role for bureaucratic politics, misperceptions, public opinion, private interests, and other internal variables, but asserts that they may modify but do not dominate the pursuit of the national interest defined in terms of security. To the extent that internal variables affect the foreign policies of the great powers, they help shape the international system.

7. This does not deny that there may exist a multiplicity of international systems functioning independently of each other (Bozeman, 1960).

8. If this was not always true for Britain it was because Britain was virtually free of direct security threats from the continent by virtue of its insular position (Morgenthau, 1967: 340).

9. I have defined these operationally as wars involving over two-thirds of the great powers and an intensity exceeding 1000 battle deaths per million European population (Levy, forthcoming).

10. Most traditional balance-of-power theories suggest that essentially all major wars result from the struggle for power among the great powers. If the concept of the struggle for power is defined broadly this hypothesis is undoubtedly true but too general to provide much explanatory power. If the struggle for power is defined more narrowly, so that the hypothesis asserts that all major wars result from the struggle for *hegemony* in the Eurocentric great power system, this hypothesis is probably false. The author is currently engaged in a major project to test this hypothesis.

11. It would be too demanding to define total defeat only in terms of permanent extinction as a political entity, for this is relatively rare historically and would leave us with too many great powers. Yet relaxing the standard to include miitary occupation and temporary loss of sovereign independence as total defeat would also create problems. The German defeat and occupation of France in 1940 would presumably lead to the exclusion of France (for it regained its sovereignty only with the help of its allies), yet Haas includes Vichy France as a major power during this period. Nor would we want to eliminate France from great power status on the eve of World War II because it was capable of being totally defeated. This suggests that military occupation is not a sufficient condition for the loss of great power rank. In addition, the Ranke and Haas conceptualizations are particularly inappropriate in the nuclear age, where all states are vulnerable to the possibility of nearly total destruction.

12. Hoffmann (1965: 135) goes further and argues that "the *main* object of a larger power is to maximize gains (defined in a variety of ways) rather than to minimize risks" (my emphasis).

13. One ingenious effort to tap the political foundations of military power has been proposed by Organski and Kugler (1980). They use an index of tax effort to measure the ability and willingness of the government to extract resources from society.

14. There is some element of circularity involved in defining great powers in terms of their interaction with other powers and their perception by other powers, but this is very useful operationally. At any given time there always exist one or two states whose great power rank is unquestionable by virtue of their military strength. These states can be used as definitional anchors to help identify other great powers.

REFERENCES

BLAINEY, G. (1973) The Causes of War. New York: Free Press.
BLASIER, C. (1976) The Hovering Giant. Pittsburgh: University of Pittsburgh Press.
BOZEMAN, A. B. (1960) Politics and Culture in the International System. Princeton, NJ: Princeton University Press.
BULL, H. (1977) The Anarchical Society. New York: Columbia University Press.

————(1971) "Society and anarchy in international relations," pp. 21-28 in R. J. Art and R. Jervis (eds.) International Politics. Boston: Little, Brown.

CHASE-DUNN, C. (1981) "Interstate system and capitalist world-economy: one logic or two?" International Studies Quarterly 24 (March): 19-42.

————(1970) "Comparative research on world-system characteristics." International Studies Quarterly 23 (December): 601-623.

DORAN, C. F. (1971) The Politics of Assimilation. Baltimore: Johns Hopkins University Press.

GILPIN, R. (1981) War and Change in World Politics. New York: Cambridge University Press.

————(1977) "Economic interdependence and national security in historical perspective," in K. Knorr and F. Trager (eds.) Economic Issues and National Security. Lawrence, KA: Allen Press.

GULICK, E. V. (1955) Europe's Classical Balance of Power. New York: Norton.

HAAS, M. (1974) International Conflict. Indianapolis: Bobbs-Merrill.

————(1970) "International subsystems: stability and polarity." American Political Science Review 64 (March): 93-123.

————(1968) International Subsystems Data. Codebook. Ann Arbor: Inter-University Consortium for Political Research, International Relations Archive.

HOFFMANN, S. (1965) The State of War. New York: Praeger.

HOWARD, M. (1976) War in European History. Oxford: Oxford University Press.

————(1971) Studies in War and Peace. New York: Vintage.

JERVIS, R. (1976) Perception and Misperception in International Politics, Princeton, NJ: Princeton University Press.

KAPLAN, M. A. (1957) System and Process in International Politics. New York: John Wiley.

KEOHANE, R. O. and J. S. NYE (1977) Power and Interdependence. Boston: Little, Brown.

KNORR, K. (1970) Military Power and Potential. Lexington, MA: D. C. Heath.

KRASNER, S. D. (1978) Defending the National Interest. Princeton, NJ: Princeton University Press.

LEVY, J. S. (forthcoming) War in the Modern Great Power System, 1495-1975. Lexington: University Press of Kentucky.

MANSBACH, R. W. and J. A. VASQUEZ (1981) In Search of Theory. New York: Columbia University Press.

MODELSKI, G. (1978) "The long cycle of global politics and the nation-state." Comparative Studies in Society and History 20 (April): 214-235.

————(1974) World Power Concentrations: Typology, Data, Explanatory Framework. Morristown, NJ: General Learning Press.

————(1972) Principles of World Politics. New York: Free Press.

————and W. R. THOMPSON (1980) "Testing cobweb models of the long cycle of world leadership." (mimeo)

MORGENTHAU, H. J. (1967) Politics Among Nations. New York: Alfred A. Knopf.

ORGANSKI, A.F.K. and J. KUGLER (1980) The War Ledger. Chicago: University of Chicago Press.

RANKE, L. V. (1833) "The great powers," in The Theory and Practice of History. Indianapolis: Bobbs-Merrill, 1973.

ROSECRANCE, R. N. (1963) Action and Reaction in World Politics. Boston: Little, Brown.

ROSENAU, J. N. (1967) "Foreign policy as an issue-area," in J. N. Rosenau (ed.) Domestic Sources of Foreign Policy. New York: Free Press.

ROTHSTEIN, R. L. (1968) Alliances and Small Powers. New York: Columbia University Press.

ROUSSEAU, J. J. (1950) [1755] Discourse on the Origin and Foundation of Inequality among Men. In Social Contract and Discourses (G.D.H. Cole, trans.). New York: E. P. Dutton.

RUSSETT, B. M. and E. C. HANSON (1975) Interest and Ideology. San Francisco: Freeman.

SPERO, J. E. (1977) The Politics of International Economic Relations. New York: St. Martins.

SINGER, J. D. and T. CUSACK (1981) "Periodicity, inexorability, and steermanship in international war," in R. Merritt and B. Russett (eds.) From National Development to Global Community. London: Allen & Unwin.

SINGER, J. D. and M. SMALL (1972) The Wages of War, 1816-1965. New York: John Wiley.

STALEY, E. (1935) War and the Private Investor. New York: Doubleday.

STUCKEY, J. and J. D. SINGER (1973) "The powerful and the warprone: ranking the nations by relative capability and war experience, 1820-1964." University of Michigan. (mimeo)

TAYLOR, A.J.P. (1954) The Struggle for Mastery in Europe, 1848-1918. Oxford: Oxford University Press.

THOMPSON, W. R. (1980) "Seapower in global politics, 1500-1945: problems of data collection and analysis." Paper delivered at the Annual Meeting of the International Studies Association/West, Los Angeles.

TOYNBEE, A. J. (1954) A Study of History, Vol. IX. New York: Oxford University Press.

VINER, J. (1948) "Power versus plenty as objectives of foreign policy in the seventeenth and eighteenth centuries." World Politics 1 (October): 1-29.

WALLERSTEIN, I. (1978) "World-system analysis: theoretical and interpretive issues," in B. Kaplan (ed.) Social Change in the Capitalist World Economy. Beverly Hills, CA: Sage.

———(1974) The Modern World-System. New York: Academic.

WALTZ, K. N. (1979) Theory of International Politics. Reading, MA: Addison-Wesley.

———(1954) Man, the State, and War. New York: Columbia University Press.

WIGHT, M. (1946) Power Politics. London: Royal Institute of International Affairs.

WOLFERS, A. (1962) Discord and Collaboration. Baltimore: Johns Hopkins University Press.

WRIGHT, A. (1965) The Causes of War. Chicago: University of Chicago Press.

9

World Order Studies and the World System

RICHARD FALK
SAMUEL S. KIM

Recent macrostructural studies of the world system have been premised on a dialectical framework of challenge and response. Characteristically, the challenge presupposes the organizational vulnerability of the present system, its inability to prevent economic and ecological deterioration as well as a drift to general war. It also presupposes the system's normative incoherence, in particular the ideological and cultural fragmentation that militates against a more cooperative and humane approach to global problems. The response, then, envisions prospects for enhanced coherence and legitimacy based on the realization of shared values. It is this perception of challenge to the present system and the need for an alternative response that lies at the core of the contemporary challenge to supplant traditional international relations with one or more variants of world order studies. Although interactions among leading states remain important ingredients of a world order approach, explicating the workings of statism is no longer the primary intellectual task.

The World Order Models Project (WOMP) is part of this academic landscape. WOMP represents an ongoing attempt by a transnational group of scholars to depict the world system as beset by interrelated problems that call for value-realizing solutions. Since its first meeting in New Delhi in 1968, WOMP has held one or more meetings each year, and has produced a steady stream of publications.[1] WOMP has been identified from its conception with the Institute for World Order, an educational foundation located in New York City. Despite the insistence of some critics, WOMP has never been associated with the advocacy of world goverment or world federalism. In fact, its main writings have been skeptical or even opposed to plans for political centralism, although they have been largely preoccupied with alternative (that is, non-Machiavellian) patterns of governance on a global scale.[2] In recent years, WOMP has deemphasized somewhat this conventional agenda of global reform and has focused more on the going dynamics of politics at the state and substate levels. Such a recentering of inquiry reflects the judgment that value realization is an outcome of the play of social forces rather than a consequence of abstract modeling of new forms of world order. In effect, WOMP increasingly focuses on and identifies with the struggles of the oppressed as a way to unify theory and practice in world order studies; the energies of the oppressed supply the potential, but are far from an assured agency, for realizing world order values. WOMP does not necessarily applaud the value outcomes of national revolutionary processes. In some instances, such as the Iranian Revolution, a struggle against oppression produces promising normative results at one stage, only to deteriorate in regressive directions at later stages (see Falk's Foreword to Farhang, 1981).

The orientation of WOMP guides our inquiry here. There is, in our view, a new approach to the study of international relations implicit in the WOMP outlook, despite its own internal pluralism. It is an approach that has grown up in reaction to the perceived shortcomings of "realism," "neo-realism," and Marxism as dominant modes of inquiry. Our effort in this essay is to depict this new, evolving approach in relation to both its contours and its developing intellectual frontiers.

A PRELIMINARY COMMENT ON "WORLD ORDER"

As is evident, the rubric "world order" is the central identifying label of this approach, yet many adherents are uncomfortable with this nomenclature for several reasons. For one thing, the stress on "order" seems misleading for an approach built around "values." The WOMP outlook, however, repudiates order as used in the phrase "law and order" and instead regards order as suggestive of a new arrangement embodying an altered set of social and political relations. The world order approach, in fact, realizes that various forms of "dis-order" will occur, and are even provisionally beneficial, during the period of transition.

Another problem arises from the perception of "world order" as a globalizing ideology emanating from an ambitious superpower. Non-Westerners have played a leading role in WOMP, but still its U.S. origins and auspices have produced suspicions, at times, even among its participants (e.g., Kothari, 1980). Idealistic rhetoric provides little reassurance, as imperial actors have often tended to cloak their ambitions beneath claims of moralist intention. These concerns rightly increased when certain scholars in the West, specifically in the United States, began to invoke the imagery of "lifeboat ethics" and "triage" to justify concentrating the responsibilities for tragedies of famine and malnutrition on Third World countries. For a while, also, leading statesmen in the United States, most notably Jimmy Carter and Zbigniew Brzezinski, and even arch-realist Henry Kissinger, associated U.S. foreign policy with the pursuit of "world order." Not only was such a claim self-serving, but it confirmed the suspicion that U.S. politicians were indeed using the symbolism of world order to promote the maintenance of the present system—that is, world order as in law and order!

A humane world order approach would have to be cosmopolitan in its outlook, establishing the identity of a global citizen without devaluing participation in a particular community specifically situated in time and space. As Americans, then, it is necessary to move beyond imperial geopolitics to embrace images of a transformed world political system based upon far greater mutuality, equality, and even solidarity.

A final problem with "world order" is that it has tended to be preoccupied with imminent catastrophe. Again, such motivations as avoiding World War III or ecological collapse reflect First World priorities, however much the literature purports to address the well-being of the human species as a whole. For most non-Western peoples the daily struggles for economic, political, and cultural survival and development at the national level remain paramount.[3] Their main global concerns are to neutralize hegemonic and interventionary pressures, whether via great power interference, multinational corporate penetration, or through the manipulations of international financial institutions and of Western information agencies. To be relevant, a world order approach needs to be as alert to neoimperial perils as to the hazards of the arms race, the dynamics of population pressure, or the upsurge of international terrorism.

Despite these difficulties, we favor retention of "world order" as descriptive of our approach. The idea of world order has been considerably purged of its adverse connotations. To shift would be to run from critics and adversaries who would, in any event, attack any successor terminology as mere camouflage. Other possible nomenclatures such as the "politics of global transformation," "movement for peace and justice," "peace research," and "cosmopolitan politics" seem either obscure or cumbersome, and in some instances, have been already preempted for work of a more specialized character (e.g., peace research). Within WOMP itself some suggestions have been made to substitute "just world order" or "just world," but on balance we believe it preferable to retain "world order" as the central identifying label.

POINTS OF DEPARTURE

The essential featurs of the world order approach can be indicated by briefly setting forth its main assumptions.

Context of Emergency/Obscenity

The world order approach arises in a context of grave social concern for the state of the world today. This concern reflects anxieties about nuclear war, ecological hazards, and the scandal of avoidable mass misery. As such, the world order approach emphasizes the inadequacy of the traditional focus of inquiry and policy that tends to ignore these problems. The world order approach puts these issues at the center of its intellectual efforts, conceiving education as social mobilization as well as abstract learning.

Normativity

Closely associated with the context of emergency/obscenity is the central idea that the global situation is seriously deteriorating as a result of *avoidable evils* (Cardoso, 1977). The world order approach establishes its identity by postulating values—peace, social and economic justice, human rights, and ecological balance (Falk, 1975b: 11-30)—and by thinking of politics as value-realizing activity. This provides a new type of coherence. Policy in a global setting is evaluated by reference to the human interests at stake rather than to those associated only with national interests (Johansen, 1980). Normativity also implies a critical stance toward knowledge (for what values or disvalued end?) rather than one based on detachment and the accumulation of skills (the sharpening of tools). The role of knowledge is to transform the context of emergency/obscenity in specified ways.

System Discontinuities

Traditional approaches to international politics emphasize the continuities and essential resilience of the state system. In contrast, the world order approach stresses discontinuities, that is, the positive opportunities for drastic global reform as well as the dangers of statist collapse. Such a study of international politics is necessarily transformational in emphasis. The world order approach is interested in alternatives to the patterns of war and repression that currently dominate international life. It seeks images and designs of what else might be coming into being in the world that could appreciably realize world order values. As such, it is concerned with assessing trends and cumulative effects arising out of existing dynamics, as well as with the description and explanation of persistent patterns of statist behavior.

Normative futurism based on the altered frameworks of comprehensive value realization can be contrasted with technocratic futurism that finds "fixes" (e.g., space colonies, nuclear fusion energy) to solve the problems of human society within existing economic, cultural, political, and ecological frameworks. To oversimplify somewhat, normative futurism tends toward progressive politics as it emphasizes popular movements for social change, whereas technocratic futurism seeks to persuade existing elites to invest capital creatively at the technologial frontier. The world order approach is wary of, although not unalterably opposed to, technocratic futurism.

Globalist Perspective

The world order approach presupposes that the world can be conceived of as a whole and that the human species shares bonds and is, in fact, bonded by a shared legacy and destiny. As such, the world's statist structure is treated as transient and conditional, a fragmentation of a potential global social reality. This fragmentation arose at a given time in human history and is in the process of being superseded. The world order approach, however, acknowledges the state's creative role in preserving national autonomy and diversity in the world as now constituted, particularly its role in achieving national cohesion (internally) and safeguarding independence (against external actors). The future place of the state in some transformed world political system is a central issue that cannot be predetermined.

For most peoples, the most notable feature of recent world history has been the struggle to become a viable state. The anticolonial movement involved the quest for formal independence, including the right to one's own flag and to participate in international arenas. More recently, the struggle has involved efforts to achieve economic, cultural, and political viability in the face of internal adversity and dissension as well as transnational penetration. Too little statism (e.g., Lebanon, post-Shah Iran), as well as too much (e.g., the Soviet Union, Argentina), poses serious value problems in the world today. Notions of self-reliance, collective self-reliance, and nonalignment represents efforts to secure the virtues of statism in the present world order system. The strengths and weaknesses of the state from a world order perspective are so intertwined at present that it is difficult to imagine eliminating the weaknesses without at the same time impairing the strengths of the state.

A globalist perspective also gives due accord to nonstate actors, including those associated with intergovernmental arrangements (e.g., the United Nations, international financial institutions), transnational activities (e.g., multinational corporations, banks), and nongovernmental operations (e.g., Red Cross, Amnesty International). The world is seen as becoming more complicated and confusing, requiring that the various trends and activities be evaluated by reference to their effect on the values at stake and by their relationship to different networks and regimes.

Globalist thinking associated with the world order approach tries to avoid "globaloney," that is, preaching pieties or touting pipedreams. It does not want to discredit holistic orientations in the annals of serious reflective or activist thought by appearing irrelevant to the practical concerns of men and women worried by the context of danger and hardship. Concrete preoccupations, however, can benefit from utopian explorations. Alternative visions of the future may help facilitate transformation. In this regard, imaginative writers and artists have more to offer world order studies than the more constrained speculations of social scientists (LeGuin, 1974; Lessing, 1975, 1980).

Praxis

The entire world order enterprise is premised on active social engagement. It is not a matter of learning for learning's sake, of fulfilling careerist objectives, or of assisting the global managers and grand strategists. A strength of Marxism is that it moves from critique to practice with a theory that explains how to realize proximate goals. World order studies has a comparable ambition, although it presently lacks a comprehensive view of praxis. It rejects romantic politics that sets forth a wish list for the future. World order politics emphasizes the credibility of its transition imagery by which the present might become the preferred future. In this regard, knowledge is purposive, to be mobilized for "the oppressed" against "the oppressor" on behalf of human interests and world order values. This partnership, challenging mainstream academic conventions about the "neutrality" of inquiry, is directly linked to the belief that current global problems confront us with an emergency situation. In this sense, the relevance of knowledge to action may not be nearly so evident in other historical contexts.

Structuralist Orientation

The nature of the challenge posed by the array of "avoidable evils" (hunger, war, repression, environmental decay) is such that the structure of international society is drawn into question. In relation to war and mass poverty, for instance, the state system, with its hierarchically arranged territorial units, cannot be expected to fashion arrangements based on nonviolence and resource sharing. World order value realization presupposes system change, that is, frameworks of institutions, procedures, and rules that give due weight to global demands although not necessarily by way of centralization. As well, a weakening of materialist incentives and a strengthening of cooperative behavior and moral incentives seems essential for a world political system that solves concrete problems in a manner responsive to criteria of the human interest. These developments should be understood as a basic change in the structural context of world order rather than as ethical imperatives.

Transformation Prospects

The world order approach has not always been consistent about its conception of positive global reform. Much of the earlier depictions of a better world political system were apolitical in the sense of having no idea about how to achieve transition and eventual global transformation. Implicit in this and subsequent approaches was an appeal or rational argument designed to persuade influential people. This top-down view of global reform has been recently supplanted by a bottom-up view based on the global potential of ongoing movements for social change and liberation. Hence, "the oppressed," to the extent mobilized for global reform, become "the proletariat," the social force potentially capable of promoting a progressive realization of values, including whatever structural adjustments are needed. Given the dangers of nuclear war and ecological decay and the refusals of existing leaders to take appropriate precautions, the oppression is universal and species-wide. Such a condition seems genuinely unprecedented, and could, in time, lead to a new politics congruent with the aspirations of world order values.

It is not claimed that mobilized movements of the oppressed are consistently or self-consciously dedicated to world order values. Their horizons are generally narrower and are characteristically focused on radical revision of domestic political structures. The world order approach nonetheless contends that these movements can have wider implications that are just beginning to be understood. Indeed, it is becoming clearer that movements of national revolution are thwarted after they "succeed," partly because of the hostile character of the existing international political system. Other movements, such as the growing West European movement against nuclear weapons and militarism, can succeed only by spreading everywhere and by adopting wider projects of transformation. Given increasingly linked global realities, partly as a consequence of technological capacity and scale, progressive changes at the national level are vulnerable to disruptive reactions. The struggle against oppression in all its forms is increasingly likely to merge with the quest for a new world order.

The Drift of History

Increasingly, the world order approach does not itself claim to be an independent force. Rather, to the extent it offers hope for transcending structures of oppression, this hope arises from an interpretation of the drift of history. Of course, "drift" is a subjective category, and the historical process does not pull all in one direction. Yet the world order approach contends that certain systemic discontinuities are taking place in international life that make its description of "reality" more satisfactory than those of the Machiavellians or Marxists. Oddly enough, then, given its stress on normativity, the world order approach is a mode of descriptive analysis that seeks to interpret the cumulative weight of emergent antistatist trends. It is this feature that deserves special emphasis: world order studies as countercultural journalism.

More concretely, the WOMP outlook interprets the drifts of history as favoring the continuing dynamics of self-determination and national revolution. More broadly, this drift is likely to unleash a widening movement against oppression that is transnationally guided, given the agenda set by the menace of nuclear war and by environmental contamination of various kinds. It is unlikely that the 1980s will end without a major transnational ecological/nuclear disaster of some kind. If so, the latent popular energies of those who feel victimized could easily become an explosive force in the 1990s. The first stirrings of popular protest are evident in Western Europe and the United States and are beginning to surface in established institutions of moral concern, especially religious organizations. As one small illustration, the Catholic Archibishop of Seattle, Raymond Hunthausen, recently urged citizens to refuse to pay 50 percent of their Federal income tax as a protest against nuclear arms, which he describes as "demonic weapons which threaten all life on earth." Lutheran, United Methodist, United Presbyterian, and United Church of God leaders endorsed this proposal (New York Times, July 13, 1981: A8).

The world order approach is not necessarily optimistic about the future. It does anticipate pervasive turmoil that will alter decisively the political frameworks for problem solving in the decades ahead, but quite possibly in a regressive manner. Those modes of inquiry that presuppose the persisting solidity of existing frameworks will not help us understand what is really happening in the world (e.g., Bull, 1977; Hoffman, 1978, 1981).

THE GENERAL FRAMEWORK OF INQUIRY

The preceding discussion suggests that the general framework of inquiry guiding world order studies is designed to perform several tasks of normative social research. Based on the methodological assumption that the transformation of global actors, values, and institutions needed for a preferred world order system is both necessary and possible, this approach involves (1) a *diagnostic/prognostic* task of describing present world order conditions and trends, (2) a *modeling* task of designing preferred futures, and (3) a *prescriptive* task of mapping a transition process, including concrete steps and an overall strategy.

Systemic Trends and Capabilities

At the heart of this particular diagnostic and prognostic task lies the following inquiry: What is the "social health" or "social pathology" of the world system today? This is a matter of describing empirical reality (the world that is) in terms of the degree to which world order values are distributed, realized, suppressed. There are several related tasks: first, that of clarifying emerging realities in relation to positive and negative trends bearing on prospects for world order values; and second, that of extrapolating from existing trends the possible world or worlds of the future. The scope of such an undertaking extends beyond consideration of interstate relations and interelite conflict. The world order approach emphasizes the complex interplay between forces of destruction and creativity that are being set loose in the world political system under current conditions. Out of this interplay, one can begin to grasp reasons for despair and hope in the present period.

The world crisis has been intensified in the early 1980s by a new cycle of geopolitical rivalries and arms competitions in the wake of the Soviet invasion of Afghanistan and the revival of U.S. interventionary activism. The conclusion to be drawn from straightforward extrapolation is, observes Johan Galtung (1980: 18) in a recent world order study, that humankind is in increasing trouble. At the same time, world order studies has become increasingly cognizant of the danger of losing credibility (and audience) by habitually crying "wolf" through the assignment of specific doomsday dates (e.g., unless fundamental change occurs, all will be lost by the year 2000 or at the end of the next decade). As will be seen later in the evolution of **WOMP** thinking, more and more world order projects seek out the latent potentialities and hidden trends that run counter to the visible deterioration of the present human condition. World order studies is a protracted movement in which there is an ongoing dialectic between long-term normative visions of preferred worlds and short-term political imperatives of the transition process.

Traditional utopian thinking was marred by a pervasive mixture of empirical and preferred realities. "World order realism" seeks to avoid sentimental exercises in wishful thinking, while at the same time rejecting the dominant perceptual paradigm of the "realist" school. The search for a credible conception of system transformation distinguishes contemporary world order thinking from traditional world order thinking. We reject the "realist" image of world order as reductionistic and anachronistic. Based on their rigid and overly pessimistic conception of human nature, the realists tend to view the present as a continuation of the past. Seeing the worst in human nature and translating such a one-dimensional view of human history into social policy, the realists lend a sense of inevitability and legitimacy to a Hobbesian world of interstate rivalry where the best that can be hoped is that prudence will encourage restraint and that muddling along will not encounter serious breakdowns of the system.

Images of Possible and Preferred Futures

As a social and intellectual movement aimed at catalyzing thought and action for helping shape the future of human destiny in a more just and humane direction, world order studies is a species of future studies. The conceptual premise of world order modeling lies in the sociopsychological principle that may be reformulated as follows: what we feel, believe, think, expect, or wish shapes not only our present behavior but also the kinds of futures we transmit and posterity inherits. This principle has found various formulations in social science research. Anatol Rapoport (1964: 30) noted that "probabilities which we assign to events become reflections of our preferences rather than of our knowledge." In a similar vein, Kenneth Boulding (1956: 6, 11) has written that our behavior depends on the image, which he defines as "the subjective knowledge structure" of any individual or organization consisting "not only of images of 'fact' but also images of 'value.'"

The image often first defines reality and only then do we see "reality." For centuries, slavery was "imagined" as an immutable part of the natural social order. It was thus "utopian" to advocate its abolition. The image holds a powerful grip on how we define the outer limits and possibilities of social change. The future can never be foreclosed; it is largely a product of political will. Everything we do or fail to do affects the shaping of our individual and collective future. Whether we realize it or not tomorrow is always present in the images of today that are operative at all levels of social reality, from the individual to the state. The sense of the future is an aspect of the "is" (the empirical reality) because we have expectations that certain things or events are to recur in a certain way and conform our behavior accordingly.

World order modeling presumes the plausibility of system change and as such differs from most futures research. Mainstream futures research largely rests on the assumption of system continuity, which is expressed in the extrapolation of possible alternative futures from past and present. This was, for example, the dominant assumption for *The Year 2000: A Framework for Speculation,* in which the authors observe that the "capacities for and commitment to economic development and control over our external and internal environment are increasingly seeming without foreseeable limit" (Kahn and Wiener, 1967: 116). Even *The Global 2000 Report,* the most ambitious and comprehensive projections developed by U.S. Government agencies of what will happen to population, resources, and environment, is based on presumed system continuity, as well as the maintenance of "present policies." Projections based on such an outlook disclose more or less similar trends: "continued economic growth in most areas, continued population growth everywhere, reduced energy growth, an increasingly tight and expensive food situation, increasing water problems, and growing environmental stress" (The Global 2000 Report, 1980: 43).

Many of the prominent global modeling exercises rely on computer technology and limit the scope of inquiry to relatively small quantifiable variables. Almost no attention is paid to specific human wants or basic human needs, let alone to the psychological, cultural, and normative dimensions of the world in which we live. The Latin American World Model (Herrera et al., 1976), developed as a Third World response to the Club of Rome projections in *The Limits to Growth* (Meadows et al., 1974), stands out as a notable exception in this regard.

The world order approach to global modeling is not designed to manipulate quantitative data and variables or to seek a technocratic fix. Its principal aim is to highlight the value premises (beliefs) and value goals (preferences) of each scenario of the future and to assess critically the extent to which it facilitates the normative, holistic shaping of human destiny. Ours is a form of *soft modeling,* an exercise in normative forecasting with a heuristic rather than dogmatic posture. Contrary to some critics, the basic thrust of the world order modeling is not apocalyptic or eschatological prophecy (Oakes and Stunkel, 1981), but an exploration of preferred futures that can be used as a road map for formulating transition steps and envisaging a positive evolution of political life at all levels, from the personal and local to the collective and global. The search for preferred futures that satisfy the criteria of normative desirability and political feasibility is an ongoing dialectical process joining inquiry of the past, present, and future.

World order studies have become increasingly aware of the hazards of premature structural specificity. Like functionalists who concentrate on specific tasks of international life, most world order scholars have grown skeptical about grand schemes or legal-institutional blueprints for a brave new world envisioned. To design a specific structure at the outset is to rigidify or even hamper the value-enhancing process. The logic and implications of world order modeling, however, do call for creative attention to problems of transnational governance, the handling of issues whose scope exceeds the boundaries of any single state. A focus on governance implies thinking about new ways to supplement statist authority and competence in a variety of areas, but not necessarily with an integrated, new general authority structure.

Transition Politics

By transition politics we mean how to build relevant and reliable bridges connecting where we are now to where we want to be in the future. Indeed, this represents the most elusive task in world order studies. Much of traditional world order thinking has been "utopian" in the sense of having been unable or unwilling to conceive of a transition process. This challenge of building transition bridges and pathways is greatly complicated by the lack of any credible (widely tested and validated) theory of system transformation (see Zinnes, 1981). The world order approach accepts transition politics as the crucial link between the present world and a more just and humane one, but it has no master key to offer. Given the contending images of preferred worlds and the uneven distribution and realization of world order values in different parts of the world, it would be misleading even to search for a master key to the transition process. Indeed, a differentiated transition strategy sensitive to the circumstances and opportunities existent in various parts of the world appears to be the best way to proceed. The targets, actors, and arenas of this transition strategy should not be too rigidly specified or given overly globalist priorities. Instead, the task of global bridge building calls for periodic reassessment of who is doing what, where, how, and with what result.

Our approach to transition politics rests upon the centrality of values. The world order approach conceptualizes transition in terms of human intervention to shape the value-realizing process. At the same time, the world order values of peace, economic well-being, social justice, and ecological balance should not be placed in abeyance pending the completion of the transition process; these values apply to the means as well as to the ends of transition politics. So many social and political revolutions have betrayed their own vision and devoured their own followers, including former leaders, because of an insensitivity to the mutually enhancing or corrupting effects of the relationship between means and ends in political behavior. Hence our approach seeks a new conception of "revolution," one that differs from "mere seizures of power, a way of circulating elites through bloody events, after which the same 'rotten things begin all over again'" (Ajami, 1980: 483). We need to look at transition with operational definitions of values that make it possible to assess the progress or regress during a given period of world politics in any of the four world order value domains.

World order studies reflects various orientations to transition. Our approach combines both actor-oriented and structure-oriented perspectives. We believe both perspectives are necessary to understand the manner in which individuals and groups at different systemic levels and in different domains may successfully intervene in ongoing social, political, economic, and cultural processes to bring about social change. A credible politics of system transformation, however, calls for both conceptual and political inputs from those who are most victimized by the existing world order. Social change may be a luxury only a few progressive elites can afford, but it is an imperative for those who suffer from the existing order. The politics of transition depends upon the oppressed becoming conscious of their suffering and developing a political will to reshape their destiny. This consciousness-raising and mobilizing activity is a crucial element in the transition process.

Stages of World Order Studies

In a critical appraisal of the promise and prospects of the world order modeling movement associated with WOMP, the late Harold Lasswell (1977: 427) observed that "the agenda for coming basic revisions will be on a ten-year cycle, and the intervals will be adapted to the occurrence of major changes." This assessment has proved on target. Since academic debates on contemporary world order studies have centered largely on WOMP, it seems useful to summarize briefly how the world order approach of WOMP has actually evolved over the years. Three distinct stages can be depicted, although these shifts in conceptual focus and methodological orientation should not obscure certain common features of the approach that have persisted since its inception.

A Law-Oriented, Institution-Building Pre-WOMP Approach

In the first stage (1961-1968), a group of concerned American scholars largely devoted themselves to establishing world order studies as a respectable academic undertaking. The general framework of inquiry was law-oriented and institution building in character. Within this framework, primary attention was given to the avoidance of collective violence through the creation of a war prevention system constituted by a core of strengthened international institutions. Despite the pronounced intention of studying war prevention in the spirit of social science, the primary focus of inquiry was on international law and international organization. The underlying assumption was that institutional centralization would come about through the consent of leading governments, who would see that their distinct national interests were better served by greater world authority than by the dangerous chaos of the decentralized and laissez-faire management of power in the nuclear age.

In effect, then, this law-oriented and institution-building approach looked forward to the formation of some form of world government. The most comprehensive and rigorous example of this approach remains *World Peace Through World Law,* conceived and written by two lawyers, Grenville Clark and Louis B. Sohn (1966). Focusing on amendments to the UN Charter, the Clark/Sohn proposals sought to transfer some functions, capabilities, and resources from national governments to a rearranged set of global institutions. The influence of the Clark/Sohn proposals on the development of world order studies during this first stage is evident in *Legal and Political Problems of World Order* (Mendlovitz, 1962) and in the four-volume *Strategy of World Order* series (Falk and Mendlovitz, 1966a, 1966b, 1966c, 1966d, 1973). In the preface to the *Strategy* series, the editors noted:

> It [*World Peace Through World Law*] is not selected as an expression of the ideological preference of the editors so much as to provide a model, specified in some detail, of what an alternative international system might be like. Such a model of one future for the international system facilitates our understanding of international society as it exists

and operates at present and informs us more clearly about the kind of changes that must be made to fulfill the objectives of war prevention [Falk and Mendlovitz, 1966a: vii].

The world order approach at this first stage embodied a number of features that now seem dubious. First, it appealed to the enlightened self-interest of the privileged to take the initiative in the transition toward a better world order. Such an approach was based on the uncritical acceptance and transference of liberal reform politics to the international scene. Second, this world order approach could be charged with wearing the mask of "world order" to disguise the imperial face of *pax Americana*, however benevolent its actual motivations. Its conceptual origin, key participants, and pedagogical materials were all American. In its legal and structural design for world order, it reflected the rather unique historical experience of the United States with its largely successful transition from the relatively decentralized condition of "state" sovereignty under the Articles of Confederation to a "more perfect union" under a new federal system. Third, this approach thought of world order primarily in terms of world law in one form or another. The implicit assumption of such an exercise in constitutional or legal engineering was a kind of intellectual utopianism through which world order scholars could escape the "messy and uncivilized" *political* struggles of forging an actual new order. Finally, this world order approach was conceptually inadequate as it defined world order largely in static terms of "order" and "war prevention." In short, the world order approach during the formative stage was conceptually inadequate and normatively provincial as it abstracted the question of system transformation in a manner unresponsive to the broader world-order agenda of the non-Western peoples of the world.

Diverse Images of "Preferred Worlds": WOMP I

The establishment of WOMP in 1968 marks the initiation of the second stage (1968-1978) of world order studies. A sense of dissatisfaction with first stage efforts brought about a restructuring of the world order approach around the idea that a broader conception of world order inquiry called for the participation of representatives from the major cultures and ideologies of the world. In both a symbolic and substantive sense, WOMP represents a new cycle in the development of world order studies. The transnationalization of world order studies through the active participation of non-American scholars of international stature resulted in the broadening of the value base of world order inquiry. The central focus on war prevention shifted to a more balanced normative framework that gave more or less equal emphasis to economic well-being, social justice, and peace, and serious, although somewhat lesser emphasis, to ecological balance. As one Third World WOMP participant put it:

> Non-Western participants in that project assaulted and challenged its Western ethnocentrism; "non-lawyers" enhanced and broadened its concerns and pushed it in the direction of political harmony and culture. Those concerned with socioeconomic justice drew attention to the fact that peace, unless rooted in socioeconomic justice, can be meaningless, stultifying, and perhaps repressive; the strong have always sought peace as a means of ensuring that their order would be unchallenged and undisturbed. The intrusion of concern for justice into world orderism was to profoundly change its thrust and essence. The hitherto legal emphasis of the movement was increasingly modified to be more self-consciously political [Ajami, 1980: 474].

Based on this broadened normative framework, WOMP participants associated with principal regions and/or actors of the world (Latin America, Africa, Japan, Europe, Soviet Union, India, United States, with indirect representation for China and for the network of trans-national actors) embarked on book-length formulations of their approach to world order. Since the values were stated in general terms and subject to a variety of interpretations, and since participants were free to propose additional values, this framework was fully consistent with pluralism in style of inquiry and substantive vision. This transnational collaborative research enterprise cut across cultures and worldviews to develop new ways of thinking about system transformation, culminating in a series of six books under the umbrella title *Preferred Worlds for the 1990s* (Kothari, 1974; Falk, 1975a; Mendlovitz, 1975; Mazrui, 1976; Lagos and Godoy, 1977; Galtung, 1980).

Although the *Preferred Worlds* series generated considerable interest and controversy in academic circles, including those outside the West (see references for debates on WOMP), its overall impact on collective ways of thinking, feeling, and acting toward a cohesive vision of a new world order has been modest. The criticisms of WOMP, some justified and some not, covered the entire spectrum of intellectual discourse, including conceptual, methodological, empirical, and political objections. Mainstream international relations research, still self-confined by the state-centric framework of inquiry, has shown the tendency of dismissing "world order" as naive, utopian, and diversionary from the mainline potential for actual global reform.

Within its own turf, WOMP has not given adequate attention to the transition problem. The *Preferred Worlds* series has not provided either a satisfactorily systematic or substantive treatment of transition politics by way of prescribing behavioral guidance for world order activists. In addition, WOMP was unable to achieve sustained, prominent participation of scholars from the Soviet Union, or more generally, from the Communist world. Third World participation symbolized the transnationalization of world order inquiry without any corresponding cohesion in research purpose, modeling design, or an integrated world order vision. This resulted in a constant questioning of the premises of the undertaking. In this respect, the views of Rajni Kothari, a leading Indian scholar, are characteristic. Kothari, (1980), while evolving his own WOMP vision of the future, remains skeptical about the "world order" enterprise, suspecting that it may, in part, be a carrier of Western hegemonic thinking, a species of cultural imperialism (see also Mendlovitz, 1981).

Now that the second stage of world order studies (or WOMP I) is behind us, it is easy to see why and where it failed to live up to its initial promises. First, generating a strong and cohesive political will toward normative goals of system transformation is almost impossible, given current global conditions. The transnationalization of world order inquiry with the purpose of finding collective (and, it was hoped, united) ways of thinking, feeling, and acting strongly suggests the proverbial story of the six blind beggars who encounter an elephant. Second, world order studies has not succeeded in breaking the virtual monopoly of the realist school in defining what is real and feasible. Many influential specialists continue to reject the WOMP dual perception of danger and transformative trends and concentrate in the name of "pragmatism" on comprehending the state system and making it work more efficiently. Third, the repeated charge of utopianism cannot be dealt with in a convincing manner unless WOMP comes up with a conception of transition politics that undergirds its call for system change and comprehensive restructuring. These criticisms of WOMP ultimately direct attention to the question of "human nature." Any definition of feasibility and workability of transition imagery is greatly influenced by our views of human nature. One inadequacy of WOMP I was its failure to base its conceptions of the future upon a coherent image of the plasticity of human nature.

Struggle of the Oppressed: WOMP II

The third stage of world order studies (WOMP II) began in 1978 when perspectives and orientations began to shift in the direction of emphasizing voices of the oppressed as the key basis for the realization of world order values. In part, this new emphasis acknowledges that past approaches to world order were overly preoccupied with formal institutions, especially the tension between states and international organizations, and insufficiently concerned about social movements and grassroots initiatives arising out of the popular sector. The new framework builds its hopes for the future around various forms of "world order populism," adapted to diversities of context and agenda.

This framework distinguishes among three intersecting systems of politics: The first system consists of territorial actors, that is, the state system and its supporting infrastructure of corporations, banks, and knowledge and news industry; the second system consists of international organizations, including the United Nations and regional international institutions; and the third system consists of people acting individually and collectively (that is, the popular sector) through voluntary social movements and associations of all kinds. This new stage in world order thinking does not attempt to convince its audience as much as it tries to show the extent to which transitional changes are actually taking place in various sectors of the world system and how these may relate to the overall quest for a new world order. This third major reorientation of world order inquiry (WOMP II) is reflected in a number of WOMP projects, including a multi-volume *Studies on a Just World Order* series (Falk, Kim and Mendlovitz, 1982; Falk, Kratochwil, and Mendlovitz, 1982; Falk, Kim, and Mendlovitz, 1983).

This synoptic sketch shows that WOMP is not status or monolithic. WOMP's continuing search for collective ways and means of thinking, feeling, and acting for a just world order system is an ongoing process subject to periodic review, genuine revision, and plural paths (e.g., some participants emphasize libertarian socialism while others stress some degree of centralization). Despite these shifts in conceptual focus and methodological orientation, certain continuities give coherence to the world order approach since its inception: emphasis on system transformation, depiction of preferred world order systems, avowal of explicit values, concern about transition politics, and a holistic conception of the global human interest.

WOMP AND OTHER GLOBALIST OUTLOOKS

As already indicated, WOMP is one of several "post-Machiavellian" orientations that arise from an appreciation of the trends toward fragility and integration at the global level. These globalist outlooks reflect a variety of concrete circumstances, including the impulse to manage turbulent geopolitical and geoeconomic forces. The purpose of this section is to comment on these globalisms from the perspective of the world order approach.[4]

In WOMP's view, the most important attribute of a political stance is its relationship to the nexus of values and organizational capacities.

Using the present stage of the state system as a baseline it becomes possible to distinguish among globalisms. As now constituted, the state system is not well adapted to the realization of world order values, and it could degenerate even further either through the intensification of "chaos" or the adoption of more regressive patterns of color.

System-Diminishing Globalism

Overt militarism is an instance of a system-diminishing globalism. Overt militarism raises even higher the risks of general war and increases the reliance on military means to achieve security. It also involves the diversion of resources from productive roles, including the satisfaction of basic human needs. Mindless industrialism may also be system diminishing to the extent that it exempts industrial actors from even the current low standards of environmental regulation or panders to excessive consumerism. Any large-scale "waste" of resources constitutes maldevelopment and is system diminishing in our view.

In general, system-diminishing attitudes include abandoning concern about human rights, renouncing efforts to complete negotiations on a new Law of the Sea, eroding support for the United Nations, diminishing support for programs designed to help poorer Third World countries, and avoiding procedures for the peaceful settlement of disputes. System-diminishing globalism is essentially imperial in conception. It premises prospects for order upon global unification through the domination of a single center of state power or through some kind of allocation of imperial authority arising out of unresolved rivalries. The basis for this globalism is military power forged into tight alliance systems. The ideology of Ronald Reagan's administration moves in these general directions. This type of globalism is most appropriately formulated in the militarist spirit of ideological cohesion and grand strategy (see Cline, 1980).

System-Maintaining Globalism

In a period of rapid change and disruption, some policy-oriented intellectuals believe a globalist orientation is needed to stabilize the present statist framework and to prevent a further breakdown of existing patterns of power and authority. System-maintaining globalism, then, is essentially a defensive posture, but one that is alert to the need for self-restraining behavior as well as for transnational coordination. It is preoccupied with economic relations bearing on trade, investment, money, and believes that military power is not a viable instrument of policy under modern conditions. At the same time, it contains neither normative energy for reform nor pragmatic demands that international stability requires major structural reforms.

The Trilateral Commission, especially in its initial phase (1973-1976) illustrates this type of antivisionary globalism (Sklar, 1980). More recently, because of the prevalence of system-diminishing globalism, the Trilateral Commission has muted its earlier conception about how to manage turmoil and has succumbed, at least for the present, to system-diminishing pressures.

System-Reforming Globalism

The energy for system reform really stems from the non-Western world and is expressed in the demands of the Non-Aligned Movement, UNCTAD, and the Group of 77 for a New International Economic Order (NIEO). To the extent that OPEC joined these forces in the mid-1970s, system-reforming globalism possessed significant leverage. Indeed, the formation of the Trilateral Commission can be partly understood as an effort to forge a neutralizing response for system maintenance. More recently, however, OPEC has joined forces with the system maintainers by delinking oil pricing policy from wider policy issues, while the system maintainers have relapsed in system-diminishing directions by emphasizing the military side of security. Post-Mao China, too, became part of the problem of shifting from the "system-transforming" to a system-maintaining approach to world order (see Kim, 1981c). As a consequence, the quest for the NIEO in all of its various forms bearing on access to capital, markets, resources, and technology has virtually lapsed, representing now nothing more than tired rhetoric.

At no point has this system-reforming globalism sought to transform the underlying framework of international society. The rhetoric in Third World arenas often resembles the WOMP call for a new world order, but their actual concerns have focused on economic well-being and even here, only on the *international* circumstances (virtually exempting from scrutiny flawed domestic modes of implementation, however regressive). Furthermore, the satisfaction of the system reformers would not have any organizational implications for world order. In fact, the most vocal voices were unconditionally statist, limiting concerns to an anti-interventionist ethos designed to protect the hard-won political independence of Third World countries. Such Third World statism has distrusted any intrusion in internal affairs whatever the pretext, although it has been generally receptive to certain supranational forms of international cooperation (e.g., "common heritage" management of ocean mineral resources), if the main effect was to give the Third World governments a better relative position in the international economic order.

Even in matters of nuclear weapons the system reform constituency has been relatively passive, possibly because the stronger or more embattled states do not want to foreclose altogether their own options. There has been some criticism of the two-tier structure of nuclear and nonnuclear weapon states and particularly of the nuclear weapons countries for their failure to persist with arms control and disarmament negotiations as pledged in Article VI of the Treaty on the Non-Proliferation of Nuclear Weapons. On balance, one can conclude that the Third World is not prepared to push hard for reform when it comes to the character of international security. This reluctance, possibly, is a reflection of perceived impotence, but it may also be a failure to take seriously the risks and global magnitude of present trends, reflecting a preglobalist form of political consciousness.

System-Transforming Globalism

In contrast to the global positions set forth above, system-transforming globalism seeks a comprehensive restructuring of the frameworks that shape our political, economic, and cultural lives. The general WOMP position was presented in the first section of this chapter and will not be repeated here. Some similar system-transforming approaches exist, including various forms of philosophical anarchism, that emphasize the dismantling of the state without necessarily building up, as an alternative, international regimes and institutions. With its stress on minimum bureaucratization consistent with world order values, the WOMP outlook shares to some degree this emphasis on dismantling.

A globalism is system transforming, in our view, if it has a normative agenda that can be realized only by comprehensive restructuring (including destructuring) and a political program for imposing its vision on the historical process. Antistatism is the litmus test of a system-transforming approach, but with the qualifications made earlier that statist forms may be selectively required at this stage to neutralize the effects of unequal state power and hierarchy. Furthermore, antistatism does not imply doing away with the state as an organizing center for national political life, but only the need to overcome the operating logic of violence and war as the foundation of relations among states. A system-transforming globalism also anticipates higher levels of productivity and resource sharing to enable the satisfaction of the basic human needs for all peoples, as well as generalized procedures for the defense of human rights and the protection of the environment. Such a reorientation of politics presupposes the diffusion of globalist belief and myth systems to support community sentiments at the global level. In effect, this series of developments would manifest what it means to think, feel, and act like a global citizen in a world where global citizenship established the political climate to an extent comparable to the way national citizenship currently dominates the political climate. We cannot be sure, especially in the countries of the First and Second Worlds, how far such globalist attitudes have spread. There may be evolving a strong undercurrent of globalist sentiment throughout the world that will remain hidden until activated by cataclysmic events or charismatic leaders alert to the needs of the time.

World Systems

The work of Immanuel Wallerstein is one example of non-WOMP system-transforming globalism. His historical investigations of world capitalism fuse with his anticipation of its demise and replacement by a socialist world government sometime deep in the twenty-first century (Wallerstein, 1979). In a neo-Marxist vein, Wallerstein interprets political patterns as derivative from economic realities, essentially, the interaction between the division of labor and control over advanced production modes.

Wallerstein extends the idea of class to the relations among states. He depicts the world system as divided among core, periphery, and semi-periphery states. Core states are at the cutting edge of high technology, the centers of advanced modes of production. Semi-peripheral states engage in intermediate levels of production, but also supply raw materials to the core and provide markets for core-country surplus production. Peripheral states have only a tiny modern sector and exist mainly in a relationship of economic dependency to the core.

In the formulations of Wallerstein, Samir Amin, and others, the global transformation in process will evolve out of the dynamics of national revolution in the periphery and semi-periphery. These dynamics will strengthen the global position of socialist values and structures. Wallerstein has not yet specified a transition path, but it would seem to involve the disintegration of world capitalism brought about by accelerating contradictions, on the one hand, and a coalition of the world's antisystemic forces (or what he calls "real worldwide intermovement links") on the other (Wallerstein, 1980).

This world system orientation is based on an interpretation of extant social forces, especially as they bear on economic organization. The world order outcome is not a matter of the observer's will, but a consequence of inherent tensions and shifting relations of forces. There may be little disparity in actual content between WOMP's recent stress on the struggles of the oppressed and the Wallerstein/ Amin world system constructions.[5] WOMP relates "oppression" to a broader category of reality than does the world system approach, which focuses mainly on the adverse effects of the international division of labor. WOMP, for example, places greater emphasis on what it means to be treated as "a nuclear guinea pig" or as ecologically expendable. WOMP also clarifies the preferred future by postulating values rather than by conceiving of the oppressed as automatic bearers of the normative content of the new politics. Finally, WOMP has been more concerned than the world systems analysts with mapping "central guidance" alternatives to either world government or statism. The world systems approach is essentially a depiction of the rise and fall of capitalism as a world force in the aftermath of the breakdown of feudalism, whereas WOMP is more of a policy exercise in discerning challenges and devising responses given the operative global setting of state sovereignty and national development. Nevertheless, these two outlooks are largely complementary and compatible. Various conceptual and normative bridges can be built to enrich both outlooks, thereby moving closer to a general conception of system-transforming globalism.

Traditional Utopography

The projection of a utopia, an alternative framework for human existence, has long fascinated men and women. The original notion of utopia was mainly connected with the ideal city, a worldly complement to the pastoral ideal of Eden. More recently, however, the utopian quest has involved conceiving of the entire world as a potential ideal city. The functions of utopography are to hold up a mirror to the deficiencies of the existing order and to suggest what life could or should be like if human potential or aspiration were to be fully realized. In the nuclear age, the idea of utopia has become mingled with arguments about human evolution and the new requirements for survival. The utopian tradition is imaginative rather than empirical; it posits a vision rather than demonstrates that the present will yield a particular future or that a given alternative vision is feasible. Hence, it has been the imagination of creative writers and philosophers rather than the exploration of social scientists that has produced the most provocative examples of utopography. Indeed, in the West, the ascendancy of analytic methods in philosophic inquiry has virtually eliminated professional philosophers from the domain of utopia and has left the field to novelists and science fiction writers.

Doris Lessing and Ursula LeGuin have made outstanding contributions to the contemporary corpus of utopian literature. Doris Lessing (1975, 1980) has investigated various dimensions of the future, especially the prospects for carrying on after the disintegration of civilization or the apocalyptic breakdown resulting from nuclear war. Her imaginings of the future, however, do not extend to constructing a framework. LeGuin in *The Dispossessed* (1974) does offer us an alternative world, "an ambiguous utopia," that is organized around a nonmaterialist, austere anarchism. She establishes an existential context of choice between worlds, the materialist world we know that is elitist and violence prone, yet rich in materialist opportunity for the successful minority, and the anarchist possibility that is posited as dreary in terms of lifestyle, yet preferable in the end. LeGuin's interpretation of the human prospect is not overly optimistic (that is, "utopian" in the traditional sense), yet it does perceive a way out of the current bind, which she, along with Lessing and many others, consider a nuclear dead end.

This kind of imaginative sweep definitely implies a system-transforming globalism. The perspectives and concerns of such authors are definitely poststatist. In fact, the state is seen as a political antique with lethal propensities. Being a citizen of the world—or more generally, a member of the human species—is taken for granted as a necessary attribute of a healthy world. At the same time, such outlooks are not escapist. Both Lessing and LeGuin manifest a deep awareness of the existing context and a determination to transcend its limitations in a humanly fulfilling way. Of course, such writers are not interested in data as it is usually understood, but only in basic structures, force fields, attitudes, and behavior.

As with world systems, the best instances of contemporary utopography are integral to the world order approach. They provide a rich source of insight that helps orient the analysis in a diagnostic sense and that gives flesh and bones to a positive image of a transformed world. To be utopian is not necessarily to be unrealistic; on the contrary, it is to portray as realistically as possible what could or may come into being. As such, utopian writing provides a context for system-transforming forms of social scientific investigation and presentation. Additional work is needed to discover and study non-Western imaginative reconstructions of possible future worlds.

Mainstream International Relations Research

Even a system-transforming globalism can benefit from system-maintaining and system-reforming investigations. Careful depictions of the resilience of the state system, such as those by Hedley Bull, Robert Gilpin, or Stanley Hoffmann, contribute to our understanding of the way in which the evolving system is operating. To the extent that a system-transforming approach emphasizes transition from here to there, it becomes essential to possess a sophisticated awareness of the dynamics of the existing order. Furthermore, from a purely normative point of view, the stabilizing and moderating properties of the state system may improve the prospects for avoiding traumatic transitions or breakdowns. To the extent that system-transforming globalisms seek to embody their values in the transition process it may be important to acknowledge the contributions of the system-maintaining approach to "minimum order."

System reformers tend to regard the challenge of global developments as structural to some degree and analyze these developments as diluting the purity of statist logic. The work of Robert Keohane, Joseph Nye, and Ernst Haas is suggestive. These authors see a functionalist dynamic of challenge and response in the realities of "complex interdependence" with new roles for international regimes, institutions, and procedures. The 1980s Project of the Council on Foreign Relations explored system reform largely with such an orientation.

As we suggested above, the main energy for system reform comes from the Third World. The Third World's grievances with existing arrangements represent one dimension of the struggle of the oppressed. Indeed, Third World pressures for economic reform, although deferential to the statist framework, embody world order values to a considerable extent. The frustration of these reformist goals, as well as the upsurge of militarization at all levels of political life, may soon disclose systemic obstacles to the pursuit of national or Third World goals. In this respect, a small reorientation of political consciousness on the part of system reformers could lead to a shift in outlook resembling that of system transformers.

A distinction can be made among various scholarly approaches on the basis of their normative premises. To the extent that the primary concern of inquiry is stability and order within current frameworks, there is a natural antagonism between mainstream international relations research and WOMP. If the motivation, however, is guided by normative goals involving the pursuit of world order values, then the inquiries are compatible even if the diagnoses and strategies are divergent.

RESEARCH PATHS: THE CUTTING EDGE OF WORLD ORDER INQUIRY

The cutting edge of world order studies at any given moment refers to the challenge of restructuring the general framework of inquiry so as to enhance its relevance for disciplined inquiry into the global problematique and to establish a closer dialogue between the empirical reality of the present world order system and the preferred reality of alternative world order systems. Five broad areas of inquiry have currently emerged as the cutting edge of world order studies.

A Struggle Theory of Social Change

A classic and influential struggle theory of social change was embodied in the *Communist Manifesto* of 1848, which called upon the exploited of all countries to rise and rebel, for they "have nothing to lose but their chains." Can we reformulate and reapply this struggle theory in terms relevant to the present world system and compatible with world order values? In the final analysis, system transformation is not so much a function of ivory tower intellectual exercises as it is of political struggles waged by oppressed peoples. The possibilities of system transformation depend on the extent to which the political consciousness of the oppressed is raised to the threshold of action and on the extent to which political struggles everywhere become oriented around the pursuit of world order values.

In this connection, the Marxist struggle theory is too restrictive as it focuses too exclusively on just one structural dimension of human oppression. The present world order system is oppressive in several respects. Adverse normative trends in recent years have accentuated the contradictions in the world system. Some forms of oppression remain "invisible," that is, not perceived as avoidable oppression by victims. Invisible oppression is largely a function of present world order deficiencies, especially those relating to the continuous threat of our lives, society and civilization, and even to our species, posed by catastrophic nuclear war. The enormity of the peril and our seeming helplessness leads us to block out or numb our awareness of the danger. Other causes of failure or refusal to see the various forms of invisible oppression are too numerous to elaborate here (see Falk, 1982). A struggle theory of social change for world order studies must be able to identify present oppressive structures and show their interconnections and global implications. Such demonstrations could influence political consciousness and eventually help mobilize millions of people for the work of devising transition tactics and strategies to achieve more humane alternative futures.

International Regimes and World Order

Although international regimes have proliferated and various regime theories have been advanced in recent years, the conceptual and normative relationships between the international political economy and world order approaches to global problems remain largely unexplored. This has brought about the criticism that "world order and future studies were fundamentally flawed in terms of both theory and action." According to this view, scholars struggling to understand the basic dynamics of global politics should provide "both a description of central structures and processes at work in global politics and an explanation of why and how these structures and processes work the way they do" (Targ, 1979: 371, 381). In response to this criticism, world order inquiry into international regimes attempts to establish a linkage between the two by placing regime research in a world order framework and by formulating and exploring a number of normative questions (Kim, 1981b).

Specifically, this approach examines the global politics of "complex interdependence" by applying the "who," "what," and "how" of Lasswell's famous definition of politics. The globalization of international relations has rendered the question of "who governs in the world system" too inconclusive and unwieldly. A more appropriate focus in "whose hands guide or govern international regimes in different issue areas?" International regimes may provide a specific setting and focus for reconceptualizing the dialectic between the conservative forces defending the existing order and the emerging reformist or revolutionary forces struggling to create a new world, especially when it is related to systemwide conflicts and contradictions. What (and whose) norms and interests contend in what ways in regime politics? What deeper social, political, and economic realities are embodied in and reflected by international regimes? To what extent is there a shared notion or several competing notions of world order that are beginning to be evident across the whole range of global institutions? What is the international regime/international organization nexus? What type and range of structural images of the future can we draw from regime politics? These are among the key questions that will be emphasized by the world order approach to the study of international regimes.

Our preliminary analysis suggests that the regime approach to world order studies has advantages and disadvantages. By focusing on the formal and informal norms and the visible and invisible structures of power that converge upon the governing process pertaining to a specific global issue, this approach promises to give us a more "realistic" picture of world politics. The traditional approaches to international organizations suffered from their exaggerated assumption about the potency of formalized rules and visible structures of power. The disadvantages of this approach lie in the conceptual evlusiveness of "international regime" and in the tendency to take a fragmented and overspecialized approach that not only reproduces the technological division of labor and specialization inherent in the management of complex interdependence but also embodies the normative bias in favor of scientific/technocratic fixes.

In substantive terms, the world order approach to international regimes illustrates the "normative power" of the global underdogs and the "material power" of the global topdogs. Dominant world actors exert powerful pressure to assess regime performance by reference to technical issues rather than in terms of values and structural transformation. As seen in NIEO politics, these dominant actors may at times acquiesce in the normative claims of the Third World at a rhetorical level provided such new norms are not embodied to any significant degree in reforms of the power structure. Regime politics also show the extent to which statism, hegemony, scientific/technocratic determinism, and a fragmented paradigm color and shape the perception of social reality in contemporary global politics. Our contention is that to tap fully the potential embedded in regime research, it is necessary to adopt a critical stance toward the prevalent "scientific/technocratic" style of inquiry. The world order approach to international regimes would place its emphasis on more holistic issues.

Comparative Foreign Policy and World Order

State actors are the principal participants in the current world order system. The case for the state's predominance is based on its competence to uphold national interests (especially territorial integrity and political independence) and its embodiment of statist values. Some of these values are procedural and are associated with the consent of the governed, representatives of the working people or their vanguard party, or the like. The international performance of state actors, however, has been rarely monitored in a systematic way. Some proposals to this effect can be found (e.g., Snyder et al., 1976), but the first full-scale study of governmental performance in the global arena was undertaken by Robert Johansen (1980) in relation to United States foreign policy. Johansen examined the gaps between the stated objectives and actual implementation of U.S. foreign policy with respect to world order values. His evaluation was based on four "cases" (SALT, foreign aid to India, human rights for Chile in the Allende period, support for international control of marine pollution), each illustrative of a world order value. Johansen's study can be read at one level as a critique of American hypocrisy and moralism, and at another, as to what shifts would need to occur if the United States were to align its foreign policy with world order values. In the background, of course, is the unresolved structural question of whether a leading state actor can genuinely pursue world order values in the present world system.

On the basis of Johansen's pioneering inquiry, an effort to extend the approach on a comparative basis has been made by appraising the foreign policy of various countries from a world order perspective (Falk, 1981). A world order appraisal of foreign policy helps establish how the wide array of states handle their participation in the world system.

The structural dimension of comparative foreign policy analysis cannot be overlooked. To what extent does the evolving structure of the world system constrain leadership at the state level? To what extent can imaginative state leadership harmonize foreign policy goals with the promotion of the human interest and the realization of world order values? What attributes of statehood (e.g., scale, resource endowment, type of polity, and so on) condition relative world order performance? Is the evolving character of the state system becoming more or less conducive to positive world order performance for various states and why?

Alternative Security Frameworks and Demilitarization

A central preoccupation of the world order approach since its inception has been the phenomenon of war. The main early response was to advocate disarmament and international peace-keeping mechanisms and to encourage an international and collective security system in place of national and unilateral security systems. Such an approach has increasingly come to appear unrealistic given the logic of state action and the hierarchical nature of the state system.

WOMP thus has tried to reinterpret the challenge of war in more politically relevant terms. In recent years, its emphasis has turned to the interlinked patterns of militarization that arise from the horizontal rivalries of the leading states, the vertical relations of powerful and weaker sectors of the world system and of various regional systems, and the domestic dominance patterns by which elites maintain control over the apparatus of government and the sources of wealth, prestige, and knowledge. The world order interpretation of militarization insists that a countermovement must take account of each of these three dimensions. The early results of this new transnational study are reported in two recent issues of *Alternatives* (Falk and Sakamoto, 1980a, 1980b).

The WOMP study acknowledges that the prospects for demilitarization are not bright in the near future. In fact, principal trends point to the intensification of militarization in all three areas during the years ahead. There are, however, some countertrends, including a growing anxiety at the grassroots level about the wisdom and legitimacy of nuclear-based security systems. The world order approach emphasizes the identification of normative initiatives that are able to delegitimize all three types of militarization. A global campaign for the prohibition of nuclear and other weapons of mass destruction may deserve a high priority at this time. Scholarly research and political activity would be mutually reinforcing in this context.

On a longer time frame, but also central to the WOMP endeavor, is the reorientation of security. We draw a contrast between *rulers' security,* whereby elites employ military and paramilitary means to secure narrowly based hierarchical relationships and structures of privilege, and *people's security,* whereby the protection of general interest in autonomy and development are upheld in the least destructive manner. The character of people's security remains to be explored in a variety of contexts. Techniques of unarmed resistance, nonviolence, and neutralism seem increasingly attractive in an age of guided missiles, rapidly deployable interventionary forces, and government units trained and equipped to administer torture as a routine matter.

Global Cultural Nexus

The world order approach, with its emphasis on values and human interests, has recently begun to examine the relevance of cultural factors. Such an inquiry is a departure from the initial stress on law and institutions as the building blocks of a new world order and the subsequent emphasis on economic development and national revolution. These earlier concerns have not been superseded but rather deepened to include the civilizational dimensions of politics and economics. The Iranian Revolution, despite its troubled path since 1978, has disclosed the potency of nonmaterialistic concerns. In fact, the leaders of this revolution have consistently subordinated materialist considerations, confusing those who assume such priorities. However perverse and misguided, the Iranian Revolution is, at its crux, a defense of Iranian cultural (including religious) integrity, no matter what the costs (in conventional ethical terms).

Locked in the history of the world's peoples are many sacred images and stories. The cultural data shape the path of legitimate development for all societies and are organically connected with any eventual hope for demilitarization. These are elusive, controversial matters. WOMP has formed a transnational group of scholars who seek to bring these issues more clealy into the various dialogues about the future of world order. One early priority of this work has been to demystify the claims of Western civilization to supplant other cultural traditions in the interests of progress and rational development. The Western role has provided authoritative rationalizations of power relations, not a rational model necessarily worthy of non-Western emulation. In fact, even within the West, there are signs that the high technology path is leading to disaster, causing acute stress in the most affluent contries even apart from the rapid buildup of geopolitical, ecological, and economic pressures that are apparently driving the world system toward catastrophic breakdown.

The search here is for a more adequate stance toward the future that draws on the richest traditions of the past, including the philosophic basis for globalist identity that lies buried in every major world cultural tradition (Walker, 1980, 1981). In a sense, the world order approach at this stage is seeking to clarify the various cultural traditions that influence the outlook and behavior of actors in international life. A more ambitious undertaking is to discern whether there is enough cultural common ground upon which to construct a cosmopolitan sequel to statism that encourages the identification with the human species as a whole without foregoing the distinctive symbols and backgrounds of each particular experience of human groups through time.

CONCLUSION

World order studies has two ambitions: to establish an enduring academic presence and to provide a basis for a movement for social change that encompasses issues of global scale. Only time will tell whether its reading of contemporary history as disaster prone and as favorable to the struggles of oppressed peoples is correct, and whether if correct, these struggles can be carried to completion without provoking catastrophe. As it is, the world order approach provides an alternative to both Machiavellianism and Marxism for students concerned about the shape of things to come in international life.

NOTES

1. The principal works associated with the WOMP project are Mendlovitz (1962), the *Strategy of World Order Series* (Falk and Mendlovitz, 1966a, 1966b, 1966c, 1966d, 1973); the *Preferred Worlds for the 1990s* series (Falk, 1975c; Galtung, 1980; Kothari, 1974; Lagos and Godoy, 1977; Mazrui, 1976; Mendlovitz, 1975); and the *Studies on a Just World Order* series (Falk, Kim, and Mendlovitz, 1982, 1983; Falk, Kratochwil, and Mendlovitz, 1982). Debates on WOMP may be found in Ajami (1980), Baldwin (1970), Beer (1979), Beres and Targ (1976), Clark (1979), Falk (1972a, 1972b, 1977, 1978, 1980), Farer (1977), Kim (1981a), Kothari (1972, 1980), Lasswell (1977), Mazrui (1972), Mendlovitz (1977, 1981), Mendlovitz and Weiss (1973), Michalak (1980), Oakes and Stunkel (1981), Sakamoto (1972), Steiner (1979), Sylveter (1981), Targ (1979), Wilkinson (1976), and Yalem (1979). Works closely aligned to the WOMP project include Beer (1981), Beres (1981), Beres and Targ (1975), Bhagwati (1972), Choucri and Robinson (1978), Falk (1972a, 1972b, 1975b), Falk and Kim (1980), Johansen (1980), Kim (1979), Lake (1973), Mazrui and Patel (1973), Morehouse (1979), Ophuls (1977), Pirages (1977, 1978), Wagar (1971), and Weston, Falk, and D'Amato (1980).

2. Some of the confusions about the position of WOMP on these issues stems from the fact that Saul Mendlovitz, the founder and leader of WOMP since its inception, has

declared his personal conviction that world government is an inevitable sequel to the state system within a relatively few decades (e.g., Mendlovitz, 1975: xvi). Furthermore, if contemplating a poststatist world political system, then some imagery of the mix between centralization and decentralization of authority (structures and functions) is unavoidable, although the implication of such discussion is not necessarily at all a net increase in bureaucratization or centralization. Most WOMP authors stress the desirability and possibility of debureaucratization and decentralization in the context of increased value sharing and global identity (e.g., Falk, 1975c; Galtung, 1980; Lagos, 1977; Mazrui, 1976).

3. The conflict between national autonomy (e.g., Kurds, Palestinians) and state autonomy (e.g., Iran, Israel) is one of the great ongoing dimensions of global conflict.

4. This section relies upon, yet alters, the framework of Falk (1977: 181-189).

5. The world system orientation is reviewed from the perspective of international relations research and theory in Hollist and Rosenau (1981), a special issue of *International Studies Quarterly.*

REFERENCES

AJAMI, F. (1980) "World order: the question of ideology." Alternatives 6 (Winter): 473-485.

BALDWIN, I (1970) "Thinking about a new world order for the decade 1990." War/ Peace Report (January): 3-8.

BEER, F. A. (1981) Peace Against War: The Ecology of International Violence. San Francisco: W. H. Freeman.

———(1979) "World order and world futures." Journal of Conflict Resolution 23 (March): 174-192.

BERES, L. R. (1981) People, States and World Order. Itasca, IL: F. E. Peacock.

———and H. R. TARG (1976) "Perspectives on world order: a review." Alternates 2 (June): 177-198.

———[eds.] (1975) Planning Alternative World Futures: Values, Method, and Models. New York: Praeger.

BHAGWATI, J. N. [ed.] (1972) Economics and World Order: From the 1970s to the 1990s. New York: Free Press.

BOULDING, K. E. (1956) The Image. Ann Arbor: University of Michigan Press.

BULL, H. (1977) The Anarchical Society. New York: Columbia University Press.

CARDOSO, F. H. (1977) "Towards another development," pp. 21-39 in M. Nerfin (ed.) Another Developmment: Approaches and Strategies. Uppsala, Sweden: Hammarskjold Foundation.

CHOUCRI, N. and T. W. ROBINSON [eds.] (1978) Forecasting in International Relations: Theory, Methods, Problems, Prospects. San Francisco: W. H. Freeman.

CLARK, G. and L. SOHN (1966) [1958] World Peace Through World Law. Cambridge, MA: Harvard University Press.

CLARK, I. (1979) "World order reform and utopian thought: a contemporary watershed?" Review of Politics 41 (January): 96-120.

CLINE, R. S. (1980) World Power Trends and U.S. Foreign Policy for the 1980's. Boulder, CO: Westview Press.

FALK, R. A. (1982) "On invisible oppression and world order," in R. A. Falk, S. S. Kim, and S. H. Mendlovitz (eds.) Toward a Just World Order. Boulder, CO: Westview.

———[ed.] (1981) Special Issue on World Order Models Project, International Interactions 8, 1-2.

———(1980) "The shaping of world order studies: a response." Review of Politics 42 (January): 18-30.

———(1978) "The World Order Model Project and its critics: a reply." International Organization 32 (Spring): 532-545.

———(1977) "Contending approaches to world order." Journal of International Affairs 32 (Fall/Winter): 171-198.

———(1975a) "Toward a new world order: modest methods and drastic visions," pp. 211-258 in S. H. Mendlovitz (ed.) On the Creation of a Just World Order. New York: Free Press.

———(1975b) A Global Approach to National Policy. Cambridge, MA: Harvard University Press.

———(1975c) A Study of Future Worlds. New York: Free Press.

———(1972a) "Can international law contribute to world order? American Journal of Internationnal Law 66 (September: 268-278.

———(1972b) This Endangered Planet: Prospects and Proposals for Human Survival. New York: Random House.

———and S. S. KIM [eds.] (1980) The War system: An Interdisciplinary Approach. Boulder, CO: Westview.

———and S. H. MENDLOVITZ [eds.] (1983) The United Nations and a Just World Order, Vol. 3. Boulder, CO: Westview.

———[eds.] (1982) Toward a Just World, Vol. 1. Bounder, CO: Westview.

FALK, R. A. and S. H. MENDLOVITZ [eds.] (1973) Regional Politics and World Order. San Francisco: W. H. Freeman.

———(1966a) Toward a Theory of War Prevention, Vol 1. New York: World Law Fund.

———(1966b) International Law, Vol. 2. New York: World Law Fund.

———(1966c) The United Nations, Vol. 3. New York: World Law Fund.

———(1966d) Disarmament and Economic Development, Vol. 4. New York: World Law Fund.

FALK, R. A., F. KRATOCHWIL, and S. H. MENDLOVITZ [eds.] (1982) International Law and Just World Order, Vol. 3. Boulder, CO: Westview.

FALK, R. A. and Y. SAKAMOTO [eds.] (1980a) Demilitarization I, special issue, Alternatives 6 (March).

———(1980b) Demilitarization II, special issue, Alternatives 6 (July).

FARER, T. J. (1977) "The greening of the globe: A preliminary appraisal of the World Order Models Project (WOMP)." International Organization 32 (Winter): 129-147.

FARHANG, M. (1981) U.S. Imperialism: From the Spanish-American War to the Iranian Revolution. Boston: South End Press.

GALTUNG, J. (1980) The True Worlds: A Transnational Perspective. New York: Free Press.

Global 2000 Report to the President (1980) Entering the Twenty-First Century, Vol. 1. Washington, DC: Government Printing Office.

HERRERA, A. et al. (1976) Catastrophe or New Society? A Latin American World Model. Ottawa, Canada: IDRC.

HOFFMAN, S. (1981) Duties Beyond Borders: On the Limits and Possibilities of Ethical International Politics.

———(1978) Primacy or World Order: American Foreign Policy since the Cold War. New York.

HOLLIST, W. L. and J. N. ROSENAU [eds.] (1981) World System Debates, a special issue of International Studies Quarterly 24 (March).

JOHANSEN, R. C. (1980) The National Interest and the Human Interest: An Analysis of U.S. Foreign Policy. Princeton, NJ: Princeton University Press.

KAHN, H. and A. J. WIENER (1967) The Year 2000. New York: Macmillan.

KIM, S. S. (1981a) "The World Order Models Project and its strange critics." Journal of Political and Military Sociology 9 (Spring): 109-115.

———(1981b) "International regimes and world order." Paper delivered at the Annual Meeting of the International Studies Association, Philadelphia, March.

———(1981c) "Whither post-Mao Chinese global policy?" International Organization 35 (Summer): 433-465.

———(1979) China, the United Nations, and World Order. Princeton, NJ: Princeton University Press.

KOTHARI, R. (1980) Toward a Just World. Working Paper 11, WOMP. New York: Institute for World Order.

———(1974) Footsteps into the Future: Diagnosis of the Present World and A Design for an Alternative. New York: Free Press.

———(1972) "National autonomy and world order: an Indian perspective." American Journal of International Law 66 (September); 257-268.

LAGOS, G. and H. H. GODOY (1977) Revolution of Being: A Latin American View of the Future. New York: Free Press.

LAKEY, G. (1973) Strategy for a Living Revolution. San Francisco: W. H. Freeman.

LASSWELL, H. D. (1977) "The promise of the world order modeling movement." World Politics 29 (April): 425-437.

LeGUIN, U. (1974) The Dispossessed. New York: Avon.

LESSING, D. (1980) Shikasta. New York: Alfred A. Knopf.

———(1975) Memoirs of a Survivor. New York: Bantam.

MAZRUI, A. A. (1976) A World Federation of Cultures: An African Perspective. New York: Free Press.

———(1972) "World order through world culture." American Journal of International Law 66 (September): 252-257.

———and H. H. PATEL [eds.] (1973) Africa in World Affairs. New York: Third Press.

MEADOWS, D. et al. (1974) The Limits to Growth. New York: Universe.

MENDLOVITZ, S. H. (1981) "A perspective on the cutting edge of world order inquiry: the past, present and future of WOMP." International Interactions 8, 1-2: 151-160.

———(1977) "The program of the Institute for World Order." Journal of International Affairs 31 (Fall/Winter): 259-265.

———[ed.] (1975) On the Creation of a Just World Order. New York: Free Press.

———[ed.] (1962) Legal and Political Problems of World Order. New York: The Fund for Education Concerning World Peace Through World Law.

———and T. G. WEISS (1973) "Toward consensus: the World Order Models Project of the Institute for World Order," pp. 74-97 in G. Clark and L. Sohn (eds.) Introduction to World Peace Through World Law. Chicago: World Without War Publications.

MICHALAK, S. J. (1980) "Richard Falk's future world: a critique of WOMP-USA." Review of Politics 42 (January): 3-17.

MOREHOUSE, W. [ed.] (1979) Science, Technology and the Social Order. New Brunswick, NJ: Transactions Books.

OAKES, G. and K. R. STUNKEL (1981) "In search of WOMP." Journal of Political and Military Sociology 9 (Spring): 83-99.

OPHULS, W. (1977) Ecology and the Politics of Scarcity: Prologue to a Political Theory of the Steady State. San Francisco: W. H. Freeman.

PIRAGES, D. C. (1978) The New Context for International Relations: Global Ecopolitics. North Scituate, MA: Duxbury.

———[ed.] (1977) The Sustainable Society: Implications for Limited Growth. New York: Praeger.

RAPOPPORT, A. (1964) Strategy and Conscience. New York: Shocken.

SAKAMOTO, Y. (1972) "The rationale of the World Order Models Project." American Journal of International Law 66 (September); 245-252.

SKLAR, H. [ed.] (1980) Trilateralism. Boston: South End Books.

SNYDER, R. C., C. F. HERMANN, and H. D. LASSWELL (1976) "A global monitoring system: appraising the effects of government on human dignity." International Studies Quarterly 20 (June): 221-260.

STEINER, M. (1979) "Conceptions of the individual in the World Order Models Project (WOMP) literature." International Interactions 6 1: 27-41.

SYLVESTER, C. (1981) "In defense of the World Order Models Project: a behavioralist's reply." International Interactions 6, 1: 27-41.

TARG, H. R. (1979) "World order and future studies reconsidered." Alternatives 5 (November): 371-383.

WAGER, W. W. (1971) Building the City of Man: Outlines of a World Civilization. San Francisco: W. H. Freeman.

WALKER, R.B.J. (1981) "World politics and western reason: universalism, pluralism, hegemony." Alternatives 7 (Fall): 195-227.

———(1980) Political Theory and the Transformation of World Politics. World Order Studies program, Occasional Paper 8. Princeton, NJ: Princeton University Center of International Studies.

———WALLERSTEIN, I. (1980) "Friends and foes." Foreign Policy 40 (Fall): 119-113.

———(1979) The Capitalist World-Economy. Cambridge: Cambridge University Press.

WESTON, B. H., R. A. FALK, and A. D'AMATO [eds.] (1980) World Order and International Law. St. Paul, MN: West.

WILKINSON, D. (1976) "World Order Models Project: first fruits." Political Science Quarterly 91 (Summer): 329-335.

YALEM, R. J. (1979) "Conflicting approaches to world order." Alternatives 5 (December): 385-393.

ZINNES, D. (1981) "Prerequisites for the study of system transformation," pp. 3-21 in O. R. Holsti, R. M. Siverson, and A. L. George (eds.) Change in the International System. Boulder, CO: Westview.

PART III

Discussion and Debate

10

The Inadequacy of a Single Logic

Integrating Political and Material Approaches to the World System

DAVID P. RAPKIN

Recent theoretical and empirical attempts to interpret the functioning of the political economy of the world system over the last half-millennium have demonstrated the explanatory potential of "grand," macroanalytic theory (e.g., Wallerstein, 1974, 1979, 1980a; Modelski, 1978, 1980, 1982; Thompson and Zuk, 1982). While these efforts represent significant extensions of spatiotemporal range and of substantive scope in relation to previous approaches, no existing theoretical framework is yet of sufficient scope to account for both the political and material processes of the world system.

The questions of the relative autonomy of the world *polity* vis-à-vis that of the world *economy* and their respective potential for contributing to our understanding of the larger world system have flared into dispute between theorists of each realm. One purpose of this essay is to demonstrate that political and materialist approaches pursue essentially different, but not unrelated, objects of investigation (questions of order, security, and war as distinct from the expansion of the capitalist mode of production, its division of labor, and uneven developmental processes) and that these two broad objectives require employment of two separate but interactive explanatory logics, i.e., sets of premises and conceptual apparatus. Substantiation of these arguments entails a critical examination of systemic theories of interstate politics, which have focused on how the behavior of states is determined by their systemic environment. A second purpose of the essay is to demonstrate that this body of theory, though sufficient to

242   *Discussion and Debate*

establish the autonomy of the political sphere, has failed, until quite recently, to apprehend its subject matter at the level of the world system. A final purpose is to explore the potential for attaining a unified theory that addresses both political and material concerns through the additive and interactive conjunction of the two logics rather than through the a priori subordination of one to the other.

A SINGLE CAPITALIST LOGIC OF THE WORLD SYSTEM: PARSIMONY, REDUCTIONISM, OR SOLE CONTENDER?

Controversy over the relationship between political and economic processes has been precipitated by the explicit contention of materialist theorists that the world system can be comprehended as an economic entity with no autonomous political processes that systematically determine crucial aspects of its operation. This perspective begins with the notion that states themselves are of a "category conceptually given by, because factually imposed by, the developmental process of the capitalist world-economy" (Hopkins and Wallerstein, 1981: 245). By extension, the system composed of such states exhibits no independent logic. The opening paragraph of Wallerstein's seminal work, for instance, asserts that the modern world system "is an economic but not a political entity" and that "the basic linkage between the parts of the system is economic" (1974: 15). The point is not that the interstate political system plays no role in Wallersteinian theory. In fact, the political pluralism represented by this system is regarded as necessary for the expansion of capital accumulation and hence as necessary for the functioning of world capitalism. But this is a rather static conception in which the interstate system is reduced to a "structural constant" (Chase-Dunn and Rubinson, 1979). Factually, the interstate system is viewed merely as a prop or platform for the operation of economic forces, while analytically it is little more than a fertile and hospitable laboratory culture within which the organism of primary interest—world capitalism—can be observed and theorized about. More recently, Chase-Dunn (1981) has acknowledged the existence of interstate political processes and their relevance to an understanding of the world system, but he claims that the logic of these processes is derivative of, and thus driven by, the logic of the world capitalist mode of production.

It is not surprising that this neglect and subordination of the world system's political dimensions has engendered a critical response from theorists of a more political bent (Skocpol, 1977; Modelski, 1978; Zolberg, 1981; Thompson, 1983a, 1983b). It is fair to say that a less contentious situation would prevail if materialist theorists re-stricted their interpretive and explanatory claims to properties of the world *economy,* while acknowledging that the world *system* encom-passes other properties that remain in need of explanation. Legitimate criticism by political theorists would then be limited to the construc-tive caution that a fully specified theory of material processes will eventually require the systematic incorporation of political con-siderations, if only in an auxiliary role. Materialist theorists, however, instead purport to offer an expansive, all-encompassing conception of *the* modern world system, with the magisterial "the" and the absence of an adjectival qualifier to the generic "system" implying that little if anything of analytical interest is left to comprehend.

I am suggesting that the impressive efforts of Wallerstein and followers to account for economic aspects of the world system with a materialistic theoretical apparatus, though ultimately underspecified, do not in themselves provoke serious boundary disputes with theorists of world politics. The notion that Wallersteinian theory exhausts that which is important to know about the world system, or that anything else of importance can be subsumed by Wallersteinian theory, is a different and more controversial matter. It is this latter, imperious claim of materialist theorists that has led specialists in world politics to assert the autonomy and indispensability of their subject matter. But assertions are not evidence and counterarguments on both abstract theoretical and historical/empirical grounds are in order.[1]

Having said this, it must be admitted that the body of scholarly endeavor concerned with interstate politics has failed to cumulate much in the way of verified (or verifiable) theoretical propositions about the long-term processes of the world political system. It is lamentable, and should be a source of disciplinary embarrassment, that the evolution of the world political system as a concrete, his-torical entity has not been deemed a necessary subject of theoretical investigation. To be sure, there is a long tradition of theorizing from a systemic perspective about the nature of interstate politics, a tradi-tion that has been termed the "classical paradigm" of the field (Ljiphart, 1974). The product of this paradigm, however, has been *systemic-level theories but not theories of the world political system.* They are systemic level theories insofar as they demonstrate how the behavior of states (parts) is determined by the anarchical nature of the system (whole) within which they exist. They are not theories of the world political system in that they are unable to account theo-retically for—indeed do not even explicitly address—the historical development of that system as an organismic whole. The expansion of the world political system's spatial boundaries, its secular trends and possible periodicities, and more generally, its movement through time have not been regarded as worthy objects of theoretical investigation.

This criticism is not meant to imply that systemic-level theories provide no general statements about enduring or recurring patterns of interstate politics. There is no shortage of propositions bearing upon such questions as when, why, and under what circumstances states will increase their capabilities, form or dissolve alliances, resort to war, and so on. But these propositions, though general in nature and enjoying some measure of corroboration, pertain primarily to the propensities and tendencies of state behavior rather than to the dynamics of the overall system through long historical time. Nor am I arguing that propositions of this form are not in principle applicable to an understanding of the processes that inhere to the larger system. Rather, the point is that in practice they have been employed ahistorically, suspended in time and space, though ready for atomistic application to single instances or short series of instances. They have not been applied to the concrete developmental course of the world political system taken as a whole. History—in fragments—has been used to illustrate theory rather than theory used to interpret history. It is as if a theory of biological evolution had been constructed to account for the short-term micro logic of evolutionary processes but was never harnessed to the macro task of explaining the long-term evolution of life in its entirety.

It is difficult, and beyond the scope of this essay, to explain the disciplinary failure to develop a theory of the world political system since its inception circa 1500. In brief, I would argue that this failure is attributable to a combination of several factors. First, there has been an espistemological overreliance on models of knowledge formation borrowed from the "hard" sciences, in which change occurs at a slower-than-glacial pace. In physics, for example, the structure and behavior of atomic particles can be safely presumed to have remained unchanged from the sixteenth century to the twentieth. Change in social phenomena is of a much higher order of velocity and, therefore, as implied above, the evolutionary approach of the life sciences would be a more appropriate model. Second, theorists of international politics have suffered from excessive present-mindedness, a tendency stemming from pressures that are both imposed and self-inflicted: the concern for immediate policy relevance and the need for quantifiable, hard data, with the latter of course diminishing in availability and reliability as we move backwards in time.

Whatever the causes of this theoretical shortcoming, it must be conceded that theorists of the interstate system do not have much to offer materialist theorists in the way of already formulated, intersubjectively agreed upon propositions about the dynamics of the world political system's long-term processes. As will be argued below, the "long cycle of world politics" framework of George Modelski represents a significant, in certain ways revolutionary, theoretical advance that attempts to rectify the deficiencies that I have described. But Modelski's work is quite recent, yet to be fully articulated, and thus should be regarded as a prototheory of the world political system. Though materialist theorists need to pay heed to Modelski's ideas, it is obviously unfair to expect an instantaneous incorporation of these still-emergent ideas to have already taken place.

What then of the criticisms directed against Wallersteinian theory's neglect of political factors? If, as I have argued, there is a dearth of systematic knowledge about the world system's long-term political processes, do the criticisms not amount to asking materialist theorists to do what political theorists have failed or not tried to accomplish? The answer is both yes and no. Certainly criticism would be most forceful if Wallerstein and others had ignored a longstanding body of systematic theory and research on the world political system. While this form of criticism is hardly appropriate in the absence of extant theory of this type, counterarguments based on Modelski's long-cycle framework have begun to emerge. Thompson (1983b), for example, demonstrates that Chase-Dunn's (1981) insistence on a single capitalist logic leads to a flawed understanding of the dynamics of the recurrent struggles for leadership/hegemony in the world system.

Short of this strongest case, however, there is still ample ground for valid criticism. The weakest form of criticism would point to a chronological sequence (or descriptive history) of discrete political and military events and short-term processes (e.g., wars, alliances) and charge that materialistic theory had omitted consideration of some of these events that were crucial to the functioning of Wallerstein's world system as he defines it. This criticism would be "weak" insofar as it would implicitly acknowledge that no theoretical order had been imposed on the descriptive history of world politics and, hence, could only charge that the corps of materialist theorists had ransacked this history in an ad hoc and incomplete manner.

A stronger form of criticism would point to the theoretical tradition mentioned earlier that addresses the interstate political system and charge that Wallerstein's failure to consider this body of theory had left him unappreciative of the competitive and predictably violent nature of the interstate system and its independent effects. Awareness of these theories would alert materialist theorists that "another system"—one governed at least in part by noneconomic forces—existed historically and analytically, although the dynamics of its long-term processes had not yet been uncovered. Moreover, appreciation of the nature of the interstate system would give the materialist theoretical guidance with which to make more thorough and adequate use of the descriptive history of world politics. Criticism of this latter (stronger but not strongest) sort is incisively leveled by Zolberg (1981), who shows that Wallerstein's (1974) failure to take account of political-strategic factors (such as the sixteenth-century French-Turkish alliance) undermines his initial conceptual specification of the world system and results in misleading empirical conclusions regarding its actual formation and operation.

The lack of prior, comprehensive theories of the world political system thus does not absolve materialist theorists of the charges that the Wallersteinian scheme neglects political factors and relies on a crude form of economic reductionism. These charges can be sustained, as Zolberg has done, by pointing to logical and empirical inconsistencies in the materialist version of the world system that stem from inattention to the political realm. The validity of these criticisms, however, does not suffice to establish an autonomous logic of interstate politics, let alone a broader logic of the world political system. The next section addresses this issue by reconstructing the logic of the classical paradigm of interstate politics, identifying its strengths and inherent limitations and arguing that Modelski's reworking and extension of classical theory constitutes a "progressive problemshift" toward a theory of the world political system.

FROM SYSTEMIC-LEVEL THEORY TO A THEORY OF THE WORLD POLITICAL SYSTEM

It should be noted at the outset that the classical paradigm of interstate politics abstracts entirely from material considerations, a characteristic that, while enabling some measure of deductive parsimony, delimits its scope and thereby renders it incapable of serving as the basis for a theory of the multifaceted entirety of the world system. At the same time, this singular focus isolates the autonomy of the political-strategic realm and thus warrants here a brief review.

The essence of the paradigm lies in the concepts of state *sovereignty* and international *anarchy.* The concept of sovereignty implies that the individual state is at the apex of a hierarchial structure of political authority within its own society and, from this position, governs and regulates political and other forms of behavior within its territorial domain toward the end of creating and maintaining domestic order. With respect to the state's external environment, sovereignty denotes the responsibility of the state for the formulation of policies toward other state and nonstate actors, with the objective of these policies being the physical security of its population, maintenance of the state's territorial integrity, and preservation of sovereignty itself against external encroachment.[2]

The state's external environment is composed of a system of similarly sovereign states, themselves governed by no superordinate authority. This system of multiple sovereignties is thus ordered horizontally, anarchically rather than hierarchically. The condition of anarchy, which frequently is likened to a Hobbesian state of nature, does not imply perpetual chaos and absolute disorder. Rather, it simply refers to the absence of any formal, centralized authority that (1) holds a monopoly or preponderance of the means of violence and coercion and (2) that is empowered to make and enforce rules or otherwise regulate and constrain state behavior in the interest of systemic order. The disintegrative worst case of war of all against all involving the absolute application of violent means, though not typical, is regarded as a perpetual boundary condition against which there is, by definition, no ultimate means of prevention.

The individual state therefore faces an environment laden with threats to the various facets of its sovereignty, i.e., threats to its survival as a state entity. These threats define a set of most unfavorable contingencies toward which state behavior must be oriented. Since there is no recourse to higher authority for protection against these threats or for redress once externally imposed injury has been incurred, the survival of each state as an independent political and territorial entity is ultimately its own responsibility, i.e., a matter of *self-help*. Self-help amounts to the amassing of military capabilities sufficient to deter potential violations of the state's sovereign imperatives or, in the event deterrence fails, to defend itself successfully when potential threats are actualized.

Self-help, however, frequently proves inadequate, as the state may be threatened by a stronger adversary or multiple adversaries. This problem provides incentives for the pooling of self-help capabilities by means of *alliance formation*. Alliances may temporarily reduce the range of immediate threats faced by particular states, or conversely, by entangling states in a multilateral web of commitments, they may serve to multiply the threats they confront. Under no circumstances do alliances allow states to escape entirely the perils endemic to an anarchical environment; at best they diminish the number of threat-exchanging units in the system. Furthermore, alliances are impermanent since they form and disband as a function of the waxing and waning of particular threats through time and space. This feature of interstate politics lends a dynamic character to the larger system as the configurations of states bound and repelled by the real or imagined hostility of others shift and reshift. *Balance-of-*

power systems, which sporadically appear as products of these alliance dynamics, may be regarded as tenuous and transitory approximations of interstate order.

Apart from the state-level imperative of maintaining sovereign independence, which by definition is generalized in the perpetuation of multiple sovereignties, intentionality plays a smaller role in the logic of the interstate system than one might expect. Consider the following scenario: Confronted with a threat-laden environment, it is only prudent for state A to build military capabilities and/or seek allies. Indeed, it may be assumed that A harbors no aggressive designs vis-à-vis other states and that it arms itself and forms alliances for purely defensive purposes. But state B cannot safely ignore A's capabilities or alliances, for defensive armies and armaments can readily be translated into offensive instruments or aggression, and A's apparent amity could switch to enmity with a mere change in A's governing regime. In response, B orients its behavior to the latent threat posed by A by also arming and seeking allies. State A, initially armed for reasons both innocent and prudent, is alarmed by what seem to be B's war preparations and proceeds to further augment its own capabilities. In short, the tendency is for intentions to be inferred from the existence of capabilities.

In this fashion, systemic anarchy enables the spiraling of both misperceptions and armaments among its constituent units. This combustible mix of subjective and objective factors in turn exacerbates the instability and insecurity intrinsic to the initial condition of anarchy.[3] Note that this phenomenon, which Herz (1976) has termed the "security dilemma," unfolds even if we assume that neither state initially possessed hostile or aggressive intentions. Each state, in pursuit only of its own security, is compelled to behave in a manner that produces the mutually undesirable outcome of reduced security for both. When generalized across the system, this phenomenon results in the condition of *collective insecurity,* which is characteristic of multiple sovereignty arrangements. Note further that we do not need to invoke flaws in human nature, genetic predispositions toward violence, innate drives for power, or pathological state forms in order to reach the conclusion of the security dilemma. Collective insecurity, and all that it implies for the behavior of states and their propensity for violent means, derives directly from the anarchic structure of the interstate system rather than from causes originating at lower levels or different functional bases of social organization.

To summarize, because of its specification of the parts-whole relationship, the classical paradigm yields what I have termed "systemic-level theory." The objective of this theory is to demonstrate how and why state behavior is shaped and constrained by the environment provided by the interstate system. It shows that this environment leads to the possession and multiplication of violent means and allows, even conduces, the utilization of those means for a variety of reasons of state, ranging from the imperative of survival to pure aggression. The paradigm thus informs us, and should inform materialist theorists, that we are apprehending a competitive system that is prone to conflict and in which force is the ultimate arbiter. These conclusions about the nature of the interstate system—derived without reference to material factors—imply that state behavior is embedded in a network of interactions that are governed by a security-oriented logic. This is not to deny that in practice this logic intersects and becomes entangled with logics associated with material ends and means. The classical paradigm does, however, provide a strong basis for rejection of the assertion that the logic of security-oriented interactions is explicable solely, or even largely, in terms of the logic of world capitalism.

If the strength and clarity of the classical approach spring from the parsimony of its singular focus, so too do its limitations. Its principal shortcomings are its bounded scope and its atomistic, ahistorical application, as evinced by its failure to produce a theoretical understanding of the long-term processes of the world political system. It identifies patterns, tendencies, and propensities of state behavior but not of the larger system that the states constitute. It reveals why the interstate political system is chronically conflictual, but it can offer only space- and time-specific explanations of why this system has been more or less conflictual at different junctures during its history. It does not suggest when, why, or under what circumstances the system has moved toward or away from the boundary condition of absolute disorder.

It might be argued that the paradigm instructs us that the interstate system tends toward war and disorder when any state or coalition of states threatens simultaneously the sovereignty of a number of others, i.e., when an attempt for preponderance or imperial domination is mounted. But this is a self-evident definitional, rather than a theoretical, statement. (It is tantamount to stating that the more people that contract a particular disease, the closer that the species moves toward the epidemiological boundary condition of extinction.) The paradigm does yield theoretical expectations about how individual states are likely to respond to such situations (increase capabilities, form alliances, and so on), but again, these expectations fall far short of the kind of theory that I am suggesting we lack.[4] These are the limitations of systemic-level theory. While such theories are useful and necessary for a variety of analytical purposes, they do not provide a logic of the world political system.

The sovereignty/anarchy paradigm, though often amended and modified, continues to frame most system-level theorizing about interstate politics. It is instructive for our purposes to consider briefly and narrowly the orthodox refinement and elaboration of the approach recently offered by Kenneth Waltz (1979). Waltz, beginning with the traditional concept of anarchy as the interstate system's fundamental ordering principle, adds *functional nondifferentiation* and the systemic *distribution of capabilities* as essential structural properties (1979: 88-101). For Waltz, as for Wallerstein, systemic anarchy is a static property, a "structural constant" of the system. He speaks of an "anarchic order," but in this usage order is little more than a synonym for system; the variable extent of order that has actually obtained through the concrete history of the interstate system is not regarded, in Waltz's formulation, as an object of theoretical investigation. Functional nondifferentiation refers to the like character of the system's constituent state units. Unlike domestic political systems, there is no functional interstate division of labor because the exigencies of the security dilemma result in the replication of sovereignty maintenance functions in each state unit. Thus by Waltz's somewhat dubious definition,[5] functional specificity, or rather the lack of it, becomes another structural constant.

At this point, one might wonder how the variable properties of the interstate political system are to be accounted for with only theoretical terms that, by definition, are invariant. Waltz avoids a totally static scheme by introducing the distribution of capabilities across states; the argument for treating this as a crucial structural property plausibly rests on the metahypothesis, for which there is considerable but inconsistent evidence, that state behavior varies with changes in this distribution. Waltz then proceeds to truncate the concept to an extent that renders it virtually useless for purposes of long-term analysis of the interstate system. Waltz relates the distribution of capabilities to the system's *stability* (the latter being a concept that in principle might be applicable to a theory of the world political system), but he defines stability so narrowly that it too is of little analytic utility. In Waltz's formulation a system remains stable so long as it remains anarchic and so long as the distribution of capabilities does not shift so markedly that a *consequential* change in the number of principal state units (great powers) occurs. Begging here the question of what constitutes a consequential change, in Waltz's view the only change between 1700 and the present that qualifies as consequential was the shift from a multipolar to a bipolar distribution of capabilities in 1945 (1979: 162). We are thus left to ponder, *inter alia,* the Napoleonic Wars, World War I, and the world depression of the 1930s as moments in a two-and-a-half-century period of systemic stability. If indeed the interstate system has been quite stable according to Waltz's definitional stipulations, it is neither very interesting nor meaningful. "The system appears robust" (1979: 162), but Waltz's theory is not, at least not with respect to the long-term processes of the system with which Waltz is concerned.

It is perhaps unfair to focus these criticisms on Waltz, since he apparently did not set out to attain (what I have termed) a theory of the world political system. In fairness, Waltz's refinement of the classical orthodoxy, by carefully moving toward formalization, has enhanced its strengths, i.e., its contributions to an understanding of the systemic determinants of state behavior. The point is that Waltz fails to escape the classical paradigm's limitations. My criticisms therefore are not directed so much at Waltz as an individual theorist as they are at the collective failure of a discipline to seek, as its principal purpose, a theory of the concrete totality of its subject matter.

MODELSKI'S LONG-CYCLE FRAMEWORK AS A PROGRESSIVE PROBLEMSHIFT

Lakatos's (1970) scheme of "sophisticated falsificationism" provides a set of epistemological criteria for resolving the problems of theory choice and the assessment of theoretical progress. In brief, Lakatos contends that a theory is not falsified, in isolation from rival theories, by the demonstration of contrary observations or refuting evidence. Rather, we should approach the question of theory choice serially. A particular theory is not regarded as "falsified" or "refuted" until it is superseded by a successor theory that possesses excess empirical content, that is, a theory that subsumes the explanatory power of its predecessor and accounts for additional, novel information as well. A theory is said to be "theoretically progressive" if it provides excess empirical content and "empirically progressive" if some of this excess content is corroborated. A new theory that satisfies these criteria constitutes what Lakatos terms a "progressive problemshift."

There is ample reason to regard Modelski's theory of the "long cycle of world politics" (1978, 1980, 1982) as a progressive problemshift in relation to the systemic theories of the classical paradigm. As will be demonstrated, the long-cycle framework provides excess empirical content and, though it is too early for definitive judgment, initial empirical research has provided some measure of empirical corroboration (Modelski and Thompson, 1981; Thompson and Zuk, 1982; Rasler and Thompson, 1983).

The theory provides excess empirical content insofar as it conceives of the global (world) political system in its spatial and temporal entirety and attempts to account for regularities and periodicities in the structures and processes that inhere to this system rather than to its constituent parts. Modelski posits that the global political system has exhibited a pattern of cyclical fluctuations between (1) periods in which a single *world power* has assumed responsibility for the provision of the public good of systemic order and security and (2) periods that lack the leadership of a single world power and in which order-keeping functions either are jointly managed in ad hoc fashion by several major powers or are simply left undone. Five such long cycles are identified, each associated with the leadership of a particular world power: sixteenth-century Portugal, seventeenth-century Netherlands, eighteenth-century Great Britain, Great Britain again in the nineteenth century, and the United States in the twentieth. Modelski's successive world powers have gained this status through a strategy based on virtual monopoly control of strategic space (the seas and later air and outer space) rather than a continental strategy of land-based conquest and domination. This control, the strategic power of global reach, is therefore functional rather than territorial in nature.

Each long cycle has consisted of four phases: global war, world power, delegitimation, and deconcentration. In brief, interstate struggle over world leadership is resolved by means of global war, with the victor emerging as a world power that leads the system through a period of stability and order. This order is subject to entropy, however, and hence tends to decay over time. As global order deteriorates, the legitimacy of the world power's leadership is challenged, its coalition of supporting states fragments, and its control over strategic space diminishes. Other major powers vie for world leadership, and a new cycle is set in motion by another global war fought to resolve the problem of successsion.

It is important to point out that Modelski subsumes the main features of the classical paradigm. Though he eschews the term "anarchy"—his prior (1972) work refers instead to the isomorphic notion of "autonomy systems"—Modelski's world system similarly begins with the absence of a single world state or overarching political authority. But instead of simply assuming anarchy and leaving it at that, Modelski addresses the questions of how order is attained in an anarchical system and why it is impermanent. Rather than regarding an anarchical order as a structural constant, the variable *extent of order within anarchy* becomes Modelski's primary object of investigation.

With global order and disorder transformed into something to be explained, rather than remaining descriptive labels, Modelski then reworks other elements of the classical approach into explanatory concepts. The distribution of capabilities is of obvious importance since the long-cycle framework implies that global order is reliant upon a high concentration of a specific type of capability—the strategic power of global reach—in a single state, the world power; periods of disorder are associated with a wider dispersal of this capability. Recall also Waltz's assumption of functional nondifferentiation as another structural constant. Modelski turns this questionable premise on its head and thus makes it an explanatory concent by postulating that global order depends on functional specialization— the world power assumes a variety of functional responsibilities for which "ordinary" states lack the requisite capabilities and incentives. The control of strategic space, for example, requires a functionally specific type of capability which, in turn, is utilized for orderkeeping, the provision of security, the organization of the world economy, and other system maintenance and infrastructural tasks.[6]

We might sketch in skeletal form the structure of Modelski's explanatory scheme: Formal anarchy at the global level creates the need for the informal provision of order. Given, as the resultant of global war, a spatially skewed distribution of specific capabilities, a single state assumes and executes certain functional responsibilities designed to create and sustain global order. Order decays as the capabilities necessary to provide it are diffused, leading to increasing disorder and culminating in another global war. In this fashion, the whole process is characterized by a cyclical rhythm.

While it is impossible to do justice to the nuances of the long-cycle formulation in such short space, the above outline of its broad contours should suffice to demonstrate its excess empirical content in relation to its predecessors of the classical paradigm. Whether or not one agrees with Modelski's specific conceptualizations, temporal demarcations, and hypothesized periodicities, it is evident that he has addressed a new set of questions that are framed at a higher (global) level of analysis. The extent of empirical corroboration of course remains to be determined, but for the time being, Modelski's "long cycles" is the sole contender for a theory of the world political system and thereby also the only challenger to the emerging hegemony of materialist world system theory.

PUZZLES FOR A SINGLE MATERIALIST LOGIC

I have argued that materialist theory can afford to ignore neither the well-established, albeit limited, logic of interstate politics nor Modelski's prototheory of the world political system. If this assertion is correct, what kinds of analytical costs are exacted by this neglect? Setting aside for the moment the question of how materialist theory might benefit from attention to Modelski's ideas, and vice versa, I shall pose several logical proglems, or "puzzles," for which materialist solutions appear to be proscribed by the reductionist character of Wallersteinian theory. These puzzles, which reference past, present, and future implications of the interstate system's security-oriented logic, illustrate the limitations of apprehending the complexities of the world system with only a materialist theoretical apparatus.

Past

If the logic of the interstate system is to be regarded as derivative of the world capitalist mode of production, then it follows that this logic must be unique to the period since the inception of world capitalism. Demonstration of the existence of the classical paradigm's security-oriented logic in precapitalist systems would therefore undermine the materialist claim. On this point, Hopkins (1979: 38) and Hopkins and Wallerstein (1981: 245) invoke the authority of Walter Dorn, citing his assertion that is the "competitive character of the state system of modern Europe that distinguishes it from the political life of all previous and non-European civilizations of the world" (1940: 1). But this premise is patently incorrect. It is precisely its "competitive character" that the modern (circa 1500) interstate system shares with several well-known, multiple-sovereignty antecedents. The logic of unregulated competition among sovereign subunits (including the role of threats, self-help, alliances, balancing behavior, and war) has been shown to have operated among, *inter alia,* the ancient Chinese warring states (Walker, 1971), the ancient Indian states (Modelski, 1964), and the Greek city-states (Mandelbaum, 1981). Chase-Dunn (1981: 33) attempts to dismiss the relevance of isomorphism with precapitalist systems by arguing, with reference only to the Italian city-states, that "these state systems were unstable . . . and tended to become world empires." It is not clear how the eventual demise of these systems vitiates the counterargument linking the prior existence of the interstate political logic with the autonomy of the political realm.[7] If we observe process A operating in isolation at one point in time, and process A and (historically unique) process B coexisting at a subsequent point in time, it requires a curious form of reasoning to conclude that A derives from B.

Present

The advent of nuclear weapons has deepened the structural tragedy of collective insecurity. It is no exaggeration to say that a multithousand megaton nuclear exchange, some small fraction of existing arsenals, would jeopardize the survival of the earth as a habitable planet (given destruction of the ozone layer, other atmospheric damage, a radioactive ecosphere, and the more immediate and calculable shock, thermal, and prompt radiation effects). There are various, more or less probable paths to this and other, less final outcomes; for our purposes suffice it to say that the probability of nuclear war or holocaust is greater than zero. In the terms of the classical paradigm, the worst-case boundary condition of interstate anarchy can now be defined as the extinction of (all) the species. It is presumably non-controversial to regard this potentiality as a fundamental problem of the contemporary world system, and it is therefore not unreasonable to expect any aspiring theory of *the* world system to at least address it.

I am not aware of, nor can I conjure, a remotely plausible hypothesis that derives this problem from the logic of capital accumulation. Without belaboring the point, the problem is readily explicable, though obviously not soluble, in terms of the logic of interstate politics.

Future

Let us consider briefly the Wallersteinian prescription and prediction of an eventual world socialism—a unitary global sovereignty that will exercise collective, substantive rationality toward the desirable end of satisfying humankind's material needs in a just and equitable fashion. We can assume, somewhat heroically but not implausibly, that the technorational requisites for such arrangements (e.g., resource allocation, regional specialization, production, distribution) are within human reach. Note that as a fortuitous byproduct of a benevolent world socialism we will no longer be bothered by nettlesome interstate problems like arms races, nuclear threats, tensions, wars, and the like. The puzzle is: *Where did the states go?* I do not mean to reify states (and the interstate system) as a permanent, pragmatically optimal, or normatively desirable form of political organization. But Wallerstein's futurology appears to depend more on faith or hope than on reasoned analysis in the absence of some specification of the political path or range of possible paths that might lead to a world state—a universal transformation of individual consciousness? Cumulatively integrative processes? The shock of nuclear war or protracted world depression? Attainment by conquest of world empire? Again, without belaboring the point, the possibility of world government as a solution to the violence and disorder spawned by systemic anarchy has long been recognized by those operating within the classical paradigm. The question of how to arrive at this theoretical possibility, as well as the myriad practical political reasons why we have not and are not likely to, has for centuries been a venerable subject of theorizing (Ljiphart, 1974). Without consideration of these political questions, Wallerstein's world socialism is but another manifestation of materialist reductionism, here reducing the future rather than the past. As such, it amounts simply to a recrudescence of the cryptic Marxian forecast of the "withering away of the state."

As a final puzzle, consider the following mental experiment: Suppose that at some future point—perhaps around the time a unitary world socialism materializes—intelligent, humanlike life on a number of other planets is either discovered by or discovers the planet earth. Assume further that each planet, by virtue of mastery of travel through (what would instantaneously become strategic) space, possesses ample capabilities for projecting force and thus also for the waging of interplanetary war. How would we describe this incipient interplanetary system? Would be a capitalist galaxy? Universe? Perhaps eventually, especially if we assume a few resource-rich, military weak planets (with cheap labor). It is easy to envisage the development over time of interplanetary markets, division of labor, core and periphery, unequal exchange, and so forth. But the point of the mental experiment is that the logic of the interstate system would apply virtually immediately. The security dilemma would arise as a consequence of the structural situation of multiple sovereignty, thus rendering the earthly interstate system a microcosmic precursor, just as precapitalist interstate systems stand as microcosmic precursors in relation to the modern interstate system.

The object of these "puzzles" has been logically to demonstrate the autonomy of the interstate political realm. Although they raise, in abstract relief, the question of which of the world system's subsystems—political or material—is the "deep" structure and which is superstructure, no claim is made here for the primacy of the political.

Wallerstein's inclusion of the political structure of multiple sovereignty as a critical element in his conceptualization of the world capitalist mode of production has proven to be a bold and productive theoretical stroke. But once having put it there, it is analytically perilous to just leave it at that. Political pluralism at the world system level is a valid and useful premise for his interpretation of the logic of the world system's economic subsystem. But it is also much more than a dormant premise; it is another (political) subsystem with its own logic. To assert that these two logics have been intertwined during the course of their development and expansion from their common North Atlantic origins is to make a historical observation. To specify theoretically and empirically the complex manner in which they are entangled, where they are interactive and where they are not, where and when one or the other is dominant, is to suggest a formidable problematique. "Codetermination," "coevolution," "mutually interactive," and "reciprocal causation" are all terms that seem to point to an appropriate place to begin the task.

TOWARD AN INTEGRATED THEORY

What are the prospects for an integrated theory that addresses both the world system's political and material processes? How might such a theory be attained and what might it look like? Despite its appeal to considerations of parsimony and coherence, a strictly materialist approach to the complexities of the world system is, in ways I have tried to demonstrate, incomplete and thereby destined to provide an underdetermined account of the overall system's long-term operation.

It follows then that an integrated theory must build upon multiple assumptions that do not necessarily reflect a tightly constructed, totally coherent world view. Minimally, we have to insist that the premises of such a theory not be logically inconsistent, but it may be heroic to ask for too much more than that. A looser, additive set of premises—encompassing both the need for security and the imperatives of capital accumulation as systematic determinants of world system dynamics—is a more realistic goal, at least initially. For a time, we will in all likelihood have to be content with multiple descriptions and interpretations of the same event, process, or period; acknowledgment of circular causation without being unable to unravel cause and effect; and, more generally, some degree of indeterminacy in the relationship between political and economic processes.

One implication of these arguments is the need for multiple research strategies and testing procedures. Given the extensive spatiotemporal range and substantive scope of world system questions (and the data availability problems that arise in consequence), there is analytical need and space for both positivist, data-analytic research strategies (e.g., Modelski and Thompson, 1981; Thompson and Zuk, 1982) and the more traditional, narrative or configurative case study approaches (e.g., Rubinson, 1978). The central issue here concerns the kinds of knowledge that world system theory is in principle capable of producing. If we are trying to gain an understanding of the concrete historical evolution of the world system, then the knowledge we are seeking must to a large degree be interpretive in nature, rather than formal explanation (in the sense of a Hempelian, "covering law" explanation).[8] To state that our knowledge of the world system must be interpretive is not at all to gainsay the role of quantitative, hypothesis-testing research. In fact, this type of strategy, if properly framed and executed, can offer a more sound and certain basis for interpretation. The point is that such strategies will prove to be, in and of themselves, insufficient; likewise for the in-depth narrative case study. The objective should be, by matching and blending, to render the two types of information complementary. Points at which the two strategies provide inconsistent or contradictory information should be regarded as anomalous and thus as points that require further scrutiny. I might add that in world system research the boundary between formal, data-analytic, and case study strategies is hard to demarcate. How, for example, would we label a time-series analysis of American hegemonic leadership in the post-1945 period? If we regard the American case as a replication of earlier instances of the same phenomenon, then a time-series analysis becomes a case study.

Our objective can be characterized as an intrepretive/explanatory tapestry of the modern world system's five centuries; the tapestry's overall design and pattern are provided by theory, bolstered with hard empirical research, and knit together and embroidered with narrative accounts. This tapestry, however, will be riddled with spatial, temporal, and substantive gaps and tears. Some periods and processes will be interpreted with less clarity of pattern and historical plausibility than others; both Wallerstein's and Modelski's treatments of the eighteenth century, for example, suggest that this period is less amenable to a neat, schematic interpretation than are prior and subsequent periods. The implication is that "grand" theory will have to rely heavily on auxiliary theories to fill in gaps, repair tears, and, more generally, to account for the diversity and complexity of human affairs apprehended at the world system level. However, auxiliary theories imply a loss of parsimony and some measure of messiness, and the criteria for assessing auxiliary theories and their bearing on the main theory at issue are rather problematic. As Lakatos (1970: 116-118) points out, the line between scientifically valid auxiliary theories and those that are ad hoc and/or pseudoscientific (and degenerative) is often difficult to draw.

The issue of world leadership (or hegemony) illustrates these problems of world system theory: the need for multiple explanatory logics and multiple research strategies, and the messiness attendant to the introduction of auxiliary theories. Without delving into the question of whether there have been three (Wallerstein) or five (Modelski) replications of this phenomenon, it is clear that a theory cast strictly at the world system level cannot provide an adequate understanding of the dynamics of world leadership. Keohane (1980) offers a succinct system-level explanation for the assumption of hegemonic leadership responsibilities: A state enjoying a systemic preponderance of capabilities, resources, and productive advantage has the largest stake in the system's orderly and stable functioning and, in this sense, will have strong incentives to undertake this role, i.e., to provide via political and economic means the (world) public goods of order and stability. Keohane also notes, however, that system-level theory is unable to predict how the candidate for world leadership will respond to these incentives. That this empirical blindspot translates into empirical difficulties is evidenced by the interwar interregnum analyzed in these terms by Kindleberger (1973) and by the period that Krasner (1978) describes as the "false start" of American leadership after World War II. In short, it cannot be predicted from system-level theory that a state possessing the requisite capabilities and confronting the "right" systemic incentives will necessarily step into the leadership position. Given the critical role of deviant cases in a universe of three to five replications, an auxiliary theory (of the hegemonic state) that focuses on factors internal to the state in question is required. Moreover, the contention that an understanding of the actual conduct of leadership, its character and duration, requires unit-level as well as system-level explanations has been amply demonstrated for the American case (Keohane, 1982; Krasner, 1982).

With these theoretical admonitions in mind, I turn to a consideration of how elements of materialist theory might be integrated with theories of interstate politics and with Modelski's more ambitious long-cycle theory. I will first examine some specific areas in which materialist theory would benefit from insights gained from political-security approaches and then will reverse the direction of potential influence.

POLITICAL LESSONS FOR MATERIALIST THEORY

The first step down the road of economic reductionism is Wallerstein's (1974) treatment of the formation and elaboration of territorial states in fifteenth- and sixteenth-century Europe. Since Skocpol (1977), Gourevitch (1978), and Zolberg (1981) have provided extensive criticisms of the aspect of Wallersteinian theory, only a brief overview of the problem is necessary. Wallerstein's critics focus on his: teleological explanations for the emergence of both capitalism and states; crude instrumentalism in viewing states largely as political machinery that exists to be manipulated by dominant capitalist classes for purposes of maximizing their share of the world product; and circularity and empirical ambiguity in his argument that attempts to derive variation in state strength from differential position in the world economy. All of these criticisms zero in on what is, for our purposes, the chief failing of Wallerstein's conception of the state—the neglect of the security motive in the formation and strengthening of states as a mode of political organization. Herz (1976: 100-101) poses the question, "what is it that ultimately accounted for the peculiar unity, compactness, coherence of the modern nation state . . . ?" and responds by pointing to

> that substratum of statehood where the state unit confronts us, as it were, in its physical, corporeal capacity: as an expanse of territory encircled for its identification and its defense by a "hard shell" of fortifications. In this lies what will here be referred to as the "impermeability," or "impenetrability," or simply the "territoriality," of the modern state. The fact that it was surrounded by a hard shell rendered it to some extent secure from foreign penetration, and thus made it an ultimate unit of protection for those within its boundaries. Throughout history, that unit which affords protection and security to human beings has tended to become the basic political unit.

Wallerstein's inattention to this fundamental dimension of statehood blinds him to the security dilemma and the other principal lessons of the classical paradigm. In consequence, all of materialist theory appears blinded to the logic of interstate politics and its crucial role in world system processes. In sum, if materialist theory is to be broadened to encompass political factors or to be made compatible with existing security-oriented theories, the notion that states are "conceptually given by, because factually imposed by, the developmental processes of the capitalist world-economy" (Hopkins and Wallerstein, 1981: 245) will have to be abandoned in favor of a more balanced and historically accurate view.

Materialist theory also suffers from a biased and incomplete conception of hegemonic leadership and the imperfect order that it provides. For Wallersteinians, hegemony, defined in terms of simultaneous productive, commercial, and financial advantage, is simply a platform that the hegemonic state uses to extract an inordinate share of the world product. While there is no doubt an element of validity in this perspective—I readily agree with Chase-Dunn's wry assertion that "U.S. hegemony has not been a picnic for everyone" (1982: 93)—it is a short-sighted conceptualization of a more complex phenomenon. Hegemonic leadership springs from the need for order (within political anarchy) as well as from the perceived opportunity to maximize competitive economic advantages. As such, it requires the organization of both strategic and economic space or, in Boulding's (1963) terminology, the management of both a "threat system" and an "exchange system." Organization and management on a global scale require a considerable investment of various resources by the hegemonic state and often entail the sacrifice of some immediate, tangible national interests in pursuit of longer-term, more diffuse global goals. That some, though not all, other states derive both security and material benefits from the exercise of hegemonic leadership is apparent in all three hegemonies identified by materialist theory. There is hence historical validity and considerable analytic utility in viewing the provision of leadership positively, as a public good.[9] I am not suggesting that the exercise of hegemony is a selfless, altruistic action or that it is not subject to abuse. In particular, the hegemonic state may extract or "consume" more resources from the balance of the system than it "invests" in the provision of order. We might regard the ratio of investment to consumption as an index for distinguishing between more or less benevolent forms or periods of hegemony. This hypothetical ratio is a variable that can be expected to decline over the duration of a particular period, or cycle, of hegemonic leadership. But this is ultimately an empirical question, and hence, to define hegemony solely in terms of its exploitative dimensions (or, for that matter, solely in terms of its positive features) is to distort and diminish its analytical potential for contributing to an explanation of the world system's cyclical processes.

Another deficient area in materialist theory is its monocausal, Leninist view of war as simply a struggle over (again) national shares of the world product. While this is not the place to recount the many causes of war, suffice it to say that greed or materialist drives are but one element of a very large set. This is a crucial inadequacy for an understanding of war is essential to a broader understanding of the dynamics, political and material, of the world system. Modelski's (1978) theoretical argument concerning the functional role of global war as a means of resolving world leadership struggles is both intuitively valid and empirically productive (see Modelski and Thompson, 1981). Furthermore, the theoretical necessity of an understanding of war for adequate comprehension of the world system's fluctuating material processes has been empirically demonstrated (Thompson and Zuk, 1982). By contrast, the tendency of materialist theorists is to regard war (minimally) as a category of events to be fit, when convenient, in narrative accounts or (maximally) as an occasional violent reorganization on a global scale of the means of production. Failure to develop or borrow a more sophisticated theoretical perspective has and will continue to circumscribe the explanatory power of Wallersteinian theory.

MATERIALIST LESSONS FOR POLITICAL THEORY

One aspect of the world system's development that is more adequately addressed by materialist theory is the question of the system's physical expansion. Since both capitalism and the state system originated in Northern Europe and eventually spread outward to encompass the entire globe, the spatial extension of these organizational modes is an important object of explanation for both material and political theorists. Yet while Wallerstein has formulated a thorough and convincing explanation of the manner in which "external areas" were incorporated into a "peripheral" position in the world system's division of labor, Modelski has left the question largely unaddressed. I would suggest that this asymmetry stems from several sources. First, it is reasonable to assert that the motor force behind European exploration and colonization was predominately material—initially the search for preciosities and later for raw materials—rather than strategic in nature. Though the naval means that enabled this expansion fall into Modelski's category of strategic reach, they are in this case simply means and do not address the motivations that lie behind the ends that were sought. To be sure, the initial European expansion was not exclusively driven by material objectives; and it is also true that, once the various extra-European areas of the world became objects of European competition, strategic locations in these areas became military ends as well. Nonetheless, it is a fair generalization that the outward expansion owes much more to economic than to political-military motivations.

Second, Modelski's emphasis on the world system's political processes follows a long tradition of Eurocentric "great power reductionism." The role of the peripheral areas in the operation of the world political system has been limited, until quite recently in world system time, to those periods during which they have been pawns of great power competition and rivalry. In consequence, the peripheries could safely be abstracted from in attempts to account for the machinations of the system's principal political actors, the European great powers. Yet it is these same peripheral areas that are an integral part of Wallerstein's division of labor that, in turn, serves as the theoretical centerpiece of his interpretation of the capitalist world economy.[10] In sum, we might say that the expansion of the world system is an issue area in which materialist theory holds a comparative advantage and that it has not left this advantage unexploited. Modelski's oceanic emphasis should be quite compatible with material theory's account of European expansion, but in order to incorporate the explanatory power of Wallersteinian theory he will have to borrow the necessary material premises.

Abstraction from the world system's peripheral areas and their role in the world capitalist division of labor leads to a second void in Modelski's long-cycle framework—it does not address the question of uneven national development. Since this question is Wallersteinian theory's primary object of investigation, it is not surprising that a wide comparative advantage is also enjoyed here. I argued earlier that materialist theory would remain incomplete as a theory of *the* world system so long as it did not address the system's explicitly political processes; the same caution applies here. While Modelski (1982) has moved toward incorporation of economic factors into his long-cycle theory, his main thrust in this respect is to account for the interrelationship between the political long cycle and cyclical fluctuations in the world economy. This is certainly an appropriate direction, but it still leaves unaddressed the question of uneven development within the world system. This question is of great importance to any prospective theory of the world system since issues of uneven development are distributional issues and, as Gilpin (1975: ch. 1) forcefully argues, distributional issues are intrinsically political issues.

CAPABILITY CHANGE AS
THEORETICAL NEXUS

The question of uneven development directs our attention to what is ostensibly a strong argument for the claim of a single world capitalist logic. Chase-Dunn (1981) has advanced the most explicit version of this argument (shared by materialist theorists) that the uneven nature of capitalist economic development has been a necessary condition for the continuation of the interstate political system. In response to his counterfactual question "what would have happened to the interstate system if the capitalist would economy had not survived?" he asserts, "Probably, it would have become a world empire" (1981: 35). It is far from evident why this transformation would "probably" have occurred. Does the argument imply that all core states (great powers) would develop *equally* once capitalism's uneven developmental processes had ceased to operate? If so, this would lead to a multipolar, balance-of-power outcome rather than world empire. Or does it imply that one core state would race ahead of the others in terms of development (and hence in terms of capabilities) and then proceed to consolidate forcibly the rest into a hierarchical world empire? But how is this to happen in the absence of uneven development?

Despite this cryptic counterfactual argument, there is an element of validity in the proposition that the dynamics of the world political system are linked to world capitalism's uneven developmental processes. Insofar as capitalist economic development provides the stuff of which states' capabilities and power resources are made, and insofar as changes in the systemic distribution of capabilities affect the world system's political processes, the linkage is apparent. At a minimum, we can say that the acceleration of capitalist development through long historical time has hastened the rate at which changes in capabilities occur. But beyond this, which is a far cry from the assertion that interstate politics would cease to exist with the demise of capitalism, what can we say about the linkage?

First note that the preponderance of Wallersteinian theory's explanatory power with respect to uneven development pertains to the developmental disparities between core and periphery of the world system. If we narrow our focus to within the core, the ability of materialist theory to account for variable rates of development diminishes. Returning to the specific question of hegemony as an instance of uneven development within the core, there is some prior materialist theorizing that bears on this issue. Chase-Dunn has assembled a set of "causes and conditions of the rise and fall of hegemonic core states" (1982: 80-85). Looking at the rise of hegemonic states, we find that all of the causes and conditions are attributes that inhere to the individual state and society: geographic centrality, innovative technologies, sufficient investment capital, diversified capital-intensive agriculture, human capital, a solidary ruling class coalition, the ability to extract taxes, egalitarian and pluralist politics, and a large home market. None of these derives from the logic of the world capitalist system. Turning to causes and conditions of hegemonic decline, we find a catalogue of factors, several of which are more systemic in nature: the diffusion of core production (and thereby of competitive advantage) to other core states, the outflow of investment capital, and, within the hegemonic state, economic aging, rising wage costs, retreat to protectionism, and weariness of the costs of hegemony. Focusing on the diffusion of core production and the outflow of investment capital (as causes that derive from the logic of world capitalism), it is evident that these factors operate so as to increase the rate of capitalist development among nonhegemonic core states and to close the developmental distance between them and the hegemonic state. Hence only the hegemonic state suffers from the systemic process of uneven development—it slows down in relation to the other core states. In sum, materialist theory cannot account in nonparticularistic fashion for the rise of states to the top of the core into a hegemonic position. *All* of the factors that lead to hegemony are located inside the state in question. Uneven capitalist development might be said to be operative on the downside of hegemony, but is this a meaningful argument if the net result of the process is to produce a *more even* distribution of capabilities across the set of core states? The single logic of world capitalism is working during a particular phase of the world system's movement, but it might be more appropriately termed "even" development. To argue that this leveling process has saved the world system from transformation into world empire, one would have to make the historically implausible argument that seventeenth-century Netherlands, nineteenth-century Great Britain, and post-World War II United States were each bent on establishing a world state under their imperial aegis.

In sum, the linkage between the uneven developmental processes of world capitalism and the shifting capabilities of states is probably the most important point of intersection between the world system's political and material processes. The crucial role of changing relative capabilities has not been overlooked by theorists of the international political system (e.g., Choucri and North, 1974; Doran and Parsons, 1980; Organski and Kugler, 1980). The common thrust of these analyses, however, reinforces Chase-Dunn's tacit admission that the loci of capability change are to be found within states rather than at the global level. Nevertheless, theoretical and empirical closure on this question is not yet in sight. Suffice it to say that the expansive claims of materialist theorists in this regard remain *ex cathedra*. In fact, it seems reasonable to conclude that the materialist theory thus far advanced makes a stronger case for the dependence of world capitalism on the interstate political system than it does for the reverse dependency. To conclude, the linkage between material processes and shifts in state capabilities remains an appropriate point for the concentration of research energies of both materialist and political theorists.

CONCLUSION

In the course of this essay, I have critiqued at length both political and material approaches to the modern world system. I hope that these criticisms have served their intended purposes, not the least of which was to establish that world politics possesses its own unique substance. Beyond that, the criticisms were intended to demonstrate that a single explanatory logic, either political or material, will not suffice for purposes of analyzing a subject as diverse, complex, and vast as the world system. If this demonstration has been successful, it follows that an integrated theory will have to be constructed with multiple assumptions, concepts, explanatory logics, and research strategies. Finally, I hope that I have pointed the way toward such an integrated theory by identifying what modifications would have to be made in order to reconcile existing political and material approaches.

NOTES

1. For historical/empirical arguments for the autonomy of the political sphere, see Modelski and Thompson (1981), Zolberg (1981), Thompson (1983a, 1983b), and Thompson and Zuk (1982).

2. The addition in recent centuries (to the set of the state's sovereign imperatives) of the objective of preserving and maximizing the welfare of its population complicates the security-oriented logic of the classical paradigm by forcing its intersection with various materialist logics.

3. For an excellent discussion, illustrated with historical examples, of the interaction between anarchy and the psychological dynamics that follow from it, see Jervis (1976: chap. 3).

4. Some might also suggest that the literature comparing multipolar balance of power and bipolar systems offers a beginning toward a theory of the world political system. But surely we would not want to advise materialist theorists to wade through that conceptually confused and empirically inconclusive tangle.

5. The definition is dubious because Waltz ignores a variety of convincing demonstrations of functional differentiation in prior theory and research. Oddly enough, Waltz subsequently relaxes this assumption and, in the process, provides a convincing demonstration of functional differentiation (1979: chap. 9). See Kaplan (1957) for a systemic-level treatment that develops role differentiation as an explanatory concept.

6. Though this aspect of his work is not presented here, Modelski's long-cycle theory reflects an appreciation of the importance of economic processes to the world political system, and vice versa.

7. It should be noted that if Wallerstein's (1980b) prediction regarding the arrival of a unitary world socialism in 100 to 150 years is correct, this would give the modern interstate system a life span roughly comparable to that of the Chinese warring states system, which endured for about five and a half centuries until its consolidation into empire in the third century B.C.

8. Hopkins (1978) expresses this distinction clearly, though in my view he overdraws to a large extent its practical implications.

9. It should be noted that Modelski's treatment of world politics as an exchange process between consumers and producers of order (Modelski and Thompson, 1981) is difficult to square with the notion of order as a public good. The theory of hegemonic stability suggests that a state with extraordinary capabilities and resources will also have the largest stake in the continued stable operation of the system; thus it will have extraordinary incentives to invest in order. If this argument is translated into exchange theory terms, the largest producer of order is simultaneously its largest consumer; this interpretation would seem to vitiate the utility of conceiving of the problem in terms of exchange.

10. This problem might be usefully thought of in terms of an interaction matrix, the cells of which contain interactions within and between core, periphery, and semiperiphery. The study of world politics would heavily fill in that portion of the matrix that records within core interactions, while filling the other cells much more sparsely. By contrast, Wallerstein's world-economy would place entries in a wider assortment of cells across the different categories.

REFERENCES

BOULDING, K. E. (:1963) "Towards a pure theory of threat systems." American Economic Review 53 (May): 424-434.

CHASE-DUNN, C. (1982) "International economic policy in a declining core state," pp. 77-96 in W. P. Avery and D. P. Rapkin (eds.) America in a Changing World Political Economy. New York: Longman.

———(1981) "Interstate system and capitalist world-economy: one logic or two?" International Studies Quarterly 25 (March): 19-42.

——— and R. RUBINSON (1979) "Cycles, trends and new departures in world-system development," pp. 276-295 in J. W. Meyer and M. T. Hannan (eds.) National Development and the World System. Chicago: University of Chicago Press.

CHOUCRI, N. and R. NORTH (1974) Nations in Conflict. San Francisco: W. H. Freeman.

DORAN, C. F. and W. PARSONS (1980) "War and the cycle of relative power." American Political Science Review 74 (December): 947-965.

DORN, W. (1940) Competition for Empire, 1740-1763. New York: Harper.

GILPIN, R. (1975) U.S. Power and the Multinational Corporation: The Political Economy of Foreign Direct Investment. New York: Basic Books.

GOUREVITCH, P. (1978) " The international system and regime formation: a critical review of Anderson and Wallerstein." Comparative Politics 10: 419-438.

HERZ, J. H. (1976) The Nation-State and the Crisis of World Politics. New York: McKay.

HOPKINS, T. K. (1979) "The study of the capitalist world-economy: some introductory considerations," pp. 9-17 in W. L. Godfrank (ed.) The World-System of Capitalism: Past and Present. Beverly Hills, CA: Sage.

———(1978) "World-system analysis: methodological issues," pp. 199-217 in B. H. Kaplan (ed.) Social Change in the Capitalist World-Economy. Beverly Hills, CA: Sage.

——— and I. WALLERSTEIN (1981) "Structural transformations of the world-economy," pp. 233-261 in R. Rubinson (ed.) Dynamics of World Development. Beverly Hills, CA: Sage.

JERVIS, R. (1976) Perception and Misperception in International Politics. Princeton, NJ: Princeton University Press.

KAPLAN, M. A. (1957) System and Process in International Politics. New York: John Wiley.

KEOHANE, R. O. (1982) "Hegemonic leadership and U.S. foreign policy in the 'long decade' of the 1950s," pp. 49-76 in W. P. Avery and D. P. Rapkin (eds.) America in a Changing World Political Economy. New York: Longman.

———(1980) "The theory of hegemonic stability and changes in international economic regimes, 1967-1977," pp. 131-162 in O. R. Holsti, R. M. Siverson, and A. L. George (eds.) Change in the International System. Boulder, CO: Westview.

KINDLEBERGER, C. P. (1973) The World in Depression, 1929-1939. Berkeley: University of California Press.

KRASNER, S. K. (1982) "American policy and global economic stability," pp. 29-48 in W. P. Avery and D. P. Rapkin (eds.) America in a Changing World Political Economy. New York: Longman.

———(1978) "United States commercial and monetary policy: unravelling the paradox of external strength and internal weakness," pp. 51-87 in P. J. Katzenstein (ed.) Between Power and Plenty: Foreign Economic Policies of Advanced Industrial States. Madison: University of Wisconsin Press.

LAKATOS, I. (1970) "Falsification and the methodology of scientific research programmes," pp. 91-196 in I. Lakatos and A. Musgrave (eds.) Criticism and the Growth of Knowledge. New York: Cambridge University Press.

LIJPHART, A. (1974) "The structure of the theoretical revolution in international relations." International Studies Quarterly 18 (March): 41-74.

MANDELBAUM, M. (1981) The Nuclear Revolution: International Politics Before and After Hiroshima. New York: Cambridge University Press.

MODELSKI, G. (1982) "Long cycles and the strategy of United States international economic policy," pp. 97-116 in W. P. Avery and D. P. Rapkin (eds.) America in a Changing World Political Economy. New York: Longman.

———(1980) "The theory of long cycles and U.S. strategic policy," pp. 3-21 in R. Harkavy and E. A. Kolodziej (eds.) American Security Policy and Policy-Making. Lexington, MA: D. C. Heath.

———(1978) "The long cycle of global politics and the nation-state." Comparative Studies in Society and History 20 (April): 214-235.

———(1972) Principles of World Politics. New York: Free Press.

————(1964) "Kautilya: foreign policy and international system in the ancient Hindu world." American Political Science Review 58 (September).

———— and W. R. THOMPSON (1981) "Testing cobweb models of the long cycle of world leadership." Paper presented at the Annual Meeting of the Peace Science Society (International), Philadelphia, November.

ORGANSKI, A.F.K. and J. KUGLER(1980) The War Ledger. Chicago: University of Chicago Press.

RASLER, K. A. and W. R. THOMPSON (1983) "Global wars, public debts, and the long cycle." World Politics 35 (July).

RUBINSON, R. (1978) "Political transformation in Germany and the United States," pp. 39-73 in B. H. Kaplan (ed.) Social Change in the Capitalist World-Economy. Beverly Hills, CA: Sage.

SKOCPOL, T. (1977) "Wallerstein's world capitalist system: a theoretical and historical critique." American Journal of Sociology 82, 5: 1075-1090.

THOMPSON, W. R. (1983a) "The world-economy and the long cycle of world leadership: the question of world system time," in P. J. McGowan and C. W. Kegley, Jr. (eds) Foreign Policy and the Modern World-System. Beverly Hills, CA: Sage.

————(1983b) "Uneven economic growth, systemic challenges, and global wars." International Studies Quarterly 27 (September).

———— and G. ZUK (1982) "War, inflation, and Kondratieff's long waves." Journal of Conflict Resolution 26 (December): 621-644.

WALKER, R. L. (1971) The Multi-State System of Ancient China. Westport, CT: Greenwood.

WALLERSTEIN, I. (1980) The Modern World-system: Mercantilism and the Consolidation of the European World Economy, 1600-1750. New York: Academic.

————(1980b) "The future of the world-economy," pp. 167-180 in T. K. Hopkins and I. Wallerstein (eds.) Processes of the World-System. Beverly Hills, CA: Sage.

————(1970. The Capitalist World-Economy. Cambridge: Cambridge University Press.

————(1974) The Modern World-System: Capitalist Agriculture and the Origins of the European Economy in the Sixteenth Century. New York: Academic.

WALTZ, K. N. (1979) Theory of International Politics. Reading, MA: Addison-Wesley.

ZOLBERG, A. R. (1981) "Origins of the modern world system: a missing link." World Politics 33 (January): 253-281.

11

"World" and "System"
A Misalliance

ARISTIDE R. ZOLBERG

Setting forth general norms for history as a nascent profession, Ranke insisted on the necessity of connecting national-level historical research with "the universal," arguing that "without this link, research would become enfeebled." But he also warned that "without exact research the conception of the universal would degenerate into a phantasm" (Stern, 1956: 62). Ranke's remarks, uttered over a century ago, are indissociable; they constitute a single admonition, which will guide my comments on the contributions to the present collection as well as on the broader trends they represent.

Transcending compartmentalization of the macroanalytic social sciences into specialized academic disciplines, disparate theoretical schools, national parishes, and ideological chapels, there has arisen a cluster of scholars who share a strong sense of dissatisfaction with the conventional notion that the world may be treated as a set of largely self-contained societal entities, coinciding by and large with international boundaries and hence suitable for an analytic treatment akin to that accorded to individual members of a species in biology. These entities are generally considered *primary* for the purposes of theory construction, i.e., logically and empirically prior to interactions and exchanges among them; the latter processes in turn are considered as forming a derivative field of activity, whose analysis is usually confined to nearly autonomous subdisciplines in economics, political science, and history (Gourevitch, 1978). It is noteworthy, in this respect, that sociology is conceptually so bound up with the notion of society that no such subdiscipline has evolved within it at all.

The dissatisfaction arises from a growing awareness that interactions among the units, as well as material, ideational, and human flows between them, do not merely occasionally determine important changes in the internal life of national societies—as a common-sense view of the historical record as well as observation of the contemporary scene clearly indicates—but that such inter-, trans-, or perhaps more appropriately yet, meta-societal processes are in fact *constitutive* of fundamental features of social organization within countries, such as the formation and transformation of states and regimes.

The issue of how to deal with such weighty, externally generated effects emerged on the agenda mostly as a result of attention to the consequences of global-level economic structures and processes for the development of the contemporary Third World. The dependency perspective constituted a genuine "problemshift"—to use the Lakatosian term that appears to be replacing Kuhnian talk of "paradigmatic change"—leading to the abandonment of the more naive versions of developmentalism, whereby the world was conceived of as a set of societies with a common genetic code, identified by placecards at the United Nations, among whom ontogeny recapitulates phylogeny, as the latest-born proceed through uniform stages of economic growth; evolve from tradition to modernity by way of movement from one set of pattern variables to another; or yet lurch from infancy to maturity in Ericksonian fashion, by way of a predictable succession of crises of political development.

Notwithstanding the rudimentary character of the propositions it generated, the dependency perspective had significant heuristic effects in that it drew attention, simultaneously, to two very different things. Most prominently, it stressed the significance of what may be termed, in the most general sense, *interpenetration* of the societal and meta-societal levels. But by taking the meta-societal level into consideration as a variable in the development of societies, it also led us back into history in the most elemental, Heraclitian sense. Given that the composition of the external environment was altered by the activities of early modernizers, the experience of countries in which apparently similar transformational processes got under way later was bound to be very different as well. One cannot step twice in the same stream. Indeed, if this logic is followed to its conclusion, it makes little sense to speak of "early" and "late" modernizers, for example, because the transformational processes experienced by each group are so dissimilar as to preclude applying the same general term to the experience of both. And if that is so, many of our theoretical constructs must be abandoned as hiding more than they reveal.

Recent analyses have extended the dependency perspective back in time, leading to a reconsideration of a variety of historical questions. Others, including myself, have insisted further that the process of interpenetration is by no means limited to the economic sphere, but occurs as well with respect to political and cultural processes. Leaving aside, for the time being, the question of how to conceptualize relationships among these distinct spheres of social activity, it is evident that when considered in all its ramifications, attention to interpenetration entails a much more general problemshift than most of us who sensed a need to cast our theoretical net beyond the societal level were initially aware.

Matters are rendered even more problematic by a concomitant dissatisfaction, among scholars dealing with the international level, with the convention that for *their* purposes, states may be considered as solid bodies whose behavior can be accounted for by an analysis of how they interact with one another *qua* solids. This is indicated by, among other things, their growing interest in "transnational" as distinct from "international" processes; by attempts to overcome the traditional separation between theories of international politics and theories of international economics, with the resulting emergence of a "political economy" perspective that is to be distinguished from the neo-Marxian school of the same name; as well as by concern with the domestic roots of activity at the international level. In short, whether initiated by "internalists" looking outward or by internationalists who realize that their table does not contain billiard balls and that is not flat, efforts to tinker with existing frameworks in order to overcome perceived inadequacies have opened up a Pandora's box from which a wide array of theoretical problems have escaped. It is no exaggeration to suggest that the problemshift under consideration massively challenges the collective ability of the social sciences to construct valid theory at the macroanalytic level.

Yet, were a nineteenth-century colleague to appear suddenly in our midst, having been preserved by some precocious but subsequently forgotten development in cyrogenics, he might well wonder what the fuss is all about. Such a question is by no means disingeneous. As the quotation from Ranke indicates, awareness of interpenetration is hardly new. Nor, would this well-informed person point out, was this confined to historians: It was inherent in the world-historical outlook, a broad-spectrum intellectual tradition associated with the Enlightenment and shared by such widely different theoretical ancestors of today's social sciences as Hegel and Kant, Smith and Marx, Weber and Spencer.

Is the recent discovery of the world and of history by social scientists then merely another manifestation of our tendency to reinvent the wheel and to belabor the obvious? The reply, as might be provided by a member of one of the principal hermaneutic circles represented in this collection, the *Review* crowd and the "long cycle of leadership" group, is that what is new is the coupling of "world" with "system." Such a coupling, they insist, is superior to previous approaches to the problem under consideration. Going beyond diffuse intimations of interconnectedness among the disparate strands of human experience and history, as well as beyond more concrete but limited observations concerning this or that aspect of interpenetration in a particular time and place, the "world system" perspective brings to bear on the issue at hand unprecedented theoretical ingenuity and methodological rigor.

Overwhelmed by the spectacle of so many other achievements since he was put in cold storage, our resurrected colleague might well be persuaded of the validity of such a claim. As for myself, I remain skeptical, and my overall position in relation to the self-assured theoretical assertions associated with the various "world system" schools might be regarded as that of an antagonistic friend or friendly adversary. Sharing the contributors' sense that interpenetration is a vitally important but unduly neglected process, I believe with them that analysis at the global level is not merely a valid intellectual undertaking but even a necessary one if we are to make progress in understanding any part, past or present, of an obviously interconnected world. Moreover, I agree that to this end it would be very heuristic indeed to *reverse* the conventional order of theoretical consideration, i.e., to conceptualize as the primary units of analysis comprehensive entities of which national societies as well as metasocietal structures and processes can be viewed as components. But I am equally persuaded that the coupling of the world-historical outlook with systems analysis, each of which is fruitful separately, produces a regressive hybrid. In short, as conceived by Wallerstein and Modelski, the universal degenerates into a phantasm, luring unwary social scientists toward a fruitless learch for elusive laws of history.

I am well aware that not all the contributors conceptualize "world system" in this manner; but as the editor's introduction indicates, the central thrust of this volume is very much a debate among a number of scholars who accept the reality of a single, all-encompassing global entity of long duration, and who view it as an appropriate unit of analysis, while differing on whether the dynamics of that entity can be accounted for by one logic, that of capitalist relations of production, or two, with the second pertaining to interactions between states, mostly of a strategic nature. Since my own earlier work in this field appears to support the latter camp, it is important to specify at some length why I find myself in approximately equal disagreement with both sides of the debate.

* * *

The mode of historical reflection inaugurated by Hegel was so powerful that it guided even his opponents. While turning Hegel on his head, Marx nevertheless adopted his agenda, the construction of a theory of history, so that from a perspective attuned to the structure of Western thought, similarities between them are more striking than differences. In somewhat the same manner, albeit setting out to overthrow the Parsonian sociological tradition, Immanuel Wallerstein adheres to the Parsonian program, seeking to erect what C. Wright Mills (1961: 22-23) dubbed a "grand theory" of the nature of man and society in the form of an abstract system. True, the world-system framework emphasizes conflict rather than equilibrium, relations of production rather than values, and diachrony rather than synchrony. But claims concerning its distinctively "real" character notwithstanding, the system is a highly formal one, and the drawbacks of such formalism are, if anything, enhanced by efforts to harness it to the Marxist quest for a theory of history.

There is no need to restate in detail the demonstration that Wallerstein's account of the origins of the Western world-system is deeply flawed by his inadequate treatment of political structures and processes. My criticism to that effect was by no means original, as indicated by appropriate references to Gourevitch, Skocpol, and Modelski, who pointed in the same direction (Zolberg, 1981a). However, as Rapkin notes in his contribution to the present volume, I went somewhat further than others by identifying, at various points in Wallerstein's analysis of the rise of the European world-economy in the long sixteenth century, a series of historical problems that could be resolved simultaneously by introducing what constitutes, from the perspective of his theory, an exogenous factor. The method I followed is akin to that of "path analysis," in that the "missing link" of the title was shown to account for a significant part of the variance with which Wallerstein is concerned.

Starting from the observation of effects, I went on to identify a generic process of which they were manifestations, and thereby came to posit a distinctive structure that generated the process. This was labeled, for short, "the system of states"—including under that term some aspects of the internal political organization of the relevant countries as well as interactions among them, involving power and ultimately force. I concluded that this political structure was "as basic as the economic" and that it was not determined by relations of production, although changing economic conditions obviously contributed to state formation and the like. The general nature of relationships between the two structures, economic and political, was captured by Otto Hintze's term "co-determination," or, alternatively, Perry Anderson's "over-determination." Equally acceptable to me is Chase-Dunn's subsequent characterization of the two as "interdependent determinants."

Less noticed, perhaps because the point was insufficiently emphasized, was the fact that the contribution of processes engendered by an interacting system of states to the formation of "the modern world-system" led me to question Wallerstein's assertions concerning the "real" and "self-contained" character of that entity and, ultimately, "the possibility of ever devising an elegant theory encompassing the origins of the modern world and its subsequent evolution" (Zolberg, 1981a: 281). I shall return to the latter, more general point in the next section. Wallerstein's insistence that his unit of analysis is to be fundamentally distinguished from the abstract "social systems" of conventional social science is basic to his general theoretical argument (Wallerstein, 1974: 3-11, 347). Upon close examination, however, this distinctiveness vanishes. Although this can be demonstrated in a number of different ways, it is easiest to do by elaborating the broader implications of political interpenetration.

As observable throughout the "long sixteenth century," this process was not only intra-European, but also involved strategic interactions between European and other collective actors. The latter included some who were to be shortly gobbled up by Wallerstein's Pac-Man, ending up in the system's semi-periphery or periphery; but there were others who effectively resisted. In short, the delineation of the boundaries of the world-system as of approximately 1650 cannot be accounted for by endogenous processes alone—the limits of economically feasible transportation—but by strategic interactions between it and actors located within what Wallerstain terms the "external" region. It follows that, when considered in its political aspect, the world-system under consideration is itself a component of some larger global entity.

The search for a social system that is "real" and "self-contained" leads to infinite regress in space and time. A moment's reflection suggests, for example, that the historical development of the European region for several centuries before and after point in time with which we are concerned was partly shaped by interactions at the level of what William McNeill (1963) has called "the Eurasian ecumene"; that the processes that lend credence to the conceptualization of such an entity were economic, cultural, ecological, and even biological, as well as strategic; and that, as between European and Asian regions within the ecumene, processes determining significant change were hardly unidirectional. Viewed in this light, the procedure involved in selecting the Western "world-economy" as a privileged unit of analysis, born around 1450, is not very different from when this is done with respect to a particular nation-state of society. The one type of social system is no more real or self-contained than the other.

My objection is not with abstraction, since that is necessary for any theoretical undertaking, but with the appropriateness of *this* abstraction in relation to the questions being asked. For example, the conceptualization of political and economic structures as "interdependent determinants" is useful as a corrective, but it hardly constitutes a significant theoretical proposition. To achieve significance, propositions must be more specific. But little progress can be made in that direction with respect to a construct such as a "world-system," whose existence spans half a millenium. Such a very large slice of time encompasses an overly broad range of variation among the factors, conditions, and outcomes that must be taken into account for the purposes of macroanalytic social theory. If the unit is nevertheless retained, theoretical efforts lead inexorably toward formalism, the statement of propositions concerning extremely abstract properties such as "rhythms" and "cycles." But if the universe to which the theory is addressed is reduced to a more specific historical configuration, such as the long sixteenth century, then the question arises as to whether anything is to be gained by referring to the sixteenth century and to the twentieth as successive stages of the same "system." In what way does this differ from the stages associated with developmentalism?

Lest I be misunderstood, I am not suggesting that no continuity at all can be found between, say, the relations of production that emerged in a textile shop somewhere in the Low Countries around 1475 and the ones Michael Burawoy (1979) observed in the engine division of Allied Corporations half a millenium later, or that nothing of value can be learned by reflecting on the two experiences. But I doubt very much that the arduous formalization of a world-system encompassing both is an efficient research strategy for achieving the goal stated by Chase-Dunn, for example, "to clarify the secret of capital as it really operates." For the reasons indicated, the world-system conceptualization may in fact obfuscate rather than clarify.

* * *

At the time of writing "Origins of the Modern World System," Modelski's 1978 essay had just come to my attention, and I welcomed it as an indication that students of international politics, hitherto isolated from the social sciences more generally, appeared to be addressing themselves to the problem of modeling that component of global interaction in a manner that would make its integration into a larger framework possible (Zolberg, 1981a: 280, n. 28). But I also questioned the heuristic value of Modelski's "cycles," a point restated in somewhat different form in a later essay, where I attempted more positively to account for patterns of state formation in early modern Europe, principally England and France, in the light of the contemporaneous formation of a system of states (Zolberg, 1980). On the latter occasion, I also stated that Modelski's approach suffered from a failure to consider exchanges between what he calls "the global political system" and other social processes at that level—such as are emphasized by Wallerstein, Chase-Dunn, and Bergesen—as well as between political structure at the international and internal levels (Zolberg, 1980: 689). The global political system thus appeared to be conceptualized as a largely self-contained entity whose dynamics of development are concomitantly internal, much as Wallerstein asserts to be the case with respect to the European world-economy (Modelski, 1978: 214-215).

Although Modelski states that the latter observation was inaccurate, I do not find in his contribution to the present volume, or in Thompson's chapter, any propositions concerning exchanges or linkages such as I indicated, except in a negative sense—the state of "global culture" makes the emergence of other forms of international order than the "leadership" type very unlikely. In the final analysis, Modelski's conceptualization of the international political field remains, in many respects, the traditional one of a flat table on which solid bodies roll about and clash with one another. The conceptualization of this field as a "system" is not unusual (e.g., Kaplan, 1957); nor is the notion that the main thrust of international relations from the sixteenth century to the present consists of a series of repetitions, i.e., of a cyclical process (Dehio, 1962). What *is* new is the combination of the two outlooks, the one synchronic and the other diachronic, within a single framework–an intellectual operation akin to the one engaged in by Wallerstein. In answer to my question, "why cycles?" Modelski asserts, "because they are there," and this is the case because a real system exists, spanning approximately the same period as Wallerstein's.

To deal with these claims, I shall apply the same critical test to Modelski as to Wallerstein, in somewhat greater detail as I am doing this for the first time in the present essay. My principal concern is, once again, to establish whether a "global political system" lasting for a half a millenium is an appropriate subject for social theory.

It is hardly necessary to insist on the importance of the very first in the series of "cycles" as a building block for Modelski's theory. Should that case be a weak one, it would drastically reduce the number of repetitions on which the very idea of a "cyclical" theory is founded; and it would cast serious doubt on the soundness of the conceptualization of the whole series as a "system." The first question is, therefore: What, exactly, is the entity over which, according to Modelski, Portugal established its leadership in the sixteenth century?

The starting point, in the descriptive account published in 1978, is control by Venice at the close of the fifteenth century of the western end of the intercontinental system of long-distance trade linking up China, India, Persia, Egypt, and points in between with Western Europe. Venice not only established a monopoly on trade with Alexandria but "also became," in the Eastern Mediterranean if not in Europe, the leading power and has since served as the model for later world powers" (Modelski, 1978: 218). Modelski then asserts that "the Kings of Portugal determined to break into that system and to take over the Venetians' highly profitable monopoly." Having already invested heavily into ocean-related technology and information, they were in a position to take advantage of a series of major wars focused on Italy to curtail the power of Venice. "By 1515 a new order had been established whose backbone was the Carreira de India, the Lisbon-Goa shipping route against southern Africa, its mainstay the spice trade, and its outposts well positioned for forming the basis of the new global system" (p. 218). Modelski very much insists on the paramountcy of Portugal, in contrast to those—including Wallerstein—who regard the sixteenth century as essentially "Spanish," on the grounds that "it was Portugal that first seized the heart of the pre-existing world system and thus drastically altered its structure" (p. 219).

On the basis of the foregoing summary, most of it in Modelski's own words it is evident that the "global system" under consideration is hardly a political one at all. However prominent they were in the area of transcontinental trade, neither Venice nor Portugal can be said to have dominated the field constituted by strategic interactions within the Eurasian zone, or even the westernmost end of it, at the time under consideration. Nor does the account provide even a minimal sketch of how that field was structured; Modelski merely asserts that at the close of the fifteenth century, "the global system was a dispersed one"; his only reference to organization pertains, once again, to trade. Neither Modelski's nor Thompson's contribution to the present volume provides any clarification of these matters. Surely it is not unreasonable to expect collaborators devoted to the same theory to do somewhat better than that with respect to its foundation.

* * *

Although we do not have a theoretically grounded analysis covering the entirety of Eurasian politico-strategic interactions in the late medieval and early modern epochs, the subject has been well explored by a variety of historians, and the attribution of an overall leadership role to Portugal is distinctly at odds with most of what is known.[1] Why then does Modelski, and following him, Thompson, insist on this? I suspect that it is because the theory stands or falls on the matter of symmetry between the several cycles. It *must* be Portugal in the sixteenth century and the Netherlands in the seventeenth because it *was* Britain in the eighteenth and again in the nineteenth, as well as the United States in the twentieth (at least from 1945 onward). As is commonly the case, the cycles on which the theory is founded are obtained by selecting quite arbitrarily one feature common to widely differing historical configurations for treatment as a formal property. Cycles of *something* are always to be found. In this regard, there are striking parallels between the present construct and that of Ludwig Dehio (1962), whose notion of cycles is tersely expressed by the original German title of his work, *Balance or Hegemony.* From the sixteenth century onward, a succession of continental powers have striven for hegemony over all of Europe; but in each case, a peripheral power, usually maritime, opportunely intervened as a deus ex machina to reestablish balance, thus preserving the integrity of the system of states as a whole. Each of the two, Modelski and Dehio, extrapolates different features of the same historical universe for constructing cycles, so that we get in the end two very different interpretations. How are we to choose between them, if at all?

What Modelski calls his first cycle, covering approximately the sixteenth century, is in reality his second, since Venice preceded Portugal in the "leadership" role. Leadership over what? The question requires us to review quickly the formation of a system of states in the westernmost region of Eurasia (Zolberg, 1980: 689-700). At the beginning of the eleventh century, when invasions ground to a halt and economic activity expanded, that region was structured on the one hand by a differentiation between religious and secular authority, leading to tension and conflict between two diffuse, regionwide political organizations, Papacy and Empire, and on the other by the parceled but more concrete domination associated with feudalism. The formation within that region of a small number of political units, more highly organized than the former and larger than the latter, thus involved simultaneously disaggregation and consolidation, the two being inextricably linked. Following Norbert Elias (1975), the process of consolidation can be thought of as akin to competition among firms within a free market, leading to an oligopolistic configuration; its main objective was control of territory and the resources it contained, particularly manpower. The competitors present at the start behaved rationally; they did not set out to acquire some predetermined entity (e.g., "France") but merely strove to control the lands adjacent to those they already possessed so as to maximize their security. The selection that operated among them may be considered, for the present purpose, to have been random. Within the resulting configuration, interaction of the same kind among the survivors in each subregion of Europe spread the struggle to an ever-wider zone.

Competition entailed two complementary mechanisms: externally, the deployment of military force; internally, the mobilization of resources that made the wielding of such force possible. This entailed a differentiation of the apparatus of domination by way of the institutionalization of new organizations. Thus, above and beyond territorial accumulation, some of the contenders underwent a qualitative transformation that can perhaps be best understood in terms of the economists' concept of "value added," resulting from an innovative recombination of the factors of production through entrepreneurship. The two aspects of change, territorial enlargement and organizational innovation, were mutually reinforcing: The one resulted in economies of scale; the other made domination over a more extensive resource base possible. In this manner, some of the units reached the level of a critical mass, at which point they acquired a determinative advantage over the residential ones, whose quest for security required that they attach themselves to one or the other of the major contenders.

By the beginning of the thirteenth century, the process had crystallized into varied patterns in each of the sub-European regions. In the North Atlantic area, the struggle revolved quite early on around a bipolar axis formed by the kingdoms of France and England, whose interactions contributed to the further breakup of previous regional structures even beyond the zone of their direct confrontations. Internal and external processes were inextricably linked; the strengthening of political integration at what was, in relation to Europe as a whole, a middling territorial level, was a decisive step not only in the transformation of the French and English kingdoms into states, but in the formation of a system of European states. Yet Europe's subregions remained for a long time relatively isolated from each other, and the outcome of the process of oligopolization was somewhat different in each of them. For example, the Iberian peninsula's political development was shaped for several centuries by strategic interactions between Christians and Moslems, a feature of the situation that amply confirms the necessity of conceptualizing a "global political system" whose spatial domain is more extensive than Europe itself. Three aggregates were built up on the basis of the several columns of the Christian advance: Portugal, Castile, and Aragon. As for the Italian peninsula, which was the zone of direct confrontation between Papacy and Empire, the process of accumulation resulted in the formation of a regional system consisting of five irreducible contenders, among them Venice.

Modelski quite correctly singles out the latter as a great power in the Middle Ages (fourteenth and fifteenth centuries), and he is right to insist that this was founded on its assumption during that period of a role aptly labeled by William McNeill as that of a "hinge" between Europe and Asia. But he fails to account for the abrupt decline of Venice at the end of the fifteenth century. Venice's power, unlike that of other major European contenders at the time, was based mostly on a mastery of *naval* warfare. Around 1470, however, not only was its fleet successfully challenged by the Ottomans, but, even more important, the very conditions that had made the rise of a maritime trading city as a great power possible were drastically undermined by the advent of "gunpowder empires, exercising local monopoly of powerful siege guns" (McNeill, 1974: 89). The Ottoman Empire itself, under Mehmed II, was but one of these; others were the United Spanish monarchy (1479) and France. It is significant that only two of these—Spain and France—appear as Cycle I actors in Modelski's Table 5.1.

The introduction of artillery was a critical factor in the formation of the modern European system of states—i.e., of a set of interacting political units, larger and with much greater strategic capability for land warfare than was hitherto the case—because of the economies of scale the technology entails. This gave a decided advantage to units of domination sufficiently well organized to extract resources from a larger territory and population (Zolberg, 1980). Concomitantly, city-states were doomed.

The three principal "gunpower empires" of western Eurasia were quick to avail themselves of the new opportunities afforded by their superiority. On the eve of the sixteenth century, the common starting point for both Modelski and Wallerstein, they pounced on the Italian prize from both east and west; concurrently, France and Spain also began competing for the Low Countries, a similarly wealthy but inexorably vulnerable array of city-states. As Dehio had demonstrated, it was the century-long struggle among these giants that formed the crucible within which the European system of states was shaped. Although the process under consideration got under way slightly earlier than Europe's overseas expansion, it naturally interacted with the latter. As recognized by Rapkin, the present analysis—particularly as it pertains to the role of the Ottoman Empire—was a telling point in my earlier critique of Wallerstein; but it is crucial here also, as it points toward a different understanding of the boundaries and structure of the "global political system" than that set forth by Modelski and Thompson.

But what of Portugal? I certainly agree with Modelski that this small maritime state was in a position to take advantage of the confrontation between the giants to acquire a good chunk of the Venetian spoils and that it quickly outdid the Venetians with respect to trade. But as measured by the new scale of international power, Portugal remained unavoidably weak. Far from exercising a "leadership" role in the emerging system, it survived as an independent actor only so long as Spain was locked into its duel with France and the Ottomans; it then reappeared over a half a century later because the reconstruction of Portugal as an independent state served the purposes of Spain's powerful enemies. In the intervening period (1580-1640), the incorporation of Portugal undoubtedly reinforced Spain; but it was hardly determinative.

However, the case of Portugal adumbrates another important feature of the European segment of the system of states. While there is no gainsaying that artillery, in combination with innovations in the sphere of political organization, was a crucial element in the formation of more powerful territorial states, it also provided a foundation for the formation of another type of strategic actor, whose emergence on the European scene drastically altered the outcome one would expect from the land-based process of oligopolization discussed earlier.

As Martin Wight (1978: 68) has pointed out, "The sea power of the Great Discoveries was already a matter of guns. The sea made artillery mobile. At a time when land guns had to be dragged laboriously across country, ships carried their cannon around the world." The combination of ships and guns can be thought of as a capital-intensive war technology operated by a small complement of skilled and versatile personnel, in comparison with land-based artillery, which required organization of a "train" involving an enormous number of men and beasts of burden, together with the supplies necessary for their maintenance, and additional troops for their protection (Cipolla, 1965; Howard, 1976). Once the appropriate nexus of technology and organization was developed, the combination of ship and gun made it possible for small but relatively wealthy coastal or island states to play a major role in world affairs. Under prevailing conditions, the necessary wealth itself could be secured by harnessing naval warfare in the service of overseas trade, including state-sponsored piracy. It was indeed the Portuguese "who invented the use of ships as artillery carriers, rather than as military transports for boarding other ships, and of guns for sinking other ships, rather than helping boarding parties" (Wight, 1978: 68). They were followed by the English, who probably invented the broadside and "developed the political uses of sea power" a generation before the Armada, when their fleet helped drive the French out of Edinburgh, thus completing the territorial sorting out that had begun in the twelfth century, and turning the British Isles into a zone of unquestioned English hegemony. The Netherlands followed suit and further perfected the strategy in the seventeenth century.

The invention of sea power was a triple turning point in world history. In one respect, it was a determinative element of Europe's ability to challenge, beginning around 1500, and over the next three centuries, reverse "the millenial land-centered balance among the Eurasian civilizations" (McNeill, 1963: 619). In another, it was the key to the establishment of worldwide European hegemony. "The discovery of the ocean," wrote the late J. H. Parry (1974: 290), in the sense of discovery by Europeans of continuous sea-passage,

> inaugurated a new age, in which control of the world's trade and to a considerable extent also political control, fell gradually into the hands of a small groups of states, mostly in Western Europe, which could build enough reliable ships to operate in all the oceans at once, and move at will from ocean to ocean. They created maritime empires, networks of trade, influence and power, on a scale formerly undreamt of.

And viewed internally, sea power provided the elements necessary to the specific coalition game known as "the balance of power system"— but which might perhaps be dubbed more appropriately, "dominate if you can" because, in its absence, westernmost Europe would have been organized into a smaller number of actors, perhaps reduced for a time to only one—if not the Habsburg Empire, then France enlarged and enriched by the addition of the Low Countries.

It is only by way of a wild stretch of the imagination, in the course of which well-documented key processes are left out of account, that the transformation of the European segment of the global political system in the early modern epoch can be attributed to some shared yearning for order rendered impossible by cultural chaos, a yearning assuaged by Portuguese leadership in the sixteenth century as well as by Netherlands leadership in the seventeenth. Both the first and second "cycles

of leadership" are phantasms such as Ranke warned against. In the overall European politico-strategic game, notwithstanding its precocious use of sea power to carve out for itself a major trading empire, Portugal in fact missed the boat, largely because Spain was able to develop both land and sea power. Later on, the Netherlands replicated the Portuguese feat of creating a seaborne empire; but, although this was an important feature of the seventeenth century, the international political system of that period cannot possibly be treated as a "long cycle of leadership" in which neither Austria, nor Sweden, nor the Ottoman Empire, appear as key actors (Modelski, Table 5.1). As for the dynamics within each cycle, or leading from one to the other, why discuss processes that pertain to a structure whose existence is in so much doubt?

Should one move forward with this sort of exercise, I believe it could be demonstrated that the theoretical framework under consideration provides an approximate fit for only one segment of the historical record, the "long century of peace" (1815-1914) when the Concert of Europe was organized under British leadership. It is hardly necessary to emphasize, however, that any explanation of the emergence of this configuration requires attention to interpenetration between internal and external processes, economic and political, among the various countries concerned. Britain's assumption of a leadership role is attributable in the first instance that what is, from the perspective of the present framework, an entirely exogenous variable—i.e., the formation within that country of industrial capitalism. The lead it thereby acquired over others insured, for a time, both paramountcy at the level of the global economic system and unprecedented mastery of the seas. Concomitantly, British leadership was acceptable to other Europeans for a variety of reasons, mostly because it indeed provided order without domination.

Yet the conditions that fostered an international regime founded on the Concert of Europe and the universal gold standard were rapidly undermined. The market economy, as Polanyi brilliantly demonstrated in *The Great Transformation* (1960), was founded on an impossible "utopia" and engendered its own contradictions at both the internal and international levels. To this must be added a factor emphasized by Barraclough (1967), among others: the formation of continent-size states, Russia and the United States, a process that provided a model for German aspirations as well. The resulting transformation of the field of global strategic interactions was as revolutionary as the one provoked by the emergence of "gunpowder empires" at the dawn of the modern era; and it is in part for this reason that Barraclough views the 1890s as the end of the modern epoch and the dawn of the contemporary age.

Whether or not one accepts this periodization, one thing is quite clear: the turn of the century marked the waning of what has been called the "Columban age," i.e., of the specific set of conditions that made sea power what it was. As both Paul Kennedy and Martin Wight have shown, Admiral Mahan, who celebrated sea power at this very moment in time, was a much better historian than he was a prophet. Although sea power continued to play a role, the twentieth century was much more the age of land power because of the enormous strategic advantages afforded by a continent-size territory now that technology and organization were available to harness the people and other resources it contained. Nor is air power in all its forms the functional equivalent of sea power, as it is much more dependent than sea power on the availability of an enormous industrial base (Kennedy, 1974). Its navy notwithstanding, Britain went the way of Venice half a millenium earlier. The logic of strategy and the concomitant conditions for the achievement of minimal international order thereby underwent profound changes long before the worldwide revolution against the sequels of European overseas expansion and the onset of the age of MAD (mutually assured destruction) altered them beyond recognition.

* * *

The ongoing debate between Wallersteinians and Modelskians might be reported in the Tuesday Science pages of The *New York Times* as follows:

As previously announced in *Journal,* the annual congress of the Society for Globology took place in the Erehwon Room of the Universal Hilton on September 31, 1982. In keeping with the program agreed upon at the last congress, devoted to the question of Space, the discussion this time focused on Time. The issue was considered particularly urgent because of the society's desire to celebrate the 500th anniversary of the founding of the present era. However, there are profound divisions among the membership concerning whether 1983 constitutes A.S. *(anno systemae)* 533 or 466, as variously maintained by the factions known respectively as Hegemoniks and Leaderniks. The conflict cannot easily be ironed out because, while agreeing that there is a system and that it is currently in a declining phase, the contending parties differ as to what it is a system of. In relation to the advancement of science, a difference of 67 years is no trivial matter, as this segment of time represents approximately 14 percent of the total life of the system—whatever it may be—to date. Less obvious to the general public is the fact that a more precise determination of the age of the system is vital for predicting the future. It is only by ascertaining which of the two factions, Leaderniks or Hegemoniks, is correct, that the society will be able to discharge its

self-appointed responsibility and reveal to an anxious world whether it
will end with a bang or with a whimper.

Notwithstanding the obvious differences between them, the two
projects are essentially similar: they are both predicated on the existence of a world system with a life of its own and on the belief that
analysis of its birth and development to date will reveal its eventual
fate. Far from a "progressive problemshift," the erection of globalism
on such a reified and organicist foundation constitutes, in my view, a
most unfortunate regression that jeopardizes the future of a promising
field of social scientific investigation.

Skepticism is naturally prompted in any scientific community by
the announcement that a simple solution has been devised for a very
complex and hitherto intractable problem that has preoccupied many
practitioners for a very long time. Breakthroughs can of course occur;
but in the social sciences, claims to that effect are so frequent that we
end up spending an enormous amount of collective time and energy
sorting throught the pile of such announcements and wading through
discards on our way to work. In this case, skepticism is enhanced by
the identification of important empirical errors of commission and
omission, as well as of significant analytic inconsistencies and distortions, in the principal publications of both circles. Skepticism gives
way to horror, mitigated only by flight into levity, when it is realized
that we have here constructs akin to the philosophies of history
denounced by Karl Popper (1950) as scientific impossibilities fraught
with illiberal political implications, and by C. Wright Mills (1959:
22-23) as "trans-historical straitjackets into which the materials of
human history are forced and out of which issue prophetic views
(usually gloomy ones) of the future." Next to these devastating critiques, Arthur Stinchcombe's (1978: 1-13) recent charge that the use
of social theory to build epochal interpretations of history entails a
profound misconception of the proper relationship between history
and social theory is a mere rap on the knuckles.

The coupling of "world" (or "global") with "system" constitutes a
misalliance because "world" implies a conceptualization of the relevant segment of human experience in an historical mode, as a singular
configuration, whereas "theory" is predicted on a conceptualization
of such experience as patterns of recurring bits and pieces. "History,"
as the term is used here, is not merely the study of the past; were that
so, there would be no distinction between it and the social sciences,
since the materials social scientists deal with are of necessity yester-
day's. In its most distinctive form, it is a rhetoric for organizing
materials in relation to the objective of providing a coherent narrative
of how something of interest to us happened, rather than for organizing

them with a view to the search for an explanation (Hexter, 1968). Guided by the needs of the story, historians have little use for concepts such as "system"; at their very best, they achieve elegance by way of a coherent eclecticism.

This is particularly well illustrated by the work of Fernand Braudel, the master of "total history," whom I single out because it is in tribute to him that Wallerstein named his center. Braudel's great achievement lies in the devising of a method for telling a coherent tale of a world, the Mediterranean in the sixteenth century. As is well known, he does so by weaving an immense tapestry out of events occurring on three different planes or levels; the "long run," meaning man's relationship to the natural environment; the "history of groups and groupings," which includes not only economic systems, but also states, classes and strata, "civilizations" (i.e., cultural entities), and their interactions as revealed "in the complex arena of warfare"; and finally "history . . . on the scale not of man but of individual men" (Braudel, 1976, 20-21). Although Braudel is committed to the notion of a hierarchy between the levels—as indicated by his materialist conclusion that "the long run always wins in the end"—and conceives the history of groups very much in terms of recurring "rhythms" and "cycles"—he stops short of any formal propositions concerning relationships within or between the levels, as demanded by theory. This is true for particular episodes as well as for the history of the Mediterranean as a whole.[2] Nor does his later wide-ranging work on the history of material change in subsequent centuries advance the claim of providing an explanation of capitalism, let alone of world history as a whole. The assertion that "the long run always wins in the end" is too vague to be of much use as a theoretical proposition; and the statement is in any case questionable since geopolitical organizations—"Spain," "France," "China"—often outlast any one episode of Braudel's "long term." Civilizations do so as well. But the assertion *is* meaningful as an admonition to Braudel's fellow historians. The admonition is akin to Ranke's in that it emphasizes the "universal"; but Braudel also goes beyond Ranke by adumbrating an historical vision that encompasses the material sphere as well.

It should be noted that the distinction I am making between history and social theory is an analytic one that does not coincide with the ongoing professional differentiation between historians and varieties of social scientists, but cuts across it; moreover, in practice, many scholars combine both modes in their work. Nor does my insistence that they are distinct undertakings entail a judgment that one is superior to the other. Rather, each of these intellectual modes has its strengths and limitations. The historical approach is particularly appropriate for grasping the multifarious circumstances that go into the making of such singular turning points in human experience as the surge forward of Western Europe in the sixteenth century, or the waning of that region's paramountcy in the twentieth. The sort of understanding to which we can aspire with respect to these is not explanation but interpretation. This is the case, as well, with such topics as the origins and subsequent development of specific forms of social organization, for example, capitalism or statism. Social theory can provide what history does not, explanations. It does so by speci-fying relationships among factors, conditions, and outcomes. But this requires a feat of imagination, the translation of some segment of reality that is perceived as unique by way of the historical approach, into a universe of recurrent phenomena and comparable cases. Social theorists have to some extent succeeded in doing so with respect to various types of social organizations—firms, parties, and the like—and even societies, economies, or polities, considered for limited segments of their existence as "cases," often to the horror of his-torians. But we can have no theory about "modern world-systems," "capitalist world-economies," or "global political systems" unless we can conceive of more than one of them, and persuade others to go along with us. It follows that we cannot aspire to discover any uni-versal principles of historical change. As C. Wright Mills (1961: 150) insisted, "the mechanisms of change we do know vary with the social structure we are examining. For historical change *is* change of social structures, of the relations among their component parts. Just as there is a variety of social structures, there is a variety of principles of historical change."

The construction of macroanalytic social theory was largely accom-plished by ignoring the unruly process of interpenetration among the cases that populate its universe. This we can no longer do. But since the construction of an all-encompassing theory at the world-historical level is an impossible dream, we should acknowledge, from the very start, the distinctiveness of history and theory, while bringing both modes of intellectual activity to bear on common problems, in a dialectical fashion.

Except in the "international" subfields mentioned in the introduc-tion, the social sciences have hardly addressed themselves to the analysis of social interactions beyond the societal level and between levels. Given our collective lack of experience in this respect, rather than fill the void by way of quick fixes, we would do well to enhance our capacity to think conceptually about interpenetration by under-taking a series of fitness exercises. Given the drawbacks of the systemic approach, it might be heuristic to think of the universe constituted by a set of societies connected by way of interactions and flows as a *field*. Borrowed from the sociological method of Pierre Bourdieu, the concept is not predicated on the assumption of a "real" or "self-sufficient" entity with precisely delimited boundaries in space and time (Bourdieu, 1982). Rather, it is a construct that enables us to encompass observable, patterned exchanges among structures, and in relation to which it is more appropriate to speak of mutual constraints than of determination. At the most general level, we can distinguish in the conventional analytic manner between political, economic, and cultural structures, without positing any transhistorical hierarchy among them. As the analysis begins, however, the principal features of the field are historical givens, forming a particular configuration.

Should we apply this method to the global level—something Bourdieu himself has not been inclined to do—it is necessary to take into consideration the fact that the course of human history in the past half-millenium has resulted in the organization of the world into a set of mutually exclusive states, and that each of them has tended to foster the formation of a more homogeneous culture within its boundaries as well as to emphasize cultural distinctiveness from its neighbors (McNeill, 1963: 632-634). In those parts of the world where this process has been going on for a long time, it has resulted in the further formation of human entities whose members share a profound belief that they are quasi-natural. Although these entities are usually called "nation-states," I prefer the more general term "statist societies," so as to allow for variation within the class between "national," "multinational," and the like. However mythical this naturalness, it entails a definition of the situation that is real in its consequences. In no way is this more explicitly demonstrated than by the control that statist societies exercise, collectively, over the movement of population across their boundaries. Although the more liberal among them allow freedom of exit, there does not exist a concomitant freedom of entry, so that in effect most of the world's population tend to be confined in the countries of their birth, a fact that largely determines their fate (Zolberg, 1981b). But at the same time, it is equally evident that statist societies have never existed in isolation; their multiplicity in the world at large is a constitutive feature of the organization of each.

Hence even if we are concerned exclusively with any one of these statist societies, it is necessary to view it as existing within a more comprehensive field; but, concomitantly, when we turn to that field itself, it is necessary to view the statist societies within them as components that interact as highly coherent entities and to recognize that as a consequence of this the processes at the level of the field as a whole are distinct from those that occur within the components. The analytic structures whose exchanges form the field encompass the intra- and extrasocietal levels, but they are patterned in different ways at each of these levels. That this is so in general stems largely from the specific patterning of the political structure. The very exist-

.ence of statist societies entails a differentiation, by way of political organization, between internal and external realms—the one a sphere of domination and membership, the other a sphere of war and peace.

Although global economic and political structures—to which I add cultural ones—interact as "interdependent determinants," each of them engenders very different effects; and those associated with the political structure occur, in their most extreme form, as cataclysmic events that make for great discontinuities between successive configurations of the global field. The occurrence of war as a type of event can be encompassed within a theoretical framework; but great wars characteristically unleashed a complex chain of singular events, best understood by resorting to the historian's craft. Upon reflection, it is evident that much the same can be said of great social revolutions, of tidal waves of cultural change, or—returning to Braudel—of profound modifications in man's relationship to the material environment.

These observations imply that social theory is a mode of intellectual discourse designed to be conducted *within* history, i.e., within the confines of one or the other of the configurations formed by such major turning points alone or in combination and with respect to which it is possible to carry out the translation of a historical situation into a set of "porperties" required for the enunciation of theoretical statements. This will not, of itself, solve the problem of conceptualizing interpenetration between social processes at the societal and extrasocietal levels; but it will ensure that our efforts to do so will be more constructive.

NOTES

1. The best introductory overview of the period is H. G. Koenigsberger and Mosse (1968). For a survey of international relations, see Lapeyre (1973). The most stimulating accounts of the origins of the new "system of states," however, remain those of the neo-Rankean Dehio (1962) and of Mattingly (1955). In none of these does Portugal appear as a "leader" or even as a "great power." Mattingly (pp. 156-157) states that "by virtue of the wealth of the East piled annually on the quays of Lisbon, Portugal was almost a major power," but then goes on to point out that the maintenance of Portugal's commercial monopoly and independence "was a task beyond the powers of diplomacy."

2. The elegant eclecticism of Braudel's narrative method is evident, for example, in his account of the expulsion of the Jews from Spain in 1492, which I have had occasion to examine in detail in the course of research for another project. He begins by giving due consideration to the "long-term" (overpopulation of Mediterranean Europe as the consequence of a resumption of demographic growth after 1450) and to "conjuncture" (the intersection of a long-term economic depression with a short-term crisis). But he then goes on to view the expulsion from the vantage point of a relatively autonomous political dynamic: Spain—he means here the emerging state—was attempting to "reintegrate itself with Europe" by shedding "its two unwanted religions. . . . It refused to become either African or Oriental in a process which in some ways resembles that of modern de-colonization." Finally, ascending to heights of idealism worthy of Toynbee, he writes of the "glacier-like movement" of distinct civilizations past one another, of Spain "toward political unity, which could not be conceived, in the sixteenth-

century, as anything other than religious unity. Israel meanwhile was carried toward the destiny of the diaspora" (Braudel, 1976: 402, 415-416, 824-825).

REFERENCES

BARRACLOUGH, G. (1967) An Introduction to Contemporary History. Harmondsworth: Pelican.
BOURDIEU, P. (1982) Leçon inaugurale. Paris: Collège de France.
BRAUDEL, F. (1976) The Mediterranean and the Mediterranean World in the Age of Philip II. New York: Harper & Row.
BURAWOY, M. (1979) Manufacturing Consent: Changes in the Labor Process Under Monopoly Capitalism. Chicago: University of Chicago Press.
CIPOLLA, C. M. (1965) Guns, Sails, and Empires. New York: Minerva.
DEHIO, L. (1962) The Precarious Balance: Four Centuries of the European Power Struggle. New York: Vintage.
ELIAS, N. (1975) La Dynamique de L'Occident. Paris: Calmann-Levy.
GOUREVITCH, P. (1975) "The second image reversed: the international sources of domestic politics." International Organization 32 (Autumn): 881-912.
HEXTER, J. H. (1968) "The rhetoric of history," pp. 368-393 in International Encyclopedia of the Social Sciences, Vol. 6. New York: Macmillan.
HOWARD, M. (1976) War in European History. Oxford: Oxford University Press.
KAPLAN, M. (1957) Systems and Process in International Politics. New York: John Wiley.
KENNEDY, P. (1974) "Mahan versus Mackinder: two interpretations of British sea power." Militärgeschitliche Mitteilungen 16 (February): 39-66.
LAPEYRE, H. (1973) Les Monarchies européennes du XVIe siècle: Les relations internationales. Paris: Presses Universitaires de France.
MATTINGLY, G. (1955) Renaissance Diplomacy. New York: Peregrine.
McNEILL, W. (1974) Venice: The Hinge of Europe, 1081-1797. Chicago: University of Chicago Press.
———(1963) The Rise of the West: A History of the Human Community. New York: New American Library.
MILLS, C. W. (1961) The Sociological Imagination. New York: Grove.
MODELSKI, G. (1978) "The long cycle of global politics and the nation-state." Comparative Studies in Society and History 20 (April): 214-235.
MOSSE, G. L. (1968) Europe in the Sixteenth Century. London: Longman.
PARRY, J. H. (1974) The Discovery of the Sea. New York: Dial.
POLANYI, K. (1960) The Great Transformation. Boston: Beacon.
POPPER, K. R. (1950) The Open Society and its Enemies. Princeton, NJ: Princeton University Press.
STERN, F. [ed.] (1956) The Varieties of History from Voltaire to the Present. New York: Meridian.
STINCHCOMBE, A. L. (1978) Theoretical Methods in Social History. New York: Academic.
WALLERSTEIN, I. (1974) The Modern World-System: Capitalist Agriculture and the Origins of the European World-Economy in the Sixteenth Century. New York: Academic.
WIGHT, M. (1978) Power Politics (H. Bull and C. Holbraad, eds.). New York: Holmes & Meier.
ZOLBERG, A. R. (1981a) "Origins of the modern world system: a missing link." World Politics 33 (January): 253-281.
———(1981b) "International migrations in political perspective," pp. 3-27 in M.M. Kritz et al. (eds.) Global Trends in Migration. New York: Center for Migration Studies.
———(1980) "Strategic interactions and the formation of modern states: France and England." International Social Science Journal 32, 4: 687-716.

12

Of Global Politics, Portugal, and Kindred Issues

A Rejoinder

GEORGE MODELSKI

OF THE GLOBAL POLITICAL SYSTEM

The major problem with Professor Zolberg's appraisal of my work on long cycles is his failure to take the necessary care to understand my concept of the "global political system." The misperception is most clearly revealed when Zolberg, in a summarizing passage ("the coupling of 'world' (or 'global') with 'system' constitutes a misalliance"), equates "world" with "global." In my vocabulary (see Modelski, 1978: 213-215), "world system" encompasses at least four differentiated levels of interaction and analysis (global, regional, national, local), and my concern is primarily with the global level. Analytically, my conceptualization of politics is as a sub-system of the world system. My mental image of the world system and its sub-systems is (in the Parsonian tradition) as illustrated in Table 12.1.

This conceptualization is in fact quite different (and needs to be distinguished clearly) from the traditional understanding of the "international system" (Morton Kaplan) and also from the Wallersteinian concept of the "European world-economy." *Contra* Zolberg, it is not a billiard table concept but rather a multilayered one on which, at different times, new patterns of global organization may be observed.

I would describe both the "international system" and the "European world-economy" as "oil-slick"-type concepts that refer to concrete entities, one a set of states, the other an "international production system" to which countries belong and that over time spread their boundaries by "recognizing" or "incorporating" other coun-

TABLE 12.1   World System and Its Subsystems

	Political Subsystem	*Economic Subsystem*	*Cultural Subsystem*	*Community (solidarity)*
Global Subsystem	Global politics	Global economics	. . .	. . .
Regional Subsystem	Regional politics	Regional economics	. . .	. . .
National Subsystem	National politics	. . .	. . .	. . .
Local Subsystem	Local politics	. . .	. . .	. . .

tries. The oil-slick concept has moving boundaries as an essential feature.

The global political system concept, by contrast, is a response to the more basic question: How is the entire world governed at the global level and how was it governed in the past? As such, it is essentially an analytical, network-type of concept that asserts that political problems at the global level (including those of world leadership, control of global war, or those of global economic organization) can meaningfully and usefully be distinguished from those arising at regional or national levels. This "global politics" concept has no moving boundaries; it is coextensive with the globe at all times; its variable property is complexity.

These analytical distinctions bring out the most important consideration (that, Eurocentrically, Zolberg entirely misses) that global interactions need to be distinguished (and analytically can be distinguished) from regional interactions in Europe. That is why it is entirely appropriate to argue that Portugal occupied a leading position in the global system even while being fully aware that it did not do so in the regional European system. That is also the reason why I have never claimed (as Zolberg maintains I have) that Portugal "dominated Eurasia" (another reason being that in any event I take care to distinguish between "leadership" and "domination"). Nor do I attribute to Portugal (as Zolberg claims I do) an "overall" leadership role but only one in global politics.

Even while focusing my own analysis on "global politics" understood as a vertically and horizontally differentiated subsystem of the world system, I am fully alive to the analytical importance of other subsystems (such as the economic), and regard it as a crucial part of my research program to try to specify the linkages between global politics and the other subsystems, and I have indicated as much in my contribution to this volume. It remains a puzzle to me why Zolberg, in his own argument, persists in refusing to recognize this ("I do not find . . . any propositions concerning exchanges or linkages") when I explicitly declare that "our analysis already points to two principal lines of interchange," namely what I have earlier (Modelski, 1981: 67) dubbed the two "Perroux linkages."

Zolberg's lack of care in reading (or citing) this aspect of my work is revealed by his comment that Britain's industrial capitalism is "an entirely exogenous variable" from the perspective of the present framework" (i.e., long cycles). Not so—had he understood the first Perroux linkage (world powers have lead economies) he would have seen that the connection between Britain's industrial revolution and its standing as a world power was not accidental but rather as predicted by theory. That same linkage had its parallels in the other cycles, obviously so in the case of the United States but also in the case of Portugal, which innovated, besides naval gunnery, two basic new types of ocean-going craft, as well as the software of long-range navigation, all based on superlative shipbuilding and shipping industries.

OF THE BIRTH OF MODERN GLOBAL POLITICS

In his singularly trivializing *New York Times* dispatch, Zolberg misleadingly implies that the only important differences between my approach and that of Immanuel Wallerstein lies in the matter of dating the inception of the modern system (even though elsewhere he maintains that we both view the origins in similar terms). To place on record my own position (which is in fact the "classical" position on this matter) I wish to say that I regard the year 1494 as marking the birth of the modern global political system.

The classical reason for choosing that particular year is the fact that it marks the opening of a generation-long period of Italian wars, a period of severe strife that destroyed the autonomy of the Italian system and thereby gave rise to the modern European system of states. That is the position of most historians, including that of Ludwig Dehio. But 1494 is also significant for another, not unrelated reason. It was the year in which Portugal signed with Spain the Treaty of Tordesillas, thereby initiating an arrangement whereby the entire global system (though not the world as such, because Eurasia was largely unaffected) was divided between those two powers in a manner that allotted the route to America largely to Spain but the remaining oceanic space and in particular the oceanic links between Europe and Asia to Portugal. The treaty marked the creation of the first regime for the governance of the global system and must therefore be regarded as the birth of modern global politics. Ever since then, we see it as a struggle to maintain and/or redefine that regime in new directions.

It is of interest to note the linkage between that global event, and the (regional) process evidenced by the struggle for Italy. Portugal succeeded in gaining from Spain, by the threat of war, considerable concessions (necessary because Spain had earlier gained special advantages by securing the inside track to Rome), principally because Spain was about to become engaged in the Italian wars against France and did not want to be distracted by a conflict in its rear over global issues. That is how the two systems, the global and the regional European, came to be differentiated from each other and made possible Portugal's role in the decades that followed (for the wars in Italy and Spain's other contests with France continued until 1559). It also made possible Portugal's successes in the Indian Ocean, at precisely the time that Spain and France were destroying the vitality of the Italian states (and of Venice and its ability to protect what until then had been its own monopoly). That is precisely the same structural condition (freedom of action in the global system for the world power, made possible by heavy regional commitments of its principal challengers) that made possible the Golden Age of the Netherlands in the next century and Britain's role in the Balance of Power for Europe of the eighteenth and nineteenth centuries.

All these considerations make it clear that we need a good deal of precision when we discuss such a momentuous process as the "formation of the system of states" in Europe, as Zolberg does at some length in his chapter. While we all know that a small number of states acquired a "modern" character circa 1500, the question of what kind of system they formed is an entirely open one and is not to be decided by *obiter dicta*. The concept of the modern states-system has been a standby of historians at least since A.H.L. Heeren's *Political System of Europe* (published in 1800 *contra* Zolberg who asserts that "historians have little use for concepts such as 'system' "). But in my view that concept is too general to remain serviceable in analyses of a social science type.

That is why I argue that, from 1494 onward, we need to distinguish between a global political system, governed over the next century basically by the Treaty of Tordesillas, and comprising principally Portugal and Spain, as well as France, England et al., and, partially overlapping with it (European and other) regional systems that would also include, e.g., the Ottoman Empire. The Ottomans do, in fact, constitute an interesting borderline case, strongly entrenched as they were at a central place of the Eurasian land mass and pressing upon the Tordesillas regime both in the Mediterranean and in the Indian Ocean, but also unmindful of the need to develop oceanic potential and a capacity for global reach and therefore incapable of offering effective competition for the control of the global system. That is also why the major part of what we know as the international politics of the modern period is in fact no more than the regional politics of Europe, a matter of perspective that we need to bear in mind continuously as we deal with global issues and one that is basically lacking in Zolberg's approach.

OF PORTUGAL'S FIRST CYCLE

Zolberg makes a great deal of the alleged "importance of the very first of 'cycles' " on the ground that the "theory stands or falls on the matter of symmetry between the several cycles." I do not know of any sound theoretical reason why the first cycle must be any more important than the others. True, we only have five cycles all told (and maybe a couple of prototypes, such as the Venetian) and that is, of course, a small number of cases. But the test of the theory (whether the cycles "are there") lies in the overall match between the model and the evidence and not just in the first cycle. All Zolberg does is to erect a straw man he hopes it might be easy to demolish.

Entirely to the contrary, what we have there is not a static symmetry between the several cycles but rather a dynamic process of the *progressive institutionalization of the role of world power.* What we observe is that each successive world power has been more populous, wealthier, militarily stronger, politically better organized, and possessed of an increasingly broad concept of the global public interest. And in a rapidly growing system, which the modern world certainly has been, how could it have been otherwise? The process of institutionalization itself is easily explainable in terms of the evident success of that role and the reinforcement thus available in the process of learning it. That is why it is easy to argue that it is the last case that is the most interesting and certainly the most important of all. That is also why, theoretically, all we ask of the first case is that the characteristics of global leadership be observable not in full but in embryo.

Are the essential characteristics in fact observable in embryo in the Protuguese case? They are. *Contra* Zolberg who claims that the "global system" under consideration is "hardly political at all," it is quite obvious that the Tordesillas regime has been the first and formative global political system. It was not just a system of trade, if only for the reason that trade never occurs in a vacuum but rather within a political framework initially provided by the world power (the second

Perroux linkage). It is Portugal that provided the greater part of that political framework: the Portuguese monarchy, clearly a political institution, organized it; it deployed significant military and naval forces worldwide, in part by the dispatch of annual fleets, and also through the maintenance of squadrons on patrol in strategic areas (e.g., Brazil, Malabar coast); it also created and kept up a network of strategic bases all over the world; and, finally, it decreed and attempted to enforce a complete regulatory framework for oceanic trade.

More often than not, what underlies the common depreciation of the role of Portugal is simple lack of knowledge. Zolberg, for instance, makes the statement that the Italian wars (1494-1516) "got underway slightly earlier than Europe's overseas expansion." That, of course, is quite wrong. Portugal's overseas expansion is often dated as having begun in 1415 (the capture of Cueta), though more pertinently it may be thought as having started with the settlement of the Azores and Madiera in the 1420s and continued with the exploration of the African coast after 1434. That would place it at least two good generations before the start of the Italian wars (which is also why an analysis of Portugal's role in the world system must begin well before 1494). But to ignore this aspect of the Portuguese role is an error of major proportions and reveals an ignorance that is more widespread than it ought to be. As two writers (Diffie and Winius, 1977: xiv) recently observed: "The contribution of Portugal to world history has been forgotten by many modern historians who write their works as if Europe consisted of only the northern countries."

This deplorable state of affairs is also evident in Zolberg's attempt to marshall evidence supporting his doubts about my attribution of a global leadership role to Portugal. He cites, in note 1 all of three "authorities": two (obscure) general texts and one (fine) monograph, on a peripheral subject (Renaissance diplomacy). No reference is made, on this question, to Portuguese historians or to other specialists in Portuguese or Iberian history, who, one would have thought, might also have opinions on the subject. The paucity of evidence thus adduced would be laughable were it not a serious matter for it is one more instance of that Northerners' conceit that finds it so hard to imagine the Southerners, those "little fellows" of dark complexion, ever doing anything worthwhile let alone pioneering a global system that they (the Northerners) then proceeded to take over.

The same considerations apply to Zolberg's comments about Portugal's standing in the "new scale of international power." That scale was a regional European one, and analytically and substantively it is irrelevant to the argument. Portugal was a sea power of the first rank during all of the first cycle, and Thompson's (1981) and my research document this fully; on the world ocean it had virtually incontestable superiority until 1580. With regard to Spain, with which it shared a land border, it held a position of equality at least until the 1550s; witness the three key treaties of Alcaçovas, Tordesillas, and Zaragoza, in each of which it got what mattered to Portugal and what it wanted.

OF RANKE AND DEHIO

Let me say, finally, that the "text," drawn from Leopold von Ranke, with which Zolberg opens his essay, does not impress me at all. Ranke talked a lot about universals but had great trouble recognizing any except a few self-sufficient nations.

The references to the work of Dehio cannot be passed over either. Zolberg implies that Dehio used the concept of cycles ("Ludwig Dehio, whose notion of cycles is tersely expressed"). This is quite misleading. Dehio nowhere in his work employs the concept of cycle but at most might be argued to be implying a process of "alternation" (balance *or* hegemony). In any event, cycles are not to be confused with repetitions or recurrences; they are a strong form of repetition and only some repetitions are cyclic.

Incidentally, Dehio's and mine are not "two very different interpretations." Dehio's is a historian's extended narrative employing the concept of "states-system." Mine is a social science enterprise with fuller conceptual equipment; while different in style and approach they are quite compatible with each other and complementary.

IN CONCLUSION

Other points could yet be raised but space is alas limited. Let me say in conclusion that propositions about cyclic regularities in the behavior of the modern global polity are not attempts at formulating "universal principles of historical change" or a search for the "elusive laws of history," as Zolberg would have it. Clearly we have outgrown those pre-social science attempts to generalize about "history" at large. Our task today is to make statements about the behavior of identifiable (hence time- and space-defined) social systems. Of course, the modern global polity is one. That is precisely what long-cycle theory attempts to do.

Social science theorizing, however, cannot rule out certain social events as "cataclysmic" and therefore beyond the scope of analysis, as Zolberg claims it ought to. I do not regard global wars as cataclysmic events beyond human reach or understanding. They are manmade disasters that are threatening to become even more disastrous, and it is time we understood them as unnecessarily cyclical events that need to be stopped from recurring. And that is not a matter either for feigned horror or false levity.

REFERENCES

DIFFIE, B. W. and G. D. WINIUS (1977) Foundations of the Portuguese Empire, 1415-1580. Minneapolis: University of Minnesota Press.
MODELSKI, G. (1981) "Long cycles, Kondratieffs, and alternating innovations." in C. W. Kegley and P. J. McGowan (eds.) The Political Economy of Foreign Policy Behavior. Beverly Hills, CA: Sage.
———(1979) "The long cycle of global politics and the nation-state." Comparative Studies in Society and History 20 (April): 214-235.
THOMPSON, W. R. (1981) "Operationalizing long cycle theory: the basic problems and some proposed solutions for the sixteenth and late twentieth centuries." Delivered to the Annual Meeting of the American Political Science Association, New York, September.

13

An Agenda for World-Systems Analysis

IMMANUEL WALLERSTEIN

Some scholars in this volume and elsewhere seem to describe world-systems studies as an arena within which two opposing tendencies contest the terrain. On the one hand, there are said to be those who (over)emphasize the economic factors; and on the other, those who (over)emphasize the political structures. Various words like "reductionism," "autonomy," and "synthesis" are used. In my view, this is an artificial (and as stated, unresolvable) debate that largely misses the point of the world-systems perspective.

The theorizing about something called world-systems cannot be comprehended unless we perceive this theorizing, and then assess it, in the light of the alternative theorizing that it intends to oppose. To be sure, in scholarship no one can copyright terminology, but it does seem pointless to discuss ideas via semantic juggling and without remembering the historical genesis, and therefore the intent, of the theorizing.

World-systems analysis (under various names) arose in the period following World War II as the reaction to the dominant view in world social science, which for this period may be named "developmentalism."[1] The basic theoretical challenge was not new. It was heir to longstanding attempts of many historical social scientists to get out from under the oppressive framework of the false methodological debate between so-called nomothetic and idiographic social science. The pseudo-debate between these presumed methodological opposites, which the majority of scholars have asserted for the last 150 years marked the essential schism within social science, could only be superseded by a "war on two fronts"—one directed simultaneously against the transhistorical universalizers on the one hand and the antianalytic particularizers on the other.

There were, it seems to me, five rejections in the countertheorizing that inspired the emergence of the world-systems perspective.

(1) Rejection of the assertion that the various organizational rubrics of scholars working in the historical social sciences were in any sense to be thought of as "disciplines" or even as currently useful groupings of scholarly activity. Stated polemically, it was the assertion: There is no such thing as sociology; there is no such thing as history; there is no such thing as economics, political science, anthropology, or geography. This rejection was quite the contrary of a call for multidisciplinary work or for a "synthesis" that would overcome "reductionism." It was a rejection of the epistemological validity of the morphology.

(2) Rejection of the juridically defined political entity, the state, as the starting point for social analysis, as the primary determinant of the boundaries of social action, as the collective equivalent (even putatively) of an "individual." Stated polemically, it was the argument that the state was merely one social institution among many, and that the state-society antinomy was a misleading premise for enquiry. This rejection was quite the contrary of denying the centrality of "political" considerations or motivations because it led in fact to seeing "political" action inside *all* social action.

(3) Rejection of both cyclical and evolutionary metahistories in the name of the "war on two fronts," and the counterinsistence that "cycles and trends" had to be analyzed as a symbiotic pair with which social phenomena may be described. Stated polemically, it was true neither that history never repeats itself nor that there were any significant social constants that were the product of "human nature." Instead, insofar as any historical system existed, there were within it repetitive patterns (cycles), for as long as the particular system existed. But all such social systems were historically time bound because the cycles reflected contradictory internal thrusts that led to and accounted for the inherent structural stresses (trends) that eventually caused the disintegration or structural transformation of the historical system as a whole.

(4) Rejection of the concept that substructures or particular processes could in any sense be "models" for parallel substructures or processes within the historical system that "came later." Stated polemically, neither Europe nor England might be said to have come "first" in the modern world in anything in which some other area or state came "second." The dynamic of the system not only was the sum of all the forces contained in it but also affected all its zones at every moment. The "development" of "comparable" subunits was therefore far more likely to be divergent than convergent.

(5) Rejection of formulating concepts as essences rather than as processes. Stated polemically, the law of the excluded middle is wrong. A is both A and non-A. If this poses difficulties for existing logics, we must change existing logics.

Each of these five "rejections" had been made previously to the post-1945 period. There were even scholars who had asserted all five of them. What was different in the postwar period was that, precisely because of the structural crisis of the capitalist world-economy, the critique of the metaphysical premises of our existing historical system, as they have found expression in the historical social sciences, began to develop a new historiography as well as a new way of theorizing about social science, both of which not only were linked to the struggle of antisystemic forces to transform the system but were also self-critical about the degree to which antisystemic forces had themselves been products of the present historical system and thereby inherently contradictory agents of its projected transformation.

From the standpoint, therefore, of these five rejections, there are occurring presently attempts (1) to restate our organizing historical myths, (2) to invent new processual concepts with which to describe and analyze our reality, and (3) to draw from such work a more efficacious program of social transformation. Let us consider each of these attempts.

One of the profoundest holds an existing historical system has on the persons located within it consists of the set of "self-evident" and virtually unexamined overall statements about the relevant historical past that permeate the cultures and the multiple educational structures of the system and which give us our categories and our priorities for analysis. These statements also dictate to us what we should and usually do ignore as historically unimportant. It is essential, furthermore, to underline the fact that even antisystematic movements normally accept, even build upon, these historical verities. Such statements are what we mean by "organizing myths."

The dominant organizing myth of the historiography of the nineteenth and twentieth centuries portrayed a premodern (precapitalist) past (first of all in Europe) in which "lords" tended to own much or most of the land. This land was in fact worked upon by "peasants" who paid "rent" in one form or another to the "lords." This premodern past was defined as a primarily agricultural, primarily rural, primarily nonmonetized social order.

Something is said to have happened in the period between 1300 and 1700 such that certain major lords, "kings," consolidated their power over larger areas at the same time that urban areas, inhabited by burghers (bourgeois), grew stronger.

The confluence of these two facts led to socio-political-economic transformations within each of the "states" (each somehow there) such that the bourgeoisie (to some degree in collusion with the monarchs) gradually ousted the aristocracy from their preeminence. As a result of this, in one state after another, there occurred an "industrial revolution."

The monarchs and the bourgeoisie were said to be equally interested in expanding the frontiers of their operations. Hence states went to war, colonized, engaged in diplomacy, and created an interstate system.

Eventually, within each industrial state an urban factory-based working class emerged and began to be restive. They formed movements. Thus politics came to be fought between bourgeois and proletarians, but aristocrats and peasants often anachronistically and annoyingly survived and complicated the system. Still, their survival was just that, a survival from the past, doomed to disappear.

I have tried to write this organizing myth, so that both liberals and Marxists and even conservatives could fill it in with their additional detail, supplying both a theory about the genesis and operation of the historical sequence and the flavor of their various moralities.

This is a perfectly serviceable organizing myth. Its cast of characters and its stock situations have informed most scholarly dramas of the nineteenth and twentieth centuries, including those of several authors in this volume. But, like all such myths, it has its drawbacks. It explains why there has been so much urbanization, proletarianization, commodification in the modern world; it fails utterly to explain why there has been so little. It explains the rationalization and bureaucratization of the world; it fails utterly to explain why the anachronisms have persisted. It explains why there have been revolutionary movements; it fails utterly to explain the behavior of "postrevolutionary" states. It explains the historical progress; it fails utterly to explain the historical regression.

It is precisely to these historiographical failures that world-systems analysis addressed itself in proposing an alternative organizing myth that would be capable of accounting for those phenomena that the alternative organizing myth could not handle.

The alternative myth started at the very same locus—Europe in the late Middle Ages, with a feudal order "in crisis." The lords were subject to severely declining revenues relative to their peasants. But here the similarity of the two myths ended.

The "something that happened" was that the upper strata sought to maintain their privilege by transforming the feudal order into a new one. "From feudalism to capitalism" thus translated into: aristocrats became entrepreneurs, that is, bourgeois. These aristocrats-becoming-bourgeois expanded the boundaries (outer and inner) of feudal Europe. They transformed their agricultural *and* industrial activities so as to maximize capital accumulation. They created modern "sovereign" states located within a political magnetic field (the interstate system) whose boundaries more or less coincided with that of the evolving division of labor between the integrated production processes of what might be termed the emerging capitalist world-economy. They were able to do this not because the kings were so strong but because they were so weak, and above all because there was in reality no Holy Roman Emperor.

These changes involved a slow and *very partial* commodification of the factors of production (including the proletarianization of labor) and a slow but steady mechanization of production and urbanization of the population. It was slow and partial because it was *not* to the advantage of the entrepreneurs that it be fast and full, since the maximization of the extraction of surplus-value depended precisely on the limited degree of commodification.

In this myth, the steady commodification was not the doing of heroic entrepreneurs but of desperate ones facing recurrent stagnations of the system and subject to pressures from below (the working strata) for *increased* proletarianization. The same stagnations accounted for the steady expansion of the outer boundaries of the system, the historical incorporation of new, low-wage production zones into the capitalist world-economy with its remolding of political entities as constituent units of the interstate system. This process furthermore was a continuous one since the sixteenth century and nothing strikingly unusual in terms of the political economy of the world-system may be said to have occurred in the late eighteenth century.

The growing worldwide restiveness of the working strata (among whom it is unwise to exaggerate the phenomenological differences of so-called peasants and so-called proletarians) gave rise to organized antisystemic movements (in many guises). By the twentieth century, the process of commodification (and rationalization) having proceeded further than was desirable from the perspective of the capitalists, these movements were able to create a level of worldwide class struggle such that the system could be said to have entered into structural crisis.

These antisystemic movements were, however, themselves caught in the web of the ideology of the system, and their various efforts to achieve transformation by seizure of power in individual states had ambiguous results, enmeshing them in the constraints of the interstate system and thereby leading them to act in ways that reinforced as well as undermined the operations of the capitalist world-economy. Still the regression in well-being vis-à-vis the historical past that was inherent in the operations of this historical system presisted and was aggravated over time, such that even the material progress initiated from below could not slow down the developing antisystemic consciousness of the working strata. And there the story stops, because we are in the middle of it, with the last act yet to be played.

It is in the light of the two opposing organizing myths that we should review the history of social scientific theorizing, which is of course nothing but the effort to systematize our mythology and thereby to make its hold more deeply rooted and more satisfying.

The emergence of the fields of study we today normally designate as "the social sciences" was a phenomenon of the nineteenth century. In 1800, none of the names of today's "disciplines" were in place as a university department, and only "history" was even a term in scholarly use. By 1900, all of our present "fields" existed in their present nomenclature, and most had developed interuniversity scholarly structures that defined, furthered, and defended the presumed "discipline."

The centrality of state boundaries in the conceptual frameworks of the disciplines, the sharp distinction between matters that were "political" and matters that were "economic," the use of "social" and/or "cultural" to categorize all concerns that did not deal directly with the decisions of governmental structures or of firms, the segregation of the analysis of the so-called great powers and that of all the other zones all derived from the premises of the liberal ideology that reflected a capitalist world-economy in which first Great Britain and later the United States were the hegemonic powers.

The absurdities and ambiguities of the resulting intellectual division of labor, the enormous lacunae of research and teaching, the conceptual morass that resulted from this division of intellectual labor, combined with the political decolonization of a large part of the world led to the great vogue of interdisciplinary and "area" studies after World War II. Such studies were supposed to resolve the difficulties. But at the same time the so-called disciplinary boundaries were organizationally strengthened by the new (usually quantitative) methodologies that led to more rigid training programs and a profusion of specialized literatures with their consequent inward turning. When being "interdisciplinary," one was supposed to bring the contribution of one's "discipline" to some collectivity of scholars, thereby reinforcing even further the logic of the morphology.

As one tried to overcome "ethnocentrism," and one became more "comparative," the "societies" one compared turned out to be more and more the sovereign states, as defined in the present and thrust backward into time.

The limitations of this set of intellectual assumptions have been assailed so often in the last 10 to 15 years that is scarcely bears repeating. I do so only because, in the context of this discussion on presumed alternative modes of analyzing world-systems, we risk losing from sight the whole point of why we're looking at the world system as the principal locus of social change.

The world-system as a concept was first of all a "concept for comparative analysis," a unit of analysis to replace the state. But it was an integral unit and it therefore makes no epistemological sense whatsoever to distinguish a "logic" of the world-economy from a "logic" of the interstate system. Indeed, it is barely possible to talk about one even provisionally without talking about the other. To try to do so is simply to return to the premises against which world-systems analysis was a protest. What should be compared or analyzed are historical systems, of which (to be sure) the presently existing capitalist world-economy is only one instance.

If then we begin to compare historical systems and establish a morphology of such historical systems, we notice that the pattern of distribution of such historical systems has been different over world time. I have elsewhere argued for a morphology that distinguishes among reciprocal mini-systems, redistributive world-empires, capitalist world-economies, and socialist world-orders.[3] I won't reargue the distinctions. Let us simply follow out the implications of such a morphology.

There was a first historical period, prior to settled agriculture, in which presumably there existed only mini-systems on the globe. We know very little about the factual functioning of such systems. There was a second period, which ran to circa 1500 A.D., in which there coexisted multiple historical systems—mini-systems, world-empires, and world-economies. From what we know (which is primarily the history of the world-empires), it seems that such world-empires were the "strong" form. They expanded and contracted following a logic internal to them. During any given expansion, a given world-empire would absorb (and thereby destroy as historical systems) many mini-systems and world-economies. During any given contraction, they would "vacate" social space within which new mini-systems and world-economies would emerge.

What is singular about the period since 1500 is that for the first time a world-economy proved to the the "strong" form. It expanded and absorbed world-empires rather than the other way around. It could thus for the first time develop fully its capitalist mode of production based on an axial division of labor located within an interstate system of "sovereign" states. This development had many consequences that are in fact the subject of analysis of the largest part of historical social science. One of these consequences, and not the least important, was the elimination from the globe of all other forms of historical systems. Thus, for the first time, a given world-system truly covered the globe.

This historical system, like all before it, is beset by contradictions and will therefore at some point come to an end. However, the fact that it is the only presently existing system means that one alternative is that it be transformed into another singular, globally extensive historical system.

This sketch of the history of historical systems has immense methodological implications. It means first of all that the units of analysis and of comparison are even more complex than prior theorizing had assumed. It means second that the most difficult phenomena to explain—the mutation in the set of historical systems circa 1500 and the present-future transformation of our existing system—are unique phenomena and therefore not amenable to any methodology that presumes a probabilistic logic based on the inductive analysis of multiple cases.

An alternative mode of theorizing thus has led us inexorably to an alternative methodology. This alternative is even less developed than the former, and even more urgent to develop. As the existing mode of theorizing finds itself under greater and more effective attack concerning both the organizing myths of its historiography and the epistemological assumptions of its theorizing, it has retreated to its ultimate rampart, the sacrosanctness of its methodological premises. The crucial terrain of struggle may well turn out to be that of methodology.

The basic premise of present dominant methodology is that scientific analysis proceeds from the complexity of reality to the unifying simplicity of correctly formulated universal theorems subject to specified modes of empirical disproof. This method was presumably the glory of the modern natural sciences and thus became the model for social science. It is therefore not without interest that, in recent years, this "Newtonian worldview" has come under attack from within the natural sciences. Against the normality of "equilibrium structures," there is now a school that argues that such equilibrium structures are exceptional and that the norm is to be located in "dissipative structures" that evolve over time as "totalities." Furthermore, this is all the more true as one proceeds from simpler to more complex structures, the most complex structures being precisely the historical social systems.[4]

Emphasis on complexity and dissipative structures must lead us, it seems to me, to a fundamental reversal of our methodological strategy. We presently start from complex empirical description and try to reduce it to simple general statements. Instead, we ought to start with simple general statements, cross-cut such statements with ever more specifications, until we arrive at utilizable concrete complex descriptions of historical structures. The test of the utility of our heuristic theorizing would lie in our consequent ability to explain and manipulate complex reality.

We end, therefore, in the realm of political practice, which thereby becomes not merely the justification for scientific activity but its object. As we become more political we become more scientific; as we become more scientific we become more political.

World-systems analysis therefore ought to lead us, if it is useful, to a longer-term and more complex view of the total social change that has occurred over time in our presently existing singular historical system. It should furthermore clarify rather than obscure the historical alternatives that are presently available and suggest the alternative consequences of ongoing social action. All of our work, each of the essays in this book as elsewhere, must be measured in this light, especially insofar as we pretend to speak to the "larger" issues confronting our historical system.

I do not suggest that this is an activity to which only the scientists are called. As war must not be left to the generals, science, using its own terms of reference, cannot be left to the scientists. Science is the social activity par excellence—that of collective thought. Given the complexity of our object of analysis and the abysmally low level of our scientific sophistication, it is not a credible proposition that most of the sagacious collective thought is or has been done by specialists. Most is and has been done in collective social organizations and the role of specialists is to theorize the practice, thereby permitting it to be effectively criticized, not so much by the specialists as first of all by the practitioners.

I say, therefore, away with semantic juggling and let's get on with the very hard work of describing complex reality in politically useful ways.

NOTES

1. I have related some of the details of this historical clash of theories in my essay, "The Present State of the Debate on World Inequality," originally published in 1975 and reprinted in Wallerstein (1979: 49-65).
2. See my brief discussion in relation to one scholarly group in Wallerstein (1980).
3. See, for example, Wallerstein (1978).
4. I have analyzed the implications of this for the current scientific and political situation in Wallerstein (1983).

REFERENCES

WALLERSTEIN, I. (1983) "Crises: the world-economy, the movements, and the ideologies," in A. Bergesen (ed.) Crises in the World-System. Beverly Hills, CA: Sage.

———(1980) "The *Annales* school: the war on two fronts." Annals of Scholarship 1 (Summer): 85-91.

———(1979) The Capitalist World-Economy. Cambridge: Cambridge University Press.

———(1978) "Civilizations and modes of production." Theory and Society 5, 1: 1-10.

About the Contributors

ALBERT BERGESEN is Associate Professor of Sociology at the University of Arizona. His present interests center on long cycles of expansion and contraction in the capitalist world-economy. He recently edited *Studies of the Modern World-System* (1980) and *Crises in the World-System* (1983).

CHRISTOPHER CHASE-DUNN is Associate Professor of Social Relations at Johns Hopkins University. He is the author with Volker Bornschier of *Core Corporations and Underdevelopment* and has edited another volume, *Socialist States in the World-System* (1982). Currently, he is working on an NSF-sponsored research project on urbanization in the world-system since 1800.

CHARLES F. DORAN is Professor of International Relations at the School of Advanced International Studies, Johns Hopkins University. The author of *The Politics of Assimilation* (1971), he has also published extensively on events-data analysis, nonlinear methods, power and threat perceptions, domestic and interstate conflict in Latin America and the Middle East, the political-economies of energy resources, international environment and commercial questions, Canadian/American relations, the cycle of relative power, and systems transformation.

RAYMOND DUVALL is Associate Professor of Political Science at the University of Minnesota and co-editor of the *International Studies Quarterly*. For the past several years, his research, supported by grants from the National Science Foundation, has concentrated on politics and governance in dependent societies.

RICHARD FALK is Albert G. Milbank Professor of International Law and Practice at Princeton University and Director of U.S. participation in the World Order Models Proejcts (WOMP). He has recently co-edited *Toward a Just World Order* (1982) and *The United Nations and a Just World Order* (1983).

ANDRE GUNDER FRANK holds the Chair in Development Studies (Social Change) at the University of East Anglia. Among his many books are *Capitalism and Underdevelopment in Latin America* (1967), *World Accumulation, 1492-1789* (1978), *Crisis: In the World Economy* (1980), and *Crisis: In the Third World* (1981). His recent research focuses on the past and contemporary economic, social, and political history of the world capitalist system and the rising tide of nationalism and religion as responses to the current world crisis.

STEVEN JACKSON is Assistant Professor of Government at Cornell University. He is involved in research in social democracy in the Third World, the global debt, state coercion in dependent countries, and the use of optimization techniques in political economic analyses.

SAMUEL S. KIM is Professor of Political Science at Monmouth College and Senior Fellow at the Institute for World Order. He has written extensively on Chinese foreign policy and world order studies. His most recent work is the *Quest for a Just World Order* (1983).

JACK S. LEVY is Assistant Professor of Government at the University of Texas at Austin. He has a forthcoming book entitled *War in the Modern Great Power System, 1495-1975,* and he has recently published articles in the *American Journal of Political Science, International Studies Quarterly,* and the *Journal of Conflict Resolution.* His primary research interests concern the causes of great power war.

GEORGE MODELSKI is Professor of Political Science at the University of Washington. He is the author of *A Theory of Foreign Policy* (1962) and *Principles of World Politics* (1972) and editor of *Transnational Corporations and World Order* (1979). The focus of his current work is the long cycle of global leadership.

DAVID P. RAPKIN is Associate Professor of Political Science at the University of Nebraska—Lincoln. He has contributed articles to various journals and edited books and has recently coedited *America in a Changing World Political Economy.*

BRUCE M. RUSSETT is Professor of Political Science at Yale University and editor of the *Journal of Conflict Resolution.* He has published sixteen books on international relations. A past President of the Peace Science Society (International), he is currently President of the International Studies Association.

DUNCAN SNIDAL is Assistant Professor of Political Science at the University of Chicago. He is currently finishing a manuscript on international cooperation and political regime formation; he is also interested in the politics of "outward-looking" development strategies.

DAVID SYLVAN is Assistant Professor of Political Science at the Maxwell School, Syracuse University. His current research interests include the "transition to socialism" and the hermeneutics of revolutionary ideologies.

WILLIAM R. THOMPSON is Professor of International Relations at Claremont Graduate School. In addition to an ongoing research interest in the evolution of the modern world system, he is currently involved in a collaborative study on the impacts of global wars on state-building processes.

IMMANUEL WALLERSTEIN is Director of the Fernand Braudel Center for the Study of Economies, Historical Systems, and Civilizations at the State University of New York at Binghamton. He is the author of *The Modern World-System* (1974, 1980) and *The Capitalist World-Economy* (1979).

ARISTIDE R. ZOLBERG is Distinguished Professor of Political Science in the Graduate Faculty of the New School for Social Research. He is the author of *One Party Government in the Ivory Coast* (1964) and *Creating Political Order: The Party States of West Africa* (1966), and the coeditor of *Ghana and the Ivory Coast: Patterns of Development* (1971). His current research interests are focused primarily on international migration policies.